THE MEMOIRS OF GENERAL JEAN V. ALLARD

A country's response to its military history and traditions has much to reveal about its central character. These memoirs of General Jean V. Allard, the first French-Canadian Chief of the Defence Staff, both recall proud victories and issue sombre warnings for complacent Canadians.

General Jean V. Allard has dedicated almost all his active years to the service of his country. Joining the militia during the Depression, he became an officer in the 1930s. His military career took flight during World War II when he distinguished himself on European battlefields and became commander of the renowned "Vandoos." The Korean War gave him another opportunity to exercise his talents as a tactician.

Jean Allard was a superb soldier (he defined himself as a "FINK"—Flying Infantryman with Naval Knowledge). He also had ample occasion to demonstrate his skill in different staff and command positions. He was military attaché in the USSR soon after the war and later commanded a British division with NATO troops in West Germany. Finally, he established one of the numerous precedents which marked his career when he became the first francophone to attain the rank of general and the summit of Canada's military pyramid. As Chief of Staff he contributed to unification of the Canadian armed forces in 1968 and created French-language units in all sectors of military activity, thus giving form to a dream he had cherished for years.

JEAN V. ALLARD is a Companion of the Order of Canada and Commander of the British Empire. He has received, for his war actions, the DSO (three times), the Croix de guerre and the Légion d'honneur militaire (France), the Bronze Lion (The Netherlands), the Legion of Merit (United States), and the Legion of Merit (South Korea). He has also received honorary degrees from five Canadian universities in recognition of his services. Both the original French version, published by Editions de Montagne in 1985, and this English translation were prepared in collaboration with Serge Bernier, historian at the Directorate of History, Department of National Defence.

The Memoirs of
GENERAL JEAN V. ALLARD

written in cooperation with
Serge Bernier

Preface by the Honourable Léo Cadieux

THE UNIVERSITY OF BRITISH COLUMBIA PRESS
VANCOUVER 1988

THE MEMOIRS OF GENERAL JEAN V. ALLARD
English translation © The University of British
Columbia Press 1988

This book has been published with the help of a
grant from the Canada Council.

Canadian Cataloguing in Publication Data

Allard, Jean V. (Jean Victor), 1913—
  The memoirs of General Jean V. Allard

  Translation of: Mémoires du général Jean V. Allard
  Includes index.
  ISBN 0-7748-0289-8

  1. Allard, Jean V. (Jean Victor), 1913— 2. Generals—
Canada—Biography. 3. Canada. Canadian Armed Forces—
Biography. 4. Canada—Armed Forces—Biography. I. Bernier,
Serge. II. Title.
U55.A45A313 1988   355.3'31'0924   C88-091186-7
                          67874
Printed in Canada

THIS BOOK IS DEDICATED TO THOSE
CANADIANS, WHO, DURING MY YEARS OF SERVICE,
ROSE TO THE CHALLENGE OF, AND OVERCAME, TO
THE GLORY OF OUR COUNTRY, EVERY SITUATION,
AND PARTICULARLY THE TWO WARS WE
PARTICIPATED IN SINCE 1939.

ALSO, TO

Simone
Michèle
Jean-Ernest†
Andrée
Louis†

Contents

Foreword

The Directorate of History, National Defence Headquarters, is pleased to have contributed to the preparation of this autobiography. We regard this book as part of a vast project that will deal, over the coming years, with the contribution of francophones to Canadian defence since 1867. Two other works, quite different in structure and method, supplement this first major contribution.

W. A. B. Douglas
Director

Jean Pariseau
Historien en chef

Preface

This is the personal story of a soldier and his equally glorious companions. It is also the book of a man of good faith, possessed both of an imaginative mind and an enthusiastic heart. I had the honour of being associated with him as Minister of National Defence, an exciting experience that he relates with a judicious choice of words. All essential details are covered.

I hope that readers—particularly francophones—will grasp the importance of the unceasing labours of a great Canadian to ensure the success of major reforms within the Canadian Armed Forces. The warnings thoughtfully given at the end of the book should also be noted. So much effort, by so many, for so long, must not be in vain. These responsibilities are handed down from generation to generation.

From my association with General Jean Allard, I retain the attractive image of a great soldier, always curious about the particulars of his trade, alert and analytical, extroverted and generous, constant and loyal, human— very human, indeed.

I am thankful to him for having written this book, and I am astonished at the fact that his memory is good enough not to lose any essential fact in this story, which is all too short. His book is but another service rendered to his people.

The Honourable Léo Cadieux

Introduction

Having reached the age at which I could think of writing my memoirs, I felt some concern, like my predecessors in this literary genre. The first issue I briefly grappled with was whether or not the idea itself was worth pursuing. The answer is now known.

Then, there were more down-to-earth issues. For instance, which events should be included in such a work? Once again, my choices were made quickly. Thus, except for Chapter 1, which is devoted to my family origins and my first years of life, my intimate personal life has hardly been touched upon. I have thus generally dealt with the public aspect of my activities, or rather with what I considered to be that public side. Nevertheless, I should state from the outset that I did not avoid facts that many may deem minor. To me, these anecdotes are important. Also, the names of illustrious unknowns are sprinkled throughout the story. Since these people played an important role in my life at some time or other, I felt I had to recognize them "officially," even if they were already well aware of my esteem. I would therefore ask the reader to bear with me on this point.

A final major question: how to say what I had to say? I opted for simplicity. I will know that I have reached my goal—writing a book accessible to all—if my comrades in arms, having read it, say that they recognize the man behind the words.

Let me say without hesitation that I am, first and foremost, a man of action, one of those who, aware of the inevitability of criticism, prefer to be criticized for what has been done rather than for what has not been done. My perception of situations, during the more or less lengthy periods of reflection that all must engage in before acting, has not been right all the time. As a result, I have sometimes followed hazardous paths. I have pointed out a few in these chapters. Fortunately, like most people, I have been much less marked by my failures than by the positive events of my life, and it is essentially about the latter that you will learn.

Preparing this manuscript has not been altogether easy. In 1973, I had prepared an outline and written a first chapter based on the general principles I have just stated. However, the fairly active life I was then living made me give up writing. In 1980, when circumstances were more favourable than they had ever been, I slowly took it up again.

About fifty pages had been written when, in early 1982, I was approached by historians of the Directorate of History, Department of National Defence, who wanted to ask me about my involvement, as Chief of the Defence Staff, in certain activities in the late 1960s through which I had attempted to improve the lot of francophones in our Armed Forces.

I co-operated fully with that study group, but this request also had an electrifying effect on me. It now seemed crucial to me that the project I had undertaken be completed as soon as possible. However, working alone as I had up to then, I could not possibly complete it quickly. I had to obtain the assistance of my former department. Fortunately, thanks to Mr. C. R. Nixon, then deputy minister, and to Chief of the Defence Staff General Ramsay Withers, the co-operation I needed was granted. That is how the Directorate of History came to be involved. Serge Bernier, one of its historians, was specially assigned to the project. He was able to write the text from my outlines and notes, from written or recorded documents that I was able to place at his disposal as well as from the archives of the department. It is therefore due, to a large extent, to the Department of National Defence that this book has been published.

I want to thank the many people who devoted so many hours to reading and commenting on the draft of this work. Some of them played a role in the story that follows, and I hope to have taken careful note of their remarks.

I would also like to thank cartographer Bill Constable for his remarkable contribution, as well as the young word processor operators whom I have not met but who, over more than two years, typed and retyped this story, which they must occasionally have found quite dull.

Both authors owe special acknowledgments to the following individuals and organizations: the Office of the Secretary of State of Canada, which subsidized the translation; Dr. Jean Pariseau, Historien en chef, Directorate of History, NDHQ, Ottawa, who with his usual acuteness checked the translation and read the proof; Dr. David Fransen who, while Historian at the Directorate of History, also unstintingly gave much of his spare time to checking the translation for accuracy; and Jane C. Fredeman, Acquisitions Editor, Humanities, at UBC Press, whose understanding and forbearance sustained us during the last year.

Two beautiful mature trees had taken root
in the soil of the Sainte-Monique region.
Around them were the young offshoots
they had brought into being.
The female tree, in the prime of life,
fell prey to a disease that vanquished it.
The children then huddled around the great male tree.
Two years later,
in the middle of winter and with no warning,
the father-tree died too.

It took a long time for spring to reach
the chilled branches of the seven little ones,
who were left to fend for themselves.

1

The Allard Family

I shall start these memoirs, quite conventionally, with a retrospective on my family and the kind of life we led during my first few years. Before tackling this subject, however, I shall digress briefly, reaching back a few centuries.

My older sister Anaïs was interested for a while in the genealogical tree of the Allards. The following paragraphs are based on the research notes she had made while consulting experts. The two-part genealogical tree shown here, however, is my work, and will not fully satisfy the experts in this field. Indeed, it is only complete from the second half of the nineteenth century. Moreover, since none of us has delved into the matter, I was unable to complete the table by retracing the origin of all the women who, having married an Allard over the last three centuries, were instrumental in allowing the name to survive.

Let us go back to the remote origins. The name Allard originates from the area of the Bergen and Trondheim fjords in Scandinavia. It was around Rouen that it took on its more French form before spreading throughout western Europe and, following the great European migrations, to America and, no doubt, the world at large.

I am part of the eighth generation that succeeded Jacques Allard, first of our branch to settle in New France. Here are, very briefly, some of my predecessors in North America in chronological order:

a. Allard, Jacques (married to Jacqueline Frérot), from Blacqueville, diocese of Rouen, Normandy, France;
b. Allard, François (to Jeanne Anguille), Bourg Royal, near Quebec City, Canada;

c. Allard, Jean-François (to Geneviève Dauphin), Saint-François-du-Lac, Yamaska;
d. Allard, Gabriel (to Elisabeth Proulx), La Baie-du-Febvre, Yamaska;
e. Allard, Gabriel (to Marie-Anne Roy), La Baie-du-Febvre, Yamaska; and
f. Allard, Charles (to Angélique Lemire), La Baie-du-Febvre, Yamaska.

This listing clearly shows that, very early on, some Allards settled in the immediate vicinity of Nicolet. I remain personally very attached to that corner of Quebec where I was born and grew up, the region that straddles the St. Lawrence between Nicolet itself and Shawinigan. Today, when the time has come, at long last, for retirement, we have returned to live at the very heart of this part of the world, in Trois-Rivières, a city to which I have been attached since childhood.

Let us return briefly to genealogy. I am able to provide more details about the next set of people than about the previous one.

Edmond, my maternal grandfather, was born in Nicolet, on January 8, 1836. A blacksmith by trade, he settled in the neighbouring village of Sainte-Monique around 1860. On August 18, 1863, he married Philomène Morel, the widow of Abraham Rousseau, by whom she had had two children, Marie and Napoléon.

From the new marriage, nine children were born, including Victorine, born on May 2, 1874. Attracted by the religious vocation, she completed her novice training with the Sisters of the Assumption and taught at the convent in Sainte-Monique. Finally, following the advice of her spiritual guide, Monseigneur Bruneau, she left that life and married Ernest Allard on October 27, 1903.

Ernest was one of seven children born to Joseph Allard and Elise Jutras. His three brothers were Joseph, Louis and Norbert. The oldest spent his life on the Cordeau Line, at Sainte-Monique. Louis stayed on the family property for more than fifty years and died in Drummondville in 1945. Norbert also settled on the Cordeau Line, but financial difficulties led him to try his luck in the city. He therefore moved to Thetford Mines, where he died in a construction site accident.

My father also had three sisters, including Marie who was married three times—first to Owen McMahon, then to François Jutras, and finally to Zoë Lemire, who had been her very first date. Another sister, Joséphine, had two husbands, Amédé Proulx and Alphonse Allard. (Of course, these numerous marriages were caused by the death of the spouse, not divorce.) The last one, Hedwidge, married Israël Bergeron of Baie-du-Febvre, and she followed him there.

Ernest was born on February 19, 1877. He was twenty-five years old when he married and settled on one of the beautiful Cordeau properties, in the

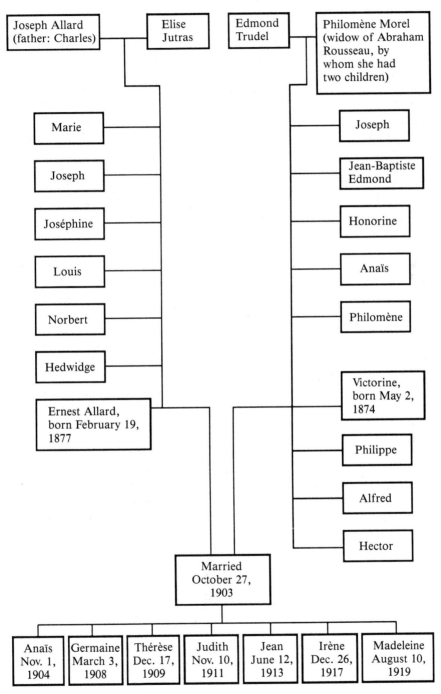

parish of Sainte-Monique, near Nicolet. He was a hard worker who constantly sought to improve his condition and that of those around him. Thus, the buildings we had just acquired had to be redone. A new house was therefore built in 1915. The following year, the barn was cemented and renovated. Also in 1916, he himself installed a hay loft and bought some farm machinery. In order to pay for these projects, he became an agent for Massey-Harris machinery and Luden stable equipment. His first major client was Joseph Descôteaux, Liberal Member of Parliament for Nicolet in Ottawa, and brother of the Sainte-Monique physician Dr. Arsène Descôteaux, who also happened to be Ernest's brother-in-law.

Never at a loss for practical ideas, my father installed an evaporator in his sugar cabin and interconnected its vats by a system of syphons that let the concentration of the maple sap proceed from vat to vat. The fire was sustained under the appropriate vat only, and the other containers, now empty, were no longer heated unnecessarily. He also had the idea of painting the outside of the sap buckets half white, half red. The colour showing indicated whether or not a bucket had been emptied. A good nationalist, when the time came to improve his livestock, he selected a bull (that nearly killed him a few months later) and cows of a Canadian breed. In 1917, he participated in the installation of an aqueduct system: using a ram pump connected to a spring, a twenty-thousand gallon reservoir was created, ensuring the water supply of several Cordeau farms. In 1918, he obtained the Canadian Postal Service contract for the Cordeau and Upper River routes. He later installed central heating, a bathroom, and a hot water tank in the house. These things were rare at the time. His business success allowed him to purchase a Grey Dart automobile.

Without any doubt, his wife Victorine was the person dearest to him throughout those years. Gentle, educated, musical and "village-minded," mother found life on Cordeau Line tedious. However, her courage and great qualities inspired the whole family, in which she instilled a taste for order, beautiful things, and, above all, music: her piano had a place of honour in our home. During the last few years of her life, she had the time to devote a great deal of attention to me. In addition to being the only son, I was the youngest in the family until the age of four, when a fifth girl, Irène, was born, on December 26, 1917. My mother showed great courage. Suffering from tuberculosis since 1915, she gave birth, after Irène, to a sixth daughter, Madeleine. Two months later, on October 10, 1919, my mother died. Throughout her illness, the exact nature of which she ignored until early 1919, she continued to raise, clothe and educate all her little ones, in addition to giving birth to two children.

My mother's death required a reorganization of our life. Left alone, my father had to provide for his seven children, including a little daughter just a few months old and another one aged two-and-a-half. Anaïs, the oldest, who had turned sixteen on the previous November 1st, was at first forced to leave the convent in order to take care of us. Later, a cousin helped us from time to time. Later still, my father hired a maid who assumed full responsibility for the household. In spite of these arrangements, he was still careworn as the loss of his companion affected him grievously.

In the meantime, he continued to renovate the house and, in the spring of 1920, he and I shared a room fully renovated to the latest standards. Unfortunately, we hardly had time to benefit from these material improvements. He died suddenly on January 9, 1921, in Sainte-Clotilde d'Horton, at the home of Napoléon Rousseau, my mother's half-brother, where he had gone with my sisters Anaïs and Thérèse for a New Year's Day visit. He left seven children, the youngest of them barely eighteen months old.

This quick overview is not yet complete: I must add a few paragraphs on what happened to the seven Allard children. However, for now, I would like to mention how these first few years went for me.

I was born on June 12, 1913, in a house that I never knew because my father replaced it a few months later. It was to the latter home, which still stands in the Cordeau Line, at one end of the parish of Sainte-Monique, that he devoted, up to the time of his death, the efforts I have already mentioned.

I would like to note an interesting fact, which I can obviously not remember myself but which is a significant one for me. In the spring of 1913, the ice had carried away the bridge linking the Cordeau Line to the village of Sainte-Monique, where the church was located. In order to go there, one therefore had to cross the river at a ford downstream from the bridge.

It was somewhat risky, but my father, a good Catholic, insisted that I be christened the very day of my birth. Under the circumstances, the number of those present at the ceremony was quite small. In fact, the cavalcade consisted of a single car. Sometimes, when I think of this event, which I was told about, it seems to me that this first difficulty I encountered was but the forerunner of many others that, fortunately, were also going to be overcome.

During the days following my birth, my father planted a few maples in front of the house where I was born. They have grown since and it is always with some nostalgia that I see them again whenever I chance to visit the Cordeau.

I have many specific recollections from the years 1913 to 1921. I will mention the few that I recall most often. For instance, there were annual maple sugar parties and hay rides at which we sat on the floor of a horse-drawn cart. Of these latter events I remember primarily that my derrière used to get wet as we went through a creek that crossed our property and that sometimes flowed over the bridge my father had built across it.

I also accompanied my father many times to the Desmarais mill, on the west branch of the Nicolet River. We went there on horseback or by car, often singing "Marianne s'en va-t-au moulin." My father occasionally had them mill small bags of grain that I subsequently fed to the calves that had been entrusted to my care.

On one occasion, I went with him to the plumbing supplier in Nicolet to pick up the heating elements for the central heating system he was installing in our home. Another time, on the way to the foundry in Saint-Léonard, father's Grey Dart lost a rear wheel, which made a lot of people laugh.

I also remember the only photograph—which I have been unable to locate since—which I appeared with my father. The picture also showed Mr. Descôteaux, my uncle's brother. We were in Sainte-Monique, in front of the Descôteaux farm, the owner of which had just bought equipment from my father for his barn.

On the other hand, my mother had laid down fairly strict disciplinary rules which her only son was, of all her children, the most reluctant to obey . . . notwithstanding the career he was to choose later. When I think of her, a few scenes come back to me. One day, while she was sitting at her sewing machine, a fox approached and killed a chicken. Another time, she refused to let me go swim in the river with my friends, the young Jutras and Raymond, who went on to drown during that outing. She was also apprehensive in a car, particularly when her husband decided to exceed thirty-five miles per hour.

I remember above all that October day in 1919 when, aged six, I was at the Corbeau Line school together with my sisters Judith and Thérèse, and Germaine came to fetch us. We had to go home, my mother was very ill. We all found ourselves at her bedside, where, gripped by fear and anxiety, we awaited her imminent passing. Towards eleven in the morning, she died away in her bed, surrounded and loved by us all.

At the time, I did not fully grasp the gravity of the event. The day of the service, it was cold and the ground was frozen. Just before the interment, a cousin took the step of opening the tomb: my last recollection of her is therefore an image of my mother in her dress of the Tertiary Order. It was a heartbreaking moment for us, the little ones, who had trouble understanding but nevertheless instinctively felt the tragedy of that moment which I was never able to forget. It was, alas, only the first such loss I was to suffer. My father, from whom the loss of his beloved wife was a mortal blow, never quite recovered from it and passed away suddenly a bare fourteen months later.

When she learned of the death of my father, our aunt, Hedwidge Bergeron, came to our house. As soon as she arrived, she dismantled the

Christmas tree and prepared us to receive the mortal remains of our father. Following his burial, our guardian, Louis Allard, our father's brother and friend, made the necessary decisions. He sold the land, the buildings, the farm implements, the house and everything in it. It was our cousin Joseph McMahon who bought the whole thing for $14,000. A portion of that money would later be used for the education of the family.

What happened to my six sisters after January 1921 and with the provisions Uncle Louis made with respect to them?

Anaïs, the oldest of the children, at first returned to the convent to complete her studies. Subsequently, she quickly became the family's guiding hand. In 1923, in spite of the scarcity of her resources, she took charge of my sisters Germaine and Judith as well as my own little self. At that time, Anaïs was an elementary school teacher at the Académie Saint-Urbain, in Saint-Laurent. She supplemented her income by giving piano lessons and by playing the organ in the parish of Saint-Laurent.

All four of us lived in Montreal until her marriage, on June 29, 1926, to Arthur Rousseau (by whom she later had five sons and two daughters). We then went to Nicolet and, after a brief stay, moved on to Trois-Rivières. Anaïs did not want to place the full burden of her sisters and brother on the shoulders of her husband alone. She therefore opened a flower shop (Fleuriste Laviolette, still in business today). The shop enabled her to finance Judith's studies and my own as well as a great many of her numerous other activities.

Towards 1931, Madeleine joined our group of Allards. In 1938, Anaïs offered Irène a study trip to Italy. At the same time, she had become deeply involved in the social and cultural life of Trois-Rivières. She devoted herself to music, and to the local concert society, and became a co-founder of "Jeunesses musicales du Canada." In recognition of her efforts, the concert hall of the Trois-Rivières Cultural Centre has been dedicated to her. In 1969, she became a member of the Order of Canada. In 1983, she received posthumously a special medal of the Ministry of Cultural Affairs of Quebec. Her life had ended in 1971 during a tourist trip to Martinique. From everywhere, the honours she so richly deserved poured in. Myself, I shall forever remember Anaïs as a great lady who left us much too soon but whose qualities of courage, tenacity and generosity have been left in heritage both to her own family and to the young people of her time.

Born on March 3, 1908, Germaine was taken under the care of uncle Louis. The very day of Anaïs' wedding, Germaine suffered a serious accident in Nicolet. For two years she was confined to a wheelchair, then she underwent an operation that left her with a handicap. Between the day of her accident and her wedding on January 23, 1932, she lived with Arthur and Anaïs Rousseau, helping as best she could in regrouping the Allards because, in spite of her difficulties, Germaine managed to earn enough money to depend on no one. She even found opportunities to exhibit her numerous talents. She had a beautiful dramatic soprano voice that made her very sought-after by the various churches and parish halls in Trois-Rivières and its vicinity. Therefore, she often sang either as a soloist or, in the thirties, with me at her side. We both have very pleasant memories of that beautiful period in our youth. Germaine was also a very gifted painter and decorator. Above all, she was a very good seamstress who shared that skill by teaching at Singer's. After her marriage to Raoul Provencher, a lawyer, and later Queen's Counsel, she gave up her outside activities and devoted herself exclusively to educating her daughter Louise. Over the years that followed, she rendered great services to the parish and diocese works. Acknowledging this, His Holiness Pope Pius XII had his apostolic nuncio in Canada, Monseigneur Giovanni Panico, give her in 1956, in Trois-Rivières, the Pro Ecclesia et Pontifice medal. Since she moved to Quebec City in 1962, she has been making ornamental ensembles for the liturgical ceremonies. The quality of her work is remarkable. To me, Germaine (perhaps the sister who most resembles our mother) is and will always be a model for the family.

Born on December 17, 1909, Thérèse never left the Nicolet-Yamaska area. Indeed, she was taken in as early as January 1921 by our aunt, Hedwidge Allard Bergeron, who, with her husband, was a landowner in the village of Baie-du-Febvre. Thérèse studied assiduously at the local convent of the Sisters of the Assumption, from which she graduated. At age eighteen, on June 12, 1928, she married Hermann Rousseau and went to live at the ancestral farm of the Rousseaus at Bas-de-la-Baie. Thérèse's dowry was the cultural heritage received from her mother and the courage that both Victorine and Ernest had had in abundance. She was first the "daughter-in-law" within the large family of Omer Rousseau and Odélie Vincent, who were still alive. Then, at age twenty, she began to raise her own children. In the end, she had five sons and three daughters who, inspired by her and her husband, would form a close, loving family. During her last years of life, Thérèse reigned alone over this little world that gradually expanded to accommodate twenty or so grandchildren. On July 11, 1982, she passed away in the house where she had lived for fifty-four years and joined Hermann in the Rousseau family plot at the parish cemetery.

Judith was almost ten years old when my father died. She then went to Victoriaville to live with her cousin Florette Allard-Milot, the daughter of uncle Louis (Florette had married the brother of her father's second wife). Judith spent two delightful years there before going in September 1923 to Sainte-Rose de Laval, where she completed her primary schooling. Then, it was on to the great convent of the Sisters of the Holy Cross in Saint-Laurent. After her secondary studies, she joined a part of the family at Anaïs' place. She decided to become a nurse and started her training at the Normand and Cross Hospital under the direction of "garde Bertrand," a legendary local figure. However, after her pediatrics training stage at the Notre-Dame-de-Liesse nursery, she gave up, announcing that she would rather be a novice with the Sisters of the Holy Cross. She still had time to become godmother to her niece, Louise Provencher, before entering the convent in Saint-Laurent. At her final vows, she took the name of Sister Sainte-Judith-des-Anges. She remained as jovial in religious life as she had been before. To this day, she knows how to make everyone around her laugh. A musician at heart, she taught the violin and the piano. Her congregation sent her to Solesme (France) to study liturgical music. While there, she also prepared a thesis on the new forms of religious expression. Skilled in many fields, she held various administrative and management positions within the order. She returned to Sainte-Rose de Laval as a provincial of the Mille-Isles Province. I call her "my little sister," which refers both to her small physical size and to her dual role as a "sister," in addition to the fact that we were personally very close, being the middle children of the family. In fact, although the circumstances of life often separated us, they were never able to overshadow our strong mutual affection.

Irène is a somewhat special case. She was only three years old, in 1921, when she had to leave the family. Her memories of that first part of her life are therefore vague. Through the mediation of Uncle Philippe Trudel, of Montreal, she was adopted by Mr. and Mrs. Frédéric Moquin, a childless couple. Mrs. Moquin was a remarkable woman and little Irène found in her the maternal affection that her natural mother could not give her. Mr. Moquin was a plumbing contractor on Balmoral Street, in the heart of Montreal. He was a dignified man who had the trust of his neighbours as well as the authorities of his parish, Notre-Dame de Montréal, of which he became a church warden around 1924. Irène's childhood, thus ran its course normally. She passed her summer at the family cottage at Saint-Pie-de-Bagot, where she became acquainted with the other members of her new family. She started her studies at the Académie Saint-Urbain, her neighbourhood school. Like my other sisters, she completed her studies at the convent in Saint-Laurent. Irène had a remarkable voice that Maestro Wilfrid Pelletier had the opportunity to hear, and he recommended that she study in Italy with a teacher who had taught his own wife, Rose Bampton. Irène sang at my wedding and left New York for Italy on January 10, 1939. Although very successful, her stay was not untroubled. Indeed, touring with the Opera Company of Parma, she was in Budapest when the war broke out in September 1939. Arrested immediately, she was a little worried and sent me a telegram. At the time, I was a captain mobilized in the Canadian Army. Having recovered from my surprise and shock, I went to the office of the

Honourable Ernest Lapointe, who led me to that of the Prime Minister, the Right Honorable William Lyon Mackenzie King, who was also in charge of Canadian External Affairs. The Prime Minister immediately phoned the British Embassy in Budapest. Released within twenty-four hours, Irène returned to Milan to continue her studies.

The war between the Allies and Germany continued without major actions on the western front: it was the phoney war. Irène, in an Italy that was still officially neutral, nevertheless got some advance information at the U.S. consulate where she was advised to take the first boat for America, just in case the Italian situation might change. Just before Il Duce decided in 1940 to join the fray at Germany's side, Irène climbed—without having made reservations—aboard the last liner leaving Genoa, the S.S. *George Washington*. The passengers had hardly reached Gibraltar when Italy invaded France across its south-eastern border. Irène therefore returned just in time, chagrined that she was unable to complete her studies in Milan but ready to continue them in New York. Finally, she returned to Quebec in 1942.

During her Italian stay she had acquired excellent technique. She was subsequently often applauded in concert and warmly congratulated by such luminaries of the music world as Milton Cross of the Metropolitan, Robert Nielher, musical director of McGill, with whom she did the famous "Exultate Jubilate" by Mozart, and the conductor of the Montreal Symphony Orchestra, Désiré Defowe, with whom she interpreted Demoiselle Elue by Debussy. The critics unanimously acknowledged the perfection of her technique and the rich tone of her voice, which did seem tailor-made for Puccini, particularly when she interpreted Liù, in *Turandot*, or arias from *Suor Angelica*. But what could one do in Quebec, in wartime, with that much talent? One gave a few concerts, sang for Victory Bond campaigns or for the soldiers. You vegetated, you taught your skill and, especially, you became discouraged. This is just about what happened to Irène. After her marriage to Emile Leblanc, a childhood friend, she raised their daughter Louise before starting to give singing lessons once again. A perfectionist, she never again sang on a great stage. Upon Emile's death, she settled in Shawinigan where she still teaches today. The newspaper *La Presse* devoted a short article to Irène in its February 7, 1984 issue, recalling her great years.

In October 1919, Madeleine was only two months old. She was a year-and-a-half when my father passed away in January 1921. Taken into the family of our Aunt Philomène, my mother's sister and the wife of parish physician Dr. Arsène Descôteaux, she lived with them for about ten years before joining her sister and godmother Anaïs. Madeleine never had much luck. Early on in her adult life, she was discovered to have serious heart problems. Afterwards, she spent a great deal of her time between the operating room and the convalescent and rest home. However, she managed to give expression to a natural talent for ceramics and was very successful, living happily in Sainte-Agathe-des-Monts.

At the time of my father's death, I was only seven years old. There was some discussion concerning whether I should be given up for adoption or sent to an orphanage. Hector Trudel, an uncle in Manchester, U.S., offered to shelter me. However, Anaïs intervened with Uncle Louis so that I would be kept around for some time longer. I think I should say here that our family had been very united up to then. These family ties were going to be kept as close as possible during the upheavals. Through her intervention, Anaïs had provided further evidence of the will to stay together. So I spent the year 1921 at my Uncle Joseph Allard's. Unlike my sisters Judith and Thérèse, I therefore did not have to change schools in order to complete that school year. At Uncle Joseph's I was warmly received by my cousins Albert and Albertine, particularly the latter who became a virtual mother to me. She had me recite my lessons and my catechism so well that I moved to the head of my class and picked up the religion prize. However, destiny took its course and Albertine, already very ill, died on October 23, 1923 at the age of twenty-two.

In the summer of 1922, I went to Lucien Allard, a nephew of my father's, who lived in Saint-Grégoire de Nicolet. It was from there that I left in August 1923 for Montreal, where I was received by a cousin, Rose Trudel, the only daughter of the American uncle Trudel. She had become the reverend sister Sainte-Marie-de-Sainte-Tharcille (congregation of the Holy Cross). At the time, she was the principal of Sainte-Brigitte School on Papineau Street. I stayed there only a few days before being transferred to the Saint-Laurent boarding school, on Côté Street, run by the Brothers of the Christian Schools. Uncle Louis and Anaïs, in spite of their very limited means, gave me that first break.

That is when I started to sing in the choir of Notre-Dame de Montréal. Also at Notre-Dame church, I served the seven o'clock mass of Father Perrin in addition to those said by visiting priests or at weddings and funerals. I have very pleasant recollections of that period spent with the Brothers of the Christian Schools, who did everything they could to enable me to have a little pocket money. This gave me some freedom, either to go swimming at the public baths, as they were called at the time, or to take the streetcar to visit Anaïs.

Two years later, in 1925, I entered Saint-Laurent College which became my true alma mater. I remained there until Anaïs' wedding, which brought me to the Nicolet seminary (I found the seven months I spent there quite difficult), and I completed my year at Académie de La Salle, in Trois-Rivières, as an external student. Finally, I returned to Saint-Laurent College the following year.

It was at Saint-Laurent that the idea of a military career first occurred to me. To this day, I cannot say exactly what led me onto this path. I shall, however, return briefly to the past to indicate how the attraction to military life had manifested itself.

The name of the priest who christened me and agreed to become my godfather in June 1913 was Rodolphe Blondin. He was a real character. Born in Baie-du-Febvre on July 26, 1848, he had managed to sandwich a tour of duty with the zouaves between studies at the Nicolet Seminary. This had given him the opportunity, in September 1870, of seeing the Piedmontese invade Rome. He had been ordained later in Trois-Rivières by Bishop Louis-François Laflèche, the local bishop but also one of the advocates of sending the zouaves to Italy. Subsequently, Blondin served as the priest of Sainte-Monique, from March 1874 until his death on December 4, 1923. He had been appointed a canon ten days before his death. I suppose that what I remember about him, except for a few brief encounters during my first few years, is my having been christened by that priest-soldier-godfather.

On to other facts I remember. During World War I, my mother or Anaïs read the news out loud for the benefit of the family. They paused at the names of those who had fallen and—mainly my mother—spoke to us about mother's cousins or people from the parish who had gone to war. The victory at Vimy as well as the explosion in Halifax harbour made a real impression on me. In addition, I had greatly admired the men I had seen parading before the small railway station of Sainte-Perpétue, where I often went with my father. Coming from all regions to the west of us, they were on their way to Halifax and the war, and I was fascinated by their khaki uniforms. They gave the impression that they were going to accomplish great feats of arms, while also symbolizing adventure. I had even noted that many spoke English, which I did not understand. Later, at the College, through our Canadian history courses, I felt a strong attraction to great military achievements, from the feats of the Marquis de Montcalm all the way to the saga of the Great War.

At any rate, at Saint-Laurent I was a member of the cadet corps, which was very well organized. I have very happy memories of it, as well as a nice picture in uniform. As the cadet officer of the Montreal region, Lieutenant-Colonel Papineau used to come and give us lectures and conduct inspections. I certainly did not foresee that all this marked the beginning of an orientation that events were going to prove decisive. All I can say is that at that stage I had a deep yearning for order, comradeship and team spirit, which I believe to be among the qualities required for a successful military career.

Nevertheless, there was nothing at the time to really distinguish me from tens of thousands of other Quebec teenagers. For example, like the overwhelming majority of them, I was brought up in a French-Canadian environment and did not not speak English. The little English I knew had been learned at the College and turned out to be quite insufficient.

My brother-in-law, Arthur Rousseau, Anaïs' husband, often repeated that in order to succeed in life knowledge of English was worth more than a B.A. He was perhaps not altogether right, but there was a lot of truth in what he said. In 1929, it was therefore decided that I would go to Kitchener, Ontario, to learn English. Why Kitchener? First of all, because Arthur knew that town, where he had had an opportunity to stay (and, as he was fond of pointing out, to be bored). Secondly, there were interesting sports activities there, including hockey, at which I excelled, and which would allow me to earn some spending money.

On the way there, accompanied by Anaïs and Arthur, I visited the Canadian National Exhibition in Toronto, which I found rather extraordinary. I also started to become aware of the beauty of Ontario. After the exhibition, we went to Kitchener. Since I was a week early, there was no place for me to stay at the college. We thus ended up at a boarding house kept by Mrs. Kuntz, whose husband had been killed fighting on the German side during World War I. I came to like Mrs. Kuntz a great deal; she had two sons, including Harry—now unfortunately deceased—with whom I became friends. My sister and brother-in-law thus left me at 47 Weber Street, knowing that I was well taken care of. At the time, my English was virtually non-existent but the circumstances would quickly correct that situation.

This brings back a memory that will be quite meaningful to any French Canadian (over thirty-five years of age, I must add). In Kitchener, the religious outlook of Catholics differed greatly from what I had known in Trois-Rivières. As a result, I found myself in a fairly amusing situation. One evening, Harry Kuntz invited me to follow him, using mostly sign language. He was all dressed up, better than usual. So I did the same and we thus left wearing our best suits. When we arrived at St. Mary's church, I followed Harry to the basement where, to my amazement, I found, under the supervision of a good priest who seemed quite Catholic to me, a group of young boys and girls who had come to dance to the sounds of a small band. I hesitated a little, because in Trois-Rivières we had been prohibited from dancing "under penalty of mortal sin." I therefore obviously did not know how to dance. But I quickly forgot my scruples; since it was all being supervised by a priest and I was in another environment, the customs of which I had to follow, I joined the party. As we approached a table with Harry, he presented me to Dorothy, a beautiful young girl. It was with her that I danced for the first time in my life . . . but not the last, for dear little

Dorothy was a charming girl. She introduced me to her parents and throughout my stay in Kitchener we continued to see each other, to dance and skate together. She was my first "sweetheart."

A little later, I took a room on the fourth floor of St. Jerome's College, run by the Resurrection Fathers. Father Dehler, president of the college and later bishop of Bermuda, was a man of great class. He was also one of the few to speak a little French. Fathers Mayer and Heiffley, in addition to their German mother tongue, spoke only English; they were both very understanding and kind to me.

A few days later, other young people arrived from Quebec, including Jean-Pierre Samson, from Lévis, who was to become one of my great friends. A certain Lebel, from Rivière-du-Loup, and the two Francoeur brothers joined the group. There was also Jos Théberge, from Saint-Siméon, near Rimouski, a gentleman, a marvellous companion (a friend to all), a "good guy" who was not very athletic but who was truly exceptional in every other respect and whom one could easily tease. Like myself, they had all come to learn English. I have remained friends to this day with Jean-Pierre Samson and Jos Théberge.

The 1929 school year began, as far as I am concerned, a little differently from previous years, in that I understood nothing during lectures. Fortunately, one of my teachers paid particular attention to my needs. One week after my arrival, things began to improve, and after three months, I mastered my second language quite well.

One day, we were all gathered outside for the selection of the football players. Since I was big and strong, I was asked whether I wanted to be part of the team. I accepted. However, I knew nothing about the rules of the game. By observing the others, I gradually understood what I was supposed to do. Finally, I ended up being a member of the college's second team. At first, I had the impression that I was forever buried under a pileup of guys who were trying to grab the ball. Since I do not like being kicked around, I managed to crawl out. At one point, the quarterback, an American by the name of Cerullo, passed the football to me and I started to run. I crossed the goal line and all my teammates congratulated me as if I were a hero. In fact, I was only dimly aware of what was going on. It was only when I looked at the scoreboard that I realized that we had just taken a big lead over the opposing team. I was, of course, very proud of myself, but it was not until later that I really knew what football was all about.

The hockey season came next, a sport I knew well. From the very first match, I was a member of the first team, then I transferred to a regional league team that wanted my services. Very quickly, I became a regular on that team. Through that club I earned a little money and gained many friends as well, including my line mates Carlo Kuntz, at centre, and

Kowalski, on left wing. I was also a member of the baseball team, at second base, a position I occupied throughout the period I practised that sport.

However, my studies gave me some cause for concern. Up to then, I had followed the classical curriculum, and I was therefore somewhat weak in mathematics, physics, algebra and geometry. I was wondering what to do about it, when a teacher offered me special tutoring courses. I completed them successfully and as a result was able to obtain satisfactory marks, passing at the end of the year.

I have always been very enthusiastic about Kitchener. In 1929, it was a friendly little town of 45,000 people, offering a wide range of activities in the arts, music and sports; in summary, a very friendly place where the little Quebecker that I was found life very agreeable.

It is now easy for me to see that Kitchener was a good start for me for many reasons. I learned English as well as certain sports that were seldom played in Quebec (football, basketball, swimming). The main effect was that I expanded my horizons. I was able to see that there were different ways in which people could be practising Catholics. The Catholicism of Ontarians seemed to me more human than ours as it was ready to grant some freedom to the young. Moreover, I saw that the English and the Irish, often despised in Quebec, were after all people like any others. I made many American and Canadian friends who did not hesitate to introduce me to their families and even invited me to their homes. In fact, in spite of my broken English in the first few months, I was always received with open arms. Some friends I made then remained friends for life.

As for the city of Kitchener, it has always treated me with a great deal of warmth. For instance, in the years that followed, the local newspaper never hesitated to announce my promotions. My Kitchener stay was mentioned with pride on such occasions. I therefore had the feeling I was a citizen of the city. About twenty-five years after I left, I was invited to return there to address the students of my old school and their parents. I was received with a huge ovation and boundless human warmth.

That stay was more useful to me than university studies could have been. One must remember that, in any case, access to university was not an easy thing at the time. University study was very expensive and the curriculum options offered were fewer than today. Moreover, in 1930, we were at the beginning of the Great Depression. It was virtually impossible for a student with no resources, as I was, to think of embarking on that path. I therefore resigned myself to this . . . all the more readily since my marks in Kitchener had not been brilliant.

I returned to Trois-Rivières in 1930 with newborn confidence in my capabilities, perhaps because I now spoke English well. I was seventeen years old. My real family was that of my sister Anaïs, her husband Arthur and their children, whom I considered my brothers and sisters. It was quite natural, as the "oldest," that I should think of contributing to the collective income. The October 1929 stock market crash, though, had by then become a financial and economic crisis. By 1930, the depression had arrived and was deepening. There were already millions of unemployed throughout the industrial world. In Canada, unemployment quickly reached 530,000, a terrible figure at the time. The wages of those who had jobs were very low, as was the cost of living.

I managed to find night work at the Reed Motors garage, at the corner of Notre-Dame and Laviolette in Trois-Rivières, where I sold gasoline (23¢ and 25¢ a gallon), parked cars, repaired flats and responded to emergency calls. I also found out about tips which, added to my weekly wage of $10.00, allowed me to go out with young ladies from time to time. Unfortunately, eight months after hiring me, Mr. Reed went bankrupt.

I was unemployed for a while until a friend told me that they were looking for part-time stevedores at the harbour. At 7 a.m. next morning, I was at the docks. Because of my name, I was the first one called. I filled in my employment card and was agreeably surprised to find out that I was going to earn 65· an hour. Although the situation was great for the moment, I knew that it was only temporary. On another occasion, I tried a new occupation, trucking, which I quickly gave up.

Another, better opportunity soon arose: my brother-in-law hired me as an accountant for his small funeral home. Once again, I earned $10.00 a week, but with room and board. I had joined the ranks of the privileged.

That job enabled me to do something I had really wanted, namely, to take singing lessons. At first, I studied music with Mrs. Vertefeuille, and later with Rodolphe Plamondon, who had returned from Europe. I loved singing and music, and my teachers also encouraged me. However, since a career was impossible I quickly abandoned that activity because I would have had to leave for New York to make a living. Room and board alone, though, would have cost more than my potential earnings with the chorus of the Metropolitan. Nor were there any bursaries that could have allowed me to go on.

Nevertheless, during that short apprenticeship I made some public appearances in school year-end recitals, then in concert halls with my sister Germaine, who had a very beautiful voice. Anaïs accompanied us in our travels and urged us on. Later, with some friends, we formed a quartet that met very irregularly for several years until the accidental death of our accompanist, who drowned in the St. Lawrence. I thus continued singing long after finishing my studies. Up to about the end of 1932, I even sang solo quite often. I also did a little amateur theatre work on the side. In fact, from 1931 to 1933, I was the treasurer of the Compagnons Notre-Dame theatre group.

Singing and the theatre were not my only extracurricular activities. I was always interested in sports and participated in funding a hockey club called the "Canadien indépendant." We practised in the Knights of Columbus skating rink, at Volontaires and Royale, which was no bigger than a tennis court.

We needed equipment, though, and most of us did not have a cent. I therefore went to see J.-B. Loranger to discuss the purchase of what we needed. Father Jean-Baptiste had a great heart and gave in fairly readily to my pleadings, so that we soon had eighteen complete outfits, including a goalie outfit. The initial cash for this transaction was provided by Mr. Loranger, while I was able to pay for my sweater, number 2. Within two months, however, each member had repaid his debt.

Our club, which had the letters CI (quite close to the CH of the better-known Montreal team) was part of the City League. We attracted a fair number of spectators and were the only ones to have "our" skating rink. It was around that skating rink, maintained by the young people of the neighbourhood, that many ace players found a sweetheart among their loyal cheerleaders.

In the mid-thirties, my life took yet another turn when Arthur Rousseau founded a funeral insurance company of which I became the first secretary-treasurer. A year later, Arthur decided to open a branch in Shawinigan and asked me to run it. My stay in Shawinigan completely changed my life: at twenty-three, I became almost independent.

I had set up the Shawinigan Youth Chamber of Commerce and I became its second president in 1937. It was in that capacity that—accompanied by my friend Gérard Garceau and a small delegation—I had the opportunity of going to advocate a cause in Quebec City. The federal government had just started offering young people an in-plant technical training programme. We wanted Quebec to approve it and even to participate in it because this would enable many young unemployed to earn some money while learning a trade. Jean Bruchési, then Secretary of the province under the first Union Nationale government, received us and explained that education pertains to the provinces and that the federal government has nothing to do with it. We therefore came back with a rejection . . . and with the promise that the bridge over the Saint-Maurice, in Shawinigan, would be rebuilt. Readers might wonder whether there is ever anything new under the sun!

At the time, although I did not know it really, I was already engaged on a path that I was to follow for more than thirty years. As mentioned earlier, I had had a stint with the cadets at Saint-Laurent College. When I arrived in Trois-Rivières, I claimed to be two years older (I was sixteen in the summer of 1929) in order to enlist in the Three Rivers Regiment with some friends from Académie La Salle. I was assigned to company C commanded by

Major Joseph Marchildon. My Kitchener stay from the fall of 1929 on cut short this budding development.

The seeds, however, had been sown. Having returned to Trois-Rivières, I was approached in 1931, at the same time as my friend Maurice Barnard, by Georges Trépanier, who invited us to take the militia officer training course that was to begin in the fall. I was quite unoccupied and accepted the proposal. Trépanier and myself, as well as Lieutenant Reginald Stanford, a World War I veteran who had fought with the Royal Newfoundland Regiment, and Philippe Goulet, an ex-cadet from Académie La Salle, went to take those courses. They were given in English with a translation provided by the regimental instructor, Sergeant-Major Claeys. Of Belgian origin, Claeys was in the infantry, with the Royal Canadian Regiment.

Two evenings a week, for more than half a year, we took military law, administration, tactics and other courses. I easily passed the various stages leading to my second lieutenant's commission. On April 23, 1933, I took my oath of allegiance to King George V, before receiving my commission from Lieutenant-Colonel J. G. Vining (who passed away in 1982 and for whom I have always had the greatest respect).

This training period continued after 1933 so that by 1939 I had become a lieutenant, then a captain. One should not forget that I was in the militia, not in the regular army. However, I can say that approximately two of the six years prior to World War II were devoted to "regular service," if one were to add up all the training sessions.

Thus, I had just been commissioned second lieutenant when I was sent to Saint-Jean d'Iberville where I served with a detachment of the Royal Canadian Regiment, then with the Royal Canadian Dragoons. Budget cuts brought me back to Trois-Rivières. My military career thus see-sawed. There continued to be, though, social activities at our regimental mess, including balls, which I liked to attend. There were also courses I had to take. For instance, for many months I had to take the train (with Majors Marchildon and Trépanier) to Montreal to attend my staff courses. I very much liked those little trips paid for by the government. I left at 3 p.m. and returned home on the night train. These courses were very useful. I met certain regular force officers there whom I was going to see again following the 1939 mobilization. I also went to Kingston to improve my knowledge of staff and military administration. All of this enhanced my career and my personality because I was required to do a great deal of reading and homework on current affairs. I also became aware of the major international events that presaged the world war.

Indeed, I was well informed regarding the probability of a new conflict. For one thing, I had direct contact with the staff of the Montreal military district. I had read during my military stay in Kingston, and had since reread, *Total War* by the German Field Marshall Ludendorf who, with Hitler, had attempted a coup d'état in the twenties. Ludendorf wanted to free Germany from the humiliating terms imposed upon it by the Treaty of Versailles. I read periodicals such as *Le Mois* published by the League of Nations, which reported faithfully the conflicting events and analyzed the impasse in world affairs. I knew Clausewitz and Liddell-Hart. I often went to listen to Bob Clark, the manager of the local newspaper, the *Chronicle*, who liked to discuss international relations with the young people of Trois-Rivières.

All these activities prepared me to assume responsibilities. The first major occasion arose in 1937. I was by then well-versed in military matters. It so happened that after years of military budget cutbacks the Canadian government wanted to re-arm. It increased the defence budget from 10 to 65 million dollars. It should be noted that the Canadian Army did not start acquiring a serious motor vehicle fleet until 1936. Up to then, for instance, our cavalry was on horseback, and that was the year when it had to abandon that noble animal and replace it with tanks.

In the fall of 1937, the Quebec Federation of Youth Chambers of Commerce held a meeting in Montreal, to which I was a delegate. At the end of the congress, when many participants were preparing to leave, I heard resolutions being read, one of which, presented at the last minute, was going to be submitted to the federal government to protest against the increase in the military budget and, in fact, to request its reduction. It was almost too late to intervene, but I managed to rally a few friends and my brother-in-law Raoul Provencher. They ran to the railway stations and to the Windsor Hotel to persuade people to come back. During that time, I engaged in filibustering to delay voting. When the assembly was fairly complete, I launched into a speech that lasted a good half hour. I urged people to vote against the resolution. After counting the hands raised, meeting chairman Roger Ouimet had to abandon the project, to the great despair of its advocates, all French-Canadian nationalists. That is how some circles thought one year prior to the Munich crisis. At that time, André Laurendeau, author of that proposal, and myself, had some disagreements. I must say that we later became friends and I came to appreciate and support his action within the Royal Commission of Inquiry on Bilingualism and Biculturalism.

I have already hinted that since my arrival in Shawinigan I had developed some independence with respect to my adoptive family. I therefore started seriously thinking about establishing my own family. I bought furniture on credit. I had a good salary that allowed me to meet the monthly instalments and quickly acquire the necessary basics which did, however, include a piano and record player—essentials for the music-lover I was.

A first sentimental disappointment did not discourage me. I had courted for some time a beautiful anglophone young lady who practised (fortunately, I would say) the Anglican religion to which she was very attached. Since I wanted to remain a Catholic, things went no further.

Then I dated Simone Piché more seriously. Simone's father Gustave was a pioneer in his field, having set up a forestry department in Quebec. By organizing the rational exploitation of forests in our province, he had not necessarily made himself popular with the forest industry, which was completely dominated by anglophones at that time. It was with great calm, extreme competence and a clear wish to serve his Quebec compatriots that Gustave Piché set up his department in spite of the well-known reluctance of those used to buying anything that might be profitable, and for whom the ends justified the means. He gave that department everything he had, and ended his life in almost complete oblivion. A plaque in his honour has been placed on the Laval University Forestry Building.

His wife, Césarine Paré, was a descendant of the Noblet-Duplessis lineage. As they say, she had class. She transmitted that quality to Simone, who studied at the Sillery convent, where she graduated. Like any young lady of good family, she learned there etiquette, music, theatre, classical drama, ballet, and so forth, in addition to the classics, which she still knows well. She made many girlfriends for life during that stint. In her opinion, the nuns of Jésus-Marie are the best educators in the world, and she is discreetly proud to have been trained by them.

After her studies, Simone had many friends because the Piché home on Chemin Ste-Foy in Quebec City, with its large grounds and tennis court, was a meeting place for the young people of the Upper Town. Val-Pichet, near Shawinigan, was another such meeting place and for a good reason: the presence of five lovely young girls.

Val-Pichet was a wooded property of 7,000 acres comprising about ten lakes. Sixty acres were cultivated. There was also a vegetable garden and an orchard. Built on the mountainside, the house had a large verandah and a long, stone staircase. The family gathered at Val-Pichet for the summer while Mr. Piché, with Simone as his driver, visited the forestry centres of the province. For the Piché girls, the days at Val-Pichet were sometimes long, but during the weekends the house suddenly filled with young men who, led by Mr. Piché, went on outings throughout the property, over the mountains or to lakes where a little fishing guaranteed beautiful trout.

I had met the third of the Piché girls at a military ball. After the party, I had driven her back to Val-Pichet and I had been invited to return. It was during that second visit that I noticed Simone, the second of the family. She had a Protestant date, which did not please her parents at all. We started to go out together.

After the usual visits, we became engaged at Val-Pichet on November 11, 1938, last celebration of the Armistice between the two wars. The Munich crisis had delayed our engagement somewhat, for I declared that I was ready to go fight at the first call. The settlement between Daladier, Chamberlain and Hitler gave us the hope that the worst would be avoided.

Simone and I were going to get married next spring but my young sister planned to go to Italy in January in order to learn singing. We therefore advanced the date to January 7, 1939. Having left Quebec City for Montreal a few months earlier with his family, Mr. Piché organized a magnificent ceremony. There were many guests from Quebec City and Trois-Rivières. The religious ceremony was held at the Saint-Jacques church in Montreal. Arthur Rousseau was my best man while Mr. Piché gave away his daughter. My first cousin Maurice Rousseau, a priest, blessed our marriage while Irène sang and George Lindsay played the organ.

Following the ceremony, we all went to the Piché home on Sherbrooke Street for a big reception. The champagne flowed, the toasts were many and everyone was happy. It was thus on a beautiful "spring" day (the temperature was 40°F) that Simone and I started our life together.

Before leaving on our honeymoon, we went to see Judith who had obtained permission to receive us in the parlour. This meeting, too, was filled with joy. We then headed for New York, where we stayed for ten days. We took advantage of it to visit the Metropolitan Opera, Town Hall, Carnegie Hall, the Metropolitan Museum and Radio City. We were at dockside when Irène embarked for Italy. Then we returned to Shawinigan, to our friends and to a life that promised to be bright and beautiful.

We had barely settled down and were expecting our first child when I was called out because the mobilization plans of our regiment had to be prepared, just in case. I left Rousseau et Frères, not without regrets, to join the regular armed forces and to start a career that was going to last thirty-three years. As we shall see, I had the extreme good luck, compared to many of my colleagues, to live mainly in Canada until midway through the war. The many changes in our life caused my wife to exhibit quickly two major qualities that she undoubtedly owed to her father, and which she would subsequently have ample opportunity to practise: her serenity and a good sense of organization.

Immediately following the start of mobilization, she moved from Shawinigan to Trois-Rivières where she spent almost the entire war and where our three children were born. The arrival of a pregnant stranger, without a "visible" husband, caused an uproar among a few of her new neighbours. However, Anaïs and Arthur were nearby, always ready to help, and this was a great comfort to her.

2

The First Years of War: The Theory

After the Munich Agreement, which ceded part of Czechoslovakia to Germany, the international situation continued to deteriorate. Mr. Chamberlain made an effort which Adolf Hitler, with his mad ambitions, found inadequate. By the end of 1938 and the beginning of 1939, it was evident that feverish preparations were underway among the Germans. The entire world lived in a perpetual state of fear.

During this period, the talk in this country centred on the possibility of peace. The country was unprepared, both mentally and physically, for war. Let us look, first of all, at the mental aspect.

As of September 1939, the Poles were dying in defence of their country but, as was becoming increasingly evident from a Western concept of civilization, they carried little weight in the discussions already sweeping Canada. We were entering upon an immense human tragedy which left many demagogues cold. Orangemen and nationalist extremists alike plunged gleefully into the vast new field of activities offered by Canadian involvement in the war.

Those who supported unstinted participation appealed to a patriotism marked, all too often, by British overtones. "For King and country!" they cried, but the country they meant was not necessarily Canada. In Toronto, where one patriotic rally followed another, voices were raised to sing "There'll always be an England." This over-identification with things British created an opening for the opponents of participation, most of them French-Canadian nationalists. To them, England represented the Empire, the Boer War and submission, while Ottawa was merely an agent of London. France was largely unknown, except as the nation that had dismissed Canada as merely "a few acres of snow." In many circles, there was open talk of using neutrality as an opportunity to grow rich, as the United States had done from 1914 to 1917.

Between these two poles were the Liberal politicians and their entourage who, election after election, had demonstrated that they were against the Conservatives and the conscription they had imposed during the previous war. The Liberals also claimed that they wanted to make Canada a great country. However, by 1939, it was clear that they had somehow forgotten to do so during their three terms in office since 1921. Nor had the Conservatives done any better during their own period in power, from 1930 to 1935. Neither of the two parties had succeeded in creating a situation in which all Canadians, from sea to sea, could agree on a few fundamental objectives.

Mentalities had changed little since 1919, and differences of opinion abounded. It would not be correct to say that English Canadians formed a monolithic block in favour of participation to the bitter end. For instance, until Germany attacked the USSR, some of the country's anglophone socialists were pacifists. In fact, a federal Member of Parliament had led anti-participation demonstrations in Toronto. In addition, contemporary anglophone historians have recorded the many rifts which existed in the supposed unanimity of English-speaking Canadians around the concept of their country's participation in a war on European soil. However, it can be said that, in English Canada, young men were generally encouraged to enlist. In French Canada, on the other hand, a man in uniform was often seen as an opportunist, or worse.

Francophones were faced with another handicap. Their country was not prepared for war. Within the Department of Defence, for example, this unreadiness was reflected in the fact that no serious effort had been made to recruit the population in general, let alone to do so in French among francophones.

In my case, although I had already made up my mind long before, it did not mean it was any easier when confronted by the circumstances. I have already mentioned some of my memories from World War I. But there were others. For instance, at the end of the war, there was the return of the local hero, Corporal Bruno Milot. A ceremony, led by Father Blondin, had commemorated the event. Yet the parish was bitterly divided on the true value of Milot's act: those who had gone into hiding to avoid conscription certainly did not share the good father's enthusiasm.

Even within my own family, feelings were mixed. The division between my father and his brothers was a definite factor. There were others, equally tangible. It was said that one of papa's cousins had entered the priesthood to avoid conscription. My mother's family, with its American connections, remained neutral. The participation of the United States, later in 1917, had done nothing to change this view.

Then came 1939 and the time for one trained in the militia to decide whether or not he was willing to serve either at home or beyond Canada's borders. I was newly married, and my wife was pregnant. Was marriage not the way to "salvation" for some? Should the family, in fact, not come first? Then too, the reputation of the new soldiers was hardly inspiring. The recruiting drive which took place during the early summer attracted primarily the unemployed; the next, in August, picked up a number of men not known for their high moral standards. Clearly, those who anticipated the worst and chose to don priestly robes were of a different stripe altogether. There was one interesting incident: shortly after a recruiting office opened in Shawinigan, a priest openly denounced the first volunteer from the pulpit as a traitor.

My period of introspection did not last long. The positive elements outweighed the rest. I must admit that once I had joined the cadets, during the 1920s, I had developed a sort of contempt for those who had avoided service after 1917. In addition, the decision I had reached long before, to serve my country if need be, had Simone's complete support, and this encouraged me in my resolve. I told Arthur and Anaïs Rousseau and the rest of my sisters and brothers-in-law of my decision.

In 1939, in many countries of the world, there were people who decided, often in the face of intense social pressure, that they wished to participate, out of a sense of international justice, in the events of history. In this country, the failure of the federal government to prepare the Canadian people did not prevent a large number of Canadians from committing themselves to the struggle against Nazism. Many of these volunteers felt that it was their duty to do so. I was one of the first of these to sign the forms agreeing to voluntary enlistment and service overseas: my father, despite certain positions he had held, had once sworn that he would never allow his son to be taken.

Canada's lack of physical preparation was merely a reflection of this lack of mental preparedness. Our country had virtually no regular army. The militia, while relatively well trained since 1919, had no theoretical or practical experience to prepare it for the Blitzkrieg which the Germans were about to unleash against their immediate neighbours. A certain urgency became evident, however, after June 1939, as preparations assumed an accelerated pace. The process that was to lead to mobilization was underway. In July 1939, for example, the various units were asked to inform Army Headquarters of their requirements in terms of equipment and space in the event of mobilization. I proceeded to Camp Borden, Ontario, where I was to spend much of the summer.

It is pitiful to think that at that time all we had were small tanks and machine gun carriers dating from World War I. In fact, we had no more than perhaps fifteen of these small, outdated armoured vehicles. A number of others were on a siding somewhere, because they had been imported from Great Britain and had not yet cleared Canadian customs. Those of us "in the field" found it shameful that a government could be incapable of co-ordinating two departments to the extent of allowing a few troops and instructors to prepare themselves during the summer of 1939 for the war that was now almost inevitable.

In fact, by the middle of August, when we returned to our units, the movements of German troops were being frequently reported by journalists and military attachés in Germany. On August 26, 1939, at my office in the drill hall, I received, as the regiment's adjutant, a "secret" telegram addressed to the commanding officer and containing orders to implement the security measures formulated the previous May. In essence, this involved calling out our men and protecting certain military objectives on Canadian soil previously assigned to us. Knowing that war was imminent, this represented another milestone on the road to mobilization, which, in fact, was soon to follow.

Clutching the message, I hurried to the home of Lieutenant-Colonel Herb Keating, our commanding officer. Together we returned to the drill hall to organize a meeting of the regiment's officers for 2000 hours that night, and to recall the non-commissioned officers and men. Sergeant Mailhot, my clerk, was with me, and with his help we prepared a list of five officers (Major Trépanier, Captains Meyers and Barnard, Lieutenants Johnson and Walker) and fifty men, who, as our most experienced members, would form the guard. Sergeant Pierre Jourdain, our quartermaster, was to assist this group. By 2200 hours, a group of six men was in position around the drill hall; they were to be relieved every three hours.

It was at this point that a certain amount of feverish activity began. Our lack of preparedness was painful to see. Fortunately, the government released funds which enabled us to deal gradually, if not always in orthodox fashion, with our most pressing needs. At first, we had to billet our men in boarding houses as close as possible to the drill hall because we did not have any buildings large enough to hold them all, or any cooking facilities. Equipment of every kind was unavailable. In particular, we were short of means of transportation. We rented a Ford truck, bought workboots for our new arrivals and handed out old uniforms from 1914-1918. Forms of all kinds, which military district No. 4 of Montreal was supposed to provide, failed to arrive. In fact, they had not even been printed. Once again, we had to improvise.

On Friday, August 29, 1939, we received a warning order that our regiment was to be mobilized with the first group of armoured regiments. We were extremely proud to be among the very first selected for mobilization. The Three Rivers Regiment was to serve within the framework of the 1st Armoured Brigade, which was also to include the Ontario Regiment and the Calgary Regiment.

Mobilization proceeded at a snail's pace, despite an intensive recruiting campaign. Officers and NCOs arrived, but painfully slowly. Men trickled in and we had to reject many of them because of their lack of education. Indeed, a technical organization like ours needed specialists: mechanics, radio technicians, and so forth. Our recruits had to have at least some basic familiarity with this type of material and the potential to be trained rapidly to the level required by each of the tasks. This meant that they had to have at least some background in terms of general knowledge and mathematics.

These requirements made our job difficult and recruitment a frustrating task. The situation soon became alarming and we were forced to accept volunteers from Quebec regiments which had not yet been mobilized. However, those who responded to the call were primarily anglophones. For those of us who had hoped to keep our militia regiment intact it was a tragic situation. We could see that our unit, which should have been French-speaking, would gradually become primarily anglophone. However, there was nothing we could do at that stage. The lack of preparation for the possible recruitment of francophones into services other than the infantry was already making itself felt. In this respect, however, it was not the federal government alone that was to blame. My experience in 1937, at the provincial level, had shown me that Quebec had not always been particularly receptive to the type of co-ordination required for the training of technicians. Some of the fault lay, too, with the primarily humanistic type of education that was offered in Quebec, and with the anti-military feeling which existed—although this lay, once again, within the realm of federal, rather than provincial, responsibilities.

The other two regiments of the brigade were already at full strength, and we could no longer afford delay. From the Quebec Royal Rifles we received two excellent officers, Captain Gordon Stanley and Major F. T. (Tim) Atkinson—the latter accepting a demotion to replace me. In fact, I learned of my promotion to the rank of major a few days after September 2, although the promotion was retroactive to that precise date. Mobilization, then, was just beginning when I became commanding officer of B squadron. Next, from Shawinigan, came Major Steve Gudgeon, a veteran of World War I, and from Montreal, Captain Cy Neroutsos of the 6th Hussars: both accepted demotions. Neroutsos, a very distinguished gentleman, served the regiment well and succeeded Atkinson as adjutant when Atkinson was promoted to major to command a group of more than two hundred men from Montreal's Victoria Rifles on Ile Sainte-Hélène. (Atkinson was to be assisted in this task by Lieutenant Frank Spénard.) We were joined as well by Captain Arthur Phelan of Montreal. A contingent of junior officers from Montreal's C.O.T.C. contingent filled in the gaps. They included Lieutenants Caron, Spielman, Gray, Bilodeau, Magny, Dubreuil, and others. From the United States, Captain Rickman, of the National Guard, joined us as a lieutenant. To complete the organization, Lieutenant-Colonel Herb Keating was replaced by Alex Dupuis, previously of the *Royal 22ᵉ Régiment*.

After a great deal of painful effort the regiment was finally mobilized. It then moved to the exhibition grounds in Trois-Rivières, where it was to complete its organization. During the first days, training consisted primarily of mounting guard. Our recruits occasionally forgot that they were holding loaded weapons: from time to time, someone would fire a shot without any idea how it had happened. Gradually, these "accidents" became less frequent. In early October, we began to repair the buildings which were to house us for the next winter. They were admirably suited to our purposes, since they could provide accommodation for nearly all our men. Other smaller buildings, which had previously housed food concessions, were converted into tiny houses, each capable of holding three or four officers. The mess was built over what had once been the swimming pool. All the men, old and new, English- and French-speaking alike, worked cheerfully together to make the project a success.

In the squadron for which I was responsible, I worked, with some success, to create a special atmosphere of mutual respect. This bilingual subunit was composed of three groups: anglophone, bilingual and francophone. The maintenance echelon was mixed. I instituted a new procedure: one day, everyone would speak English, and the next day, French; in this way, everyone had a chance to improve his language skills.* My squadron was very proud of its bilingualism. Spirit was excellent and understanding almost perfect, a situation which probably made it much easier for everyone to learn his job. In fact, over the years, this company has produced a large number of the regiment's fine officers. Unfortunately, I did not stay long with these men.

Early in 1940, the regiment moved to Westmount and the grounds of the Montreal Athletic Association. Following our arrival, Lieutenant-Colonel Dupuis was transferred and command passed temporarily to Major Trépanier. All of us wondered what was going to happen. After lengthy deliberation, the authorities called on J. G. Vining, the regiment's previous commanding officer, who by then was retired. To our great delight, he

---

* The *Collège militaire royal de Saint-Jean* was to adopt a somewhat similar bilingual system when it opened in 1952.

joined us in Westmount and Trépanier became his second-in-command.

Even with Vining's arrival, the men from Trois-Rivières were becoming a minority in their own regiment. Links with their city of origin were practically cut. Their unit was already over 50 per cent English-speaking and this proportion increased again after another move, to Borden. And until the end of the war, when Lieutenant-Colonel Fernand Caron assumed command, the regiment was to retain this largely anglophone nature.*

I was sent to Kingston for a refresher staff officers' course. Staff officers were in great demand and I had already taken the Militia Staff Course. This period in Kingston was to mark the beginning of a new phase for me. But before I go on, let us go back in time a little.

On October 16, 1939, during the initial phase of mobilization, our first child, Michèle, was born at Normand and Cross Hospital. A few days later, she was baptized at the Saint-Philippe Church. Her grandparents Piché became her godparents. Her Aunt Pierrette, Simone's sister, carried her to the baptismal font. Michèle thus became the first of Ernest and Victorine's grandchildren to bear the name Allard. She was greeted, of course, with joy and pride. Like her mother, she had to learn to live with the confusion that accompanies war. Michèle spent the first years of the war between Trois-Rivières (where Simone was involved in the war effort, in addition to raising her baby), Val-Pichet and Montreal.

In the spring of 1940, then, I left my family in Quebec and presented myself at the Royal Military College in Kingston for the staff officers' course, which was to last one month. There I met a large number of officers of my own rank with whom I was to be deeply involved in the years to come. The course was excellent. The instructors, headed by Lieutenant-Colonel K. C. Burness, were experienced and of high calibre. The students came from all the mobilized regiments in the country. For me, it was a marvellous experience. The commandant of the college at the time was from Trois-Rivières, Brigadier Kenneth Stuart, later Chief of the General Staff. His presence added to the general quality of the teaching because his lectures were extremely interesting.

On completion of this course, I was chosen to continue my training in some of Britain's specialized schools. At that time, the Germans had already invaded Belgium, the Netherlands and France. When I boarded the *Empress of Australia*, en route to Great Britain, I knew, as did my many Canadian comrades in arms, that we were going to learn the art of war as much as to provide reinforcements to a Great Britain all too painfully aware of its tragic situation.

---

* Jean-Yves Gravel's *Histoire du Régiment de Trois-Rivières* (1982) is eloquent on this subject.

I arrived in Great Britain a few weeks after the evacuation from Dunkirk and was immediately sent to the communications and technical training school. From there, I went on to Linney Head, where I did further training as a gunner for another month. Next, I travelled to Bulford, on Salisbury Plain, to improve my knowledge of tactics. There I had the opportunity to measure myself against trainees from the British army. It was a new and enriching experience, and one that was to be of enormous value to me. The people of Salisbury welcomed us warmly. The town had long been a major garrison centre, and the soldiers of the Canadian Expeditionary Force of 1914-18 had assembled and trained there before going on to the French front. Here I had the impression of being "in the thick of things." Some of the Canadians I met in Great Britain were to become close friends: one was Murray Johnson, whom I still see. The same was true of the British, a number of whom were to serve with me later on various occasions.

To put all this theoretical experience into practice, I was assigned to one of the British army's armoured regiments, the 4th County of London Yeomanry, which was part of the 22nd Armoured Brigade, itself part of Britain's First Armoured Division. The role of this division was to defend the southeastern coast of England.

The situation was critical. The defeat of the French army and the miraculous retreat of the British forces from Dunkirk had shaken the British considerably. In addition, Italy was threatening the Near East, an area of vital importance to Britain. The British, who, until that point, had not taken the war very seriously, began to mobilize their forces and their industries to replace the equipment lost in France or to produce the items they had lacked since the beginning of operations.

My role in the defence of England was to serve with C squadron of the 4th County of London Yeomanry. Here again, we had only light tanks. Our heaviest equipment consisted of one Besa machine gun. The regiment, composed of recruits from London and the surrounding area, was proud and spirited. It included lawyers, notaries and veterans from 1914-1918, come to serve the King. In general, they had no desire for command, preferring to leave this role to the regulars. In fact, the regiment included a number of officers from the regular army, including Major George Kidston, who headed the squadron of which I was a member.

We prepared systematic plans for the defence of England's southeastern coast. The region assigned to us was a likely spot for an invasion: it lay between Rye and Folkestone, almost directly across from Dunkirk. Our defensive role was, therefore, generally recognized as an important one. Indeed, we were well aware of the fact that we would be in the front lines in the event of a German landing.

We performed many drills. I recall that one day, General Norrie, the

G.O.C. of our division, told us to lay out tracks through all the fields so that the Germans would think that Great Britain had many more armoured vehicles than in fact it did. This, it was hoped, would deter them from attacking. Tactics like these were almost the only effective means of defence available to the army. Consider the situation. Of twelve armoured vehicles, my squadron kept three available for HQ. With the other nine, we covered a front of . . . twelve miles. So out we went into the fields, to the dismay of the farmers, who had to be satisfied with my explanation: "It's all right." My English was still rather shaky at the time! We went through with the manoeuvre, however, doing as little damage as possible.

The German reconnaissance planes included a number of English-built Lysanders, which had been abandoned in France following the disaster at Dunkirk. After we had thoroughly marked the area out with our tracks, the area was declared off-limits to all RAF Lysanders. Adventurous souls or straying pilots were systematically fired on. The Lysanders, both German and British, disappeared from our air space.

After a long series of drills, we felt that we were prepared to defend our sector. Our confidence was unshaken by the fact that we had very few tanks, no infantry and little or no artillery. Clearly, in 1940, the British Ministry of Defence was not much farther ahead than its Canadian counterpart in terms of its material situation. But what a difference there was in terms of morale, for the British formed a solid unit which would obviously prove difficult to shake, even under the worst circumstances. During my time there, the British displayed a noble example of courage and determination. The high command, too, demonstrated remarkable intelligence. The officers who made it through the preliminary selection process were extremely talented. I was happy to serve with them.

During this period, the Germans were bombing all areas of England. At first, they met little opposition. However, the Royal Air Force gradually rose to the challenge. From time to time, a Hurricane or a Spitfire would hurl itself against four or five German fighters. Whenever an aircraft went down in flames, the anxious question was whether it was German or one of ours. Fortunately (and this is a tribute I have long wanted to make), the pilots responsible for Britain's air defence were skilled and courageous.

Railway centres were favourite targets of German bombing and this caused considerable disruption and some inconvenience. Like most people at the time, I frequently travelled by train and it often happened that the repair crews had not had time to clear the tracks. In the stations, members of women's groups would then serve us tea and doughnuts while we waited. We often missed meals, but we never went hungry.

At this stage, I would like to explain briefly which aspect of British attitudes struck me most during this—my first—stay in Great Britain. Let me first quote a great French thinker who, on June 22, 1940, four days after Pétain's France abandoned the fight, wrote:

England was never greater than during these days when, all alone, it defends world freedom. Upright, sword in hand, it stands on the rock that is both her foothold and shield. Today, it is also the last bastion of the West. She surrounds herself with her men, her cannon, her ships and her great iron birds. She does not have to appeal to the spiritual strength of her sons: they exhibit it in abundance.

. . . these are the men, and this is the country, that will put an end to Germany's mad dream, that will bring back to humanity the tribes of the Metal Age, that will cause History to triumph over Prehistory.

. . . Hail intrepid England, upright in combat, facing the war and fighting the powers of darkness.*

This testimonial was written in Buenos Aires, far from England, but having seen the situation for myself I can state that Focillon knew what he was talking about, that he knew intimately Great Britain and her inhabitants. Shortly after my arrival in England, I had the opportunity to see Winston Churchill, an extraordinary man whose speeches had roused his people's morale. The British were reduced to fighting without the equipment they needed. But, to defend British soil, they were prepared to use anything that came to hand: picks, shovels and pitchforks. The sentiment was repeated everywhere: "The Germans will never conquer this country." This admirable determination on the part of the British made a strong impression on me.

I was in London the night the city was bombarded with incendiary bombs. It was an experience I shall never forget. London was in flames and servicemen on leave were required to assist the firemen and police. I was assigned to traffic control. The most extraordinary thing was the total composure of the civilians. Many went down into the air-raid shelters and then back home quite naturally, if indeed their homes were still standing. The bombardment continued all night. There was no panic, not the slightest sign of discouragement in the magnificent people of London.

The next morning, debris lay everywhere. All day long, we worked to clear the streets. That night, when I returned to my regiment, my heart was filled with rage at this savage and senseless attack, which was totally unjustified and would not change the course of the war. The Germans had committed a serious error. Instead of crushing British morale, they had raised it to a new

* Henri Focillon, "Salut à l'Angleterre," in *Témoignage pour la France* (New York: Brentano's, 1945), pp. 33-36.

peak. After this bombing, the British were more determined than ever not to permit a German victory.

Living among the English, for a Quebecker, was an enriching social experience. Accustomed to the language of English Canadians, I soon realized that there were some startling differences between the language of the British public schools and that heard in a Canadian officers' mess. The vocabulary, the accent and the phrasing were totally different. I became used to it, but it took time. The language spoken by the people of Wales, Ireland, Scotland, or even the Midlands was different in each case. The English accent of each of the groups forming the mosaic of the United Kingdom was often difficult to understand. But it was the cockney slang of London that was the most intriguing aspect of spoken English. It was an enormous surprise for a French Canadian already having his problems with English. But I became used to it because I had no choice. And my posting to the 4th Yeomanry was extremely useful in improving my knowledge of English. In fact, I enjoyed my colleagues' sense of humour so much that I soon found myself wishing that I spoke the same way.

The British mentality, too, was different from that of the English Canadian. The English were reserved; sometimes they seemed almost shy. Once you got to know them, however, they were friendly and enormously funny. At work, they were serious. At play, they were aggressive, staunch defenders of what, in cricket, they described as "fair play": they were formidable opponents. Their patriotism was beyond suspicion. They never questioned a rule, but would apply it to the letter, with all the self-sacrifice demonstrated more recently in the Falklands. The British people, in general, were disciplined. Nothing could have stood in the way of their defence of the beautiful country they call their home.

During the difficult period I have described, it was this discipline that seemed to be the unifying characteristic of the entire nation. Recalcitrant people (and there are always some) were quickly put in their place. Everyone was prepared to help the less fortunate. During the bombing of London, I had an opportunity to observe and admire this traditional discipline and calm. The ruling people we French Canadians have frequently known only through our local anti-British propaganda became a people to be admired. They were a people who would still go to Albert Hall to hear Sir Henry Woods conduct the London Philharmonic in his Promenade Concerts, even when the performance was sure to be interrupted by the battery in the middle of Hyde Park going into action against planes coming to bomb London.

Elderly soldiers and pensioners who had been rejected for mobilization, because of their age or health, formed the Home Guard, their military equipment limited to hunting rifles, gasoline bombs and steel bars. They provided useful service by performing guard duties which military personnel would otherwise have been obliged to handle. This elderly guard would probably have offered more resistance than might have been expected, for there was not one of them who would have chosen to survive an English defeat, as every one of them I met told me.

Nonetheless, my stay was over. The regiment to which I belonged was preparing to leave for the Near East and I was told that I was to return to Canada. On the morning of February 25, 1941, I said good-bye to my companions, many of whom were to die in North Africa. Then, with some regret, I presented myself at a Canadian detachment stationed in Great Britain, which sent me by train to Greenock, Scotland. There, accompanied by Lieutenant-Colonel Alex Dupuis, I boarded a Polish ship, the S.S. *Batory*, which set sail at 1910 hours on the 27th. After a number of adventures, we reached Halifax at 1100 hours on March 9, 1941.

Despite the friendship and admiration I felt for England and its courageous people, I was glad to be home. Simone and Michèle were waiting for me on the platform at the Trois-Rivières station when I arrived several days later. Interestingly enough, thanks to the excellent job Simone had done, showing Michèle my pictures, she recognized me when she saw me, although she was only seventeen months old.

There was another reason for our happiness: Simone was expecting our second child near the end of the month. My return was well-timed, then, and we thanked Providence for arranging things so well. Homecoming celebrations were kept to a minimum. We settled down to await the new baby's arrival, with some patience given the circumstances. Unfortunately, the experience I had acquired in Great Britain was needed by my regiment, now at Camp Borden under Vining's command, and I was recalled. Pierrette, Simone's sister, stayed with her for the final week of her pregnancy.

On March 19, I left for Borden, arriving the next day. I presented myself at brigade headquarters, where I was told that I was to be appointed second-in-command. My main responsibility would be to organize the training of our troops. Working from the experience I had acquired in the British army, I formed specialized training groups and appointed instructors, with well-defined programmes for them to follow. At first, the programme involved one-third of the men but within a short time, the entire regiment was included. Essentially, instead of developing the training around the individual within a squadron designed for this purpose, I enlarged the horizon so that the entire regiment became a school. As a result, we were soon equal to any of the other Canadian armoured regiments.

On March 25, I received a message announcing the birth of my son. Like Simone, I was beside myself with joy. I seized the first opportunity to return home and, on March 30, our son, accompanied by Arthur and Anaïs

Rousseau, his godparents, and held in Pierrette's arms, was taken to the Saint-Philippe Church for baptism. He was named Ernest in honour of his grandfather. On April 3, I returned to Borden to resume my activities.

By this time, our training programme was successfully under way. Towards the end of March, communication exercises, performed in the Ontario countryside, had in fact demonstrated that the regiment was built on solid foundations. An outstanding officer joined us at this time—Major Melville Gordon, who agreed to begin with us as a captain. This excellent officer came from Ottawa, where he was an engineer and a lawyer. He was promoted to major shortly thereafter and was to serve the regiment with distinction.

In midsummer 1941, Lieutenant-Colonel Vining was sent to England for specialized courses. I replaced him on a temporary basis. A week later, my regiment received orders to prepare for the transatlantic crossing. Preparations were well underway when I was suddenly informed that I would not be leaving at once. It had been decided that I was to go to the staff college at Kingston. I admit that it was difficult for me to leave my unit. But the opportunity I had been offered was one I could not refuse. Among other positive effects, I would have the chance to spend a few more months in Canada and occasionally to see my wife and children, who were spending the summer of 1941 at Val-Pichet. Little did I suspect, however, as I said good-bye to my comrades in arms on the station platform, that I would never serve with the Three Rivers again. In fact, it was the end of a period in my life.

The course in Kingston was the first staff course to be offered on Canadian soil for officers of the regular army.* Unlikely as it seems today, at the time it was another milestone in the movement of the Canadian army towards total independence from the British. This independence began around the end of 1916, with the formation of the Canadian First Army Corps, in which the units, command and staffs were largely Canadian. In 1941, this independence was extended with the establishment of the institutions required for the training of Canadian officers and NCOs.

This course was an extremely important one because it would determine which young officers were to replace the elderly veterans of World War I. It was these older officers who were then commanding our overseas army, which was one day to serve in the liberation of the European continent.

My stay at the college offered all sorts of advantages. For instance, we had the opportunity to meet and get to know new officers with whom we would

---

* In fact, the first Canadian course was given in England under the direction of Lieutenant-Colonel G. G. Simmonds. Starting with the second course, the decision was made to move it to the Royal Military College in Kingston.

serve during the most active part of the war. It was also a time for making friends—friendships that have lasted through the years. I met a number of French Canadians there as well: Majors Croteau (Hull) and J. N. E. Grenier (Quebec); Captains C. R. Payan (Saint-Hyacinthe), O. E. Delorme and J. P. L. Gosselin of the *Régiment de la Chaudière* (the latter, unfortunately, was later killed in Korea). There was also Major L. F. Trudeau, who later served under my command, rendering great service to the *Royal 22e Régiment* during the Italian campaign. Through the years he has remained a staunch friend. Finally, there was Dollard Ménard, who had recently returned from India, but seemed to be having some difficulty settling in with his fellow French Canadians.

The course was extremely interesting. Its purpose was to prepare us to think in terms of the huge Canadian units, based on the British model, which were to be included in armies and army corps. It was given entirely in English, which did not disturb any of the French-speaking participants. Since the staff operated in English and it was impossible under the circumstances, to do otherwise, it would have been useless to protest. We simply worked a little harder. In any event, both anglophones and francophones had to struggle to absorb correctly, in fifteen weeks, the various staff functions of a division in action. We had to prove to our instructors that we were equal to the challenge. Some of the trainees had to use their evenings and weekends to prove their abilities, and there was little time for our families.

I would like to pause briefly at this point to describe the role and general composition of an infantry division in order to make the two following chapters more understandable. Let us assume, first, that the division I am going to describe with the assistance of a table is, with one or more other divisions, part of an army corps. The corps, generally in combination with at least one other, will form an army. During the war, Canada's contribution to ground forces, the First Canadian Army, consisted of two corps, including a total of 3 infantry divisions, 2 armoured divisions and 2 armoured brigades. In addition, many Canadians served on an individual basis with foreign units. Finally, some Canadian land units served with large British units while at the same time a number of foreign units were included within our First Army. I should mention too that Canada also made major air and naval contributions during this conflict.

The following table, then, shows the units within an infantry division.

INFANTRY DIVISION
Division HQ

Royal Canadian Armoured Corps	One reconnaissance regiment
The Royal Canadian Artillery	Royal Canadian Artillery HQ Three field regiments One antitank regiment One light AA regiment Anti-mortar section
The Corps of Royal Canadian Engineers	Corps of Engineers HQ One field park company One divisional bridging platoon Three field companies
Royal Canadian Corps of Signals	Divisional signals
Canadian Infantry Corps	One machine gun battalion One defence and services platoon Three infantry brigade HQs Three ground defence platoons Nine infantry battalions (three per brigade)
Royal Canadian Army Service Corps	Service Corps HQ Three infantry (brigade) companies One divisional troops company
Royal Canadian Army Medical Corps	Three field ambulances Two field aid stations One field sanitary section
Royal Canadian Ordnance Corps	One ordnance field park
Royal Canadian Electrical and Mechanical Engineers	Electrical and Mechanical Engineers HQ Three infantry brigade workshops One light AA workshop Eleven recovery units
The Canadian Postal Corps	One divisional postal unit
The Canadian Provost Corps	One provost company
Canadian Intelligence Corps	One field security section

DIVISIONAL ADJUNCTS TO CORPS TROOPS

Royal Canadian Ordnance Corps	One advanced ordnance park
	One mobile laundry and bath unit
The Royal Canadian Army Pay Corps	One field cash office

I have taken this long detour primarily for those readers who may wish to have their memory refreshed or simply to learn something of the general structure within which our infantry fought.

In addition to this instruction regarding the division, the Kingston course included many other elements. We had to know the number and capacity of various weapons, and the logistic and administrative requirements of a force of this nature. We also studied the enemy's organization and logistics. Then there were theoretical studies of the various phases that a battle may take: defence, retreat, attack, pursuit. We analyzed specific cases and the conclusions we drew were evaluated by the instructor and then discussed within our work groups.

The course was designed primarily to examine the operation of the various branches of a division staff and to help us understand all the functions associated with each specific position. We looked at communications (radio, dispatch riders, liaison officers, telephone). In particular, the work groups were set up as staffs, with each member required to perform one of the functions of an operational headquarters.

We were required to prepare maps for distribution to the commanding officers of subordinate units, on which we would indicate the possible manoeuvres of the enemy from the most recent information based on contacts made by our patrols, visual observation, aerial photographs and assessments by our intelligence services.

Finally, we prepared operation orders for our subordinate commanding officers. These documents had to include a number of elements: the context of the proposed operation, the objectives to be reached, a plan for the support to be provided to the infantry by the artillery and armoured units, and plans for logistics and medical support.

All these theoretical exercises were designed not only to assess the candidates but also to prepare them for the roles they were soon to fill. They were followed by a practical exercise in the field, to help us understand more clearly what we were doing and to recognize any errors in analysis which we might have made in class.

One week before the end of the course, I was assigned to operations (G3) at the headquarters of the 5th Canadian Armoured Division (an armoured division contained almost the same support units as an infantry division, but there were far fewer battalions of infantry since its fighting strength was based on three armoured regiments). I was very pleased with this assignment.

For the entire period of the course my family life had been neglected despite all my hopes to the contrary. However, I was able to spend two weeks and a number of weekend leaves at Val-Pichet, where Michèle soon became my "little sweetheart." I could not pretend, though, that I really knew my daughter, and even less my son. Thanks to a friend in the air force, I was able to return to Montreal on November 9, 1941. I had less than two days to say good-bye to my family, whom I did not expect to see again soon. Then, on November 11, I caught the train at Rockland Siding for Halifax, where I boarded the *Orcades*, a very comfortable ship of the Maritime Oriental Lines.

The 5th Division left Halifax at 1712 hours on November 13, on seven ships travelling in a convoy of nine. Ours were named *Orcades, Duchess of Atholl, Andies, Durban Castle, Obiensky, Hollandais* and *Windsor Castle*. In addition, we were accompanied by two freighters. All of us were under the protection of a battleship, two cruisers and five destroyers of the American navy; this escort, however, accompanied us only part of the way, since the United States was not yet at war. In all, the crossing was a pleasant one, punctuated by bridge games, submarine watches from the bridge and making new acquaintances.

We arrived in Liverpool on November 24, 1941. The staff officers disembarked immediately and boarded a train travelling southeast, towards Aldershot. For the next few months, we were housed in the Royal Pavilion, located in a beautiful park in the centre of town. Aldershot had been a military garrison town for over a hundred years, and the units that formed the division, including nearly 20,000 men, were easily accommodated around the pavilion in permanent barracks. Finally we were able to take delivery of our equipment and begin training to take our place in the First Canadian Army Corps, which played an important role in the defence of the United Kingdom.

Our G.O.C. was Major-General E. W. Sansom, whom I knew well from the days when, as a young member of the militia, I had taken courses in Montreal. I received a friendly welcome from this dynamic and pleasant gentleman. My first job was to inspect the various units as they arrived, for our staff was determined to establish control of the situation as rapidly as possible. The general wanted me to get to know the commanding officers of the brigades and of the subordinate units. It was a pleasant assignment and I soon made friends.

Because I had already spent several months with the British First Division,

I was quite familiar with the equipment we would be receiving. The organization of the units was also familiar to me. I was warmly received wherever I went. Because I knew something about the technical characteristics of the armoured vehicles the units were receiving for the first time, I was able to solve a number of problems fairly readily, and thus to assist them with their training. I admit, however, that I had some difficulty in adapting to my new role as a staff officer. However, my companion from staff college, Major W. C. Murphy, of Vancouver, who remained a close friend until his death, helped me to settle in.

One of the first problems I had to solve involved the control of the tanks' turrets, which was slowing reaction time to the point that the German tanks always seemed to get off the first shot, with results so disastrous that the problem could not be ignored. Reports from the Near East, where my old regiment had been demolished in the battle of Agedabia the previous January, provided convincing evidence. The difficulties were confirmed following tests at Lulworth's armament school. I carried out two analyses of the problem, one relating to the procedure followed by the crew and the other to the mechanics of our tanks. The preliminary conclusions which I reached seemed fairly convincing.

I spoke to General Sansom, who authorized me to continue my study. I then discussed with my friend, Major Fox, an idea I had had which might make it possible to correct the situation; he assured me that my solution was feasible. And so I set to work. When I had completed my design, I contacted the armoured corps' research centre at Chobham to have a prototype produced by their technicians. Returning to Lulworth, I installed it in a tank and began a series of practical tests.

Before I go on, I would like to explain briefly what my little invention consisted of; it will be readily apparent that there was nothing very amazing about it. In tanks of that period, the gun crew included, among others, a tank commander and a gunner. Suppose that the tank was travelling along when the commander suddenly noticed a target on his right. The procedure was then to say to the gunner: "right, right, right," etc., until the gun was in line with the target. Depending on where the target was located, a number of seconds might elapse between the tank commander's instructions, the gunner's response and the moment when the target and the gun were finally lined up. My invention consisted of an electrical system connecting the commander's periscope with the gun. When a target was sighted, say, in this case, to the right, the commander would call out: "right." The gunner would start the gun moving in that direction and the gun would automatically stop when it came into line with the periscope. In certain cases, this gadget could give the tank the three or four seconds necessary to destroy, for example, an antitank gun sighted before it could fire. My system was just one more electrical circuit to be added to those already present in our tanks.

At Lulworth, a number of minor problems arose during the installation process. Still, the correction mechanism I had devised was so simple (see drawing in appendix A) that with a few adjustments it was ready for use. I then taught a team of trainees to use it as part of a combat training course. The result of the first test was more than satisfying: my men hit seven targets out of ten, when the previous average had been three out of ten. I then selected a new route and sent out an unmodified tank with a crew of instructors, followed by a second tank, modified and with a crew of trainees. The results were amazing, with the trainees beating the instructors at a rate of two to one. I then submitted my report to General Sansom who, in turn, mentioned it to General McNaughton. General McNaughton called me in to explain the system. When I had finished, he asked me to demonstrate it for the commanders of the Allied armies. I did so. It was on this occasion that I first met General de Gaulle, a brilliant tank officer, who tried out the device personally. He seemed somewhat surprised to be addressed in French by a Canadian.

This second stay in Great Britain left its mark on me in another way, too. I recall that it was during this period that the Canadian government announced that a referendum would be held to determine whether Canadians were prepared to release the government from its commitment not to impose compulsory overseas service. I was torn between the two sides of the issue.

This was another painful time for me. I was the only French-Canadian officer on the staff of the 5th Division, and I felt that I was under some scrutiny to see how I intended to vote. I had never doubted what my own vote, or, for the matter, that of our French-speaking troops would be. My office mate, Bill Murphy, found it difficult to understand either the reason why I would feel torn by this decision or my remarks once the overall results became known.

From my viewpoint, things seemed as follows. On the one hand, there was the democratic freedom I felt I was defending alongside my English-speaking compatriots, who had become my friends and who remained my friends after the referendum. There were also my British army comrades who fought for the same cause and gave their life in North Africa. There was, finally, the United Kingdom which, from June 1940 until December 1941, when the United States entered the war, courageously accepted to carry on the fight virtually alone. I could only admire that country and wish it victory, with the full co-operation of Canada as a whole.

Yet, what was happening in Canada in 1942? The country had become sharply divided at the very time when unity was a must. I do not wish to repeat the arguments used by both sides, many having already done so in various ways. Suffice it to say that I found them unacceptable, whether their advocates were Ontario Orangemen or Quebec nationalists, for they fuelled a dispute that was out of place.

The fall of France in "The Sixty Days that Shook the West" (the title of a book by Benoist-Méchin) led me to draw a parallel with Canada's difficulties. In the 30s, serious divisions had occurred between the right and the left. During the French-German hostilities, the French Communists maintained their neutrality in accordance with the German-Soviet pact of nonaggression. At the same time, there was a current of French Fascists who hoped for an agreement with Germany. The "real" French, despite their efforts, could not contain Adolf Hitler's attack when it came. Of course, these were not the only reasons for the French defeat, but the ideological struggle which, at the opening of hostilities, had been going on for several years had played a major role in France's lack of preparation.

Nevertheless, when one had lived in Quebec, as I had until 1939, and was involved in what was going on, could one really condemn the attitude taken by a large portion of its population at the time of the referendum? Indeed, was it not normal for Quebeckers to follow those who claimed to anyone who would listen that the Liberals had betrayed their confidence? Suffice it to recall the pressures and promises of Mackenzie King's representatives sent to Quebec in 1940 to persuade people to replace Duplessis' Union Nationale with a Liberal government. However, I found it unfortunate that the people of Quebec seemed to refuse openly to participate in a moment of history as grave as this war of civilization which had been going on for nearly three years. For me, the quarrels of 1837 and 1917 were things of the past. I could not visualize a future based on the denial of duty towards democratic freedom. To my eyes, the great social movements now meeting on the fields of battle were more important to the future of all Canadians than the family quarrels which lay behind Quebec's refusal.

In summary, even taking into account certain understandable frustrations of Quebeckers, despite my awareness of my obligations to my wife and to my two small children, I regretted the "no" my people had given. Although I was prepared to continue to the end, I also vowed, with God's help, to correct the abuses and errors committed by our leaders, who had forgotten Canada's duality. In my position as a staff officer, I saw that very few French-speaking officers were able to function in this environment where English was the sole working language. I knew too that it was too late to correct these problems. In any event, I could do nothing to reverse a situation which had existed for so many years. Instead of allowing myself to become discouraged, I used my bilingualism to acquire new skills.

The year 1942 was well underway when, on July 13, I was informed that I had just been appointed an instructor at the staff college in Kingston. The next day, I boarded the S.S. *Argentina* and arrived in New York on the 19th.

It was a new life that I was beginning, and this time my family was with me. I was able, first of all, to spend a few days with them at Val-Pichet. We then packed our bags and set out for Kingston. It was a totally new experience for Simone and the children to be able to accompany me. As an instructor, I was entitled to what proved to be comfortable housing. In Kingston, there was a house waiting for us on Hogan's Alley. After a quick trip to the market, we moved in. It was not perfect yet, but we were so happy to be together again that it was easy to ignore a few minor inconveniences.

I had expected to start teaching in September; however, immediately following my arrival in May, I was asked to replace Major Charlebois, who had been ordered to England. I was happy to do so. True, I was coming in right in the middle of a course, but it gave me an opportunity to become familiar with the situation.

Two days after my arrival, General H. F. H. Hertzberg, the college's commandant, whom I had known before the war, called me into his office. He gave me a letter from Ottawa asking me to go to Washington with my file on the Synchro-switch I had developed for our armoured vehicles. I proceeded to Ottawa, where I met Colonel Graling, the American military attaché. After a brief discussion, he gave me a message and some airline tickets. The next morning, I was at the Canadian embassy, where Colonel Bud Drury welcomed me. I was presented to the Minister-Counsellor, Lester B. Pearson, before being taken to the headquarters of the American army.

My stay was busy and interesting. I discussed the matter in detail with the local experts. They decided to send me to the Armored Board, at Fort Knox, Kentucky. I was very well received. But they needed a model of my device which would fit American tanks. Within a day it had been built. I then installed it, following the procedure developed in England and demonstrated it. After a complete tour of the military base at Fort Knox and a brief visit to the American gold reserves, I was warmly thanked. I then boarded a train for the trip back to Detroit, Toronto, and Kingston. My mission was accomplished. About ten days after my return to the college, I received a very kind letter of thanks from President Roosevelt.

Nonetheless, my contribution, as such, was never used. Of course, nearly all of Britain's armaments were manufactured in the United States. The Americans, working (I believe) from my concept, developed an electric control system by which a needle in the gun's sights fell into line with another in the periscope. This produced the same result, using a system which was slightly more complicated than mine, but which had the advantage of being more accurate and, in particular, easier to use for the new recruits on whom our armies were based. Still, I was proud of the contribution I had been able to make, primarily on the basis of my analysis of the relationship between man and machine and my success in improving the results of the interaction between the two.

Graduation ceremonies for the students of the fourth staff course were held on August 15, 1942. I had one month to prepare for the next course, which was to be quite different. It was a challenge because the new programme involved exercises on the various phases of battles, the organization of amphibious operations and movements over long distances. The exercise fields had to be changed and the instructors had an enormous amount of work to do ensuring that everything was ready in time. I was responsible for developing the long-distance exercises and for assisting the head instructor with the defence exercise. I found the work fascinating and threw myself into it with enthusiasm.

Almost the entire group of instructors was changing. As a result, I again encountered some of the friends I had made during my student days in 1941. They were Majors C. N. Clark, C. W. Ferguson (later killed in France), H. A. A. Parker, W. G. N. Robinson and Ken Southern (later killed in Italy, just a few hundred yards from my command post). Like myself, they had taken advantage of their return to Canada to have their families join them. All of us lived on Hogan's Alley. Our children, who were largely the same age, played together. We, the parents, got to know each other by visiting back and forth.

Finally, on September 16, the course began. We attacked it with enthusiasm. New faces appeared. But only six of the seventy-three candidates were French Canadians. The fifth course, which was a great success, ended on January 16, 1943. The sixth started at the beginning of February and ended early in June. Major Jean-Paul Carrière was one of our new instructors. Our students included Majors Paul Sauvé and Hugues Lapointe, two distinguished candidates who earned excellent reputations at the college. Both had a marvelous sense of humour: the fact that they were political adversaries added bite to some of their comments. It goes without saying that they did very well.

During this course, we performed an experiment. One exercise called for two enemy headquarters to operate for seventy-two hours. Adrenalin pills were given to certain students to measure the degree of working efficiency that staff officers, who did not sleep for the entire period, were able to maintain. One-third received real pills, while another third were given placebos. The final third worked without pills. The results were not particularly conclusive since it was impossible to measure the long-term psychological and physical effects involved. The scientists, however, went away satisfied. Our candidates were then given a full day's rest.

On June 1, 1943, I received a new assignment. I had been transferred overseas to the HQ of the First Canadian Army Corps. I was to be staff operations officer (GS02). I had the great pleasure to work there under the direction of General H. D. G. Crerar.

My experience in Kingston had been enriching in a number of respects. The social activities with my colleagues and the staff of the college had made life very pleasant. The children had grown and, for the first time, had had time to get to know their father. The activities of the college were interesting in themselves. Young militia officers were always passing through. They came from every walk of life—lawyers, accountants, engineers and countless others. The great majority were from the western provinces and, in particular, Ontario. Some were from Quebec: these included Sauvé and Lapointe, as I have mentioned, who were to return to politics after the war. But there was also Captain Tellier, who was to achieve the rank of lieutenant-general in the regular army as a result of a remarkable wartime service record: he won the Distinguished Service Order (DSO) for commanding, with distinction, a company of the *Royal 22e Régiment* during the Italian campaign.

During the fall of 1942, our family also had the pleasure of entertaining Lieutenant-Colonel Dollard Ménard, who had returned from Dieppe with the DSO. It was a great pleasure for us to do so. He was the only one of the battalion commanders at Dieppe to return to Canadian soil. Although he had been wounded during the first moments of the landing and so had not been able to participate as fully as he would have wished in the action of his regiment (the Fusiliers Mont-Royal), he was still one of the rare Canadians to have encountered the Germans since 1939. In addition, he had faced the hell of Dieppe. His account of these events was extremely useful to students and instructors alike.

The college was a constant whirl of activity. Trainees came for three months at a time in groups of seventy-five, and had to work very hard to satisfy their course requirements. The instructors worked equally hard. But all those who passed through (trainees and instructors alike) were proud of their work and profoundly anxious to return overseas to play a role in what was to be the final victory against Nazism.

But nothing lasts forever in an army at war. When I left Canada for the third and final time during the period 1939-45, I left Simone and the two children behind, at Trois-Rivières. This third separation occurred on June 12, 1943, on the platform of the Drummondville station. It was my thirtieth birthday. Simone, composed as always, was at the station. Without a tear, she said good-bye. We watched each other disappear in the steam as the locomotive pulled away and on to Halifax.

Simone returned to our home at 412 rue Bureau, where, with the two children, she was to spend the most difficult days of the war. Fortunately, Mr. Laperrière, our landlord, was extremely kind and devoted. Mr. Saint-Louis, the grocer, always had special treats for her. Arthur and Anaïs, Germaine and her husband Raoul Provencher, were there to help her. Still, she was alone, with a little maid who helped her but could not console her in her solitude. Our separation was to last for two years and four months, during which time the children, of course, continued to grow.

I had noted, as I was leaving, that Michèle, the elder child, seemed to be very aware not only of the coming separation but also of the risks I would be running while I was away. It was interesting but, at the same time, painful to see how this child, not yet four years old, dreaded the moment of my departure almost as if the rather unusual circumstances under which we were living had forced her into emotional maturity before her time. Jean Ernest, of course, was far too young to feel any concern.

On June 13, I boarded the S.S. *Anders* to begin my fifth transatlantic crossing in wartime. The weather was clear and warm. I took advantage of the opportunity to catch up on my rest: it had been a marvelous year but one that had required a great deal of effort on my part. I wondered frequently what my new post would bring. This time, it was to be the "real" war for the Canadians, for it appeared that our army would be going into action in the very near future.

Following my arrival in Britain on June 23, I proceeded by land to my new post. The light truck in which I was travelling turned down a long entrance way lined with fine trees before coming to a stop at the door of Gravetye Manor. This splendid estate provided accommodation for staff officers up to the rank of major and was halfway between East Grinstead and Wakehurst Park, which together made up the headquarters. Two batmen took my bags and carried them upstairs to an oak-panelled bedroom with an enormous fireplace and luxurious adjoining bath. The rest of the manor was equally magnificent. The gardens, with their rockeries and beautiful flowers, were maintained by an old gardener. It was hard to believe that we were at war. Wakehurst Park Manor, where the division's operational branch, including, of course, our offices, was located, was much larger. But the maintenance, which was handled by military personnel for reasons of security, did not provide the same view we had from our rooms in Gravetye Manor. Still, it was very pleasant.

The next day, June 24, I presented myself to Brigadier-General Churchill Mann, who handed me a pile of papers and said: "You're from the staff college . . . sort this out for me." "This" was the report on the Dieppe raid. A few days later, I attended a conference under the direction of Major-General E. L. M. Burns at Second Division HQ: as a result, I was able to prepare the final report. This operation taught us several lessons which enabled us to modify a number of procedures we had previously followed.

Mann left us shortly afterwards to assume command of the 7th Brigade. He was replaced by Brigadier W. (Bill) Megill. Megill was an old acquaintance, having served in Montreal during the 1930s. Almost at once, he assigned me the job of planning Exercise Whale, which involved troop movements towards England's southeastern ports. These movements were designed to mislead the Germans while the First Canadian Division was embarking for the invasion of Sicily. We had to distract the attention of the German army and make them believe that a landing on the French coast was imminent. The exercise proceeded very well.

On my return to HQ, I read the second part of the routine orders and discovered that a number of officers from my corps, who had studied under my direction at Kingston, had recently been promoted to lieutenant-colonel. I immediately called the director of the Armoured Corps, Brigadier-General Rutherford, whom I knew well. I wanted an explanation. He was not there but the staff officer who answered, and whom I had taught at staff college, told me that he did not know who I was: according to him, my name did not appear on the Armoured Corps' list. At the same time, he told me that Lieutenant-Colonel Lesley Booth, of London, Ontario, had been named to replace Vining at the head of my regiment, now the 12th Armoured Regiment (Trois-Rivières). I was insulted, and I say so even after all these years. I immediately arranged an appointment with Crerar to find out what was going on. In the heat of the conversation, I told him that if this was the way I was going to be treated, I would prefer to return to Canada and finish out the war near my family. In any case, I believed that I had served the Armoured Corps well until then. My interest was clear, and had been demonstrated by, among other things, the technical innovation I had designed for turret control. I was known, moreover, as a good technical officer. I was furious at the behaviour of the people who headed this Corps, and I never wanted to see them again. The general asked me first of all to calm down; he assured me that he would look into the matter personally. He himself was getting tired of the cavalry, but for other reasons. He felt that most of them were not "mechanically minded", as he put it. It was his impression that some of them were playing games with the armoured vehicles entrusted to them.

The next day, the general called me in to ask whether I would agree to move to the infantry. I said yes! Less than twenty-four hours later, I was second-in-command of the *Régiment de la Chaudière*.

3

The Harsh Practice of War, August 1943-May 1944

When I agreed to move to the infantry as second-in-command of what was already a well organized regiment, I learned that for some people I was not a welcome addition. My arrival had destroyed certain hopes of promotion. In a sense, what had happened to me in the armoured corps was being repeated among my colleagues in the infantry. In addition, I knew almost no one here, whereas in the 12th Armoured, despite my prolonged absences, I could always return to a group of old friends or rapidly make new ones. Finally, while war is war whatever the branch of service, in terms of tactics I was better prepared in August 1943 to lead an armoured squadron into combat than an infantry regiment. In short, although I would soon be joining an entirely French-speaking regiment, a situation I had not experienced since the opening of hostilities and about which I was essentially very happy, I could not help feeling some apprehension.

However, I remained optimistic. My time at the staff college, both as a student and as an instructor, had enabled me to become familiar with all the activities of the commanding officer of an infantry regiment. Moreover, in 1943, very few Canadians had, in any event, any experience at all with operations under fire and my new regiment was not earmarked for immediate combat. Finally, the senior authorities of the division had confidence in my ability to meet the challenge. I could not see myself disappointing them, particularly since I did not feel truly handicapped by the negative elements of the situation I have described. In fact, I felt ready to assume greater responsibilities of command. I therefore prepared myself psychologically to deal as quickly as possible with the frustrations that were certain to exist and were, to a certain point, legitimate. Obviously, it would be up to me to take the first steps to win my men's hearts.

I collected my weapons and luggage and proceeded cheerfully, despite the minor difficulties I anticipated, to join my new regiment. I assumed command on August 13, 1943, in the absence of the incumbent commanding officer. Two days later, I received orders to move the regiment close to Horsham, where I had served with the British army in the 4th London Yeomanry. The move went smoothly. As soon as we were settled, I took the opportunity offered by the upcoming transfer of four of our officers to organize a regimental dinner. My primary intention was to get to know my fellow officers in the course of this function, which, while formal, was still quite jovial. The officers leaving us to join the *Royal 22e Régiment* in Sicily were Majors Georges Sévigny and Michel Gauvin, Captain Louis Rousseau and Lieutenant Yves Gosselin. The event went well and the general process of mutual adaptation was well underway when I received further news. Those four officers were to remain with the *Régiment de la Chaudière*, while I had been transferred to the R22^{e}R, where I was to become second-in-command, as of August 23. I was stunned.

Although the appointment was good news, I knew what it would mean. All the "negative" elements I have mentioned would have to be faced again. In addition, instead of having time to become familiar with a unit which was involved in final preparations before going into action, I was to be plunged into the thick of the fighting as a member of one of the country's most respected regiments.

During the last week of August 1943, I boarded a plane at Land's End, in Cornwall. During the flight, I had plenty of time for reflection. I remembered the image I had of the man who led the *22^e Bataillon* (C.E.F.) for part of the Great War: General Tremblay, revered by all French-speaking infantrymen, even those from other regiments. The officers and men who had served under him had imbued the unit with his legend during the inter-war period, when the regiment had been maintained within the regular army. I also reviewed the organization of an infantry regiment and the tactics on which infantry warfare is based. These two elements, while they had been discussed extensively in various courses, remained extremely theoretical in my case as may well be imagined. However, it was with continued confidence in my lucky star that I turned to meet this new challenge. Once again, I allowed myself to believe that the obstacles before me were no worse than those I had already faced in the past. I felt certain that with effort I could surmount them, and I intended to do so.

The first part of the flight which was to take us as far as Gibraltar was not without incident. As we flew over neutral Spain, antiaircraft batteries opened fire on us. Before the plane could climb out of range of the Spanish guns, a shell pierced the fuselage and passed through the back of the seat occupied by General McCreary, Alexander's chief of staff who, fortunately, had just leaned forward to pick up a blanket that had slipped off. Resuming his normal position, he said to me: "They never go through the same hole twice," and promptly went back to his reading.

The plane was unheated, and it was very cold at the altitude we were maintaining. The blankets were barely enough to keep us warm. Fortunately, we arrived at Gibraltar and, within a few minutes, the temperature rose from -10°F to +104°F. It was a little hard on the system. After a one-hour stopover, the plane took off again for Algiers. During this leg of the flight, I made a "dramatic" gesture: I threw my black Armoured Corps beret into the Mediterranean, as proof to myself that I was done with it forever. What I did not know was that, a quarter of a century later, I would be back in it in another capacity, for reasons related to the rejection I had just suffered.

From the airport in Algiers, the group was taken to the HQ of the 15th Army Group (under Field Marshal Alexander), which was responsible for the overall direction of operations in Sicily and the planning of the landing on the Italian mainland. I spent three days there, then took the train to Philippeville. There I boarded a flight, with a number of others, for Syracuse. We were greeted by a hail of shell splinters from Allied navy antiaircraft guns which were defending the fleet against an attack by the German air force. Wearing a steel helmet and accompanied by two Red Cross girls, I headed inland at top speed in the jeep that was waiting for me. We stopped in a lemon grove to regroup. The night was spent under the trees. The Red Cross workers, who were terrified, did not get much sleep. It was the first time I had experienced fire from such close range.

The next day, we climbed into a light truck for the trip to Catania, where the 5th Canadian field hospital was located. From there, I travelled to Taormina and on to the headquarters of the R22^{e}R. I presented myself to Lieutenant-Colonel J. P. E. Bernatchez, who commanded the regiment.

I knew no one in the R22^{e}R, with the exception of Captain Ovila Garceau, a native of Trois-Rivières and a childhood friend. Nor did I expect to receive an enthusiastic welcome from a group of officers who had lived together for more than three years and whom I had never met on other staffs or at the college. There was, within the R22^{e}R, a sort of Lower St. Lawrence chauvinism which created barriers to my relationships. The challenge facing me was clearly greater than I had anticipated. Because I was second-in-command and hence a possible successor to Bernatchez, some officers were even more distant. Bernatchez himself seemed annoyed and said very little to me during those first days.

None of this changed the attitude I was determined to take. I had been chosen by the highest authorities and I had no intention of letting myself be put upon by anyone. However, I chose discretion and felt my way slowly and

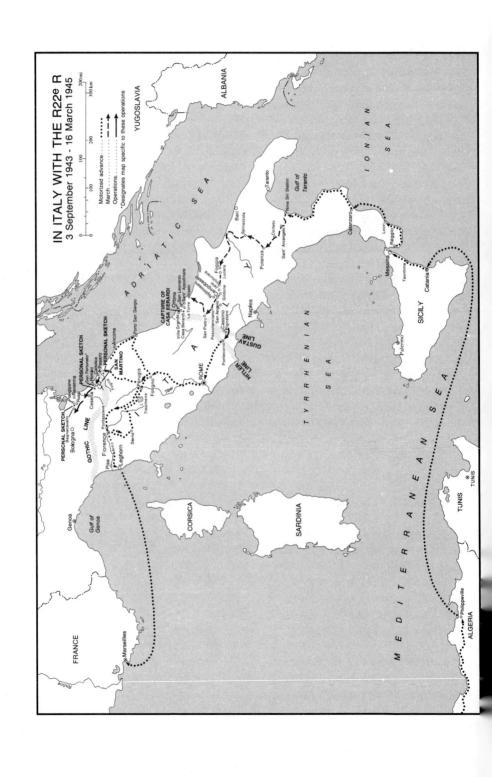

IN ITALY WITH THE R22e R
3 September 1943 - 16 March 1945

very politely among the officers, the NCOs and the men. Finally, when Captain Paul Triquet broke the ice, I knew I had chosen the right approach. From that day on, I felt that I was part of the group.

To help those unfamiliar with these details and, at the same time, to expand on the more general information provided in the previous chapter, I shall review briefly the structure of the 1st Canadian Infantry Division, in which my regiment was fighting.

1st CANADIAN INFANTRY DIVISION

Royal Canadian Armoured Corps:
    4th Reconnaissance Regiment (4th Princess Louise Dragoon Guards)

The Royal Canadian Artillery:
    1st Field Regiment (Royal Canadian Horse Artillery)
    2nd Field Regiment
    3rd Field Regiment
    1st Antitank Regiment
    2nd Light Antiaircraft Regiment

Canadian Infantry Corps:
    The Saskatoon Light Infantry (MG) (machine gun battalion)
    1st Infantry Brigade:
      The Royal Canadian Regiment
      The Hastings and Prince Edward Regiment
      48th Highlanders of Canada
    2nd Infantry Brigade:
      Princess Patricia's Canadian Light Infantry
      The Seaforth Highlanders of Canada
      The Royal Edmonton Regiment
    3rd Infantry Brigade:
      Royal 22e Régiment
      The Carleton and York Regiment
      The West Nova Scotia Regiment

I should also explain what the regiment's B echelon was. A realistic policy instituted by the British Eighth Army, which included our First Division, required that a certain number of officers and NCOs be left in the rear, outside the combat zone, to form a reserve in case disaster were to strike the combat units. In the trade these were known as the LOBs (Left Out of Battle). The second-in-command was in charge of this echelon. If the regiment's command post (C.P.) were destroyed, the second-in-command would be in a position to replace his commanding officer and, with this reserve force, would have a good chance of avoiding the complete dislocation of the unit.

Near the LOBs and also under the direct authority of the second-in-command, B echelon contained a number of highly skilled specialists: the dentist, the paymaster, the quartermaster, office and supply clerks, the armourer, shoemakers, etc. There was also the Knights of Columbus canteen and its canteen keeper. All of them had, in addition to their profound devotion to "the boys at the front," a cheerful side that helped us relax. They represented the pleasant side of life in a wartorn foreign land. Obviously, the work was somewhat administrative, as compared to that of the fighting man. It was necessary work, however, for order and control. We lived in tents or "borrowed" houses. We ate three meals a day. We put our affairs in order and caught up on our correspondence. In the evening, we might play a good game of bridge, cribbage or hearts. The men tended to prefer poker . . . and occasionally I let myself be talked into a game. Let us now return to our primary concern.

On September 3, I participated, as second-in-command, in the landing on continental Italy. I accompanied the unit's HQ and the mechanized column towards the airport at Reggio. In the area we disarmed hundreds of Italians who surrendered, shouting: "Finita la guerra." With my group I then proceeded along the road running northeast towards Locri where I was to await the fighting portion of the regiment which had advanced against a number of objectives in the mountains. Finally, after a long march of some forty miles through the Calabrian highlands, the companies joined us: HQ, transport and B echelon were ready for them. After their long and difficult march, the men were footsore; a swim in the ocean did wonders for them.

Italy capitulated on September 3 (the announcement was not made public until the 8th). This changed matters considerably for Field Marshal Kesselring, who, with only his German troops and a few loyal Italians, was required to defend the boot of Italy. He had no choice but to retreat before the Allies. The British Eighth Army had used landing craft to reach Reggio. It would be several days, however, before they could clear the harbour and bring in large ships with munitions, equipment and food. In addition, since marine transportation resources were limited, it would take some time to bring in the approximately one thousand vehicles our units needed to guarantee their mobility. Kesselring knew this. Along his retreat routes, he therefore organized a series of easily defended points where he could put up heavy resistance. He also had large quantities of antitank mines sown in the riverbeds, which otherwise could have easily served as access routes for our troops and enabled them to bypass the points of defence he had chosen.

His plan of retreat made it clear that Kesselring was not going to let himself be caught in the trap we had set for him. In fact, the American Fifth

Army was supposed to land on September 9 in the Bay of Salerno, on Kesselring's rear flank. If the landing was to be a success, the Fifth needed the enemy troops to be kept in Calabria as long as possible. However, Kesselring's intelligence had noted the absence, at Reggio, of the American Fifth Army, which, with the British Eighth, formed Field Marshal Alexander's 15th Army Group. He could therefore deduce that the Fifth Army was planning to land somewhere within the Allied fighter planes' radius of action, at a place where the beaches were accessible: Salerno or the Bay of Naples. The question of co-ordination and timing between the two armies which formed the 15th Group may have been debatable, but, under the circumstances, Kesselring was certainly not going to risk endangering his troops to defend southern Italy. His efforts during those first days, then, were not focused on holding back the Eighth Army.

To compensate for our shortage of vehicles, the High Command had decided to transport troops by sea wherever possible, with the aid of landing craft. It was therefore decided that a group from the 3rd Brigade would form three mechanized columns which would advance from Locri along the access roads to the north. Meanwhile, some of the infantry from the three battalions forming our brigade would board landing craft and, with the support of the Royal Navy, would land at Catenzaro, approximately sixty-five miles farther north. This group, which I was to command, left the beaches of Locri at nightfall. We hoped to reach our destination before dawn. Everything went well until we reached the beach selected for the landing. There, I decided to risk only my own landing craft on the first approach. It was a fortunate decision, even though we ran aground on a sandbank and were unable to reach the beach; on checking the depth off the bow, I discovered that there was barely twenty-five feet of water. We had to try another landing site. An Italian fisherman told us that the beach one kilometre farther north was in deep water. A destroyer rescued my landing craft from its predicament, and the group proceeded on to the north. The good Italian was right. However, the sun was up by the time we reached the site, and our armada felt slightly exposed. As it happened, the beach was defended by a large-calibre gun mounted in a casemate on top of a mountain approximately three miles from the landing site. At my request, the Royal Navy observation officer who had accompanied us asked for assistance from a support vessel. A few minutes later, a salvo from all its large-calibre guns destroyed the casemate, leaving only a single gun pointing forlornly skyward.

The landing proceeded without further incident. The companies then spread out in a semi-circle around the beach and each sent out reconnaissance patrols around the perimeter of this bridgehead. Since I could not yet contact 3rd Brigade HQ, to which I was attached, and had no means of transport or other support, I simply placed the troops on defensive alert. Then I awaited radio or physical contact. Towards the end of the afternoon, the advance guard of the R22eR column met one of our patrols. Our regiment was soon reunited. The companies from other regiments which had accompanied us returned to their own units.

On September 18, 1943, the Canadian division was split in two. Our regiment was part of what was known as B Force, or, essentially, the 3rd Canadian Infantry Brigade. On that date, leading a reconnaissance group from the R22eR consisting of the carrier platoon, sappers and the companies' reconnaissance officers and NCOs, I advanced along a route parallel to that taken by B Force. We encountered a number of obstacles, demolitions and mines. As a result, our progress was slow. We bypassed San Arcangelo, following the bed of the Agri River, and moved on towards Corleto. Suddenly, I caught sight of a puff of smoke and the silhouette of a vehicle. Since we had already encountered a certain amount of German resistance a few miles earlier, I told myself that it was Jerry waiting for us. I called a halt and deployed the few men I had with me. We circled around, then stepped out, guns drawn, to confront the enemy. Surprise! I found myself face to face with Marcel Ouimet, a war correspondent for the CBC.

- "What are you doing here?" I asked my friend Marcel.
- "I slept here," he replied.
- "Have you seen Jerry?"
- "No."
- "You're lucky, buddy, because we just chased him this way."
- "Too bad we didn't see anything. Come and have a cup of coffee and rum."
- "Make it fast because I've got to go after him."

A few minutes later, I left Marcel and his companions and hurried on towards Potenza. I could not help thinking about those men who, with no weapons and no special precautions, had at some time in the past few hours been behind enemy lines. On my arrival at Potenza, I found B Force, commanded by Lieutenant-Colonel Bogart, engaged with the German resistance which was blocking the access routes to the town. I reconnoitred the area, as planned, in preparation for the deployment of the regiment on its arrival. I then sent the men who had been selected as guides to meet their companies and direct them to their respective sectors. Meanwhile, I reported to my commanding officer, Paul Bernatchez, and returned to the rear to resume my post as second-in-command.

While the administrative zone at the rear was far from the combat zone, it was by no means dull. Here a newcomer like myself could familiarize himself with the administration, the administrators and the Left Out of Battle (LOB) portion of the brigade. In fact, the friendly relations I established with Majors R. Danby, of the Carleton and Yorks, and Ron Waterman, of the West Nova Scotia, were to prove useful, since both later became the commanding officers of their respective regiments, which were members, as we were, of the 3rd Brigade. Friendship is always useful when you are fighting side by side.

During this period I also realized that my regiment was in urgent need of replacements for its fleet of vehicles. These replacements, which I managed to obtain, were required as a result of the shipwreck between Scotland and Sicily the previous July of the ship transporting the R22^{e}R's B echelon. The lost vehicles were replaced by English vehicles which the Eighth Army had used in the deserts of Africa. Since there was no alternative we had had to make do. Until the arrival of the new vehicles the old ones would continue to serve us well, thanks to our excellent mechanics, and particularly Sergeant April, who often worked night and day to keep them in running order.

Beyond Foggia, on Highway 17, the regiment advanced from victory to victory, across the mountains, towards Gambatesa, Jelsi and Campobasso, which it captured after occupying Monte Gildone the night of October 11-12. This was the end of one phase of the battle and B echelon rejoined the regiment. The men were allowed to go into town. One of them, Sergeant Denifrio, managed to locate his grandparents, who were fine people, like himself. He and his family had a great celebration; unfortunately, it was to be his last, for he was killed, in December, in the advance towards the Arielli.

At the end of October, the regiment advanced, occupying without opposition, the small town of Ripalimosani, northeast of Campobasso. It was fall, the weather was cold and we were still in our summer uniforms. During this well-earned rest, with the men billeted in requisitioned houses, we were able to change our uniforms and attend to the equipment and weapons, which had been neglected during the long dash towards Campobasso.

The people of Ripalimosani were generally happy to welcome the regiment and joined in the celebration. Most of them were co-operative. An excellent officers' mess was set up and we discovered a man who was to remain a friend of the regiment for many years: Antoni Di Paulo. This Italian-American, who had spent a number of years in Chicago, spoke perfect English. He was extremely likeable. His ability to get along with people was to serve him well. The town's Fascist mayor, who had refused to co-operate with us, was forced to resign by the people. By a curious coincidence, our new friend was then elected with an overwhelming majority. Democracy had to be served, and it was with the assistance of Di Paulo that the mess was able to serve a good meal to celebrate the visit of the new general commanding the First Division, Major-General Chris Vokes, who had been promoted to replace the excellent Major-General Guy Simmonds. On the menu: fresh pork, drippings and chicken, all washed down with plenty of wine.

Our stay was a pleasant rest but it had to come to an end. New objectives awaited the regiment. A few days after celebrating the Armistice (November 11) we resumed our march to the northeast, towards the upper Sangro. This was a new sector and, this time, it lay in the Apennine snows. The Sangro was a rushing torrent and its waters were icy cold. The front which the regiment was to cover was an extremely wide one. However, on the other side of the river, the Germans were no more numerous than we were. They limited themselves to raids and bombardments, one of which brought home to me just how senseless war could be. Lieutenant Pellerin, from Shawinigan, had dropped by the regiment's command post for a little chat with me, and I greeted him with pleasure. On his way back to his own company, a mortar shell, probably fired at random, landed in front of him and killed him. Incidents like these left me at a loss for words. Today, however, I cannot help occasionally making an analogy between these meaningless losses and those caused by traffic accidents every day.

On November 5, we moved into San Pietro, not far from Castel de Sangro, for three weeks. On the 26th, I received orders to assemble the men under my command at Vasto, on the Adriatic coast, where, after only a few days, I was detached from B echelon and the LOBs and ordered to San Leonardo, approximately three miles southwest of Ortona. Here preparations were underway for a battle which was to become famous in Canadian military annals.

It was now December, and the weather was particularly miserable. It was cold, and it rained and snowed. The troops were constantly in the mud, and everything seemed hostile. The terrain was very hilly, and with the slightest rain, streams flooded their banks, river levels rose and the strength of the currents rushing down the mountains made operations extremely difficult.

Around us, the news was generally good. The Germans, hoping to stabilize the front for the winter, were resisting the 1st and 2nd Brigades. Operations appeared to be bogging down. The regiment, deployed around San Leonardo, was in reserve. B echelon joined me and was deployed at the top of a hill, approximately three miles to the rear of the Regiment. From this promontory, I could see the front some eight miles to the north. In good weather, I could see Chieti, northwest of Ortona. The echelon, while out of range of the enemy guns, was still close to the front. At one point, an enemy aircraft penetrated as far as our position, but did not attack us. Fearing that we had been discovered, I ordered my men to disperse more widely and to apply more camouflage. The sentries too became more vigilant. The front was unstable and, after all, we were too close to take any unnecessary risks.

The concentration of the First Canadian Division was now complete. It was preparing to open the approaches to Ortona, its first objective. The task was assigned to the 1st and 2nd Brigades. The 3rd was to be held in reserve. The final objective was Pescara, at the eastern end of a road that wound across the peninsula to Rome.

Faced by the Canadian threat, Kesselring reinforced the troops in the sector with a regiment of paratroopers. The tenacity which these men displayed represented a serious obstacle. The two brigades attacked, incurring heavy losses. The attack was halted, however, on the heights above a ravine which blocked access to the Orsogna-Ortona road. On December 13, the 3rd Brigade went into action with an attack to the left of the area which the 1st had attempted to take. This attack too petered out on the slope, still south of the ravine. It seemed impossible to go any farther without taking the north side of the ravine. Brigadier Graham Gibson, who now commanded the 3rd, decided to send in his reserves; the R22^{e}R was to go into action, faced with a difficult task ahead of it.

Concerned about the consequences of the daring attack he was planning, Lieutenant-Colonel Bernatchez called me in, at about 2200 hours on the 13th, to explain what he intended to do. I also attended the meeting during which the details regarding the execution of the operation were passed on to the company commanders. As a result, I was completely familiar with the objectives to be pursued. Bernatchez then said to me: "It's a big risk, and if my command post is destroyed, you'll have to take over." I returned to the echelon on the hill and organized my jeep with the necessary radios. A small truck carried radio No. 21, which connected me to the brigade's net and enabled me to serve, if necessary, as a relay post. Accompanied by my driver, a radio operator, a clerk, my batman Private Bujold, and a load of shovels, ammunition, a Bren gun and several boxes of rations, I set out along the axis of advance to be followed by C Company, under Triquet's command. I found a suitable location, set up my alternative command post and awaited the advance.

At about 0330 hours, on December 14, I saw C and D Companies moving towards their start line. I called out to Garceau to wish him luck and spoke briefly to Triquet, who enthusiastically told me: "We're really going to get Jerry." Major "Snuffy" Smith and his two tanks, followed farther back by another four armoured vehicles—all from the Ontario Regiment's C squadron—advanced behind them. Thirteen Platoon, commanded by Lieutenant Marcel Richard, was at the point and advanced towards the bridge that crossed the ravine. A few minutes later we heard the first shots. The battle was underway and our radios, which had remained silent during

the approach, now crackled with information of every kind. The artillery's radio net provided a number of interesting details. It soon became apparent that the day would be a long one. The battle was raging around a group of houses on the Orsogna-Ortona road, at a crossroads perpendicular to C Company's axis of advance. Suddenly, I heard an explosion and the firing seemed to stop. Major Smith's nasal voice announced that two German tanks had been immobilized and that another was hightailing it to the east. A few minutes later Lieutenant Richard arrived at my command post. He was on foot and white as a corpse. Summoning all the discipline for which he was already recognized and which would continue to distinguish him later, he requested permission to be evacuated. He had been hit in the right clavicle—forcing him to salute me with his left hand—and he was still bleeding. His dressing was readjusted and he was taken to the aid post by jeep. He had time to tell me that Sergeant Rousseau had taken over and that his platoon was now moving east along the road.

The situation had become confused and it was difficult for me to determine exactly where the troops were. On the road and paths leading to Casa Berardi, men lay dead or wounded where they had fallen, with no one to help them. The wounded were soon brought in. Some of the men from the companies involved got lost in the brush along the ravine and never reached their objective. Triquet and eleven men, however, with the help of four of Major Smith's tanks, managed to reach it and took possession of the Berardi house, which was solid and well situated. Meanwhile, Garceau and D Company, who had advanced along the south side of the ravine, arrived, with their numbers severely reduced, to the right of the Casa. There were now about forty of them. B Company, commanded by Captain André Arnoldi, who had been wounded, reached the southwest perimeter. The objective had been achieved, but at what cost!

From my position at the temporary command post, I had the impression that there were fewer than one hundred men within the perimeter. The situation was clearly precarious. Gibson called me in to ask if I could round up some men to reinforce the position. I managed to collect about a hundred: LOBs, administrative services, maintenance, and so forth. I then set out towards a rendezvous which Bernatchez had assigned me by radio. From that point, under the guidance of Bernatchez, who had decided to set up his CP within the perimeter, the group, of which I was not a part and which by now included the sappers, the medical officer (Captain Guy Latour), the stretcher-bearers and artillerymen, set out. The movement provoked a reaction from the Germans, who showered the sector with artillery and mortar fire. As the little group approached the position, it suffered a counterattack and was slightly delayed. The regiment, despite its limited manpower, held the position all day through December 15. Bernatchez managed to effect a sort of consolidation. In the midst of repeated counterattacks, it was difficult to know exactly how things were going. We had many dead and wounded. During the night of December 16-17, Gibson sent me out to replace Bernatchez, whom he called to a conference. The next morning, Gibson sent me another message saying that I was to assume temporary command of the regiment. Bernatchez was going, in spite of his protests, to Cairo, Egypt, for a well-deserved three weeks' leave. I suspected that my superiors would be using the weeks to come as a test of my ability to lead the regiment.

At this stage of the battle there was not much I could do. Since I had been able to rest the night before outside the immediate combat zone, I decided to go out, amidst all the confusion and enemy activity, to check the layout my predecessor had left me. I had full confidence in his judgment, and I did so more for my own information than with the intention of changing anything. With my natural optimism, I found, in fact, that everything was in order, given the circumstances.

The command post and aid station, which had been set up under the Roman arches of the Casa Berardi's cellar, were an easy target for the Germans. But the debris that accumulated each time the house was hit made our shelters less and less vulnerable. The aid station, set up in what had been the stable, was equally solid. When we moved in, we had had to turn the cows loose. Some were killed and the rest wandered off. But it was in a good cause. The wounded lay on the hay, safe and warm, and this, together with the excellent care they received from Dr. Latour and his team, saved a number of lives. After a successful attack by the West Nova Scotia Regiment against a high point to the south of the ravine, the little path connecting the R22^{e}R to the rest of the brigade became more usable. That night we were able to evacuate the wounded on muleback in relative security.

The layout of the battalion was simple: to the west, A Company, commanded by Major Jos Trudeau; to the northwest, B Company; to the northeast, C Company, under Paul Triquet; and, to the east, D Company, commanded by Captain Ovila Garceau. The sappers, commanded by François Laflèche, formed the rearguard for the command post. Pierre Chassé's 3" mortars were adequately camouflaged by haystacks behind the command post to escape the enemy's attention. Major Smith's tanks remained north of the Casa to provide support to any of the infantry companies as required. This perimeter, which formed a half-moon against the ravine, was no more than 300 yards deep.

The battalion had been severely weakened by its losses. But because it still had all its automatic weapons and means of communication, it could react

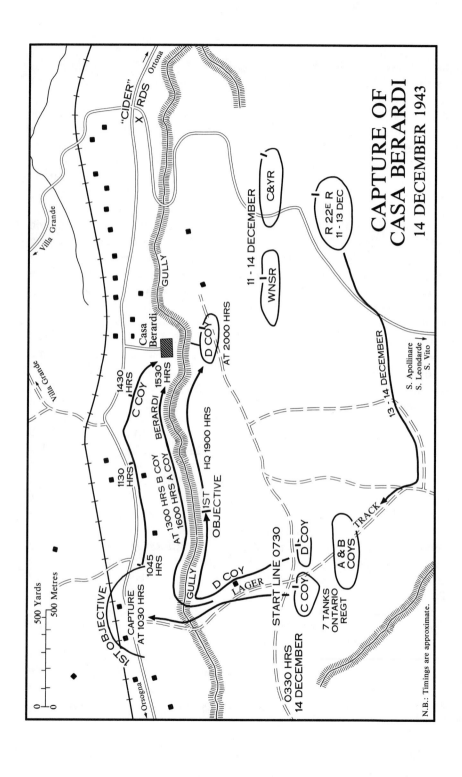

CAPTURE OF CASA BERARDI
14 DECEMBER 1943

N.B.: Timings are approximate.

as vigorously in case of enemy attack as if it were at full strength. German reconnaissance patrols drew heavy fire which led them to believe that the battalion was still intact.

When the sappers succeeded in mining the Orsogna-Ortona road, our position became even better. The artillery, under Major Duff Mitchell, a great friend of the regiment, was finally able to provide defensive fire around the perimeter, and this ended the enemy's minor incursions. Mitchell established an observation post in the debris of the second floor of the house which, despite everything, was still standing. He spent a great deal of time there during the day in order to familiarize himself with the enemy's layout.

As I have said, the command post, with its radios, occupied a small room in the centre of the cellar. On one occasion, Triquet* lay down for a rest on a makeshift bed there and slept for twenty-four hours. Captain Guimond was more innovative: he slept on his feet, still wearing his earphones. The signals sergeant and two men maintained communications with the companies, but telephone lines were out of the question.

To the rear, along the ravine, an Italian civilian was manning a machine gun for the Germans. A good Fascist, he controlled access to the house, particularly the front door. It was his last "political" act. A patrol, under the command of Corporal Vallée, eliminated him. Unfortunately, Vallée also died in the exchange.

To the right of our position, under Garceau and his three lieutenants, Coderre, Châtillon and Chicoine, activity was intense. This sector was forced to repulse a number of patrols and counterattacks. During my second night the Germans organized a heavy action around three Panzer IVs. The first tank went straight through our position only to find itself stuck among the mines to the west where it was destroyed by one of A Company's PIATs.* The other two met Major Smith's tanks. Smith, guided by Corporal Eglington, who led the tank by walking just in front of its treads in the dark, destroyed one of the Panzers. The other retreated without awaiting further developments. Meanwhile, Garceau's men drove back the infantry and order was re-established. For his gallantry, Eglington later received the Distinguished Conduct Medal. Unfortunately, Lieutenant Chicoine was killed during the action.

For the next three nights, the companies remained extremely vigilant. They sent out numerous patrols beyond the perimeter to determine the

---

* Triquet's courage and leadership were largely responsible for this difficult victory achieved by the R22eR, which opened the Ortona road for the Eighth Army. Promoted to major, Triquet also received the Victoria Cross, the highest military honour awarded by Great Britain, for his brilliant role and his indomitable will.

* Projector Infantry Anti-Tank, used by infantrymen for anti-tank purposes; the weapon launched 2½ lb hollow-charge projectiles.

amount of pressure being maintained on us by the enemy. One of these patrols, commanded by Corporal Piuze, encountered the enemy at a point northwest of our position. Following a brief exchange, Piuze was taken prisoner, while the others were able to withdraw. Before dawn, however, Piuze made a daring and clever escape. Another patrol, commanded by Captain Létourneau, followed the railway tracks west. A few hundred yards away, he observed a number of the enemy. On the way back, he was severely wounded in the left heel when he stepped on a landmine. Captain Létourneau courageously returned, unaided, on his shattered heel. Captain Dumont, sent out on patrol to probe the German posts to the north, failed to return. We never learned what had happened to him.

In this precarious situation, I visited my companies only during the early hours of the morning. Since our positions extended for only about a hundred yards, inspections were brief. On my second morning, I was caught by surprise by a German machine gun that could certainly have brought me down. Fortunately, my "bodyguard," Chiasson, was a crack shot: with a single shot, he dropped first the machine gunner and then his assistant, who was attempting to take over from his fallen comrade. The brave Chiasson never missed a shot, as we used to say. The new commanding officer of the R22^{e}R would probably not have lasted long under the machine gun fire had it not been for him.

On the fourth night, Brigadier Gibson called me to brigade HQ. I set out with an escort and a convoy of mules carrying several of the wounded by the ravine path, which was now relatively safe, at least at night. At the end of the path my jeep was waiting. I had no difficulty reaching the headquarters near San Leonardo. After I had reported to Gibson on the situation, which was gradually stabilizing in my sector, he told me that the 1st Brigade would be launching an attack from west to east between Villa Grande and the junction of the roads to Ortona. "Morning Glory" was to take place in the early hours of December 18. I returned, the jeep loaded with ammunition, along the road Triquet had taken (with a great deal more difficulty) four days earlier. Along the way, we were fired upon by a German machine gun, which punctured two tires. To proceed, carrying the ammunition,would be extremely dangerous; yet we had to have it. In any event, the Germans fired too low and the jeep travelled too fast to present a good target. Two valiant officers, Captains Potvin and Picard, accompanied me on this "escapade." A few minutes after my return, I called my people together to inform them of the plans the division had in mind. Finally, after a week of waiting, the front was going to change, and we would be leaving our relative isolation. We were to be in reserve. It was excellent news, but knowing the hazards of war, we waited to see it happen before we started celebrating.

The operation began as planned at 0800 hours on December 18 with a

heavy barrage of artillery fire to the northeast. An hour later, the Royal
Canadian Regiment (RCR) arrived in front of C Company's position
(Triquet), but its momentum appeared to have been reduced by concentrations of German artillery reaching our positions, particularly that of D
Company (Garceau). The fire became more and more intense. The RCR,
which had suffered heavy losses, was stopped along the edge of a small
ravine running north and south ahead of Garceau. There was no way we
could rescue D Company from the hell in which it now found itself. In fact,
given the RCR's lack of success, we now had to expect a counterattack. To
prepare for this possibility, I placed the regiment's sapper platoon under
Garceau's command. He sent them along the edge of the ravine, to protect
his right flank. At about 0900 hours, Major Burt Kennedy arrived at the CP
to tell me that he had been ordered by his commanding officer,
Lieutenant-Colonel John Pangman of the Carleton and Yorks, to clear the
valley. Since the RCR's advance had been halted at the same level as D
company, I felt that any operation to clear out the bottom of the ravine was
out of the question. I contacted 3rd Brigade and the Carleton and Yorks and
told them so, asking that they wait until the RCR had achieved its objective.
My suggestion was rejected. With the support of our mortars, Kennedy, like
the good soldier he was, then launched the assault. As I had anticipated, his
company had not gone very far before it was in serious difficulty. Because he
had, fortunately, albeit without permission, placed himself under the
protection of the R22^{e}R, with which he was in radio contact, Kennedy
informed us that the carnage had to be stopped. We transmitted the message
to the Carleton and Yorks, who were no longer in communication with him.
Brigadier Gibson then intervened and ordered Kennedy to stay where he was.
An hour later, the RCR successfully resumed its offensive, and the Germans
moved out of the ravine. Kennedy was then able to advance unopposed.

On December 22 we withdrew from the front, having held a precarious
position for eight days. The regiment was sent to rest in the little village of
La Torre, where we all hoped to spend Christmas. Our first priority,
naturally, was to let the men get some rest and, after all our losses, to
undertake a complete reorganization. Major Fernand Trudeau, acting as
adjutant, organized the Christmas party while I put the regiment back into
shape. We rested as well as we could. On the 24th, I was summoned to
brigade HQ, where I was told that the R22^{e}R was to be transferred
temporarily from the 3rd to the 1st Brigade. We were to occupy a defensive
position northwest of Casa Berardi. Since we had only a few hours before
returning to the front, we had to cancel the Christmas party, which our
chaplain, Father Gratton, had so carefully prepared, and turn our attention
to the reinforcements we had received directly from Canada and, particularly, from the *Voltigeurs de Québec*.

These men, who had no experience of active war, were nonetheless extremely able soldiers. They took their places unhesitatingly within the R22^{e}R alongside veterans already hardened by six months of combat and received their baptism of fire almost at once.

We were soon back with our brigade, which asked us to take the plateau at the forks of the Riccio, between Ortona and the Arielli. On December 29 we advanced and were met by rolling fire from the left bank of the Riccio. Nonetheless, we achieved our objective and consolidated it. The next step was to cross the Riccio to improve the situation at the front of the brigade (with which communications had been cut). I ordered a reconnaissance of possible objectives, but decided not to do anything until the next day.

C and D companies, supported by a barrage of artillery fire, crossed the Riccio near its source. We did not go far because the Carleton and Yorks had not yet taken Torre Muchia, and our right flank was therefore somewhat exposed. On December 31 I reconnoitred the area towards the Arielli and discovered a spur that commanded the enemy lines all along the front of the brigade. It was during that recce action that I received my first wound, but this did not prevent me from staying on to launch a company attack against this point. The attack was totally successful and I could therefore cancel the orders for the participation of my two other companies.

New Year's Day dawned cold and miserable with chilling rain, icy winds and enemy shells to greet us. I inspected the companies at their positions and shook hands with all my men as I offered them my best wishes. Hot meals—something we had not had for several days—were served to a majority of the troops.

Until January 13, we remained in static positions. That period made an unforgettable impression on me. First of all, on January 5, I was promoted to the rank of lieutenant-colonel and I officially assumed command of the R22^{e}R. Next day, Lieutenant-Colonel Bernatchez, on his return from leave, came to say good-bye. Between these two happy events, there was a dramatic incident. Some sectors of our position had been at the mercy of a machine gun nest that we had been unable to pinpoint. A patrol undertook an attack on it in the evening of the 5th. Its leader, Sergeant Fortier, was one of those who had arrived from the Voltigeurs ten days earlier. During the day, I took him with me to the outposts and showed him clearly what the task was and how it was to be done. At nightfall, Fortier left at the head of his group, going to his objective. When he heard voices, he stopped his patrol and continued to advance, accompanied by only one of his men. He was almost immediately hit by a bullet and left for dead.

His companions came back and made their report. I then learned that Fortier had miraculously managed to return to B Company and that he was asking to see me. With great difficulty, through the mud and under the rain,

I went to the tent where he was lying. As soon as I reached him, he gave me a report that was subsequently found to be most accurate. Then he asked me whether I was satisfied with his mission. I had hardly time to tell him that I was before he died. Based on the details he had provided, his new comrades-in-arms from the R22^{e}R quickly avenged him.

Another significant event occurred at the end of that stint at the front. In early November, the 5th Canadian Armoured Division had arrived from Great Britain. By January, its infantry brigade (the 11th) was considered combat-ready. On the night of January 13, the 11th therefore came to relieve us. The change-over was going to be done man-for-man. However, the regiments of the 11th were at full strength while those of the 3rd, including ours, had been reduced by six months of combat. I heard a few neophytes from the 11th grumble because they had to dig their own trenches since we had not left them enough. They were going to learn quickly. Indeed, three days later, the 11th launched an attack that was a complete failure and cost 200 men. The brigade withdrew immediately, ceding the terrain to the 2nd.

From January 14th onward, the R22^{e}R was again placed in to the reserve, in the small village of San Apollinare. The rest was well earned and gave us an opportunity to appoint new officers and NCOs and to resume training. The newcomers, of course, needed the time to settle in. I used it to send my company commanders, qualified NCOs and a number of sergeants and men south on leave, to Bari or Naples. Administrative duties were left to Major Charlebois, my second-in-command, and the company captains.

Our losses among the corporals and sergeants had been heavy, and I was concerned. I decided to use our rest period to train an instruction group which would be responsible for giving lessons in tactics to replacements and newcomers. Lieutenant Côme Simard and some of my good men, playing the role of the enemy, helped me in operating this makeshift school. For a week, each corporal in turn became section commander. We presented them with different situations involving advance, attack, consolidation, defence or withdrawal, and varied them by changing the terrain of manoeuvre and the enemy layout. This course was extremely helpful. First of all, I got to know the men who, when all is said and done, win the battles. We absorbed each other's way of seeing things; I learned to know the limitations of each person as well as his perception of a tactical problem and his response to it. Through their effectiveness as section leaders, I believed corporals could play a major role in combat. They had therefore to learn to command, that is, not to "carry" their sections by doing everything themselves, often at the cost of their own lives. They had to learn how to manoeuvre their men in action for maximum results. This course forged a bond of friendship and respect between my subordinates and myself that was to last the rest of the war. Our subsequent achievements and my later friendship with Lieutenant

Simard were closely linked, in my opinion, to those two weeks of work.

During this respite between battles, I also managed to attend the Opera San Carlo in Naples, where I heard *Cavaleria Rusticana* and *Pagliacci*, and had the opportunity to hear the famous tenor Taviliavini for the first time.

Our two weeks of rest over, the regiment returned to the front in the Villa Grande sector. Our new command post was well located, in a small house behind a long slope. The companies also had excellent positions just in front of another slope overlooking the Arielli, a small river slightly to the north of Villa Grande and Ortona. There was only one precarious position, an outpost held by a platoon approximately 300 yards in advance of D Company. It bore the code name "Blue Bird." Since it was located only 75 yards from a German position, it was frequently attacked by enemy patrols. During an attack by the Hastings and Prince Edward Regiment in December 1943 the 14th Tank Regiment had lost a Sherman tank on a mine. This tank, which had suffered only exterior damage, provided excellent shelter for the platoon's command post and a first class radio station. This "advantage" enabled it to maintain its position.

One evening, the Germans launched a serious attack which, although halted once, was immediately resumed. The post's commander sent us an SOS: he had very little ammunition and could not hold out for long. I sent Corporal Armand Hébert and one of his men with a muleload of ammunition. Hébert, a tall young man, strong and dedicated, hurried to deliver his precious bundles. He accomplished his mission and in his haste to return climbed onto his mule while his companion walked on ahead. However, the mule stepped on a mine and was turned instantly into mincemeat. Hébert was thrown up in the air and back into the mine crater. He had lost both legs and his left arm; his right elbow was shattered. His companion too was seriously wounded. The news reached us a few minutes later. The stretcher-bearers went out to look for them in total darkness, but could not find either of the two men. I was, I must confess, very upset. I decided to go myself, with Sergeant-Major John Tremblay and the same two stretcher-bearers. Some time had elapsed since the incident. Nonetheless, we soon located the private, who was lying near the path. The stretcher-bearers picked him up and delivered him to the aid station. Then we began to search for Hébert, whom we found in the crater. Seeing his condition, I said to Tremblay: "He's dead." But Hébert, who didn't move, heard me and replied weakly: "I don't know much, but I'm not dead." Tremblay had a stretcher. I picked Hébert up and placed him on it. Then, after securing him to it, we raised the stretcher to our shoulders and carried him to the aid station. The poor fellow was by then unconscious. Tremblay and I looked at each other with the unspoken thought that, if he were not already dead, he soon would be. An emotion charged night eventually ended. Hébert regained consciousness and, with his companion, was sent to hospital. Both survived. Their action had not been in vain because the Germans did in fact attack the outpost a third time. They were repulsed thanks, in part, to the ammunition which our two men had transported.

The winter was divided into periods of two weeks at the front, at the Villa Grande position, and one week of rest, usually in the San Pietro-San Lorenzo region. Each time we went to the front, we knew that danger was lurking, as we have just seen, although we were only there to hold the positions (no major attacks were launched in our sector before spring). Opportunities arose once in a while, though. In early February we were temporarily attached to a British brigade. While carrying out the usual reconnaissance I noticed that there did not seem to be anything between us and the village of Crecchio, where it appeared that the Germans had taken shelter from the weather. I decided to organize a raid that I entrusted to Triquet and his company.

Crecchio was located on a hard-to-reach spur from which one could exit quickly at only two spots. Our tactic was to block those two exits and cause the Germans as many losses as possible. Things went very well. When our men started going from house to house, the Germans ran out in a panic to take up their combat positions. In most cases they were quickly felled by our small arms. We inflicted many losses and captured a few prisoners before leaving. We suffered only light casualties. Daring and momentum had carried the day during this raid. This action made me wonder whether our superiors had been right in doggedly attacking Ortona head on with the ensuing heavy losses. Would it not have been better to bypass Ortona completely in order to hit Pescara—that, after all, was our objective—at the rear, which would have forced the Germans to withdraw from Ortona anyway?

Over the course of the winter, our command post received a number of distinguished visitors, including Field-Marshal Harold Alexander who, in addition to seeking information, enjoyed speaking French to the men, with whom he spent a great deal of time. At the command post he liked to discuss various projects. General H. D. G. Crerar, accompanied by his aide-de-camp, Captain Henri Tellier, also visited his former staff officer, now in command of a regiment. On one of his visits, Tellier asked me if I would accept him in the R22^{e}R. "With pleasure," I answered. "But since you have no experience at the front, you'll have to start at the bottom." Tellier, who trusted his former staff college instructor, replied that that was part of the job. I spoke to General Crerar and, a few days later, decked out with his beaver badge and the red, yellow and blue shoulder flashes of the R22^{e}R, Tellier presented himself at the command post. As I had promised, he was sent, despite his captain's rank, to replace the lieutenant at "Blue Bird." For his first experience at the front, it was a good one. On several occasions, the Germans took it upon themselves to make it even more exciting. He acquitted himself well and, at the end of the week, I brought him back and sent him to A Company as second-in-command.

General Crerar visited the R22^{e}R fairly frequently, almost invariably arriving just before lunch. Naturally, I would invite him to stay because I suspected he was fond of the cooking his only French-Canadian regiment prepared. He probably did not suspect that our cook was the blacksmith from the sappers' platoon. The waiter was the devoted Private Bujold, a Gaspé boy who was also my batman. These two fellows always found some way of cooking up a meal that included soup, fish, meat and dessert, washed down with plenty of locally "liberated" wine. Thanks to them our relations with the High Command were excellent.

The command post also received other visitors. Captain Yvon Beaulne, the press officer, who later had a brilliant diplomatic career, often dropped in with journalists. Bill Boss of the Canadian Press and Moe Desjardins spent a great deal of time with us. Painter Robert (Bob) Pilot, an old friend, stayed with us for several weeks. The French Army's liaison officer to our army corps, Captain Jacques Noetzlin, enjoyed talking to the officers of the regiment and became a good friend. One day he came running to tell me that Vesuvius was erupting. "That sounds interesting," I replied. "Yes," answered Noetzlin, who suddenly realized that I was not particularly excited by the news. He then explained to me that, in civilian life, he was a vulcanologist, normally attached to the University of Geneva and responsible, on behalf of his association, for studying Vesuvius. As such, he wanted to fly over the volcano, which was in the liberated zone. Noetzlin did not speak English very well and when he had attempted to make that request to the Canadian liaison officer, he had been told just to calm down a little. Knowing that I would understand, he had come to see me. One hour later, the two of us boarded a plane loaded with cameras. A few minutes after takeoff, we were above the volcano, which Noetzlin filmed to his heart's content until he finally asked us to land at Naples. I did not see him again for several weeks. He did not come back to see us until after the fall of Rome, with a copy of his report for "his friend Lieutenant-Colonel Jean Allard." We were to see each other often in the years to come.

On April 13 we received great news. The previous commanding officer of the R22^{e}R, Paul Bernatchez, had returned from England with a promotion to brigadier. He was to replace Gibson in command of the 3rd Brigade. He was one of our own and we all celebrated. But we needed a present for him. The regiment was in the San Pietro-San Lorenzo position. Nearby there was a German outpost. I called in Sergeant Piuze and his chum, Corporal Ducharme. Piuze said:

"If you want to give him a prisoner for a present, I'll go and get you one. When do you want him?"

"Tomorrow, if possible."

The next day, at about 1000 hours, I went to brigade HQ to greet Bernatchez, who was just arriving. Close behind me was another jeep containing Piuze, Ducharme, and two prisoners who were rapidly escorted to the POW cage which had been standing empty for some time. I approached the commander and told him: "There's a present for you, and an extra one for good measure." Major-General Vokes, who was taking Bernatchez to his new command, had the surprise of his life.

Piuze later explained that at about 0800 hours, on the 14th, he and Ducharme had observed two soldiers from the German outpost sleeping in the sun. He had then indicated to Ducharme which one he would take and left him to handle the other. Piuze had said to the German as he woke him, "Coming, little fellow?" Ducharme had followed suit. They had then returned by the little path through the ravine which the two prisoners had been responsible for guarding.

The winter, spent alternately along the shores of the Arielli and in the little Italian village of San Apollinare, had taught me a great deal. Our frequent visits to the front had helped me to get to know my men. The rest periods among the Italians had given me the opportunity to sing and joke and enjoy myself with my officers. Since I had never before served in a regiment which was entirely French-speaking, and a regiment of the regular force at that, I had needed this opportunity to establish contact with my people in this youthful spirit that breathed through us all. I was curious to know all these men, from the Gaspé, Acadia, the Lower St. Lawrence, the Saguenay, Quebec, Trois-Rivières, St Maurice, Ottawa, Hull, Manitoba, Edmonton and Montreal. Their backgrounds and education were different; all they had in common were their names and their language. Yet they all acted like brothers. It was in fact more than that. The spirit of the R22^{e}R had been born during World War I in sacrifice and blood. The solidarity and gallantry of 1914-18 had been the first occasion in the history of Canada when Canadians, under their own commanders, had learned to know one another and to march to combat with their heads held high. For the first time, after three centuries of French or British domination, Canadians had been able to fight under officers from their own land: men like Tremblay, Dubuc, Chassé, Archambault and many others. The seed sown by these brave men had taken root and grown. Its fruits were now being enjoyed by all of us, the "youngsters," who had assimilated the principal quality: the spirit of the R22^{e}R.

It has frequently been suggested to me that it must have been difficult to command the R22^{e}R. I have always said it was not. Not when you knew the unit well. After all, it was not all that unusual. The entire British regimental system had been based on the recognition of groups such as the Scots, the Irish, the Welsh and the Midlanders, who, with officers of the same origin, had also developed the atmosphere necessary for effective service. In 1939-1945 it was the strength of the old R22^{e}R Battalion that was evident. Discipline, while inspired and even regulated by British manners and customs, was not applied as it was elsewhere, even in other Canadian units. The famous English "spit and polish" made our boys laugh, although they applied it as well as their counterparts, but without the degree of seriousness they felt they saw in their English-speaking neighbours. If one of our men appeared to be slacking off a little too much, officers rarely shouted at him. We tended to use ridicule instead: the fellow would soon feel isolated and his "regimental pride" would bring him back into line. This was, and still is, for all its apparent triviality, one of the differences. The language that best expressed this spirit was, of course, the French of Canada, as understood by the boy from the Gaspé and the Albertan alike.

The pleasure of commanding men like these has no equal, for their dedication and pride were written on their faces. The price of this pride in command was the loyalty that the men expected of their officers. We were perceived by the troops not as aristocrats or the rightful possessors of all wisdom and authority. Rather, the officers were chosen from among the men because they had the same spirit and the ability and courage to refuse meaningless adventures and to embark upon only those actions, regardless of the risks involved, in which they themselves were prepared to participate. This willingness on the part of the officers to share everything and to command by example created a unity of spirit which was, and still is, the strength of the R22^{e}R.

The regiment included some marvelous illiterates. Despite what the psychologists, then just coming into vogue, seemed to think, these men did not run from danger. In fact, the men who did not know how to read were often those who demonstrated the most prodigious memories. They were able to use the terrain, often better than the rest, and to follow contours on a map. They were frequently excellent mechanics. Their greatness of soul was unparalleled. What a pity it was to reject them, I had said, when this question had been put to me during my brief period with the *Régiment de la Chaudière*. And so, to my great delight, all those who had been classified as illiterate, but whom I had then recommended for service, were assigned to the R22^{e}R during the reorganization. The months that followed proved that I had been right.

As the winter of 1944 drew to a close, we were informed that an Indian division would be relieving the 1st Canadian. Where were we going? It was a "secret." After several days of reorganization at the rear, during which we enjoyed the beautiful Italian spring, we were sent west. We arrived at Jelsi, several miles from Campobasso. It was the first time I had a battalion at full strength, with 837 officers and men. During the first two days at Jelsi we worked on our muscles, going on long marches through the mountains. We also used the time to check our weapons, do a major cleaning and change our clothes: our winter battle dress was replaced by the summer uniform. It was announced that we would be visited by Georges Vanier, Canada's ambassador to de Gaulle's Free France and a hero of the R22^{e}R during World War I. We greeted him with a guard of honour before treating him to a somewhat rustic dinner. After inspecting the companies in their rest sectors he spoke to them and returned to Algeria. I have to admit that the men, in the midst of all this relative pomp and circumstance, were somewhat preoccupied by our final destination, which was to be announced the next day.

We boarded our vehicles the next day for the trip to the Monte Cassino sector, several miles south of the Rapido River. No sooner had I arrived than I was called to a conference. The commanding officer of the British Eighth Army, General Sir Oliver Leese, addressed the group of commanding officers gathered together for the occasion. He began by saying that at 2300 hours, on May 11, 1060 guns of all calibres would open fire on the positions of the Gustav Line, north of the Rapido and of the Gari (the former being a tributary of the latter); 45 minutes later, two divisions of the Eighth Army would launch an attack on those rivers. This was to be the beginning of the battle for Rome, along an axis comprising the wide valley of the Liri which rises towards Rome but which is dominated over virtually its whole length by mountainous areas, a few miles away on either side of the river. Initially, the 1st Canadian Division was to be held in reserve.

However, during the night of May 15-16, it relieved the Indian 8th Division with orders to advance on the Hitler Line, seven miles north of the Gustav Line, which had been breached. Bernatchez's 3rd Brigade relieved the Indian 21st Brigade and set out. The R22^{e}R was to the left of the Carleton and Yorks and accompanied by C squadron of the 12th Armoured Regiment (Trois-Rivières). Resistance was heavy and progress slow. The next day we were halfway to our objective but our advance seemed to be becoming easier. The regiment halted on a slope south of the Aquino, a creek at the bottom of a wide ravine that blocked our advance over a large stretch. A patrol sent out to our right, towards the British 78th Division, informed me that the British had not yet come up to our level. We consolidated our position for the night and sent patrols out ahead, towards the river, and along our flanks. Since German resistance had been sporadic in the last few hours, I was not surprised to find that the patrols failed to make contact. The Aquino River, which was visible from the advanced posts, told us nothing. Before organizing a major attack, I felt it would be wise to ensure that it was really necessary. The next morning, at about 0400 hours, I went out myself to see what was going on. I was accompanied by my batman, Private Bujold, with a submachine gun and my driver, Private Denis, who, carrying a submachine gun for the occasion, had to watch the front and the right side of the road and drive the jeep at the same time. I advanced towards a small flour mill along the edge of the river. Everything was perfectly still. Since we could not take the jeep across the river, I left Denis behind and went ahead on foot with Bujold to a farm located approximately 300 yards away on the other side. A few minutes later, Denis, who, on his own initiative, had improvised a bridge, arrived at the farm with his jeep, accompanied by two other men from B Company whom Potvin had sent, just in case. On their arrival, and in order to ensure our safety, I sent Bujold and the two men to check out the buildings. A few minutes later, they returned with two prisoners whom they had surprised behind a haystack. We had come upon a picket that was supposed to be protecting the left flank of the German front facing our 1st Brigade, which was advancing towards Pontecorvo on our left. It was a bit of luck for us, but it did not prevent the German guns just ahead from withdrawing at top speed towards the Hitler Line, approximately two miles to the north. In view of this situation, I asked B and D Companies to come and meet me at the farm. Because they were already in a state of alert, Potvin and Garceau were able to set out immediately. A few minutes later, Bernatchez joined us. Together, we examined the approaches to the Hitler Line and decided to push on with these two companies to the outskirts of an olive grove. The two companies proceeded rapidly to the area and Brigadier Bernatchez authorized the advance of the rest of the regiment. The command post was then set up in the farmhouse. I immediately ordered a reconnaissance of the front, which was now no more than a mile from the defensive fortifications of the Hitler Line. On my return to the command post, I received a report from the army corps announcing that in the difficult mountain sector to the left of our 1st Brigade, General Guillaume's Moroccan *goumiers* had achieved a spectacular breach in the Hitler Line which was not as heavily fortified at that spot as in the valley (but the terrain was much more difficult). The French Expeditionary Corps was therefore behind the Hitler Line and, according to the report, it was possible that the Hitler Line sector in front of us had been evacuated. We were to press forward swiftly. Towards the end of the afternoon, we received orders to make a reconnaissance in force at dawn the next day. The front was too calm for my taste, and I could not believe that the fortified points had in fact been abandoned. The support we were to receive from the artillery was minimal: a single battery, to begin with, and one squadron of tanks from the 12th Armoured Regiment.

On May 19, at 0630 hours, A Company (on the right, Tellier) and D Company (on the left, Garceau) advanced, accompanied by a tank unit. They progressed fairly rapidly at first, with no appreciable opposition. Within a few minutes, a thick fog had descended over the field, severely limiting the vision of the tanks' drivers. They were now approximately halfway to the fortifications; I decided to halt these companies and to continue the advance with B (Potvin), which was to pass through D's positions, on the left, while C (Bellavance) passed through A's on the right. We were able to carry out this manoeuvre under cover of the fog. I suspected that the fog would lift with sunrise; but the change at least placed D and A Companies in a position to provide back-up support and even to expand rapidly on the penetration which B and C Companies were now preparing to effect.

An hour later, when the mist had dissipated, the two companies found themselves within sight of the fortifications. Accompanied by their tanks they began the attack. On the left, Major P. Potvin had advanced only a few yards when he received his first wound. His point platoon on the left, under Lieutenant Harry Pope, advanced, suffering heavy losses; then a German counterattack captured Pope and his remaining men. At the same time, Potvin received a second wound, this time serious. His right platoon continued the advance but its lieutenant, St-Onge, was killed almost at once. The company passed to the command of Sergeant-Major Drapeau. He ordered the reserve platoon to form a defensive position to which the survivors of the point platoons would rally. This reserve was commanded first by Lieutenant Audren and then, when he was wounded, by Sergeant Couturier.*

The situation was no better for C Company (Bellavance). Moving along the Aquino River, which slanted off to the right it was raked by fire from two machine gun nests. Lieutenant Claude Gagnon was pinned down with his platoon while Lieutenant Roger Piché took a bullet in the arm. After visiting Sergeant-Major Drapeau and what was left of C Company, I realized that the situation was equally serious for B Company. I called again for artillery fire against the German positions. I was told that most of the artillery, with the exception of my own support battery, was out of range. Instead, I was offered a number of 4.2 inch mortars, which I could hardly use on the German advanced posts for fear of hitting my own men. Seeing that it was

---

* During this action, Captain Keith Saunders of the Royal Canadian Horse Artillery exposed himself frequently to enemy fire in order to ensure the effectiveness of the artillery battery that accompanied us. He assumed command of Potvin's company, all the officers of which had become casualties, and enabled it to withdraw in good order. Upon my recommendation, he received the Military Cross.

useless to attempt to go any farther, I fired smoke pots at the German strong
points and hurried to explain the situation to Brigadier Bernatchez. Before
leaving, I instructed Major Tellier to decide on a plan of retreat with Major
Garceau. On the way, the windshield of my jeep was shattered by a burst of
machine gun fire. Private Denis, my driver, who had been sitting beside me,
was hit, but I was not. I threw myself into the ditch alongside the road and
continued walking back towards the rear. However, a few minutes later my
escort, Private Geonais, managed to get the jeep going again, under fire
from the same machine gun. He set it slowly in motion while he himself
crawled along on the protected side. Once out of range of the enemy, I took
the wheel, drove Denis to the aid station, and hurried off to the brigade.

Bernatchez had already halted the advance of the Carleton and Yorks at
the edge of the olive grove. As a result, he was able to contribute an artillery
battery to support the R22^{e}R. This was far from enough, however, and he
realized that it was useless to continue the attack, since our mission had
already been accomplished. After consulting with Major-General Vokes,
who seemed difficult to convince, he finally obtained permission to
withdraw the R22^{e}R from its precarious position.

I returned to the regiment where Tellier and Garceau had prepared a
complete plan of retreat during my absence. On my return, I quickly
withdrew the tanks, which were beginning to run short of fuel. Garceau took
charge of what was left of B Company. Major Potvin was missing and
presumed dead. Garceau withdrew through Tellier's company, which then
assumed responsibility for the sector. C Company (Bellavance) withdrew
behind a smokescreen. Satisfied with the results of the retreat, I ordered
Tellier to fall back in turn. We regrouped around a farm approximately a
mile and a half behind the position we had reached that morning.

The day had been a costly one. We had more than fifty dead and wounded
and still had not managed to breach the fortifications presented by the Hitler
Line. I felt that my regiment had been the victim of the recklessness of the
High Command, which had sent it on a dubious mission on the basis of
relatively limited information and without artillery support to surprise the
defenders. Moreover, we had had no real support from the air force, which
could have bombarded the lines, in preparation for the attack. Nor had the
division shown much imagination in assuming that the Germans would
abandon such well built fortifications which enabled them to contain the
advance of the Eighth Army with minimum forces when they were
attempting at the same time to hold back the French on their right flank and
the Poles at Monte Cassino on their left. It seems that our commanders had
overestimated the assistance the French could have given us. The latter were
stretched very thin at the end of communication lines that were long and
vulnerable in view of the terrain and of the fact that our stretch of the Hitler

Line had not yet fallen. Similar to what was done at the outset of the offensive against the outposts of the fortifications forming the Gustav Line, the segment of the Hitler Line in front of us should have been attacked without hesitation by a thousand guns, as it was in fact attacked a few days later.

Under the circumstances, the R22^{e}R had reason to be proud of its effort. As a former staff college instructor, I was left with a bad taste in my mouth about the whole affair. I looked on those who had analysed the intelligence reports as ill-advised bureaucrats. And after this event I retained serious doubts about the competence of commanders who had blindly made the decision to hurl us, without preparation, against lines supposed to be abandoned shortly anyway. My friend and comrade Paul Bernatchez, who had reluctantly transmitted the order, silently shared the same opinion. He was as deeply affected as I by the losses his former regiment had suffered, losses that were to contribute very little to the eventual victory.

At rest, our command post was set up in a farmhouse. A sudden artillery attack caused us eight wounded, including a soldier who was sleeping in a haystack that caught fire. The poor devil was about to be engulfed in flames when I caught sight of him. I barely had time to extricate him from his situation. Later in the evening, a patrol from the Carleton and Yorks heard someone calling for help in French. Major Jos Trudeau, my adjutant, volunteered to take out a patrol to see what was going on. He found Major Pierre Potvin who had managed, despite severe wounds, to follow a small ditch back to the edge of the olive grove. Jos carried him on his back to the aid station where he was evacuated to the hospital and treated. What a relief it was to know that he was alive and had a good chance of recovery, especially since Potvin, a humble and even shy man, was extremely popular and well liked. The news of his return spread quickly and helped us forget something of the blow we had suffered the previous day.

The battle was not yet won, and we spent four days preparing for the final assault. The division was now to attack head on with its three brigades. The 1st (Spry) on the left, towards Pontecorvo, was to act primarily as a diversion; the 2nd (Gibson), on the right, where the R22^{e}R had been repulsed on May 19, was to spearhead the effort, and the 3rd (Bernatchez), minus the R22^{e}R which would be the divisional reserve, in the centre along a newly opened axis, but with the Carleton and Yorks as the only regiment in direct combat while the West Nova Scotia Regiment remained ready to exploit any potential breakthrough by the Carleton and Yorks.

On May 23, at 0500 hours, after placing the battalion on one hour notice, I proceeded to 1st Division HQ and placed myself at the disposal of Major-General Vokes, as provided in the plan of attack. I was extremely anxious to learn the results of the attacks by the 2nd Brigade. The 3500 yards of front (approximately two miles) that had been chosen for the penetration were pounded by 810 guns. Progress was very slow, and although the 2nd Brigade suffered heavy losses, it was unable to reach a casemate. By 0900 hours, no appreciable progress had been made.

In the centre, the 3rd Brigade (Bernatchez) was advancing. The Carleton and Yorks had succeeded in demolishing the turret of one of the casemates and the West Nova Scotia had opened a breach in the barbed wire, mines and two of the twin machine gun turrets protecting the casemate. Because of this success, Vokes returned the R22^{e}R to the command of the 3rd Brigade. Bernatchez was delighted and decided to send us into the breach. We lost a great deal of time, however, because once we reached the position we had to wait for Bernatchez's orders, do a reconnaissance, assign the troops to the selected axes of advance, prepare a plan for artillery support, bring up the tanks from the 12th Armoured to join the lead infantry companies, establish liaison with the West Nova Scotia, which was holding the breach open, and move the three assault companies to their jumping-off positions.

The plan I developed on this occasion was to penetrate along a very narrow front, with D Company (Garceau) on the left and C (Bellavance) on the right, closely followed by A Company (Tellier); Garceau was to penetrate beyond the fortifications; C was to swing right behind the blockhouses and casemates and take them from behind, followed by A, which was to advance to the west along the left flank of C, as it cleared the fortifications.

Not until mid-afternoon could we start to move. Rain was beginning to fall and delayed our progress. Accompanied by my faithful artillery officer, Major Duff Mitchell, I advanced between the two companies. Suddenly, we found ourselves in front of a fortified house, containing an 88 mm gun which fired at us, the shell passing between Mitchell and myself. The two of us, along with Corporal Angillillo and Bujold, were out of our vehicles in record time. Corporal Berthiaume, a member of the 1st Anti-Tank Regiment, Royal Canadian Artillery, in charge of a 17 lb. gun, immediately went into action and fired directly into the loophole of the house, destroying the enemy gun and gun crew.

A few minutes later, I stopped near a house where my childhood friend, the outstanding and popular Major Ovila Garceau, lay with a fatal wound in the abdomen. As soon as I saw him, I knew he was dying. I did not ask him what had happened. Garceau, who was still conscious and lucid, said to me: "You know, Jean, old buddy, it's an honour to die for the Van Doos. Tell my mother I died happy and say good-bye to her for me. Say hello to Jos Trudeau for me." We laid him onto a stretcher; he died on arrival at the hospital. Garceau's death was hard to accept. He had given his all, like thousands of other Canadians before him, in a war far from home, a war that would go on without him.

But what had become of D Company, which had been sent into the heart of the fortifications? Already I knew that one of the platoons was not following its axis and was no longer in touch. Where was it going? Fortunately, Captain Vaugeois, with his reconnaissance platoon, which was in reserve, was close behind me. I sent him ahead with his group with orders to assume command of D Company. Within a few moments he was on his way. He soon located the brave Sergeant-Major Roy, who had already taken matters in hand and reorganized his command post while preparing to advance against the objective. With Vaugeois in command and communications re-established, the company took up its position beyond the fortifications, where it was soon firmly established. I was then able to turn my attention to Major Bellavance's C Company. It was advancing behind the fortifications to the east, taking them from the rear where they could not defend themselves. The job was done, the breach was wide open, and Tellier's A Company, covering C Company's left flank, was mopping up in the rear. B, in reserve, took up its position around a blockhouse where we established the regiment's HQ. But it was already late, and we had to consolidate our position for the night. Suddenly, from the roof of the blockhouse, the observer spotted a battery of German guns firing on units of the 2nd Brigade which were located on the right flank of A and C Companies. Although it was well camouflaged in a fold on a mountainside, Mitchell was able to respond with approximately 200 guns. His first shot was from a 4.5 inch gun, and the shell landed precisely in the middle of the position. Noting this extreme accuracy, he ordered each gun to fire three rounds. When the dust had settled, all I could see were burning trees and vehicles. To our right the front was suddenly silent. Meanwhile, C Company had made contact with a platoon of Princess Patricia's Canadian Light Infantry (PPCLI), and A Company had reached a hillock commanding our position. A burst of artillery fire enabled us to determine the exact position of A Company, which was beyond the Hitler Line, approximately 1500 yards northeast of the command post. The regiment had thus opened a breach over a mile wide and felt satisfied that it had avenged its defeat of May 19. Consolidation for the night began.

This fine victory, of which the R22eR had every reason to be proud, had, however, exacted a high toll. Between the crossing of the Rapido, on May 13, and the piercing of the Hitler Line, on May 23, we had lost approximately 200 men, including 28 killed (one major, one captain, two lieutenants, one sergeant, nine corporals and fourteen privates). Nor was that to be the end of it. The next morning, Lawrence Cannon, who had come to replace Ovila Garceau in D Company, was hit in his jeep by a German mortar shell. He was killed instantly. Captain J. P. Martin, who was with him, was seriously injured and was to spend several years in hospital.

But Monte Cassino had been overrun. The Poles had taken it and the road to Rome was finally open. The 5th Canadian Armoured Division passed through the opening we had made. Subsequent engagements in this sector were minor. Our division had won a well-deserved leave, during which all the regiments were reorganized.

4

May-December 1944

New officers had to be named for the R22^{e}R, and NCOs replaced, particularly the brave corporals who were always the first victims and, proportionally, the most numerous among the dead and wounded. To replace Major Garceau, who had been killed, and Potvin, who was seriously wounded, two future pillars of the regiment arrived: Major Louis-Frémont Trudeau and Captain A. E. (Tony) Poulin. They were sent to C and D. Some of our weapons and equipment had to be replaced. In fact, we were issued Vickers machine guns, which I had been recommending for several months.

One fine morning someone arrived at the door of my tent. It was about 0600 hours. I got up and, to my great surprise, a young officer saluted me. It was Lieutenant Harry Pope, who said: "I've escaped with four of my men." With Pope, you had to expect anything. I told the men to go and get something to eat. Then I invited Pope to have breakfast and asked him to tell me his story. At the mess everyone stared at Pope as if he were a ghost. He and his men had jumped off the train that was taking them into captivity. They had then joined partisans near Florence. Naturally, Pope had found time to become engaged to the most beautiful girl in town, who, he claimed, was a Medici. Suspecting that I did not believe him, he said: "Wait! I'll introduce you to her when we get to Florence." Two months later, he came to see me, accompanied by the most beautiful blonde in Italy: she was indeed, as he had said, a descendant of the Medici.

In any event, after our meal, I announced the good news to General Vokes. He asked me to send all the returnees to him for interrogation. Pope was to provide some extremely valuable information on the layout of the

Gothic Line. Eventually, he was appointed aide-de-camp to Lieutenant-General E. L. M. Burns, an old friend of his father. In fact, Harry was well known to the upper echelons, since he was the son of General Maurice Pope. However, he wanted nothing to do with generals. Our friend, suspecting that his father had arranged the appointment, and also somewhat bored with his new life, made General Burns's life so miserable that one morning Burns called me to ask:

"Will you take Pope back?"
"Yes, with pleasure."
"Good! Come and get him right away."

His method of "disheartening" Burns had been to apply every regulation to the letter. A few minutes later, Pope, an excellent regimental officer who had wanted to remain with his friends, was back with us. He had won. Perhaps he was impossible at times, but I enjoyed his intelligence, his gallantry and his great ability. In short, I was very happy to have him back. I never had cause to regret my action, and several years later, in Korea, I was to have the pleasure of awarding him the ribbon of the Military Cross for gallantry and services rendered.

This rest period was a particularly busy one for the regiment. Pope Pius XII, for example, granted us an audience. It should be mentioned that, with few exceptions, the members of the R22^{e}R were devoutly practising Catholics. Most of them took communion once a week. The chaplains made every effort to serve their flock everywhere. There was no shortage of volunteers (including myself) to serve mass. This state of mind explains in part why we were all extremely moved at meeting the Pope, a frail, ascetic giant. After his kind words to us, in French—which were recorded and have been kept in the regimental archives—a special mass was said by our chaplain. The sermon was given by Father Théodoric Paré, a Franciscan, who was at that time posted to Rome and who had arranged the papal audience. Ambassador Vanier then addressed us briefly in St Peter's Square.

The next day, I had the privilege of being granted a private audience with the Pope. He asked me about my family. I noticed that his intelligence service was excellent, for he knew a number of astonishing details about those close to me. Also in Rome, I visited Father Perrin, the director of the Canadian College there. The good father had a little trouble remembering me as an altar boy at his 7 a.m. masses at Notre-Dame some twenty years earlier. And finally, I was invited to a dinner attended by the flower of future Italian politics, Aldo Moro, Alcide de Gasperi and Benedetto Croce. I heard these men speak with enthusiasm and hope of the democracy to be established in their country.

A few days later I received an invitation from the Vaniers. I caught the service flight to Algeria. Unfortunately, the day after my arrival I suffered an attack of malaria and I was taken to hospital where I remained for several days. The Vaniers and Colonel Maurice Forget, who had planned a busy schedule for me, including receptions and visits, had to cancel everything. The day before my return to Italy, however, I managed to attend the most important of these functions organized by the embassy. My most vivid memory of this visit was the excellent care Madame Vanier gave me that first night, when I was delirious with a fever of 105°. I thank her for it again whenever I see her.

On my return to Italy, we were informed of the impending visit, on July 31, of King George VI, colonel-in-chief of our regiment. It was a great honour for us. The regiment arrived at San Angelo the day before, donned its finest uniforms and, on the 31st, was reviewed by George VI. The march past was perfect; the King congratulated us warmly in excellent French.

Then it was time to prepare for our return to the front. We did not know exactly where or when our next battle would be. It was at this time that we were entrusted with a special mission. We were sent to Florence, where we were to replace a number of French units which had been withdrawn from the Italian front. These soldiers, under the command of de Lattre de Tassigny, were to set sail for Saint-Raphaël, in the south of France, where they were to undertake the liberation of part of their own country. En route to Florence our convoy was attacked by a German aircraft and several men were wounded. To deceive the Germans, who were to remain ignorant of the departure of the French as long as possible, since they would also have a fairly good idea of their destination, the departing forces left a number of signallers with us. Radio exchanges at all levels were handled by these men. In this way, German listening posts would have no reason for suspicion about the origin of the messages, if they managed to intercept any. We remained in Florence for about three days. Although we mounted no attacks and experienced no counterattacks, the Germans were very close. They blew up every bridge in the city—with the exception of the Ponte Vecchio— during our brief stay.

After this interval, we received orders to proceed to Perugia; the First Division was returning to the shores of the Adriatic. We reached the front lines about five miles south of the Foglia River. The 5th Division was on our left. The Polish Second Army Corps had moved along the hill to the right and seized the heights south of the river. The regiment was fit and at full strength. The company commanders were Tellier (A), Dubé (B), Trudeau (C) and Poulin (D). Captain Maurice Trudeau commanded the support company and my artillery officer was still the devoted Major Mitchell. While not entirely completed, the German defence works offered the defenders substantial protection and posed a serious problem for the attackers. One glance at the map was enough to indicate that it would be difficult to pierce the defensive line established on the other side of the river.

The approaches to the Foglia, captured by the 1st and 2nd Brigades in the last days of August, enabled the 3rd Brigade (Bernatchez) to take up a position on the heights just south of the river and the enemy's defence system. According to the original plan, the West Nova Scotias, still under the command of Lieutenant-Colonel R. Waterman, were to seize a bridgehead about a thousand yards west of Borgo Santa Maria. We were not to go into action until the next day, September 1, when we were to continue the advance by passing first through the positions taken by the West Nova Scotias. Everything should have gone normally. Unfortunately, the West Nova Scotias, after descending a long slope towards the river, became bogged down in a minefield protecting its banks. There it suffered heavy losses and had to stop without completing its mission, which had been to open a path through the mine field. Even though the 5th Canadian Armoured Division had managed, on August 31, to breach the Gothic Line, far to our left, the defences facing our brigade held throughout the day on September 1.

The operation by the West Nova Scotias had begun at about 2300 hours. Earlier in the evening, on the 31st, in anticipation of a morning operation beyond the bridgehead, I had set up my command post close to Waterman's and installed an observation post on the heights opposite the area where the West Nova Scotias had been expected to effect their penetration. I was therefore well aware of the disaster occurring in the valley. When, at about 0100 hours, Bernatchez asked me to meet him at Waterman's command post, I placed the R22^{e}R in a state of alert and notified my officers to meet me at my command post at 0200 hours.

On my arrival at Waterman's command post, I realized that my colleague was severely rattled. Bernatchez asked me to relieve him. To avoid adding to the confusion, I asked him to "freeze" the West Nova Scotias where they were and to simplify liaison, always a problem at night, I told him that I would take a different route. I went down the slope leading to the river with Bernatchez and easily found another crossing point. Bernatchez approved and I hurried back to my command post to give my orders. On my arrival I found that the regiment was already prepared to move out. After examining the terrain I felt that it would be useless to endanger my infantry by asking it to clear the area of mines. I therefore called upon the carrier platoon, which would be responsible for supporting and protecting the sappers of the 4th company of engineers, which, in turn, was to be closely followed by B Company, commanded by the courageous Yvan Dubé, to whom I assigned the task of capturing hill 105 as soon as the road was clear. B was to be followed closely by D, with Major Poulin, who was to occupy point 113, to Dubé's left. Once these areas had been occupied, Dubé was to return towards the south to attack Borgo Santa Maria from the rear. During this operation the artillery was to keep the enemy occupied by slowly engaging points 105, 113 and the road to Borgo Santa Maria. Everything went as scheduled and at 0600 hours the sappers and carriers occupied point 105, replacing B, which had attacked and captured it at around 0530 hours and was now advancing southward to take Borgo Santa Maria. This task was completed by about 0645 hours. Meanwhile, D had taken point 113 where it remained to protect Dubé's rear. In relieving the West Nova Scotias, the R22^{e}R had saved the 3rd Brigade from apparently imminent catastrophe. A great deal remained to be done, however, when it was decided that my two reserve companies were to be loaned to a temporary command formed of the

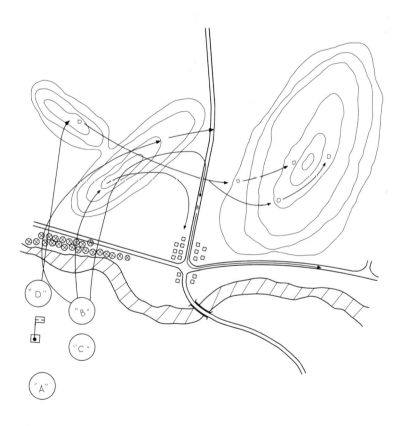

48th Royal Tank Regiment and the Royal Canadian Dragoons. As a result, my plan had to be carried out by the men already committed, who had spent the night clearing the area of mines and expanding the bridgehead.

We still had to capture point 137 and mop up the region to the south and to link up with the Poles to the east. This mission, which was entrusted to Captain Yvan Dubé, was essentially a continuation of the previous one. But Dubé was wounded; his replacement, Captain Gérard Payette, suffered the same misfortune a few minutes later. Finally, it was my operations officer, Captain Côme Simard, who captured the objective. The most difficult of these operations, the taking of point 131, which commanded the roads to the north, was entrusted to Major Gaston Poulin and D Company. It was an enormous task to undertake with such limited resources. In fact, this 425-foot mountain was the principal point of defence for the sector. It had a number of works which were well dug in and camouflaged and gave the defenders a marked advantage. Since I had no choice at this stage, all I could do was consider how to provide Poulin with the support he would need.

The enemy's outer defences were so well camouflaged that they were not spotted by our lead men until the very last moment. Only the determination of the platoon commanders, Lieutenants Pelletier and Laflèche and Sergeant Vézina, enabled them to overcome this first obstacle. In his book, *696 Heures d'enfer avec le Royal 22e Régiment,** Poulin gives a very detailed account of this battle which was all his own and for which he earned my full admiration. In fact, it was his first real battle at the head of D Company. By this success, he proved himself a worthy successor to the legendary Major Garceau.

After this first assault he advanced quickly to the summit, where he encountered a number of casemates. He sent Sergeant-Major Roy to ask me for assistance. My command post was just at the foot of the mountain so I knew what was going on. Roy wanted tanks, which neither Bernatchez nor I had. As a last resort, I sent for Captain Vaugeois with his platoon of carriers and placed it under the command of D Company. Meanwhile, Bernatchez detached a company from the Carleton and Yorks and placed it under my command. Adding to the bad luck, the artillery officer, Captain Howard, who was accompanying Poulin and D Company, was killed and his radio knocked out of commission. Poulin's had suffered the same fate. Left without communications for several minutes, Poulin felt totally alone. Vaugeois's arrival, however, re-established communications with my command post. In addition, the brave bombardier accompanying Howard succeeded in repairing his own set. Communications ceased to be a problem, but the battle was still not won. The final assault had yet to begin.

* *696 Hours of Hell with the Royal 22e Regiment.*

Meanwhile, the company from the Carleton and Yorks had joined battle on Poulin's rear right flank; it was progressing slowly, meeting the same resistance Poulin had experienced earlier that afternoon. For the moment, this movement was no help to D, except that it made a German counterattack rather hazardous. At 1700 hours, I heard a number of explosions and bursts of machine gun fire. Poulin had launched the final assault using the carriers as tanks. Half an hour later he informed me of his victory.

Simard, commanding B Company, had also had to face fierce resistance. Nonetheless, he too was successful. The Gothic Line had thus been pierced around Borgo Santa Maria and the opening consolidated. The night of September 1 began, then, with victory, a victory lost in the great account of the action of the 1st Canadian Army Corps, but one that still reflects honour on those who made it possible through their courage and determination: Officers Poulin, Dubé, Simard, Laflèche, Pelletier; Sergeant Vézina and Corporal Nadeau; and, above all, the teams of individuals from B and D Companies, those men, almost anonymous forty years later, who were, nonetheless, the true heroes of this feat of arms.

Simultaneously, our A and C Companies, which had been withdrawn from my command, had attempted to cut off the Germans' retreat to the north by occupying Cattolica, approximately seven and a half miles behind the German lines. However, they were too weak, and without support they were unable to contain the Germans. Our arrival the next day came too late to be of any assistance. Another major battle therefore lay ahead.

The few days we spent at Cattolica enabled the regiment to rest and re-establish some degree of order. We all expected to be returning to the front lines within a few days. The regiment was very comfortably housed in the barracks of the Italian navy, and this was fortunate because for two days, warm and dry, we watched the rain fall in torrents. Anticipating the work which surely lay ahead of us, I took advantage of this time to study the topography through maps and reconnaissance of the terrain. To our left, I could see San Marino, perched in the mountains; to the right lay Rimini. Between these two towns were a series of hills, including a small one near Rimini occupied by the village of San Fortunato. It was an ideal defensive position whose outposts could be protected by the little Marano River. Normally, it would have been possible to ford the river but the rain that was falling at the time might make it difficult. Paul Bernatchez, who had arrived in our sector with his HQ, rapidly reached the same conclusions. Wanting to inspect several points as closely as possible, he boarded a reconnaissance plane which crashed on takeoff. He suffered a serious jaw fracture and had to be hospitalized.

His brigade major, M. Robinson, asked me to replace him. However, because the regiment had no second-in-command, I preferred to return to it as soon as possible. And when Lieutenant-Colonel "Pat" Bogart arrived, I returned to the R22^{e}R and resumed my study of the terrain.

The morning of the 7th, I received orders to move to a new sector north of the Conca where we were to establish a new defensive position. The regiment moved out at 1600 hours and we were soon dug in. This was fortunate because the Germans, who were anxious to learn our intentions, sent out a large number of patrols. The nights of September 8 and 9 were extremely active. In fact, we were there simply to create a diversion. With us were the staffs of a number of Greek units that were arriving at the front for the first time and wanted to become familiar with Canadian methods. The Greeks were extremely nervous. Despite the language barrier, for they expressed themselves with a little French, a great deal of Greek and a little English, I managed to calm my successor. On September 9, in the middle of the night, their troops arrived at the front, making such a racket that our only concern was to get out of the sector as fast as we could. At dawn, my troops moved out, I handed over the position to my Greek successor, leapt into my jeep and high-tailed it out of there.

Our new waiting area was approximately two miles south of the Marano and one mile west of the Greek brigade. I had barely finished setting up my command post in a house when a bomb hit the roof and killed Corporal Bernier, who was doing intelligence work on the second floor. It was a shock to find this dedicated young man dead in a place which was well back from the front and was supposed to be safe.

Our orders to advance arrived on September 12, as the Carleton and Yorks was mopping up the south bank of the Marano. My companies stopped to wait, approximately 1000 yards to the rear of the Carleton and Yorks. So that I would not have to move during the coming engagement, I set up my command post in a farmhouse along the south shore of the river, which was protected by the presence of the Carleton and Yorks. Shortly after our arrival, I went with my counterpart from the Carleton and Yorks to inspect the riverbanks, which I discovered were muddy, thick with reeds and difficult to reach. It was useless, too, to attempt a crossing in the vicinity of the bridge. As I walked along the bank, I found an area that seemed to offer better access, 1500 yards from the Carleton and Yorks. I returned to my command post and told Poulin and Tellier, who went to examine it. They agreed that it offered certain advantages but felt that it would still be a difficult crossing, particularly since it led to a fairly steep bank on the other side. As a result, they were not especially enthusiastic. But, like the good soldier he was, Poulin, who was to make the first assault, told me that it could be done. After the withdrawal of the Carleton and Yorks, the

Germans, hidden from view behind thick masses of reeds, reoccupied some of their advanced posts. The situation was becoming critical. In addition, we had just received a map showing the new German layout, north of the river, and it was hardly encouraging. If I were to launch this attack, I could expect the worst. However, I had unbounded confidence in the quality of my officers and men and, in point of fact, no other choice; I therefore decided to go ahead.

It was pitch black at 2300 hours, on September 14, when D Company advanced into the underbrush. With enormous difficulty, it found the place where it was supposed to cross. It was greeted by desperate resistance on the north bank. Losses were heavy, but Poulin hung on and gained a small bridgehead on the other side of the Marano. A Company, which followed, received the same reception on the left flank and made the crossing, but its situation was precarious. On the left flank of the regiment, the West Nova Scotias had not yet succeeded in crossing when daylight arrived. By this stage, I was no longer in communication with Major Tellier, and contact with Poulin was intermittent. In addition, two of Tellier's platoons had not reached the rendezvous on the bank. Early in the morning, these two platoons from A Company, accompanied by seven tanks, arrived to join their leader. With them they had a "Tankdozer," which helped the tanks to get down to the river and up again on the other side. It was nearly 1000 hours and, of course, the enemy was pounding the entire sector.

The situation was extremely difficult in our bridgehead. I had two choices: fall back and try again the next day or risk everything with a very slight chance of success. It was noon and the West Nova Scotias were still south of the river. After deep reflection, I concluded that the situation would be no better the next day, that I could not risk leaving A and D alone all night at the mercy of possible counterattacks, and that, after all, since the road was open, a breakthrough towards the northwest might still be possible. The best choice thus appeared to be an attack. Majors Smith (tanks), Trudeau, with C Company, and Captain Simard were near my command post. I told them that they were to attack to the northwest around 1400 hours. Their companies were to take up positions at once near the ford south of the river. Each was to be accompanied by a troop of tanks. B would go first, followed closely by C. C would take the road to Rimini, and continue until it reached a tiny hamlet southeast of a large hill and across from Pallazo des Vergers. The support artillery would act in response to their calls, but until I had a signal from them, it was to engage all the known posts with a mixture of explosives and smoke. I wished everyone good luck and Mitchell immediately began to shell the enemy positions.

At 1400 hours, Simard crossed the river and set out, followed by C, with Trudeau at its head. The Germans were so surprised that they did not react immediately. Simard and his men cleared everything in their way while Trudeau protected the rear and flanks. All of them were extraordinary; nothing could stop them. I then ordered Tellier to leave the bridgehead. I was to meet him at the junction of two roads, one of which followed the Marano while the other led towards Rimini. I told Poulin to stay where he was to protect our rear. An hour later, B encountered relatively serious opposition. Our tanks acquitted themselves well against three enemy tanks sent out to meet them: we lost one but destroyed two. Simard and Trudeau continued to advance. By 1700 hours, they had both reached their objective, approximately three miles north of the river.

I moved my command post forward and spent the night with A Company. I was extremely worried that the enemy would strike back violently at dawn. However, I was confident that Simard and Trudeau would be able to defend themselves. Still, it was impossible to sleep and, with Mitchell, I remained on alert all night. At dawn, we had a few skirmishes in which the tanks distinguished themselves. However, everything remained relatively calm. The West Nova Scotias were still south of the river, and fearing a surprise attack, I moved A forward near the other two companies. My command post was to join them. Phase I was completed, but the situation remained unstable. With three companies and a squadron of tanks, however, we were capable of defending ourselves. The element of surprise had been almost total. Ahead of us, the enemy front was beginning to crumble. However, we could not stay where we were at the bottom of a hill and at the mercy of those who held it. When I reached the area, I decided, once more, to attack.

In preparation for this attack, it was more important to ensure the security of the command post than to protect our rear with D Company, which had remained on the shore of the Marano. I therefore ordered Major Poulin to disengage and to move his company up to the hamlet around my command post. Poulin, who for two days had been fighting a tenacious and desperate enemy, asked what he was supposed to do with the Germans. I told him to leave them there: "If they don't have anyone to fight, they'll have to pull back." This is exactly what happened. Meanwhile, A Company was to protect the command post, which was not located in a particularly restful position: an antitank gun post was discovered less than 100 yards away but was taken and destroyed by one of my patrols. Meanwhile, the West Nova Scotias had finally managed to cross the river and were being fired upon by the defenders of San Lorenzo on the southern point of the defensive layout more than a mile behind us. The brigade asked me to assist this regiment, but my position was so precarious that I could not take risks in that direction. From our position we could, however, direct artillery fire. For the rest, the West Nova Scotias would have to take care of themselves. Unfortunately, in doing so they managed to cause some consternation in

Simard's company. Indeed, the West Nova Scotias asked for, and obtained, air support. But they were our positions that the planes attacked—and missed.

It was now noon, September 16, and we had been fighting alone, as a spearhead, for two days. The important thing now was to capture and occupy the area north of the slope in order to cut off the communications of San Lorenzo's defenders. I called in my officers, with the exception of Poulin, who was busy disengaging his company from our previous bridgehead. Trudeau, Simard and Tellier arrived, all three convinced that I had to be dissuaded from undertaking another attack on this next objective. I knew how they felt and made them wait, but kept any ears open to what the three brave officers had to say among themselves.

While we were getting ready to discuss our strategy, Major Smith, commander of the tank squadron, arrived. As he emerged from his turret, this gallant Briton, who was supporting us with tanks from the 48th Royal Tank Regiment, was hit by an antitank shell which took off his head. His second-in-command immediately took over and we were ready for orders. Before beginning, and before my three company commanders could speak, I said to them: "Today is September 16, the anniversary of the battle of Courcelette. Like our predecessors, and in memory of those among them who fell, we must make this one final effort." No one dared say anything and I started to explain my plans in detail. The plan was simple and the objective was to be split into two parts. The central point was to be Palazzo des Vergers, which would be attacked by B Company (Simard) accompanied by a tank squad. The northern sector would be taken by an oblique attack by C Company, also accompanied by a troop of tanks. A Company and the carrier platoon were to remain in reserve to assist in case of difficulty. The artillery was to open the battle with intensive bombardment of the two objectives, and the usual support thereafter would come at the request of the forward observation officers accompanying each of the companies. H-hour time was set at 1450 hours, that is, 40 minutes after my company commanders had left. Mitchell, who had already passed on his orders for the initial concentrations of artillery and smoke, accompanied me to the second floor of the house. Through the northwest window I pointed out a few additional objectives. Suddenly, a German shell exploded on the windowsill, seriously wounding Mitchell in the face. I helped him go downstairs and lie down on a stretcher, while he tried to explain his plan of fire to me by pointing at various spots on the map. However, the combined effects of his wound—a shell splinter had gouged his nose and cheek—and of a morphine injection made his speech increasingly slurred and he fell asleep. I had lost an excellent artillery officer, a faithful companion and a friend. Fortunately, his signaller was unscathed and the radio in his jeep was still working. I had an extension cord run up to the second floor, and through the narrow window, I was able to notify the artillerymen of Mitchell's condition and to direct the supporting fire. The battle progressed rapidly, and I could see my two companies advancing towards the objective. Despite opposition, Simard and his men were moving up the hill and within a few minutes they were around the palazzo. Trudeau, on the right, had gotten off to a fast start when he suddenly lost two tanks. The company came to a stop halfway to its goal. They had just discovered three antitank guns deployed in a triangle on the side of the hill. Suddenly, from the platoon on the left, I saw three men dash forward.

The first fell almost at once; the second, carrying a Bren gun, had gone barely a hundred paces when he in turn was hit and dropped his weapon. The third quickly seized it and advanced towards the first casemate. I had just recognized him as Sergeant Yvon Piuze. In a few seconds, he wiped out the crew of the first casemate and moved on to the next, which he destroyed in less than five minutes.

Unfortunately, as he turned to come back to the third, he was hit by a burst of machine gun fire and killed instantly. The firing had come from a fourth casemate, which had not been spotted. The destruction of the first two casemates had, however, opened the left flank. The company advanced and the other two casemates were raked by fire and destroyed. C then resumed its advance. A few minutes later, it reached the heights commanding San Martino. With this phase completed, B Company advanced and dug in on the left, slightly to the rear of C, while A took up its position around the castle. Maurice Trudeau, then officer commanding the support company, destroyed the German antitank guns. The Vickers machine guns and mortars were set up on the southeast flank of the hill. The pioneers organized protection for the command post. The victory had been won. This final effort was extremely valuable, because we now commanded the network of roads leading to Rimini and the entire surrounding plain. We anticipated a counterattack, which we were prepared to stop. With the arrival of Poulin and D Company, the command post was safe.

The outcome was positive, but we had lost a number of our comrades, including, in particular, Sergeant Piuze, to whom I wish to offer special tribute. To us he represented everything that was gallant; he was truly one of the bravest of the brave. His death was felt as an enormous loss. He did not receive his country's highest honour, which I attempted to obtain for him posthumously, only because the authorities failed to recognize the importance and valour of his action. Without his sacrifice, C Company would probably not have achieved its objective that day, and the enemy would have had all night to reinforce its position and even to drive C Company back down the hill. I then say to Piuze, with many of our comrades who witnessed his extraordinary action that day, thank you, from the bottom of our hearts.

The next day the front was realigned. The West Nova Scotias had finally reached San Lorenzo. We were all exhausted. I took advantage of the opportunity to inspect our new position. It was a good one, although a spur to the northwest was still held by the Germans. It was essential that the area be cleared out since it prevented the free circulation of our men on the left flank of the hill we occupied and might even provide access to the centre of our layout, defended by only one company. It was no easy task that I entrusted to D Company which, it will be recalled, had suffered severely two days earlier in holding the bridgehead on the Marano. But it was essential for us to hold that point which, after the loss of the hillside we now held, had become the central point of the enemy defences in the sector. I had made my decision and since only one company was involved, I gave Major Poulin full freedom to plan his approach route, his supporting fire and the disposition of the tanks.

At 1720 hours our artillery began to pound the enemy positions, and at 1940 hours, two concentrations preceded the company and its tanks as they approached their objective. The advance was rapid and proceeded without opposition until they reached a belt of barbed wire interspersed with a few mines. The area was covered, of course, by machine gun cross fire which the tanks of the 48th Royal Tank Regiment were able to neutralize while Poulin's men took the objective, losing only one man in the course of the operation. I had never thought that it would be difficult to capture that sector, but holding it would be another matter. Unfortunately for the morale of the men, who felt protected by the presence of the tanks of the 48th RTR, they had to withdraw during the night for maintenance and refuelling. It was at this point that the real battle began. Without the legendary courage of all the men of D Company and the intelligence of its officer commanding, the day's small victory might have ended very badly.

While the Germans were being kept busy by D Company, the rest of our sector was relatively calm. Even so, B and C were attacked by enemy patrols. Several houses in the vicinity of San Martino changed hands a number of times. But it was D that worried me. The next day the tanks from the 48th returned. They arrived in time to provide support for Poulin who, although he was in a very difficult position, had kept his cool. He had just asked me to fire on his position. I asked no questions, and gave the order. As it turned out, he had tricked the Germans by altering the layout the enemy patrols had scouted. Our gunfire thus separated the enemy's tanks from their infantry during the attack. Meanwhile, Cardin and Meunier were successfully defending the new perimeter from the German infantry. This was not, however, the last of this series of local counterattacks, all of which were successfully repulsed.

With the exception of Brigadier Bernatchez, who often visited his subordinate units, we in our sector rarely saw high-ranking officers or staff officers from the brigade, division or corps of which we were part. For example, during the battle I have just described, which lasted ten days, I saw these people only when I visited headquarters. That visit caused me some anxiety. During the entire advance beyond the Marano I had followed an axis of advance which failed to observe the artificial inter-unit boundaries imposed on us in any major action. There was nothing wrong in doing so since we were alone, five miles ahead of the closest unit of our division. To my mind, and under the circumstances, only the topography was important. The "chinagraph boundaries" could and should be changed, depending on the circumstances: it was the staff's job to stay up to date. In this case, I found that D Company might have found itself doing battle with the PPCLI, one company of which had been assigned the exact spot occupied by one of my companies as its objective. The maps at the division level were certainly not up-to-date, as further evidenced by the attack "in support" of the West Nova Scotias the air force had made against us. But who was responsible for that error? I had many other reasons to be unhappy with what was going on at the divisional level, and I was not alone in being dissatisfied.

Following the failure of the German counterattacks against D, activities against B and C became more numerous. We were somewhat exposed since the Germans still held San Fortunato, above us. The enemy artillery shelled the three companies constantly, and there were numerous German patrols. Being in a defensive position relative to our objective, we were unable to move. With the arrival of the PPCLI on our left flank, A Company was able to form our only reserve. It in turn was preparing to counterattack. It was under these conditions that the Seaforth Highlanders of Canada arrived to relieve us on the night of September 18. This relief operation, effected without prior reconnaissance, without co-ordination and in the midst of all this enemy activity, was difficult. It was almost impossible to effect the handover on a man-for-man and post-for-post basis. Liaison was less than perfect. With my completely exhausted regiment, I could only think of ensuring the security of my men and of the territory, which I handed over to my successor, Lieutenant-Colonel Thompson. As soon as he told me that he was in position, I gave my companies the order to withdraw, whether they had been relieved or not. In the confusion, a German patrol managed to seize a position that we had vacated but the Seaforth Highlanders had not yet occupied. I should have been held partly responsible for this loss of terrain because of the hasty departure I had ordered. The fault, however, was attributed entirely to Thompson. A few days later, he lost his command (was this the only reason? I could not say). Personally, I believed that Thompson had done the best he could under the circumstances. Who had given the sudden order for the Seaforths to come, in darkness, relieve a decimated and nervous regiment that was in a hurry to get a well-deserved rest? No easy judgment could be possible under such circumstances.

For us, this was where the first phase of the battle to pierce a new German defensive line, the Rimini Line, should have ended. Happy at the prospect of a wash, a hot meal and a good rest, the regiment withdrew several miles to the rear. Before daybreak, it was asleep in the middle of an olive grove. The men had earned the rest after five days of intensive combat during which time they had had no proper sleep and nothing to eat but bully beef and hardtack. By the time I arrived at 0530 hours I too needed a rest. I had not been asleep more than half an hour when my faithful Bujold woke me to say that I had been summoned to brigade HQ. I was still fully dressed so I hopped into my jeep.

Along the 3rd Brigade's front the situation was not encouraging. The Carleton and Yorks had taken a bridgehead the day before beyond the Ausa and had effectively stabilized it, but the consolidation attack against Monte Covignano by the West Nova Scotias and the Hastings and Prince Edward Regiment had failed. Major-General Chris Vokes, however, wanted to take San Fortunato without delay. He had even set zero hour for 1100 hours. The R22eR was to do the job. That decision made me wonder. A few hours earlier we were withdrawn from combat in the chancy manner already described. We of the R22eR all believed that we had earned a good rest. We were now required to return to the front within six hours, in a sector where two battalions had just been broken. Disobeying orders was out of the question, but I quickly decided that, for my men, the time of that attack would be delayed as much as possible.

I proceeded at once to the area where the assault was to begin. Here I found the Hastings in a defensive position to the right of the road across the mountain and approximately 1000 yards behind the original start line. On its left, the West Nova Scotias were in total disarray as a result of the complete failure of the attack it had attempted at dawn. Turning around, I saw that the approaches were completely bare, more like a pool table than tactical terrain. Leaving my men to rest, I returned to the brigade to ask that our attack be delayed. Vokes agreed to 1600 hours. Realizing that an attack at 1600 hours, still in daylight, made no more sense than one at 1100 hours, I pretended to agree and returned to my command post to prepare a plan which would benefit from darkness. I waited until 1300 hours before announcing the news to the regiment. After a brief conference with my company commanders, I asked them to take their men about 1000 yards to the rear of the West Nova Scotias and to join me in a ditch 100 yards behind the start line. I remained absolutely convinced that an attack at 1600 hours would be suicide. Thus I decided to delay operations by assigning a false rendezvous to the tanks which were supposed to support us but which were not part of my plan. At 1500 hours, my company commanders met me. I took them aside one by one and told them what I expected of them. It was a somewhat unorthodox operation which, carried out in darkness, still had a good chance of success. The commanding officers of C and A, Trudeau and Tellier, were then to explain my plan in detail to their platoon and section commanders.

In order to appear as if I were keeping to the schedule, I opened a preliminary bombardment of the German positions at 1550 hours and ordered it repeated at 1600 hours. Naturally, nothing else happened. I then advised the brigade that the tanks had not arrived. They showed up finally at 1700 hours; immediately I ordered them to be camouflaged as well as possible behind the houses along the road which was to serve as our start line. I then had the same artillery pattern repeated, but once again we stayed put. I had set up my command post and my communications in a little house along the line of departure without apparently attracting the enemy's attention. My intelligence officer, Lieutenant Joe Girolami, was keeping an eye on the front from a second floor window. My new artillery officer, Major Cameron, was with me, along with my operations officer and my

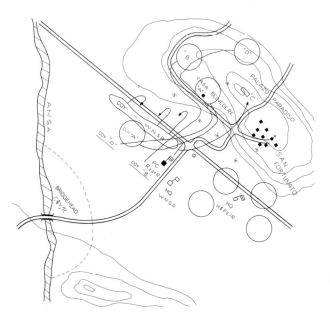

signallers. Until I gave the order, all noise or movement was strictly forbidden, as was radio communication. At 1830 hours, I had the artillery repeat the plan of fire.

At dusk, I told Louis Trudeau and Henri Tellier to go to it. In silence, Trudeau, followed by his company in single file, went up the mountain without opposition to Palazzo Paradiso, his objective. Tellier did the same, taking a path which led him, after a short battle, to Casa Belvedere, halfway up the southeast flank of the mountain. Both reached their objectives without losses. The Germans, taken by surprise, surrendered by the dozen. I sent Côme Simard with B Company to take up a position on the left. D, under Major Gaston Poulin, advanced through B to cut off, if possible, the retreat of the last defenders. Captain Maurice Trudeau and his support company remained below, ready to act if necessary. I then decided to move my command post up into the middle of A Company, in Casa Belvedere. On my arrival at the top I discovered the extent of our victory. The cellar of the Casa was already full of prisoners. In the area lay dozens of German dead and wounded. We had only two or three wounded and one dead. Once installed in Casa Belvedere I proudly reported the position of my command post to brigade HQ. Surprised and believing that I was mistaken, they made me repeat the message twice. The second time, they replied that the Germans must surely have withdrawn before we arrived. I said they had not and that, in fact, the battle was far from over. A few minutes earlier I had had the searchlights of our anti-aircraft batteries turned on to light up the battlefield we had just won. We spent the night under their light. Poulin, with D and two Vickers machine guns, had managed to reach the northwest side of the mountain. I warned all my people that I expected a violent counter-attack and that we had to remain in a state of alert. At 0700 hours the next morning the attack came. But Poulin had taken the necessary precautions. After effecting a brief penetration as far as C Company the enemy was driven back. A few Germans managed to escape from the prisoners' cage before order was restored. The victory was won.

The German army had lost hundreds of men in this short battle. We had had only one officer and six men killed and three officers and forty-five men wounded. A fine page had been added to the history of our regiment, and we received congratulations from all quarters. The past days had demanded the courage and gallantry of so many that it is impossible for me to name them all here. I can only raise my hat and tell them all: "If you were on the Rimini Line, you are part of the legion of the brave."

I would like to pause here to express to the artillerymen, engineers and signallers the affection and profound admiration I feel for them. Many of them fell in the line of duty or were wounded as a result of their unstinting dedication to their task of supporting my men.

Special mention must go to the North Irish Horse Regiment and the 48th Royal Tank Regiment, which assisted us during this period and, in so doing, lost some twenty tanks and a number of officers and men. Without their courage and determination we would never have succeeded in the difficult task that had been assigned to us. These men had been a part of the magnificent team around me during this long battle, a team that merited all my heartfelt gratitude.*

Within the infantry, Majors Tellier, Trudeau, and Poulin, and Captains Simard, Girolami, Trudeau and Lahaie, who had followed my orders without question, were the true architects of this victory. I can only thank them. Unfortunately, other heroes will never have the opportunity to learn how much admiration I had felt for them: these were the 56 officers, NCOs and men who gave their lives so fearlessly for the glory of their country and for the civilization they had sought to defend.

After this series of battles, the regiment needed time to restore its strength. It withdrew from the front lines and returned to Cattolica and the naval barracks there. These were not perfect, but they represented a considerable improvement over the trenches. A few officers and men were then sent on leave to see Rome and Florence. Major-General Chris Vokes visited the regiment, congratulated it and officially passed on messages of congratulations from Prime Minister Winston Churchill and the commanding officer of the Eighth Army, General Sir Oliver Leese, which we had already received by telephone a few days earlier.

During this rest period the regiment received reinforcements and, in particular, a deputy commander in the person of Major Gilles Turcot, who had accepted a demotion to come to the regiment. I did not know Turcot, but I soon realized that he was an excellent officer. He readily took over the administration of the regiment, which had been neglected since the departure five months earlier of Major Charlebois. This instantly took a lot of weight off my shoulders. In addition, Gilles was a pleasant and cultivated young man who quickly became a friend. I soon learned to rely on him completely.

It was during this rest period that I accepted an invitation from Monsieur and Madame Couve de Murville, the French Ambassador, and his wife. Accompanied by my good friend, Captain Jacques Noetzlin, I travelled to Rome, where we were treated like kings. During my visit I was able to play golf with my hosts and visit a number of museums, including the Vatican Museum, with Father Morin. I also attended a number of concerts and visited St-Paul-beyond-the-Walls and St-John Lateran. I took advantage of the opportunity

* In fact, Captain Clone, British Armoured Corps, received the Victoria Cross on my recommendation for one of the numerous feats he accomplished during the Palazzo des Vergers episode. I thought that this deserved to be recognized officially in the manner his superiors would deem fit. When I learned that he had received the highest British military distinction I felt the same pride as if he had been a member of the R22^{e}R.

to visit some of my men in the 5th Hospital. I found that they were being well looked after by, among others, two nurses from home, Lieutenants Madeleine Sanschagrin, of Trois-Rivières, and Camille Desbiens, of Grand-Mère.

Back at the regiment I found everything in perfect order. I also learned of the impending visit of the Minister of National Defence, the Hon. J. L. Ralston, and that of the Archbishop of Quebec, Cardinal Rodrigue Villeneuve. We were all very happy to see the Archbishop. During the two days he spent with us he officiated at the consecration of the cemetery where our men had been buried and sang a Requiem Mass for the repose of their souls.

This visit was marred, however, by the display of an incredible lack of tact on the part of the authorities of the 1st Canadian Corps. The cardinal was escorted by Major John Leclerc, a former brigadier-general who had been reduced to the rank of private for having insulted the cardinal on a train from Quebec to Montreal. From private, he had been promoted to sergeant-major and had joined the R22^{e}R in Sicily. Bernatchez had sent him back. Finally, he had reappeared with the rank of major, wearing the kilt of the Seaforth Highlanders of Canada. I had the surprise of my life when I saw him with the cardinal. He managed to attract attention to himself in front of the cameras.

For my part, I did not find the joke—if one wanted to call it that—very funny. Leclerc was known in the regiment and the men might well conclude that you can get away with anything if you have enough nerve. It was thus a very bad example to set and a demonstration of stupidity on the part of the authorities concerned. It humiliated the cardinal in front of the people of Quebec and was something of a personal insult to the population of the entire province, who could see Leclerc strutting about in the newsreels, when many were aware of the vulgar way in which he had behaved earlier.

The war, however, continued. After the capture of Rimini, the Germans retreated, abandoning what was left of the Rimini Line. The autumn rains had not let up and the Germans had had time to establish themselves farther north, on the Savio. The 1st Brigade had followed them to a point two miles south of the river. In order to regroup our division, the 3rd Brigade had been sent to replace the 1st on the left flank. During the night of October 18-19, the regiment replaced the Royal Canadian Regiment on the extreme left flank, next to the British 56th Division. The relief was carried out very rapidly. Our advanced companies did not appear to have come into contact with the enemy. In order to give Majors Tellier and Poulin some rest, I had them replaced by Captains Denizet, of Winnipeg, and Langlais, of Quebec.

As soon as the relief was completed, and in an effort to make contact with the enemy, I sent out two patrols approximately 100 yards ahead of our positions. They were to remain where they were if they encountered no opposition. That is what happened. I therefore moved B Company forward and continued this little stratagem until morning. Finally, a patrol stuck its nose into the town of Cesena, still with no opposition. I was preparing to occupy the town, when I received orders to move a thousand yards to the right and leave the town to the 56th Division.

During this manoeuvre we had lost one man of whom I was particularly fond: Sergeant Caron, killed by a mine at the junction of the roads leading to Cesena. Caron was a rather unusual fellow. As sergeant of the sappers' platoon he was responsible for defending my advanced command post. During the waiting periods, I often talked to him. He was firm but kind to his men, who feared him but loved him enough to follow him anywhere. He was a "natural leader" with an unusual philosophy of life. One day, I had asked him what he did before the war. He had replied, quite nonchalantly, that he was a bum.*

"What are you going to do after the war?" I asked him.
"I don't have any education," he told me. "I think I'll go back to being a bum."

I had laughed because by then I knew him well enough to be aware of his many skills. He was a dedicated man, who had made the best of the Great Depression of the thirties by travelling around, working as a dishwasher on ships or catching rides on freight trains. In this way, he had travelled around America and much of Europe. When I saw him dead beside the road, I rendered homage to a good friend.

The regiment soon reached the eastern side of the railway line running west of Cesena and, as they approached a river, the advanced platoons began to encounter increasingly fierce resistance. Our artillery was finding it difficult to hit the machine gun nests which were deeply dug into the north bank of the river. My command post, which was following A and B Companies, was also attacked by the German artillery; communications with the brigade were cut off and those with the companies became intermittent. Suddenly, everything seemed difficult. A Company, temporarily headed by Trudeau, who was replacing Captain Denizet, wounded by the first shot fired at us, crossed the tracks behind a smoke-screen. It continued east for approximately 1000 yards, then swung north towards a hamlet where it was greeted by several bursts of machine gun fire. Trudeau immediately attacked and destroyed the nest before going on at once to another. During these two attacks two of his platoon commanders, Lieutenants Laviolette and Rousseau, were killed. B Company, again under

---

* Thousands of young Canadians had become vagrants during the 30s, in the midst of the 20th century's greatest economic crisis.

the command of Major Potvin, who was now back from the hospital, was experiencing little more success. As it too advanced to the north, it received the same treatment as A. Lieutenant Leblanc was able to reach the river before he was also seriously wounded, as was his companion, Larochelle. We had, however, driven the enemy back north of the river. Brigadier Bernatchez asked us and the Carleton and Yorks on our right to feign preparations for a crossing. We moved our tanks, Bren gun carriers and trucks up towards the river. The ruse succeeded, and the Germans, whose forces were generally weak, abandoned the north bank. The next morning, Lieutenant Harry Pope swam across the river and confirmed the fact. I immediately sent one company to the other side. Since the engineers would not be able to build us a bridge for two days, we improvised one ourselves and thus were able to bring another company and adequate antitank defences across. Everything was calm once more, the enemy having withdrawn to Forlempopuli.

During this series of skirmishes our mortars had played an important role. They did so in a number of ways. First of all, they had supported our companies. Later, however, an officer of a British regiment had come to ask me whether we could assist him just before an assault he was to make, after crossing the river, against a reinforced position. We were to open fire just as he was making the crossing. I told him that we would be happy to help. We determined the targets and exact times. Then, at the appropriate moment, Captain Létourneau and his men rained 1500 81 mm bombs on the two casemates in question in less than thirty minutes. The Germans surrendered to their attackers without firing a shot. The Briton later came to thank me and to ask how on earth I had been able to offer "such generous shelling." I explained to him that we had captured a number of German mortars and that the bombs came from the German stocks on hill 139, which we had captured at the beginning of September. Our intervention had therefore cost us nothing of our normal allotment. He thanked me profusely. I answered: "Heil Hitler."

Once again, the regiment returned to the rear. Concerning the overall situation, I was beginning to wonder what was going on. Since September the 1st Canadian Division had been involved in a series of battles, all of them successful. After each one, however, we spent long periods waiting. It seemed to me that at this pace we would never reach northern Italy. I felt that we ought to do away with these delays. Naturally, it was not my job to criticize the decisions of the high command. We had to be content, then, for an overall view and with the reports we received from the BBC, which appeared to have completely forgotten the Italian front since the Normandy landing.

At this point, I would like to venture an aside which may be of interest to decision-makers, civilian or military. General opinion to the contrary, the most difficult time for a leader is not the process leading up to a decision. It occurs, instead, just after the decision, that is, following exhaustive analysis of the situation, when the orders for execution have been given, for this is when doubt sets in. In 1943-44, my doubts took the form of incessant questions running through my mind. Had I analyzed all the factors thoroughly? Was I sure of the nature of the reaction I had anticipated from the enemy? Was the terrain onto which I was sending my men really what I thought I had seen or interpreted from a map? Often I wished I could start over again from the beginning. Yet I know it would have been an error to do so. There were, there will always be, some imponderables. They were implicit or explicit elements of the situation under study and of the response we had organized. The decision-maker, therefore, must become accustomed to the anguish associated with the doubt that is forever plaguing him, if only to prevent it from infecting his subordinates. To overcome this doubt and in an effort to forget it (never entirely successful), I often found solace in reading poetry, and I recommended similar distractions to my subordinates. Just before the battle, I would return to my place at my command post, ready to deal with the imponderables. I later learned that, at other levels as well—less important levels, because they do not directly affect human lives doubt continues to follow decision, and that there too it is essential to carry on along the path selected, however winding and difficult it may become. Let us return now to the harsh reality of ground warfare.

It was already November 28, 1944, and, after a period of torrential rain, good weather had returned. The 3rd Brigade's new mission was to push the enemy back beyond the little town of Russi and to capture the bridges across the Lamone. The area consisted of marshes that had been drained; in the process, the rivers coming down from the mountains had been diverted by means of a system of elevated canals some thirty feet above ground level. In cross-section, they looked like this:

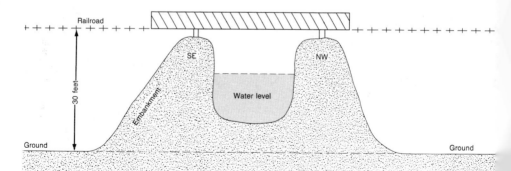

These structures offered magnificent observation points, given the fairly flat topography of the region. As defensive positions, however, they were difficult to penetrate. In addition, the railway lines were also raised on embankments to the same level as the canals, and formed a grid that could not be ignored. It was these obstacles that slowed the advance of the 1st Canadian Division, temporarily under the command of Brigadier J. D. B. Smith.

In our sector, there were deep-rooted German defences entrenched in a ditch ten feet wide, approximately 300 yards south of the Russi. The second line was dug into the northwest embankment of the Lamone.

The 3rd Brigade's plan was fairly simple at first, but it was to become more complicated as the troops advanced towards the Lamone River. Bernatchez had placed the West Nova Scotias on the right, with the town of Russi as its objective. The Carleton and Yorks were to be held in reserve while the R22ᵉR was on the left with a squadron from the Royal Canadian Dragoons watching our own exposed left flank. The objective assigned to the R22ᵉR was the railway junction northwest of Russi and the railway bridge across the Lamone. It was an excellent plan which allowed me to act without worrying about my right flank. After a study of the terrain and, in particular, of its manmade structures, I knew the risks we would be taking.

The most difficult role was reserved for Louis F. Trudeau's C Company: the other three companies were to open a path for him. A and B fought well, but the axis of advance had still not been cleared. A German platoon, supported by at least three Panzers, was still holding the bridge and putting up bitter resistance to an attack by one of A company's platoons. I told the commander to withdraw his platoon and ordered Trudeau to take his entire company and crush this defence, immediately following a concentration by our artillery. Accompanied by a troop of the North Irish Horse, flamethrowers and everything I could give him, Trudeau attacked. He was driven back, having lost several men, including Sergeant-Major Bérubé, who had already been wounded three times with the company and should have been sent home. However, in choosing to remain with his friends until the end of this battle, he had sealed his own fate.

Trudeau attacked a second time, then a third, with the same result. I was present for this last assault, and after examining the terrain, I asked Trudeau to withdraw and to resume his advance after swerving approximately 1000 yards to the left. A Company would take the axis to keep the defenders occupied. Under cover of a concentration of artillery fire, mixed with a number of smoke bombs, C rapidly regrouped and was on its way within a few minutes. It crossed the canal without opposition and picked up the axis of advance approximately one mile beyond the canal, then pushed on alone towards the junction about two miles ahead. Following the report of this initial success I lost all radio contact with Trudeau and was naturally very concerned about what might be happening. In any event, the defenders of the bridge were taken by surprise and abandoned it without being able to destroy it. A immediately occupied it. I then ordered Potvin to follow Trudeau. He informed me, however, that he was still dealing with heavy resistance. I asked him, nonetheless, to disengage himself and to proceed through another breach he had opened earlier. I would send D to handle his opposition. With his usual energy, Potvin set out, but since the West Nova Scotias had not yet crossed the canal he had to be careful, watching his right flank and, if possible, avoiding any serious engagement. A Company, which was by then under the command of Captain André Dubé, who would lead it almost to the end of the war, launched its assault on the canal and succeeded in taking it. The front was beginning to crumble. I still had no communication with Trudeau and his company. Suddenly, Potvin announced that he could see them advancing along the main axis we had selected. I waited with my command post at the approaches to the bridge until I received the radio message: "Hello 3, China." It was the code word to indicate a cemetery near a railway junction northwest of Russi. I immediately ordered a general advance; Potvin was to proceed to "China" while Trudeau advanced at once to seize the railway bridge. I hurried ahead in my jeep to join them. Potvin made good progress; so did Trudeau, but the bridge he was to capture was destroyed a few minutes before he reached it. Following this entirely understandable failure he took up a position on the left of the embankment while Potvin established himself around a monastery to the right of the debris of the bridge. A and D followed and set up to the rear of the first two companies. But the regiment was still alone, and there was no reserve: we could be attacked at any time and from any direction. We spent the night as a lonely outpost.

In the confusion created by this rapid attack a number of Germans had remained in their positions. It was some time before they reacted. I had not had the axis of advance cleared and did not feel that it was necessary to waste my time doing so. I had reached my objective, and I was too far from the West Nova Scotias, who were advancing very slowly, to risk losing the ground we had won by spreading my men out.

In any event, the Carleton and Yorks were attacked by machine gun fire from a group of houses I had passed earlier in my jeep with no opposition. Could some Germans have been hiding there at the time? Or perhaps they had arrived after we had gone by and hidden among the houses. When the C and Y, slightly annoyed, informed me of this fact, I was far too busy organizing the defence of our sector to worry about what seemed to me a dubious matter, and I told them so. In any event, the defenders surrendered, a few minutes later. The regiment then advanced without further opposition to take up a position opposite the Lamone, to our right.

The Germans were still well entrenched along the railway line and on the other side of the river. Every movement on our side of the bank was met by a burst of machine gun fire. It was by no means peaceful, although I now realized that there was very little possibility of a serious counterattack. Still, we had to watch for patrols from the direction of the river and on our left flank. The rest of the 1st Division moved rapidly up to our level. Meanwhile, the 5th Armoured Division was hurrying north in an attempt to cut off the retreat of the German 114th Light Infantry Division. In our sector, the enemy was receiving reinforcements, as demonstrated by two attacks against D and B.

At 2300 hours on December 5 Brigadier Calder's 1st Brigade, with the RCR on the left and the Hastings and Prince Edward Regiment on the right, passed through our position and attacked the Lamone. It met only weak resistance. The two regiments were positioned between a railway embankment on the left and a deep ditch on the right. Everything was calm. Brigadier Smith, commanding the division, then ordered Bernatchez to send the R22^{e}R across and to resume the advance.

The RCR, however, which was ahead of us, had not yet brought its fourth company across; nor had the 48th Highlanders, the 1st Brigade's reserve regiment, made the crossing. I found this strange and told Bernatchez that I wanted to have more information on the situation in the RCR's sector before relying on its support in any advance. In fact, according to Potvin, who was watching from the second floor of his monastery, the fourth company of the RCR, which had finally begun to advance, appeared to be engaged with an enemy on its left, under a railway viaduct. The officer commanding of this company was not yet across and appeared to have lost contact with his lead element. There was no way that I was going to send the R22^{e}R into this confusion in the middle of the night. Bernatchez then came to see me and, when I had told him of the information I had received from Potvin, he told me that we should go to RCR HQ, some 1000 yards to the rear of our position. On our arrival, we were informed that the commanding officer was asleep and was not to be disturbed, since everything was calm on the front. Bernatchez informed the division of my objections and Smith asked Brigadier Calder to meet us at RCR HQ. He arrived a few minutes later and asked what was wrong. I wasted no time explaining; the commanding officer had just woken up, and I asked him if he could give us a report on the situation. His operations officer told him that everything was calm. I insisted that they check. He took the radio and called each of the companies: none of them replied. A call from Potvin confirmed that the Germans had recaptured the northwest bank of the river and were even firing on him. On the right, the Hastings and Prince Edward Regiment had suffered the same fate: two battalions of the 1st Brigade had suffered terrible casualties. In the course of this disaster, two of my young officers, Falardeau and Poirier, who had been seconded to the RCR, lost their lives. Peter Hertzberg (the son of the general, whom I knew well), who had asked me two or three times for permission to serve in the R22^{e}R, had also been killed.

On December 9, however, I witnessed a masterpiece of tactics. It had been planned by none other than Paul Bernatchez. His plan was a classic and deserves detailed description because we were the ones who benefited from it. As I have indicated, the already excavated banks offered two important advantages: trenches to accommodate machine gun posts at the top and, on the flank of the reverse slope and below, shelters where the men could hide in case of heavy bombardment.

For the attack and the river crossing Bernatchez selected the West Nova Scotias on the left and the Carleton and Yorks on the right. The R22^{e}R, held in reserve, was to expand the bridgehead to be formed and protected by the other two battalions. To precede the attack he devised a ruse in which artillery was to play the major role. He ordered a very conventional bombardment by the divisional artillery, which was to handle the river, and by a 4.5 inch heavy artillery regiment, which was to provide counterbattery fire. During this shelling he pulled his two assault battalions back 500 yards. Then, after the initial bombardment, he had the divisional artillery continue firing, and instead of launching the attack as usual after two or three minutes of silence, which normally gave the defenders time to return to their positions on the surface, the 4.5 inch guns began an intense linear concentration along the northwest bank of the river, catching the defenders unprotected as they returned. After five minutes of pounding, the two battalions launched the attack and crossed the river unopposed. A solid bridgehead was established, enabling me to push on to the next canal. The entire operation had been extremely well planned. I still wonder why my friend Paul received no official recognition for this feat. The mystery may perhaps be explained by the many changes that occurred simultaneously in the higher command: Smith, instead of receiving the promotion he expected, was sent to replace Calder, and Major-General Foster replaced him as the commander of 1st Division. In addition, Lieutenant-General Charles Foulkes replaced Burns at the head of the army corps.

Our advance towards Bagnacavallo proceeded without too much difficulty as far as the canal separating us from the village. As the sun rose we found ourselves opposite a brick factory. On our right, the 2nd Brigade was advancing towards the Savio and had almost bypassed Bagnacavallo to the north. In our sector, a series of large ditches and canals made progress more difficult. In addition to these obstacles, the flat terrain complicated daytime movements and created risks that were unacceptable when weighed against the forces we were facing. We stopped on the Fosso Vecchio and one of Major Tellier's patrols brought in a prisoner who confirmed the presence of the 114th Jaeger Division and the 356th Infantry Division. In accordance with German tactics since the beginning of the Italian campaign, both divisions would hold out just long enough to force us to make a substantial effort. Having destroyed the momentum of our advance, they would then withdraw to another likely obstacle. Until that time I had always refused to ask for additional support from the larger formations. Moreover, in December 1944, because of the new front in Western Europe, such support was limited by the rationing of artillery ammunition. However, in the case of the brick factory, I had to ask for help from the air force and the 4.2 inch mortars of the Saskatoon Light Infantry which, after an intense concentration, crushed the few defenders who had held back the entire regiment.

A series of small and often disproportionately costly actions brought the regiment to the Senio, another river like the Lamone, with the same problems and the same topography. For an entire month, which had begun with a spectacular breakthrough, the regiment had advanced, by a series of frustrating battles through natural and manmade obstacles which the enemy had used to maximum advantage. On December 22 the regiment was withdrawn from the front lines. We were to celebrate Christmas among the civilian population of Piangipane, a few miles east of Ravenna.

I did not know it, but I had commanded my last battle at the head of the R22^{e}R, one year and five days after taking over at Casa Berardi. What a road we had travelled together. Looking back, I could not help remembering all the brave men who had backed me through the most difficult times in the regiment's history. I had given it everything I had in terms of knowledge, imagination and loyalty. It had responded with generosity and with all the strength and intelligence of which it was capable.

My mission, then, was accomplished. I would soon be leaving the regiment, remembering all those who would be left behind in Italian soil forever as a testimony of their devotion to the cause of freedom. I remember them, and all those who, during this difficult period, carried on the tradition of our French-Canadian regiment, the glorious tradition which lay in the valour and the generosity of the men who had been part of it throughout its brief history. I left the R22^{e}R, I must admit, filled with pride, a pride that came from having shared this time with hundreds of our own young men, the cream of French Canada's fighting men.

5

An Unexpected Promotion

In January 1945, the regiment took part in the first skirmishes along the Senio. We expanded our sector, fighting alongside a battalion of Italian partisans, who fought very well. Then, the chief medical officer asked me to report to hospital for a complete medical examination. I handed the regiment over temporarily to my second-in-command, Gilles Turcot. Three days later, I was given one month's leave. I did not know exactly what was going on, but I began to suspect that my time with the R22^{e}R was over.

Following this leave I represented the 1st Division on a study group planning the end of the Italian campaign. I travelled to Florence for these talks with Lieutenant-Colonel John Tweedsmuir, who was representing the 5th Division. John was a pleasant companion and we spent ten days at the Excelsior Hotel overlooking the Arno. Between working sessions it seemed to me that we were living like millionaires. Our meals were accompanied by the finest Italian wines and enhanced by the music of a 35-piece orchestra. There were also interesting visits to the great historical sites of the magnificent city of Florence.

Then it was time to return to the regiment. I learned that it was leaving the front lines and was to go to a small town named Porto di San Giorgio, on the Adriatic coast. It was the end of February 1945, and the weather was beautiful. On March 1 we celebrated St. David's Day in honour of the Welsh patron saint. It was our affiliation with the Royal Welsh Fusiliers that provided us with this welcome opportunity to let off steam.

Two days later Paul Bernatchez told me that we were through in Italy. We were to proceed to Livorno, then by sea to Marseille and on to Belgium and the First Canadian Army. It was a long trip that was to take us through

France from south to north along the valley of the Rhone and into Burgundy before bringing us to Brussels. During the final portion of the trip we passed through towns and villages whose names had been inscribed on the regimental colours since World War I. We were greeted by Major-General Vanier in the forest of Fontenay-Tressigny where, as Canadian Ambassador to France, he formally welcomed us. The regiment continued on to the north. On our arrival at Cambrai, where we were to spend the night, I received a message asking me to present myself to General Crerar at First Canadian Army HQ near Nijmegen. I did not know what to expect. I considered a number of possibilities and concluded that I would not be returning to the Van Doos. In fact, I was almost certain that I would be sent back to England, with a promotion to colonel, where I would find my old friend Dan Spry. I did not want to return to England, even with a promotion, while my regiment was fighting in Holland, and I rehearsed the answer I would give the general.

I crossed Belgium nonstop. When I reported to First Army HQ at around 2100 hours, I was greeted in the mess by a group of old friends: Major-General Mann, Brigadiers Lister and Walsh and Colonel Bill Anderson. Someone took charge of the faithful Bujold and my driver, Gionnais, who disappeared with our jeep. My modest luggage was placed in the visitors' trailer.

It seemed to me that the people who greeted me were hiding something. Still, nothing happened, beyond a warm welcome, during the few hours I spent with them, drinking, eating, and especially, having one cognac . . . then another. The drinking told me nothing. Utterly exhausted, I asked to go to bed. I was shown to a luxurious trailer, where I quickly fell into a heavy sleep. At 0700 hours, someone knocked at my door to say that the general would see me in an hour. To my surprise, I was not even hung over. The batman on duty had prepared my uniform, and after breakfast, I proceeded to Crerar's office. The general greeted me warmly and said, with a smile: "Hello. Have a good sleep? Sit down!" I barely heard him, because I was trying to remember the answers I had rehearsed the day before. Once again he asked me to sit down and began by congratulating me for the excellent work I had done with the R22^{e}R. He added that he was glad he had sent me there. I thanked him. The conversation continued for a while along these lines until suddenly he announced that he was giving me a promotion. I said to myself, "This is it." But I could no longer remember my answers. Thank goodness! He went on to say that he had decided to make me a brigadier and to give me the 6th Brigade. Realizing that I was speechless, he burst out laughing and wished me good luck. "Major-General Bruce Matthews is waiting for you," he added. I gave him the worst salute I had ever given in my entire career and went off to see General Matthews, who presented me with the red band that I was to wear in future on my cap and all the insignia identifying my new rank. He congratulated me and welcomed me to the 2nd Division. I was to return to the R22^{e}R to say good-bye and return in two days to his HQ near Putte. But before I left, my companions from the previous night joined Matthews to congratulate me. I was offered a glass of champagne as a token of friendship. At 0930 hours I was on my way to join the R22^{e}R which had just arrived at Putte, a small town between Brussels and Antwerp. The news of my promotion had preceded me. Gilles Turcot, in fact, had just learned that he was being promoted to lieutenant-colonel to replace me. Both these events were joyfully celebrated by the entire regiment.

Nonetheless, it took me a long time to tell these men all that was in my heart as I left them. I remembered all those I had known intimately who, under my orders, had faced enemy fire and died. Among the officers: Garceau, Cannon, Young, Bilodeau, Letarte, Charlebois, Dumont, Chicoine, Saint-Onge, Vincent, Pellerin, Laviolette, Hogan, Dussault, Comeau, Cardin, Poirier, Rousseau. Among the non-commissioned officers: Sergeant-Major Bérubé, Sergeants Piuze, Caron, Gauthier, Danofrio, Corporals Patenaude, Vallée, Villeneuve, Braconnier, Boulianne, and others. To say nothing of all those anonymous men whose faces were still before me and who were part of the mosaic of French Canadians from Western Canada, the Maritimes, but especially, from every corner of Quebec, each of them with his own typical turn of phrase to which I had gradually become accustomed. All of them, the living and dead of every rank, passed through my mind at that moment. I saluted the legion whose devotion had given me access to the highest ranks. Without them, this honour, which reflected on French Canada as a whole, would not have been possible.

Following the ceremony marking the transfer of command, I congratulated Gilles Turcot and offered him all my best wishes. I then proceeded to division HQ where Major-General Matthews waited for me with the commanding officers of the various battalions of the 6th Brigade: Lieutenant-Colonels Jimmy Dextraze (Fusiliers Mont-Royal), Vern Stutt (South Saskatchewan Regiment) and "Burt" Kennedy (Queen's Own Cameron Highlanders of Canada), and my future artillery officer, Lieutenant-Colonel Dale Harris. The division's staff officers were represented by Lieutenant-Colonels Peter Bennett and Morry Pocock. My visit was brief. But General Matthews and Peter Bennett had time to brief me on the division's plans. In fact, my brigade was to cross the Rhine under the command of the 3rd Division, of which General Keefler had recently taken command. With Vern Stutt, the brigade's temporary commander, I proceeded to the 6th Brigade HQ to take over my trailer. I wish I had a picture of my batman's face when he saw what looked to him like a palace on wheels. Bujold had faithfully followed me from the R22^{e}R: although he was still a private, he looked as if he too had received a promotion.

After a rapid tour of the operations centre to meet my staff, I set to work studying the plans. Then I reported to General Keefler to receive his final instructions. Vern Stutt and my staff had done an excellent job of preparation and I assumed my command with confidence. A rapid inspection of the units confirmed the quality of the men I would be heading. I knew at once that I would do so with a great deal of satisfaction.

According to the 3rd Division's plan my brigade was to cross the Rhine just behind the 9th, under Brigadier Rockingham, and then swing east to take up a position on an axis which, eventually, would be followed by the 2nd Division. As soon as I was beyond the 3rd Division's bridgehead, I was to come under the direct command of Lieutenant-General G. G. Simmonds's 2nd Army Corps, while still retaining a direct link with my normal division, the 2nd. The plan was extremely simple and suited me perfectly. During the night of March 28-29 we crossed the Rhine near Rees and set up briefly within the bridgehead before going on to complete our mission, which was to open a path to the north.

This second phase began badly. The 6th Brigade had advanced completely to the other side of the Rhine but had no exit road from the bridgehead. Indeed, the northern part of the sector had been flooded by the Germans to cover their retreat. Our left flank was completely blocked by the 3rd Division, which was attempting to advance towards its objective, Emmerich. In the course of a reconnaissance I discovered a small road along the eastern boundary of my sector, and in the middle of the night, I decided to use it since it would enable me to concentrate my brigade north of the obstacle which the water presented. My units set out, followed by my HQ. They had almost completely moved out when I realized that this road was in the sector of the neighbouring division. I therefore proceeded to the HQ of the 43rd Division (Wessex) to request permission to use it. Major-General Thomas greeted my request with a flat no and a minor scolding. I responded with mocking obsequiousness. Nonetheless, I used the road to reach my HQ. I got away with it, but I did not appreciate the Englishman's attitude.

With enough logistic matériel to last several days I ordered the brigade to move north. The Fusiliers Mont-Royal (FMR) were on the right, the South Saskatchewan Regiment (SSR) on the left and the Queen's Own Cameron Highlanders of Canada (Camerons) in reserve, following the advance and slightly on the left. I soon learned to appreciate the quality of my regiments. Vern Stutt and Jimmy Dextraze were both excellent leaders. The advance was swift and drove back the German opposition in short order. Because I was used to a mobile battalion command post, I found brigade HQ a cumbersome nuisance. In the type of operations in which my troops were engaged, I did not see how I could manage to drag along all this bureaucracy. In keeping with my concept of rapid reaction and immediate decision, I detached from HQ a group of "essential people" to form a command post which would follow me everywhere and serve me until the end of the war.

Following the first advance to the north, I received orders to probe Zutphen's defences. The response was immediate; the Germans were defending the town and only a major operation could dislodge them. General Simmonds assigned the task to the 3rd Division. My brigade then resumed its movement along the axis of advance leading to Groningen.

My brigade was now on the Twente Canal. The operation I was planning would recall the fighting in which we had been involved in Italy, where we had had to fight our way from river to river and mountain to mountain for over a year. There was one major difference, however: despite its canals, Holland was good flat country with a network of paved roads that permitted rapid advances. Our patrols had provided us with excellent intelligence, and under cover of the final hours of the night, we were able to crush the enemy and seize the north shore of the canal.

We soon encountered another obstacle: Holten, where missile launchers had been installed. The task of capturing it was assigned to the 5th Brigade. My own was to bypass Holten on the right and move as rapidly as possible towards Beilen. We had a solid advanced guard, flanked on the right by a squadron of the 8th Reconnaissance Regiment and on the left by a squadron of the Royal Canadian Dragoons, commanded by Major Prospère Gauthier. The brigade, with the Camerons in the lead using every possible vehicle, including every available space on the tanks of a squadron of the Fort Garry Horse, bypassed Holten and crossed a canal and, within a few hours, was en route to Hogeveen. There, the entire population turned out to greet us with open arms and bottles of gin. I had followed close on the heels of the advanced guard and suddenly found myself in the middle of this crowd, which recognizing the red band on my cap and the flag on my jeep, surged around me. Without the help of the Dutch liaison officer who was accompanying me, I do not know how I would have gotten through. Flags appeared at every window and people began dancing in the street. We had to use loudspeakers for several minutes to persuade the crowd to disperse because the Germans were still nearby. Indeed, the enemy had merely withdrawn to a point behind a bridge they had demolished. When our first two companies arrived at the canal, not far from the town, the Germans opened fire. My men quickly spread out along the south bank.

The Dutch Resistance, however, had anticipated this manoeuvre on the part of the Germans. Suddenly, I saw two big barges appear, loaded with men and the materials required to build another bridge. A patrol from the

Camerons having managed to drive the few remaining enemy forces from the area of the canal, our Dutch allies set about building their bridge. A few minutes later, leaving the Camerons to defend the bridgehead, I despatched the Fusiliers Mont-Royal as the advanced guard. It continued the advance, followed by the 6th Regiment of Field Artillery; these units had been ordered to deploy one mile farther on. The Fusiliers, with Dextraze in command, rapidly covered the first five miles. As they approached Spier, they recognized the French Parachute Battalion which had been dropped a few days earlier to block the road south of Beilen. Commandant Vallières said to Dextraze, when he saw him: "Thank God, we fired our last bullets a few minutes ago and we were just about to surrender." Dextraze realized that the Germans had decided to defend Beilen. He deployed his battalion near an adjacent village, which he had just taken. Meanwhile, the 8th Reconnaissance Regiment was reporting progress on our right flank. On the left Major Gauthier was encountering resistance. However, he had just trapped a German infantry company which had thrown itself into the middle of his tanks on the run. Gauthier had manoeuvred his machine gun carriers so well that he had soon surrounded the infantry and put it out of action.

All these separate reports coming in failed to give me any clear overall idea of the battlefield. I therefore jumped into one of our observation planes to see how my troops were actually doing. They were all where they were supposed to be. From the air I could see that the enemy had left a small bridge standing over the canal that would take us to the north shore and give us ready access to Beilen. I asked Dextraze to send a patrol to check the bridge's carrying capacity. Half an hour later, the patrol held the bridge and estimated that it would support up to eight tons. I already had a plan in mind, and with this assurance, I prepared to put it into operation.

The operation was to involve two phases, with the first to begin at dusk. At that time the FMR were to set out along the road, cross the little bridge and, once on the other side, circle around behind. Once he was behind Beilen, Dextraze was to inform me. The Camerons would immediately advance towards the demolished bridge at Beilen and act as if they were preparing to cross the canal, throwing planks into the water while the artillery pounded the town. The real battle would be fought by the FMR, using the advantage of surprise. To assist him, I placed under Dextraze's command a machine gun company from the Toronto Scottish to protect his rear as he returned south.

Phase II was to consist of an attack to be mounted by the SSR a mile and a half east of Beilen. Its mission was to form a bridgehead and install a Bailey bridge in order to open the road to the division and to heavy traffic. If necessary, it would also provide assistance to Dextraze and his troops.

Everything went smoothly, and an hour after the beginning of the

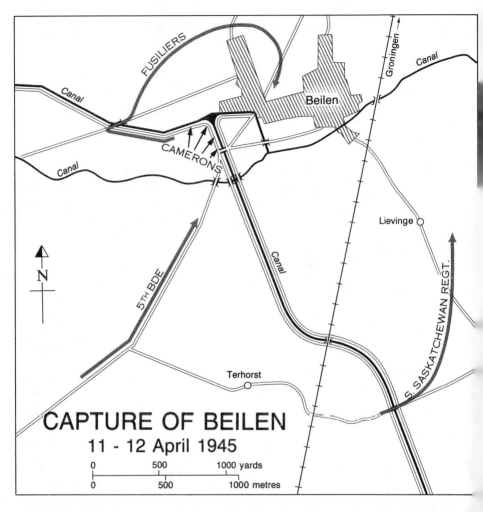

CAPTURE OF BEILEN
11 - 12 April 1945

operation, Dextraze told me that he was ready behind Beilen. The Camerons then began their feint, well supported by a concentration of artillery fire directed against a dozen casemates along the canal. Meanwhile, Dextraze, with his Bren gun carrier platoon, tricked the German sentries by returning a light signal he had noted earlier, which was being used by them. After wiping out the pickets he took the enemy completely by surprise a few minutes later by penetrating the town. The real fight began. The casemates, taken from behind, became useless. The defenders could not stop the Fusiliers. Following the first reports, I withdrew the Camerons from the bank and implemented the second part of the plan. Lieutenant-Colonel Vern Stutt set out, and an hour later his regiment was north of the canal.

(Right) Returning from their father's funeral in January 1921, at the top, left to right: Anaïs, Germaine, Thérèse; bottom: Judith, Jean Victor, Irène and Madeleine.

op) At the age of 4, I was dy for the calvary.

(Left) My parents, Ernest Allard and Victorine Trudel.

(Top) Member of the hockey team, Trois-Rivières.

(Left) Simone in November 1938. You can see why she won my heart.

(Right) Michèle and Jean-Ernest, March 1944.

(Top) This command post was close to Villa Grande. The photo was taken in March 1944: Captain Bernard Guimond, Major Gérard Charlebois, Major Paul Triquet, Captain Pierre Chassé, Captain P.F. Potvin, Major Ovide Garceau.

(Left) With Pope Pius XII.

(Right) Visit to the Italian Front of Cardinal Rodrigue Villeneuve, April 11-12, 1945.

(Top) Colonel the Honourable
J.L. Ralston, Minister of
National Defence, enjoys a
joke with R22^{e}R members,
September 29, 1944.

(Left) George VI with the
Regiment, July 31, 1944.

(Right) J.-V. Allard and the
journalist Bob Pilot,
December 1944, Rocca di
Giovani.

◆

(Top) Civilian reception committee at Dorval, September 1945.

(Left) Simone and Michèle, skiing in Moscow.

(Right) Jean-Ernest, walking towards our summer camp near Moscow.

(Top) R22ᵉR being inspected
by Brooke Claxton, Minister
of Defence.

(Left) Military parachute
training.

(Right) At left, Colonel
Marcellin Lahaie. With us,
two officer-cadets from CMI
soon after its opening.

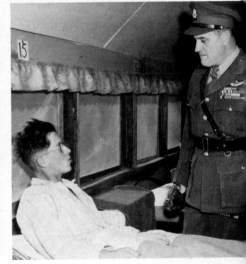

Top) In Cyprus, with Chief
Warrant Officer Léo Boudreau,
who had accompanied the
family to Moscow as a
corporal in 1946.

(Left) Anniversary of the
Russian Revolution, November
7, 1947. Left to right, front
row: my Mexican and
Chinese counterparts; at back,
with a cigarette, my Danish
counterpart.

(Right) Visiting a Canadian
military hospital in Korea.

(Top) Louis St. Laurent lays a wreath on the war memorial in Seoul. On my left, U.S. General Maxwell Taylor.

(Left) Talking to villagers at Chin Mok Chon, a re-established village in the forward area. To my left, the interpreter, Lieutenant Pak Kwan Ho.

(Right) Some of the Chinese prisoners who refused to return to their homeland.

The engineers, under the command of Major W. Summerville, were then able to begin construction of a proper bridge, which they completed in record time. Since it was still dark, I asked the commanding officer of the SSR to send a company to seize the bridge across another canal, five miles farther north. An hour later it was reported that the bridge had been demolished but that the company had managed to cross this second canal. Since the bridge over the first canal was now completed, the SSR sent its train across and advanced to join its company on the next canal. I then sent the Camerons and my command post through the opening.

Meanwhile, the FMR were engaged in house-to-house combat within Beilen. The enemy, its back to the wall, showed no sign of surrender. My company of engineers was preparing to build a second bridge. It was at this point that the 4th Brigade, under the command of my friend Brigadier Freddy Cabeldu, invested Assen, a few miles ahead of us towards Groningen. The surprise and confusion of the Germans were so complete that we took many prisoners still in their night clothes.

The FMR finished mopping up Beilen. As they were regrouping I had the entire sector cleared. During the search one of my patrols discovered a concentration camp containing thousands of political prisoners, most of them Jews. The German SS, assisted by a few Dutch collaborators, were preparing to load them into trucks for transportation to some unknown destination. After a brief exchange of fire the guards surrendered. The prisoners were free. There were several thousand of them, all in the most pitiful condition. I had no time to take care of them, but I issued rations and turned them over to the civilian authorities. But that vision of horror remains with me to this day.

After this emotional experience, I ordered the brigade to move out once more. The next morning, it entered the outskirts of Groningen. During this advance, Prince Bernhard joined us. He knew the region and the Resistance there. The information he was able to provide me proved to be of enormous assistance. I was surprised, however, to see him contact members of the Resistance by public telephone. As we entered the southern outskirts of the city, my brigade relieved the 4th along the banks of the Eems Canal, which circled the downtown area. After several probing missions I realized that the battle would not be easy. The approach we were to take was to begin from a railway marshalling yard. We were facing the canal, which was fifty feet wide with sloping sides ten feet high in this area. Any movement along the canal drew an immediate German response. The bridges had all been raised, and the control booths were all on the German side. I could have shelled the approaches to the enemy positions and even the downtown area. But the people of the city were prisoners in their own homes. It would have been a senseless massacre. After examining the bridges it seemed to me that it might be possible to lower one, if the Resistance could handle the job. Prince Bernhard checked before replying that he had the team we needed, that although the operation would be very risky, it was worth the cost. We agreed that the attack would take place the next morning, at a time of which he would be informed. All that night I had "the" bridge watched.

The plan of assault was relatively simple. Control of the battle to follow, however, would be more difficult. And its success would be based entirely on the speed with which our armoured vehicles could cross the bridge. Two companies, each from a different regiment, interspersed with tanks, were to make the crossing. Once on the other side, the first company was to spread out to the right of the main street, along the canal, and the second, to the left. Everything depended, of course, on the success of the Resistance.

The night was spent organizing the troops so that they could file across the bridge in the proper order for deployment on the other side. The FMR was to take the lead and the SSR to follow.

At 0700 hours, as planned, three men suddenly emerged from a cellar. They advanced on the run towards the unmanned control booth. Two were wounded when the Germans reacted with machine gun fire. However, with incredible courage, all three entered the booth. They lowered the bridge by means of the manual system which the Germans had not damaged. Within a few minutes the way was clear for us to cross and my two companies were able to reach the north bank behind a light smoke-screen. The rest of the two regiments followed close on their heels. The battle for the downtown area was now underway. Using the buildings along the first cross street, the enemy put up stubborn resistance. Our progress was slow but systematic. The morning passed without substantial gains. Nonetheless, by the end of the afternoon, our two battalions, very ably manoeuvred, were in possession of the main buildings along the first street and advancing towards the city centre. Unfortunately, civilians began to emerge from their homes, and a number of people were killed during exchanges of fire. The battle continued all night. In order to prevent the enemy from regrouping I kept the market square and the central park under fire by the 4.2 inch mortars of the Toronto Scottish. The fire was effective in cutting off the communications of the German command post.

Fighting resumed the morning of the second day. At this point Lieutenant-Colonel Jimmy Dextraze, carrying a white flag and standing on his command carrier, took the initiative and presented himself at the enemy command post to ask the commanding officer to surrender. Since he was no longer in communication with his colleagues, the German commander decided to come and negotiate terms with me. Dextraze brought him to my command post. I wasted no time. My gun was in plain sight on my table as I told him there were no terms to be discussed and that he would be well advised simply to surrender. I added that his counterpart in the northern sector of the city was about to do so. He agreed and, accompanied by our men, went to order the ceasefire. The downtown was ours. The Camerons immediately began mopping up the eastern part of the city and the outlying areas. Groningen was then entirely in our hands. In order to avoid a surprise attack, the Camerons sent patrols east towards Ten Boers. We had only to clear the streets of a few isolated strongpoints which were still putting up resistance. This was the end of a thrust of more than eighty miles that my brigade had accomplished, from the crossing of the Rhine on March 29 to the surrender of the Groningen garrison on April 15. Accustomed to the short distances we had covered in Italy, I regarded this exploit with a great deal of satisfaction. In fact, on one occasion, we had advanced sixty-five miles within twenty-four hours, a record for a Canadian infantry brigade in this war.

Two days later the 3rd Canadian Division arrived in our sector. I then received orders to rejoin the 2nd Division, which was preparing to attack Oldenburg. In order to avoid the rear of the 4th Canadian Armoured Division and of the 1st Polish Division, we had to make a wide detour to the south before advancing towards Delmenhorst. On April 20 I arrived in the area and received orders to advance on Kirchhatten, which lay towards Oldenburg. We moved rapidly despite the falling snow. Young cadet officers in Oldenburg at first responded forcefully, but the noose was tightening around them. Two of my regiments, supported by C squadron of the Fort Garry Horse (FGH), machine guns from the Toronto Scottish and two regiments of artillery, surrounded them and gained the upper hand without too much difficulty. The FMR proceeded to carve a path along the left flank and soon reached the Küsten Canal, in the vicinity of Oldenburg. Skewing to the right, the FMR reached the southern outskirts of Oldenburg. The SSR too was approaching. But the bridge on the main street, joining the two parts of the city, had been raised and mined.

At low tide, the stone slopes of the canal made it impossible to cross. But on the extreme left of our front, now controlled by the FMR, it appeared that it might be possible to cross with a few boats. I assigned the mission to Dextraze, who succeeded in doing so before daybreak. However, without vehicles or support weapons, he was extremely vulnerable to counterattacks. Nonetheless, he sent a patrol to the entrance of the bridge and captured it before it could be blown up. Major Summerville's engineers rapidly climbed up the structure and reported that the lowering mechanism was beyond repair. On the second floor of a building across from the bridge, I discussed a number of possibilities with Summerville. We concluded that we had to destroy the screws that were used to raise and lower the bridge. Within less than an hour, the sappers had cleared the bridge of German mines and were ready to blow up the screws. We evacuated the sector and the sergeant of the engineers pressed the button. I heard an enormous explosion. There was dust everywhere. When the dust had cleared, we saw the bridge fall heavily into place. After thorough examination, I ordered the FGH to make the crossing. They did so with no problem. The Cameron Highlanders then followed. We met little resistance. It was May 3 when I was asked to advance towards the airport, located north of the city. A few minutes later my troops were deployed there. We took the usual precautions before settling in for the night. The next day we received orders to cease fire at daybreak, May 5. Exhausted, I collapsed into bed, where I slept a good twelve hours. It was the end of the war for us and the end of the crushing fatigue under which we had all laboured.

Certain precautions had to be taken, however. The German army was fairly disorganized by this stage; had it managed to transmit the message to all its troops? Would the fanatics listen? We stayed where we were for several days—just long enough to discover the German air force's wine cellar, which was quickly transferred to our own trucks. A few days passed and I was ordered to move my brigade to Aurich, where we took possession of the naval barracks. My troops were spread out along the Ems-Jade Canal to receive the Germans being evacuated from Holland. It was a beautiful spot but there was one problem. It was the site of a Russian prisoner-of-war camp. Were we to release our allies without a roof over their heads, keep them in their barracks, or have them transported across the Elbe and returned to their own people? I chose the last option.

There is nothing sadder than watching the procession of a defeated army. That is what we saw every day at Aurich. These German soldiers came from Holland, from where they had been expelled. Unlike the Russians, who had preceded them in the camps, they were disciplined. They had, however, lost the arrogance which had characterized them and which we had observed in the past. We ordered them to clear the mine fields. Hundreds of thousands of mines were soon piled up in an area about three miles from Emden. The mountain of 750,000 Teller-type mines covered approximately 300,000 cubic yards. One morning, I felt the earth skake and heard an enormous explosion. Almost 5,000 tons of TNT had exploded. For 1,000 feet around what had once been a minefield, everything had been levelled—
trees, fences, buildings. It was a foretaste of Hiroshima. None of our men were killed, but several were injured.

The brigade remained at Aurich for approximately a month and a half before returning to Holland, where it was to be demobilized. As I travelled across the country we had liberated, I was disgusted to see young people carrying signs which read: Liberate us from our liberators! For those of us who had been in Europe for five long years, it was no laughing matter. On several occasions we had to protect these good-for-nothings from our troops when they had the audacity to come too close with their insults.

Another difficulty arose from the fact that Montgomery, flying in the face of all logic, had forbidden his troops to fraternize with the Germans. It was one thing to order us to restrict our drinking to tea. But to prohibit young soldiers from fraternizing with German girls, on pain of court martial, was plain stupidity. Fortunately, demobilization proceeded rapidly and the great majority of our men were repatriated. The rest were assigned to the occupation force.

After turning over the reins of the brigade to one of my commanding officers, I took leave. I travelled first to England, where I was invited to Buckingham Palace to receive my three DSOs (Distinguished Service Order) from King George VI. Next, I was to act as a witness to Paul Bernatchez, who was marrying a Toronto nurse, Joan Ward. The lovely Joan, who had learned to speak French within a few months, showed courage in meeting her fiancé's friends. The gang, of which I was a member, along with Paul Mathieu, Paul Triquet and a few others of the same stripe, was not particularly reassuring. The stag could have been a problem. Joan managed to control the situation, apparently, because Paul arrived on time for the ceremony.

The day after the wedding I travelled to Paris to meet Colonel Maurice Forget, then Military Attaché to the Canadian Embassy. It was my first trip to this city. I took advantage of the opportunity to attend a number of shows, eat at some of the fashionable restaurants, say hello to the Vaniers at the Embassy, and visit a few Parisian friends, including Mademoiselle Lejour and her brother (friends of our family) and Renée Nizan and her father. Renée was a concert organist who had toured Quebec with her father in the early thirties when we were both eighteen, and we had gone everywhere together. During my stay we visited Notre-Dame-de-Boulogne where, on the organ her father normally used, she played Widor's symphony. Alone in the nave, I thrilled to the music. The perfection of her playing was almost beyond belief. Unfortunately, Renée was to die in an accident the following December.

6

Military Attaché in the Soviet Union

Simone's life had not been all roses since 1939. In fact, as we shall see later, things were not to improve until the spring of 1946. Nevertheless, the worst of her worries (about me) and of the separation was over . . . at least, that is what we hoped.

There had been several occasions for rejoicing in Trois-Rivières: my two promotions in the field, certain feats of arms, eulogistic newspaper articles and decorations. But these highlights were also received with some concern. Indeed, there had also been unpleasant surprises. The following cables are included primarily to show the highly detached manner in which injuries were announced. The description used left a great deal of doubt in the minds of those who read the cables in Canada.

CANADIAN NATIONAL TELEGRAM

6M0MK 86 NL GB 2EX

OTTAWA ONT 24

MME SIMONE PICHE ALLARD

REPORT DELIVERY 312 RUE BUREAU TROIS-RIVIERES QUE

19332 MINISTER OF NATIONAL DEFENCE SINCERELY REGRETS TO INFORM YOU LIEUTENANT-COLONEL JEAN VICTOR ALLARD DSO OFFICIALLY REPORTED QUITE SERIOUSLY WOUNDED IN COMBAT DATE AND NATURE OF HIS INJURIES NOT YET REPORTED STOP WHEN WRITING TO HIM ADD THE WORDS IN HOSPITAL IN LARGE LETTERS ABOVE HIS NAME TO ENSURE QUICK DELIVERY STOP WE WILL SEND YOU IMMEDIATELY ANY ADDITIONAL INFORMATION RECEIVED STOP IN ORDER TO AVOID INFORMING THE ENEMY DO NOT REVEAL

THE DATE OF HIS INJURY OR THE NAME OF HIS UNIT.
DIRECTOR, MILITARY ARCHIVES

836A

CANADIAN NATIONAL TELEGRAM

42M0 JA 61 DL 2 EX9 GB

    OTTAWA ONT 655PM 11-44

MME SIMONE PICHE ALLARD

    REPORT DELIVERY 512 RUE BUREAU 3RIV QUE

21624 MINISTER OF NATIONAL DEFENCE WISHES TO INFORM YOU LIEUTENANT-
COLONEL JEAN VICTOR ALLARD DSO PREVIOUSLY REPORTED QUITE SERIOUSLY
WOUNDED IN COMBAT NOW REPORTED QUITE SERIOUSLY WOUNDED ACCIDEN-
TALLY IN COMBAT DATE OF HIS INJURY CONFIRMED NOV 18 1944 NATURE
REPORTED AS WOUND TO THE LEG STOP WE WILL PROVIDE IMMEDIATELY ANY
ADDITIONAL INFORMATION RECEIVED.
DIRECTOR, MILITARY ARCHIVES

949PM

Tens of thousands of documents of this kind were sent. I had had a little scare myself, and I was quite lucky to keep my left leg when I was injured for the second time.

Like the overwhelming majority of my comrades, I had also been more concerned about the fate of my family than about my own during those two years of active warfare. That concern was to continue until we were to be reunited once more.

During the summer of 1945 I was asked whether I would accept the position of Canadian military attaché in Moscow to replace Brigadier Lefebvre. Personally, I agreed, but External Affairs insisted that I first had to stay there for six months before making a final decision and bringing my family there. This was a condition that required consultation, so I cabled Simone. With her customary fortitude she agreed.

In September, I returned to Canada. The family was waiting for me at Dorval. Simone was there with Michèle and Jean-Ernest but also with Anaïs and Arthur. The welcoming committee also included a number of comrades-in-arms, such as Paul Triquet, V.C., Roger Piché, Guy Vaugeois, Guy Laframboise, Yvan Dubé, Gilles Turcot and the good Colonel Chaballe, a veteran of World War I. After a few friendly exchanges, they all understood that I was in a hurry to begin my home leave.

In Trois-Rivières I made a quick visit to my relatives. Then, invited by Jean Crête, we left with him for a hunting party in the Upper St. Maurice, in the company of Raoul and Germaine Provencher and my good friend, Canon Hervé Trudel, the priest of Saint-Pierre. The best guides of the

Mauricie, including Edouard Lemieux, were at our disposal . . . and they were no slouches. We returned with a moose that Jean Crête shot at the very last minute. The leave passed very quickly. It seemed that I had just arrived when I had to prepare to leave again. This separation was going to be less difficult than the previous one because we knew in advance how long it would last.However, Simone announced that she was pregnant. Once again she had to spend most of her pregnancy alone.

A few days following that news, I went to Ottawa to receive what turned out to be rather brief instructions from Defence HQ and from the Department of External Affairs. Then I returned to Montreal for a medical examination and the required vaccinations. The doctors decided to reopen my wound in the left leg to extract some shell splinters and repair a muscular hernia. The whole thing went very well. Back home, though, I suffered a strong reaction to penicillin and had to return to the hospital, but I was able to leave for Christmas.

Two weeks later I boarded the *Queen Elizabeth* in New York to sail to England. In London I met Dana Wilgress, Canadian Ambassador to Moscow. He gave me the broad outlines of what was shortly to become the celebrated Gouzenko affair. Igor Gouzenko was a Soviet cypher clerk who had fled from the Soviet embassy in Ottawa and requested political asylum in Canada, taking with him a great deal of information that flushed out a network of British, American and Canadian spies working for the USSR. Gouzenko was taken under Canadian protection during the first week of September 1945. The whole affair remained highly secret until an American newscaster mentioned it openly in early February 1946, no doubt as a result of an indiscretion by the entourage of President Truman (to whom Mackenzie King had communicated the matter).

The Canadian government response was to hush up the affair for the time being and to make it public only when the USSR had received a message that I was given under seal by Wilgress in London. I had to take that document, the details of which I did not know, to Léon Mayrand, our chargé d'affaires in the USSR. In turn, he would forward it to the Soviet authorities and Mackenzie King would then reveal this spy affair. Wilgress took advantage of the opportunity to predict to me what the Soviet attitude would be once the truth was out, and he was right on.

Following that meeting, I went to Hull and boarded a cargo ship sailing for Denmark. In Copenhagen I had the first unpleasant surprise of a trip that was going to have many of them: the baggage handlers were on strike. I borrowed a cart and went into town with my luggage. Once there, I found out that the ferry which was supposed to take me to Malmö, in Sweden, was also on strike. With a Dane I had met who had the same problem, we decided to go to the fishermen's harbour, where a fisherman took us aboard.

From Malmö I went to Stockholm by train. From there, I was supposed to go to Helsinki aboard the M.S. *Bore* but because of the cold the ferry was forced to go to Turku, on the Baltic. It was February and temperatures were way below zero Fahrenheit. After a few hours the ferryboat stopped. Stuck in the ice, it called for the assistance of an icebreaker. We finally arrived eight hours late and two hundred miles from Helsinki. It took five hours to reach the capital by taxi, because the car had to make a large detour around the Soviet base of Hangö. I had to wait two days in Helsinki before I could obtain a place on the train to Leningrad. I took advantage of the lay-over to see the city.

As I boarded my train I found that the Finns, no doubt in order to thumb their noses at the Soviet generals who were on the train, had organized an honour guard for me on the station platform. Somewhat embarrassed, I reviewed the guard under the gaze of the Soviets. We slowly got underway to the Soviet Union, following the peninsula along the Gulf of Finland. We stopped at Vyborg, where workers were repairing the tracks. That was the point on the Mannerheim Line where the small Finnish army had held the Soviets at bay for several months during the winter of 1939-40. Following Soviet officers who were as curious as I was, I was able to see a part of the battlefields where the Finnish fighters had given such a good account of themselves. The train waited for eight hours and food became scarce. Finally, we arrived in Leningrad, where I found an Intourist guide who led me to the hotel.

I discovered the skyline of the beautiful city of Peter the Great. To my great surprise, it did not appear to have been damaged by the war. At any rate, its fine buildings and its huge squares were in perfect condition. I also noted, for the first time, the presence of the NKVD (Department of the Interior) police, which had guards patrolling the railway station with mounted bayonets. I had the feeling that I was entering a concentration camp. As soon as the passport and mission order formalities were completed, a guide brought me to the Astoria Hotel. Although my room was clean, it was cold (about 45°F), since only the large common areas were heated. Fortunately, I had a bottle of good cognac in my luggage, and a few swigs made me feel warmer. I kept my clothes on when I went to bed.

Next day, my guide took me for a tour of the city in a taxi. We first went to the Hermitage, the old Winter Palace of the Tsars, since transformed into a major art gallery. Many of the world's most famous paintings by celebrated painters such as Rembrandt and Monet were there. Some painters of the Russian school were also impressive. The visit included the cathedrals (which were closed), including the famous Holy Grace, the Smolnie Schools, the university and the places where the mounted Imperial Guard had often charged the crowd. It was a highly instructive tour that disproved propaganda claims that the core of the city had been razed.

Next evening, I took the Red Arrow train to Moscow. The trip, which was supposed to take twelve hours, in fact took more than twenty-four because some of the wartime damage to the tracks had not yet been repaired. My only food was a small box lunch prepared at the hotel at Intourist's request. This was hardly sufficient for a single meal. My compartment had three bunks. I took the bottom bunk; the middle one was occupied by a Red Army officer, and the top bunk by a woman 6 feet tall, wearing a uniform and looking more like a wrestler than the beautiful Soviet women of the Bolshoi ballet which I had the pleasure of seeing later in my stay. After a night spent sleeping with my head on my attaché case, I woke up somewhat tired during one of our many stops. Although it was already 8:30 a.m., it was still dark. There was no point in trying to go to the washroom, as the corridor was filled with those waiting. Like many others, I decided to take a visit outside. The cold was deadly, and I quickly returned to my compartment. The Soviet officer had also gotten up. He had folded his bed away and seemed to be waiting for me, sitting on the bunk. He said something resembling hello and, with a big smile, invited me to sit next to the window. He was not stupid, because, in view of the incredible cold, the window was precisely the place to avoid. Anyway I took out a small English-Russian dictionary and I found in it the expression "dobre din." The man replied with a sentence I completely failed to understand. So I lent him my glossary, where he found what he wanted to tell me: next to it, I could read the English equivalent. The conversation was launched. A little later, seeing that I had nothing to eat, the Russian opened a satchel and offered me a piece of bread and sausage. I accepted with a "spasiba" which he seemed to understand. Although difficult, our exchange continued with the help of the little book.

In mid-afternoon the train finally entered Moscow station, where Mr. Mayrand was waiting for me. It was a great joy, after so many days, to find someone who spoke French. We jumped in an embassy car and a few minutes later, the trip was over.

Mr. Mayrand quickly gathered the members of the staff in order to introduce them to me. Although they were not many, they all seemed happy to welcome the newcomer. In addition to Mrs. Mayrand (of Italian-Armenian origin) and to the three Mayrand children, there were Mr. and Mrs. Jack Thurrett, third secretary, Miss Oram, head of the secretariat, Miss Josephine Miller, whose brother was an army officer and who was acting as Thurrett's secretary, and Miss Myra Powell, who was going to be my secretary. I then met the service staff. A French woman, Miss Suret, the Mayrand children's governess, Vera Andrevna, receptionist and interpreter; Mr. Kostaki, the ambassador's driver; Yasha, who was going to be my driver, and Petronelle, the cleaning woman. Since no lodging had yet been set aside for me, Mayrand decided that I would stay at the embassy and have my meals at his home with his family.

We then had to get on with the serious matters. As soon as Mayrand received the communication I had mentioned, he made an appointment with Molotov, the Minister of Foreign Affairs, who set an appointment for midnight. Business was often done very late at night over there. Maybe the forces of darkness had a hand to play in this? In any case, the chargé d'affaires asked me to accompany him. The meeting only lasted three minutes, just long enough for us to hand over our message and to receive, in English, Molotov's glacial "thank you." Mackenzie King then went into action. Arrests, trials, criticism in the House of Commons and the press followed.

As Wilgress had predicted, a certain pressure was exerted on us in Moscow for some time. The morning following our meeting with Molotov the number of policemen at the embassy's doors doubled and we now had four of these guardian angels. With an innocent air, I went out, wearing uniform, for a morning walk. Two men immediately started to follow me. When I came back, one hour later, Josephine Miller told me that she had thought I was a goner. With a smile, I replied that we had to keep our cool and the storm would blow over.

My first mission accomplished, I went on to my next task, namely, visits dictated by protocol. With the Soviets, this only involved meeting General Koutouzov, responsible for the armed forces Foreign Relations Bureau. When he received me in his office, he was flanked by two officers, one of whom acted as the interpreter while the other did not utter a word. Because of the precarious diplomatic situation now prevailing between Canada and the USSR, the meeting was very short, devoid of any warmth and limited to the customary formalities. The other visits, to embassies, were almost always followed by a lunch with the military attaché and his assistants. The British and the French were particularly agreeable. In the case of the British, the air attaché, Air Commodore Wincott and his wife, as well as the naval attaché, Captain Duncan Hill and his wife, quickly became friends.

Major-General Alex Gatehouse, though, was another story. His reception was courteous but without any follow-up. My old friend and comrade from the Italian campaign, Army Corps General Augustin Guillaume, was the French military attaché. His assistants, Colonel Charles Ailleret, Commandant Georges de Bouteiller and Captain Georges Leloup as well as air attaché Guy de St-Marceaux became my companions throughout my stay. Many years later, we would always be happy to meet again. Our relations with the Americans, while excellent, were nevertheless a little more official.

Among the ambassadors, I hit it off immediately with Sir Maurice and Lady Peterson, of Great Britain. Sir Maurice remained a friend until his death. On the French side, General Georges Catroux and his wife, "Queen Margot," were extremely nice and always showed a great deal of affection towards me. U.S. ambassador General Walter Bedell Smith was a pleasant fishing and hunting companion. However, my best friends among the ambassadors were without question Antonio Lovink and his wife Clara, from Holland, as well as the entire Dutch delegation, including Baron Mausits Van Karnebeek and his wife Dorithey. The commercial attaché, Henk Goemans, his wife, and their daughter Eileen would also remain friends and sincere companions for many years. It was with them that I went skiing and to the Bolshoi for opera and ballet, and it was also them whom I joined when I went to the numerous diplomatic receptions.

I had far too many acquaintances among the foreigners in Moscow at the time for me to be able to name them all. I will add to the above, though, the names of Manlio Brosio and his wife Clotilde, from Italy; Colonel Carol Benedich, Swedish military attaché, General Knudtzon, Danish military attaché, and Admiral Matteson, the naval attaché of the same country. I recall with sadness one of those names, that of Czech ambassador Doctor Horak, an ex-professor at the University of Prague, and his wife, who were soon to fall victim to the abominable Communist government imposed upon their country. They were quality people, heroes who did not fit into the new communist mold. They had remained loyal to the idealism of Benes and of the founder of their country, the famous Thomas Masaryk, and to his son and successor Jan who apparently committed suicide in 1948, at the time when the USSR forcibly imposed its hegemony in Czechoslovakia. The memory of the Horaks always reminds me of the ugliness of communist policy. Regardless of the motives, I will never forgive communism for the atrocities it has committed (and is still committing) throughout the world, for far too long now. However, it is somewhat of a consolation to me, in thinking of the Horaks; that I contributed to saving from the same fate Colonel Klan (the deputy air attaché of Czechoslavakia), his wife and their son, who managed to escape to Vienna in 1949. Seeking a sponsor to enable them to reach Great Britain, they appealed to me through the British authorities. Subsequently, I was able to see them again in London. I am proud of having such people as my friends and of having been able to contribute to their happiness.

A few days after my visit to General Koutouzov, I was invited by the Red Army to participate in the 30th anniversary of its founding on February 23. On the eve of the event, the embassy received a telephone call from Koutouzov's office, suggesting that I refuse the invitation. After thinking about it for a short while, I nevertheless decided to go. Koutouzov's office was advised of my decision. In my opinion, we had to show that we did not fear these pressures.

On the evening of the reception, I was received at Krasny Dom by a Lieutenant-Colonel Studionov, who led me to the concert hall to hear the Red Army Choir. Still guided by Studionov, I then went to one of the three rooms where the reception was being held. There, I found myself in the company of the aides-de-camp. Commodore Wincott and his wife came to speak to me, but they were politely escorted to the other room, where most of the military attachés were and where I ought to have been as well. Faced with this situation, I started walking towards the other room, but the door was suddenly barred. I felt that there was no point in insisting for the time being so I gave up. After all, I had decided to come in spite of advice to the contrary. Studionov offered me a glass of vodka. I had taken the precaution of swallowing a few charcoal pills before leaving the embassy, since they help absorb some of the alcohol one drinks. I therefore gulped down, Russian-style, that first glass, which was followed by a mountain of caviar served on a crepe. Another vodka soon materialized. We were up to five or six and I noticed that Studionov did not seem at all concerned by the amount of alcohol, which we were drinking like water. After another plate of caviar, I grabbed the decanter and invited my hosts to toast the leaders of the Red Army. We began with the marshals. Since I was holding the decanter, he felt he had to keep up. After my last marshal, I noticed that Studionov had trouble speaking. So I proposed a toast to Stalin and the poor man, after swallowing the vodka, fell face down on the ground, completely drunk. Four officers came to carry him out of the room. While awaiting the sequel, I took another "large" portion of caviar. I had hardly finished it when Koutouzov himself came to apologize for his officer. Then he asked me, very innocently: "Why don't you dance with the others?" Playing the same game, I claimed that, being alone and unable to speak Russian, I had trouble finding a partner. Koutouzov then asked me to follow him to another room where some people spoke English and French. Then he introduced me to a beautiful Russian girl, a Bolshoi dancer, who spoke to me in excellent French. We entered the ballroom at the very instant when the band started playing a Viennese waltz. I said to my partner: "If you don't mind, I'm going to dance this my way." She very kindly accepted, without suspecting that my main wish was to avoid whirling around too much with all the vodka in my stomach. We later went to the marshals' room where my companion introduced me to Marshal Zhukov and to a few other Soviet heroes. Then we joined the generals. The rest of the evening was spent very pleasantly in her company. Around 3:00 a.m., General Guillaume, who was getting ready to leave, told me that he could take me home if I wished. I left my dancer and, happy with my performance, followed Guillaume to his car. On the way, he asked me whether I wanted to go skiing the next day, and I accepted. Back at the embassy, I found that I was still quite conscious in spite of all the vodka.

I had the feeling that I had won the first of the many social battles my new function was going to require.

The next day, a Sunday, I went to mass. Afterwards, the Guillaumes took me skiing. I felt rather drunk and found the day very long. The whole thing was capped by a spectacular fall at the bottom of a run leading to a ski jump ramp that I had fortunately managed to avoid. Because of the cold, the oxygen slowly overpowered the vodka. After a good dinner at the Guillaumes', they had me driven to the embassy. The last twenty-four hours had been an initiation to the life of the Moscow diplomatic corps.

In early March, I obtained a suite in the Savoy Hotel. This was a rather austere place that was certainly less secure than the embassy. There was always a risk of dirty tricks. Many diplomats lived there, mainly military personnel. We all agreed that a certain signal rapped out on the radiators indicated that the person giving the signal needed help, and the first of us who would be available would then run to assist his colleague. This caused the police to be cautious and no nasty incident occurred on our floor.

It was important for me to learn Russian. Through the diplomatic office, I was assigned a teacher who gave me three lessons a week. Those who had done the classical curriculum in high school (as in my case) have an enormous advantage when learning Russian because the alphabet and declination closely resemble those of classical Greek. Moreover, I realized that Russian contains many words related to vocabularies of European languages that I already knew to some extent. Thus, I was able to read Russian very quickly and could soon understand the newspapers. Speaking, however, was another matter altogether, particularly since contact with the population was difficult and opportunities were rare. With some effort I nevertheless managed quite well. Since I liked everything connected with music, recreation in Moscow was easy to find. I quickly learned how to go to the Bolshoi, to its annex, the Tchaikovsky room, and to the conservatory, where I had the pleasure of hearing the greatest works of the classical repertoire. Three times a week I went to one of these great concert halls to admire the quality of operas, ballets and concerts. Even there, one had to watch oneself because compromising incidents sometimes occurred. I understood that, being alone, the risk for me could be even greater. In order to protect myself I took along my secretary. When the Russians, on my second visit, noticed that my companion was "only a secretary," they refused my ticket. This tends to prove that Soviet society is classless—but some classes are better off than others. Subsequently, my love for music made me take the risk—not really that great—of going alone to those shows.

Relations with the Soviet armed forces were non-existent for all intents and purposes. We were regularly promised visits to military establishments but these never materialized. Co-operation failed even in small matters.

Thus, I received one day a letter from a Canadian family whose son, a flyer, had been shot down in the Archangelsk area during World War II. He was therefore probably buried locally, and his family wanted to have a photograph of his grave as a souvenir. I visited the office of the military attachés to ask whether I could obtain that picture or whether I could go identify that grave myself and take a picture of it. Neither option was considered by the Soviets, who seemed to pay no regard to the importance this request had for the victim's family. In fact, my request was rejected outright one month later.

Although matters involving individual cases received such scant attention, mass events were frequent in the Soviet Union and were organized with dramatic precision. The first one I saw was on May 1, 1946. For the occasion, the diplomats and military attachés were given a place of honour on the benches placed on either side of Lenin's tomb. Red Square was completely covered with banners, flags and four enormous portraits of Marx, Engels, Lenin and Stalin. Stalin, Bulganin, Molotov, Beria and others were on the rostrum. It was a beautiful day and the military attachés met before 10:00 a.m. in order to avoid the crowd. I noted that my invitation bore the number 022, quite a coincidence for the former commander of the *Royal 22e Régiment*. The Soviet troops, commanded by Marshal Koniev, paraded for two hours. The crowd itself passed before us for four hours in a "spontaneous patriotic demonstration of the peasants and the people" (for which they had been training almost every evening for months). I was staggered by these human masses.

My second invitation was to a concert to take place on Red Square on the evening of that same May 1st. Once again, the attachés were all in place when the group of bands of the Moscow military region as well as the Red Army Choir made their entry. Conducted by Major-General Alexandrov, they played the Slavic March and the famous 1812 Overture by Tchaikovski. The show was magnificent. Included in the show were the bells of the Kremlin and the AA guns that showered gold stars upon Red Square lit up by AA searchlights. The whole thing was capped by the aerial deployment of a huge Soviet flag and a picture of Stalin. An unforgettable view; because the music of more than one thousand players and the synchronization by the conductor of the Kremlin bells and guns were admirable, I wanted to jump up and congratulate the people involved. However, the impenetrable barriers that had been set up quickly cooled my enthusiasm.

Among the Soviet authorities, there was great, and legitimate, pride in their feats of arms. It was often accompanied, however, by a certain arrogance that was misplaced. Thus, on that May 1, 1946, General Koutouzov asked me what Canada had done as compared with the millions of men the USSR had lost. My reply was pointed: "We do not measure effort by the number of people sacrificed."

By this time, our diplomatic relations had once again become more or less correct. The police guard of the embassy had been cut back to two men and the standards that prevail in that type of dictatorship were respected. Mr. and Mrs. Wilgress had returned to Moscow and a change in personnel was announced. Léon Mayrand would be replaced by Robert Ford. Since the Canadian government had now decided to allow my family to join me, we were assured of being able to occupy the Mayrands' lodgings in the embassy yard.

In May 1946, there was a conference of Commonwealth prime ministers in London. Wanting to hear a personal account of events in the Soviet Union after the announcement of the Gouzenko affair, Prime Minister King asked me to join the Canadian delegation in London. After giving me an exit visa, the Soviets offered me a Moscow-Berlin passage aboard one of their DC3s. In the morning of June 6, I went to Vnukovo airport, where I was received by a protocol officer who introduced me to the captain of the aircraft. I was by then beginning to manage quite well in Russian, and I immediately felt that the trip would be quite pleasant. Entering the aircraft, I saw that its interior arrangement was most basic: two cloth benches, one on each side of the plane and, in the middle, six 45-gallon barrels tied down by cables. The captain pointed out my seat, adding that the barrels were full of the "benzene" that was to be used for refuelling in Kaliningrad (previously Königsberg, in East Prussia). This was not very reassuring. A few minutes later, a truck approached one of the engines and attached a starter shaft to the propeller in order to make it turn. This procedure seemed perfectly normal to them and both engines were soon running. The aircraft then slowly taxied towards its warmup area. At that point another passenger who looked like a moujik took out a cigarette and lit it by first striking his match on one of the fuel barrels. I was stunned. The man was puffing on his self-rolled cigarette during take-off. Used to our own precautions, I was somewhat unhappy with this. His cigarette finished, he threw it on the ground and squashed it under his foot.

At one point, the captain invited me to sit in the copilot's seat. I accepted gladly. Here I was, in the cockpit, chatting (with some difficulty), when he handed me the controls and lit up a cigarette. In spite of these "hazards" and of my incompetence in Russian, we reached Kaliningrad without incident. While the contents of the barrels were being transferred by the "bowlful" to the DC3's fuel tanks, the flight captain asked a policeman to show me around town. The policeman complied readily—and I was shown around at the expense of the NKVD. I thus had the pleasure of touring the old town of the Teutonic Knights; although partially demolished, it still gave an idea of what that faraway, historical period had been. The captain was waiting for me when I returned. I sat down again in my copilot's seat. He explained that the runway was a little short but that everything was going to be OK (at least, that is what I understood). The plane lined up on the runway and its engines ran up to full speed. Suddenly, as if someone had cut a retaining chain, we dashed away at full speed and began ascending very slowly, missing a row of trees by only a few feet. Flippantly, the captain turned to say a word that I did not understand well but which seemed to be "hurray"! Still pale and not quite able to hide my fear, I answered: "hurray"! Before long, we were over Poland, at approximately 5,000 feet, on our way to Berlin. It was a beautiful day, and having recovered from my fright, I resumed the conversation. In mid-afternoon, we arrived in Berlin where a car from the Canadian mission was waiting for me, fortunately, since I did not have a kopeck in my pockets. I thanked the captain and went to the Canadian mission where I was pleased to see again Lieutenant-General Maurice Pope. He and his wife were great people. They were the parents of Lieutenant Harry Pope, who had served with me in the R22^{e}R during the Italian campaign, and they received me with warmth and kindness.

The next morning, I told Pope in his office about my impressions of the Soviet Union. He then invited me to visit West Berlin and the various Western missions in the sector. Back at his office, he told me that King wanted to visit Berlin. Knowing that I would be with him in London, Pope wanted me to try and dissuade the Prime Minister from making the trip. Having myself felt the unhealthy atmosphere prevailing in Berlin, I promised I would do so. He then asked me whether I needed anything. I told him that the Soviets had required that I leave their country without taking away any of their money. He gave me 200 marks. Since I did not know the real value of that amount, I thought it was enormous. In the afternoon, I went to the British officers' club, and after a good meal and drinks for less than 5 marks, I could begin to gauge the value of my marks. When I was invited to play some poker, I was able to even better appreciate the real value of that money. Indeed, I left the club with over 500 marks in my pocket. The next morning, before I took the plane for London, I repaid General Pope. He was quite surprised, then laughed at the luck I had had the previous evening. As soon as I arrived in London, I went to the exchange office, where I was given about 30 pounds sterling (then about $150). At that point, I started thinking about the financial catastrophe that could have occurred had I been unlucky in Berlin.

At the Dorchester Hotel I went to the suite reserved by the Canadian delegation, where I was welcomed by Mr. James Gibson, head of the Prime Minister's secretariat, with whom I was going to have dinner. After a good martini prepared by Norman Robertson, I went to see Mr. King who was waiting for me: he did not take an aperitif, since he virtually never drank alcohol. During the meal, conversation revolved entirely around two topics: the Soviet response to the announcement of the Gouzenko affair and the feasibility of visiting Berlin. On the first point, I have already stated the gist of what I remember. On the second, as promised to General Pope, I stressed the difficulties a prime-ministerial trip to Berlin could cause, including the possibility of unpleasant incidents. Convinced of my sincerity, he concluded that the trip would probably be untimely. Robertson, the Under-Secretary for External Affairs, was happy about my intervention and readily concurred with his boss. After I had left King, Robertson thanked me warmly and asked me many questions regarding our relations with the USSR and its armed forces.

Following two days of meetings and a visit to the War Office, I was offered a trip to Canada with the delegation. We left on the S.S. *Queen Mary* on my 33rd birthday, celebrated with great enthusiasm by the entire delegation. I had a bad hangover the next morning, of course. Along the way, my luck held. I won the shipboard lottery three days in a row, and as Norman Robertson's bridge partner, I gave up counting my earnings. Before arriving in Halifax, King said he wanted to welcome the war brides, the overseas women our men had married during the war who were arriving in Canada for the first time with their children aboard our ship. He asked me to mingle with the crowd in order to hear the reaction to what he said. It was a beautiful day and most passengers were lying on deck when Mr. King's little speech was announced. Later, I had dinner with King in his cabin. There were three guests, James Gibson, Norman Robertson and myself. Mr. King spoke very little, then suddenly asked for opinions regarding his speech. We agreed, all three of us, that it had gone very well. Without any exaggerations, we congratulated him. Suddenly, he turned to me: "While I was speaking, a lady whispered something in your ear. What did she say?" Without thinking, I answered that she had asked, "Who is that old man?" King smiled. The thought immediately occurred to me that my diplomatic career had perhaps just ended. In fact, that was not the case.

After arriving in Halifax, he invited me to continue the trip to Ottawa in his private railway car. I regained my composure after understanding that he wanted me with him primarily while he was crossing Quebec, where he was going to be welcomed by delegations in Rimouski, Lévis and Drummond-ville—he wanted next to him a French-speaking general in uniform. In Ottawa, I spent two days at Army HQ before returning to Trois-Rivières where my wife and children were waiting. Since I had won more than $1,000 during the trip, I did not submit a claim for travel expenses to my department.

The next task was to prepare the family to leave. Before that, however, we waited for the birth of our third child. A little girl, Andrée, was born on July 4, and was baptized at the Saint-Philippe church in Trois-Rivières. Her mother had to recover from the delivery, so we delayed preparations for a month. Simone and the children passed the month of August at Val Pichet. The country air gave them the strength required for the long trip to Moscow.

After a five-year wait, after the concerns, solitude and great responsibility of raising the children alone, Simone had indeed deserved what she was now offered. Still, her hitherto difficult role was not going to be made easier just by the fact that we were now going to be reunited. Between the day we were married and the day I retired we moved 18 times and travelled 26,927 miles merely to go from one place of residence to another.

As for the trip to Moscow, the first one undertaken by our complete family of five, it was not going to be all roses. First of all, in Moscow, there was a shortage of everything. Our planning had to be for a stay of at least two years with a baby who was only three months old, a small boy of five and a little girl of seven. We needed clothes for every season, we had to ensure that Andrée was not going to lack food, and so forth.

I should point out at this stage that the children of a career soldier do not lead a stable life. Their fate is not always enviable. Because of numerous postings, they must quickly adapt to ever-changing environments, schools, school curricula and friends. This is particularly difficult in the teens, which is the period when lifelong friendships are made. Michèle was the first to suffer the full impact of these vagaries.

When we boarded the S.S. *Aquitania* for Moscow, via England, I was accompanied by a batman, Corporal Léo Boudreau of the R22^{e}R. Brought up in a large Acadian family, he knew how to take care of the little ones and took charge of them, paying special attention to our little Andrée. Regarding Léo Boudreau, let me add that, a mere corporal in 1946, he reached the highest rank attainable by an NCO within the Forces, that is, Chief Warrant Officer. Following that Moscow stay, during which he lived with us, Léo was always considered family. Much later, as a sign of both respect and affection, Andrée, who had the fondest memories of this good soldier, invited him to her wedding.

Having arrived in London, the family was housed at the Dorchester Hotel and had its first contact with the beautiful British capital and the Old World. The Dorchester was splendidly located facing Hyde Park, where the children could run around safely. Thanks to Léo's presence, Simone and I could get away to visit London. This new life made the whole family very happy.

Unfortunately, things were soon going to get less pleasant. The reservations had been confirmed on a Soviet ship, the S.S. *Sobiensky*, which we were supposed to board ten days after our arrival in London. However, the

Soviet embassy had not received permission to issue an entry visa to Corporal Boudreau. We were certainly not going to leave him fend for himself in London, so we therefore decided to wait for things to sort themselves out. The reservations at the Dorchester Hotel, though, had expired and we had to leave. But where to? There was a shortage of accommodation in London. Fortunately, resort hotels were empty and we found the Connaught at Herne Bay, on the Thames, approximately fifty miles from London. We stayed there for a week even though the day after our arrival the Soviets issued Léo's visa, because the *Sobiensky* had left by then and we had to wait for the next ship. The Connaught was very comfortable and we had a good rest.

Another misadventure was soon to befall us. On the eve of our departure, since I wanted to ensure that everything would be ready on time, I went to London to deliver the luggage to the ship at Pier 10. Next morning, a car from the military mission, along with a guide, left for Herne Bay in order to pick up the family and take them to the ship before noon. I was waiting on board with the luggage, and the cabins were ready. The guide, however, took a wrong turn and the family got lost somewhere in the south of London. We waited for one, two, three hours but nobody showed up. The ship's captain, no matter how sympathetic, could not linger. I left the luggage on board and disembarked. Having heard nothing from my family, I had to be patient. When they arrived on the docks, the ship had been gone for over an hour. For the second time, we had to find a place to stay in London, and this time we had no reservation. Finally, we found two small rooms at the Normandy Hotel. Air Vice-Marshal McBurnie offered his DC3 to fly us to Stockholm where the British air attaché picked us up and took us to the Grand Hotel of Saltza-Baden, in the suburbs. The few days spent in Sweden allowed us to celebrate Michèle's 7th birthday on October 16. Four days later, our ship berthed in Stockholm and the family finally embarked for Leningrad, via Helsinki. We spent two days in Leningrad, subsequently taking the Red Arrow and reaching Moscow after a full month on the road.

Setting up the family in the military attaché's residence was relatively easy. The residence was in the yard of the embassy. Since the place was under constant police surveillance, the children could play freely. The house was completely furnished and we unpacked quickly. The loyal Corporal Boudreau, whom the children now regarded as an older brother, was always there. While we were awaiting the arrival of the governess from France, Corporal Boudreau took care of the children.

The domestic staff selected by the dedicated Vera Andrevna arrived. Petronelle, a good-hearted peasant, took care of maintenance, laundry and heating. Nadiejda was the cook and Adelina our first maid. In May 1947, the ranks were swelled by the dedicated Elizabeth, a descendant of an old aristocratic family from Georgia (under the old system, she would have been a princess). Elizabeth took charge of Andrée, in an exceptionally efficient manner. All of these women were very devoted to us. Of course, we had to expect that they would report our activities to the police. I was already used to that and it did not bother me.

When planning my time, I intended to reserve Saturdays and Sundays for family and friends. In the big embassies (United States, England, France) there were arrangements for the children of those nationalities. Ours were soon able to join those groups and make new friends. They handled the experience very well. Michèle and Jean were of school age, but there was no suitable school for them. Through Mrs. Vanier, whose husband was ambassador to Paris, we found a French teacher who was qualified and willing to make the trip. Mademoiselle Ménétrier came from Saint-Dié, in Alsace. She was good to the children but caused us some unexpected problems during the last months of our stay. Not all these details of our daily life, however, could be sorted out before diplomatic life resumed.

Socializing among Western diplomats was intensive. There were receptions day after day. Friendships were quickly established, but contact with the Russians was virtually nil. The local population was fearful, and we wanted to avoid incidents.

When we arrived, the Western community was waiting for us. The activities began with a big cocktail given in our honour by the Canadian chargé d'affaires. This was the occasion when Simone was introduced to the diplomatic society within which she would very quickly feel at ease. I found some old friends and met some newcomers, including Walter and Betsy Cronkite, who were then the representatives of United Press and with whom we established a lasting friendship. In fact, we were warmly welcomed by those within the Western and Asiatic communities who were still free, whereas the representatives of socialist countries received us correctly but coldly. To them, we were just another bunch of spies.

As soon as we were settled, I resumed my work. But what kind of work? The first invitation from the Soviets was for the big November 7 parade, second in size to that of May 1. To me, this was just a repeat of the previous performance. On the other hand, our travels were still restricted. The Soviet Minister of Defence kept promising that we would be able to visit military establishments, but nothing of the kind materialized during my stay. We were forbidden to have personal relations with members of the Red Army. To have an idea of what was going on, one had to rely on the opinion of observers or espionage. Canada, however, had formally prohibited us from spying, a fact that had been clearly emphasized to me in Ottawa in 1945. Moreover, the policy of our country was not to co-operate on any project of the major Western powers and to exchange nothing of substance with their military attachés. I allowed myself a mild violation of this directive.

During my recent stay in Canada, I had visited the chiefs of the intelligence service that our Army was setting up at Ottawa HQ. On that occasion, I had the opportunity to speak to those who were going to receive my reports. I told myself at that time that I would send something with each diplomatic pouch—and I kept that promise. But what kind of document would I be able to prepare in view of all the constraints I was facing? First of all, they could ask me to confirm, in a general manner, or—very rarely—to deny information Ottawa had received from other sources (primarily American and British). Furthermore, I had to provide any information that could have any value to our government and its armed forces. To my mind, this second part of my instructions could provide a very broad field of research, although the sources seemed for the time being limited to official Soviet communiqués, a rather lean diet.

The first element that allowed me to stay abreast of Soviet policy was the weekly meeting of Commonwealth ambassadors and military attachés, held at the British embassy. It was very interesting and, thank God, I was allowed to sit in. The British, always well informed and highly competent in diplomatic and military affairs, gave us each week a summary of world activities, focused on the USSR and its external relations. Sir Maurice Peterson, the ambassador, or Sir Frank Roberts, the embassy counsellor, presented erudite analyses of Soviet current affairs and their likely evolution. The participation of the various other members of the group was also interesting and relevant.

In addition to this, there was my lonely work on a fairly specific topic: the present and future Soviet Army. Indeed, we knew little about it except for the fact that it had crushed the German Army from 1943 on. The most important question in 1946-47 was how it might be used in the face of U.S. nuclear power. Another issue was its capability to undertake and sustain a potential conventional war.

Without becoming a spy, I began to familiarize myself with this issue by reading the military books that I could buy in bookstores. I also went to the big Lenin Library, where I read military reviews. At the office, I received the military journals, *Krasnyy flot* and *Krasneya zvezda*. As my Russian improved, I began piecing together the jigsaw puzzle. At first, the results were not very encouraging. I told myself that patience and work would triumph in the end. In order to have some assistance, I hired a Russian translator who was undoubtedly a spy. I believe that I was able to mislead her about my interests by asking her to translate a great variety of subjects that I picked from journals and reviews. This hard work started to bear fruit after many months and I was able, by inductive reasoning, to understand the comings and goings of Soviet troops. I began to have a fairly accurate picture of the shape the Red Army was gradually assuming for the kind of peace preached by the Soviet government. This became very interesting, and assisted by some friends, I was able to confirm the validity of some of my deductions.

My very specific objective was to discover the organization of the Department of Defence, the basic structure of the armed forces and their deployment throughout the country as well as in the newly conquered countries. Finding out about the organization was relatively easy. Military journals and reviews provided me with the bulk of the data. Through my colleagues, I obtained some more. Getting the rest was a little more complicated.

One day, while I was walking in the street, I saw on the sidewalk a bunch of carbon paper sheets. I put them in my pocket and later realized that they came from the Academy of Artillery Science. By deciphering it, I discovered a great amount of the mission information on the artillery arm and its relations with General HQ and the field formations. I also found there the likely use, under combat conditions, of guns, mortars and rockets of various calibres. It was quite a find, and it enabled me to complete a good portion of the organization chart I had drawn up and to understand the manner in which the Soviets' firepower could be used.

The structural and territorial organization of the army was relatively easy to piece together. By means of the articles and news in the *Krasneya zvezda*, I was able to complete the configuration of the military districts quickly. The number of troops stationed in each district was more difficult to obtain. I seemed to be unable to unearth that secret until, one day, an article gave me an idea. It was stated there that every soldier would be eligible to receive, for a special task successfully accomplished or for good conduct, a holiday trip to Moscow. I told myself that, everything else being equal, there must be a proportional number of soldiers arriving every day from the various regions. The difficulty was in knowing where each of them was coming from. On the railway map, I saw that the various Moscow railway stations were of dissimilar size. By watching arrivals very closely, I subsequently discovered— based on the volume and unit identification—interesting statistics. These were only percentages, but combined with other information, they became highly useful and gave me a picture of the situation.

Other areas yielded information more rapidly. Thus, in May 1947, the Red Army, which had now become the Soviet Army, unveiled at its May 1st parade its new armament including tanks and various vehicles. Obeying the rules, I took no pictures but next day the Tass Agency gave me whatever I wanted.

Nuclear research, production and tests had become of paramount importance for the Soviets. After the defection to the USSR of scientists who gave it the information required to manufacture nuclear weapons, I quickly became convinced that that country would successfully run a first test. This was confirmed to me in early 1947 by the clandestine visit of a former German scientist, who came to see me one morning at the embassy. He was one of the slaves the Soviets had brought from Germany to work on the production of heavy water. When I reported the matter to Ottawa, General A. J. L. McNaughton—then the Canadian representative to the U.N. Atomic Energy Commission as well as chairman of the Canadian Atomic Energy Control Board—told me that it would be impossible for the Soviets to succeed before ten years. I preferred to believe my intuition as well as the information provided by my contact. Indeed, on November 7, 1947, 30th anniversary of the revolution, following the failure of a first explosion, Molotov announced that nuclear weapons no longer held a secret for the Soviet Union. And, in 1949 they successfully carried out a test. Altogether, in all these areas, I was quite proud of my accomplishment. I just hoped that my efforts would be of use to Ottawa, and I later found out that they were.

During my stay in Moscow, work proper only took a small proportion of my time, although I did more than what was expected of me to keep up my spirits. We had a great deal of free time, which we spent as best we could. Our relations with the British were always correct and very friendly. Indeed, we felt "at home" at the British embassy, the tenants of which were friends who regarded us as compatriots with whom they could share information and to whom they could suggest certain orientations. At Christmas 1946, my whole family gathered there at the invitation of Lady Peterson. I sang Christmas carols with the choir. We were all very happy at that gathering, which made us forget our isolation, always difficult for good French Canadians, during this holiday season.

Officially, the Soviets did not celebrate Christmas. However, Christian traditions remained close to the heart of the people, who always managed to remember the great event through discreet celebrations, which, organized in the midst of desperate straits, were that much more sincere. The people managed to transmit to the foreigners in their midst a profound sense of their traditions. The tenacity of their feelings made itself felt at Easter 1947, when the government authorized a religious celebration. The crowd that came to the Orthodox cathedral in Moscow was full of religious fervour. The diplomatic corps were invited, but the thing to see were those thousands of Soviets. After the Resurrection ceremony, they piously paraded in the streets carrying to their poor lodgings the torch of the new light.

In the evening, assisting Father Laberge (a Franco-American) at the Saint-Louis-des-Français church, I had the honour, during the Easter Saturday ceremony, of ringing the bell for the first time since the revolution had silenced it thirty years earlier. I was deeply moved by the import of the moment.

There was also a sad side to that religious renewal. This was the story of Mrs. Hotte and her daughter, both very devoted to the cause of the only Catholic church in Moscow. Mrs. Hotte was the widow of a French professor who had taught literature at Moscow University before the revolution. One day, while the good man was doing his work at the university, revolutionaries entered the classroom and crucified him against the wall, killing him like a dog. Imagine the heartbreak of his wife, who had a little baby, born in Moscow. She sought refuge at the French consulate. When the situation returned to normal, she requested permission to return to France. The Soviets granted her request since she was French but refused to issue an exit visa for her daughter, claiming that she was a Russian subject. Poor Mrs. Hotte refused to leave the country and the French embassy, which had followed the Soviet government from Petrograd to Moscow, hired her as a receptionist. She was never able to see her country again. During the first part of the war—when the Germans and Soviets remained precariously at peace with each other—she was interned as a foreigner. Afterward, she was able to resume her job at the embassy.

When I met her, she lived in a little walk-up apartment not far from the embassy and the Saint-Louis-des-Français church. At the church, she played the organ, while her daughter conducted the choir. A group from the French embassy, which I joined, provided the hymns during the ceremonies. When these two ladies could not attend, the practices were held at my home. Thus, we had prepared a mass to celebrate the Immaculate Conception on the morning of December 8 1947. I went to the church but Mrs. Hotte and her daughter were not there. Commander Guy de St-Marceaux decided to look for them at home. He found two policemen at her door. Next day, we found out that they had been arrested for espionage during the previous night. The French embassy tried unsuccessfully to have them released, and we never saw them again. I was told later that Mrs. Hotte had died in a concentration camp and that her daughter had simply disappeared. I must confess that an event such as this affected me greatly. That day, and ever since, I have not had enough epithets to curse that terrible regime which could stay in power only through the force of its police, through spying and oppression. Moreover, it gave nothing to its people. In fact, it took everything away from them, even the most basic dignity.

In 1947, there were two major events in Moscow. The first was a conference at which the British, the Americans, the Soviets and the French tried to agree on a peace treaty with Germany. The meeting did not produce anything concrete. However, I witnessed three facts related to that conference that I shall state briefly, if somewhat disjointedly. On March 15, U.S. General Mark Clark, whom I knew, asked me to be his interpreter during a reception. He wanted to tell General Guillaume that he was not very happy with the positions taken by the French delegation. Guillaume later made a comment to me to the effect that "the Americans are pessimists."

Two weeks later, on a Sunday, I noticed Georges Bidault (head of the French group) and his wife at mass. I could not help noting in my diary that great men who are churchgoers are few and far between. I saw Bidault again later, since he went to church regularly, but also at a reception at the French Embassy.

On March 30, I was at a reception provided by our country to the various delegations that were in Moscow for the conference. On that occasion, I noted that British Foreign Minister Ernest Bevin exhibited an incredible vanity. He boasted that he had predicted as early as 1918 that there was going to be a Second World War. According to him, Lenin should have been in Versailles in 1918-19 to prevent the mess that treaty turned out to be. He added that he was going to remind the Soviets that in 1917-18 he had prevented his longshoremen's union from loading ammunition ships sailing for Archangelsk to resupply troops fighting against the young revolution. That argument, he believed, was going to be very useful in the talks. Events in due time proved otherwise.

There is one more observation I must add. In April, while talking with Egyptian high officials, I was struck by their utter lack of trust in British socialism which, according to them, would fail to respect institutions, much like the other known socialisms. I must say that, at the time, I feared almost as much as they did the potential excesses of British Labourites.

On April 25, I went to the Byelorussia railway station to witness Bevin's departure. Before climbing aboard, Bevin sang a little song to his host Vyshinsky. Bevin apparently liked carols.

The second major event of 1947 was the 800th anniversary of the founding of Moscow. While the people lacked food, the government spent millions to prepare the celebration. Hundreds of workers were engaged in decorating Moscow. All the houses on Gorki Street were repainted, trees were planted along the sidewalks, the domes of the Kremlin were gilded anew. The members of the Politburo received new seven-passenger Zim automobiles, which were copies of the American-made Packard. The stores were filled with merchandise at prices people could not afford. Huge patriotic demonstrations were planned, which my wife and I were invited to attend.

The first was a grandiose mass gymnastics show at Dynamo stadium on July 20. The entire diplomatic corps was there and there were invited guests from every republic of the USSR and the new satellite countries. Also present were communist leaders of various national parties throughout the world. During the spectacle, announcements and comments were made to the crowd, but not a single word of command was issued to the young performers, who put on a magnificent show. Depending on the segment involved, up to five thousand young gymnasts were accompanied by the bands of the Moscow garrison, which directed their movements. We saw an enormous, incredibly precise ballet. The image I remember to this day is that of the Ukranian Republic performers who covered the entire stadium area and imitated a field of wheat undulating in the wind. During that fifteen-minute event, the gold-coloured costumes worn by the gymnasts changed colour, darkening momentarily in the trough of the waves. It was unforgettable! The performance of the other Soviet regions was every bit as impressive. The final picture was a palette of colours from which an accurate portrait of Stalin suddenly emerged. What a day! What discipline on the part of those Soviet youths.

The second demonstration was put on by the Soviet air force at the Vnukovo airport. It was a beautiful day. When I arrived with my wife, the inimitable General Koutouzov asked me: "You do not have your camera?" I replied that obviously I did not, but I did not tell him that his newspapers were going to give me the next day all the pictures I would need. On that occasion, I saw the new MIG jet come out of the sun before overflying the parade stands at 500 miles per hour. All participants performed with precision at the controls of transport, fighter or bomber aircraft and helicopters. The event was capped by a massed flight about 10,000 feet above us. This was followed by an enormous buffet, after which we returned to the embassy.

On July 27, it was the turn of the Soviet Navy to show its mettle. We were therefore invited to Khimki. It was obvious, however, that at that time the Soviet naval arm did not receive as much attention as the other two. The show was pitiful. There was really nothing to learn there except that the Soviets had removed the submarines from the Fleet Command and included them in a strategic command.

The summer of 1947 was not devoid of interest. In order to provide the children, who were often sick, with a little fresh air and recreation, I rented a *dacha* about twenty-five miles from Moscow. My wife went there almost daily with them. The village was not particularly beautiful and one had to fetch water from the common well. Still, it was better than nothing. The family that rented to us had moved to the shed. They were good people who worked on a collective farm. They were very poor, and as is often the case with such simple folk, they were very generous to us. Their children came to see us every day to give us flowers or sell us vegetables.

The surrounding region was interesting. For example, less than two miles away, there was a camp of German prisoners-of-war who spent their spare time singing beautifully as a choir. Also in the vicinity was Marshal Budionny's *dacha*, surrounded by about ten acres of grounds and guarded by a company of soldiers. The house was surrounded by a fence at least ten feet high, with barbed wire all around. We could see the house from afar but we could not get close. Stalin also had a *dacha* in the area. As a result of this particular situation, there was a policeman every 300 yards all the way to the highway leading to Moscow.

Our walks outside the embassy were often very revealing in terms of the repression people suffered from. One day, I went out with Jean-Ernest, who was then five years old. Along the street, we saw men in chains being herded towards an enclosure. They were prisoners going to work on a nearby building site. This made a very strong impression on my son, and I had to explain to him, as best I could, what this meant. In the evening, he had great difficulty falling asleep as a result of this unfortunate incident, which he later often recalled.

On Sundays, we usually went for a walk in the countryside with a group of friends and their children. We were sometimes thirty or so sharing a picnic. We thus spent a few very pleasant hours before meeting again, in the evening, at one of the embassies, or else at Spasso House, the U.S. Ambassador's residence, to see a movie. Following such a long day with our friends, I was usually ready to resume the official week.

My relations with my embassy colleagues were usually good, in spite of some quite normal conflicts. With Mr. Wilgress, I had no major problem. In fact, I appreciated the man with whom I was later to work again. Among other things, he taught me how to communicate my thoughts in writing concisely. He would quickly reduce one of my three-page memos to a single page that contained all the necessary facts. With Wilgress, there was a mutual exchange of services that everyone appreciated. I am not certain that I shared his views regarding the USSR. According to him, the Soviet privileged class that had risen over the last thirty years wanted a long peace in order to consolidate its gains. Undoubtedly, he was a brilliant man, and it is only fair that he should be included, as Professor Granatstein has done, among the first generation of mandarins of the federal civil service. Following the Gouzenko affair, his view of the USSR was difficult to justify to the disappointed Canadian authorities. Since he had to leave his post during the summer of 1946, our association was fairly short-lived.

After his departure, I found myself with an excellent chargé d'affaires, Robert Ford, whose wife was of foreign origin and not yet aware of all our customs; this sometimes led to certain misunderstandings that were difficult to accept at the time but which, everything considered, were quite minor.

By the end of two years in that post, I had seen many diplomats and military men come and go. I had also acquired a good reputation among foreign diplomats. My wife and I were highly sought-after. Because of all these connections and with a little jogging of my memory, I was able to recognize the names of the overwhelming majority of foreign diplomats posted to Moscow, some of which were often quite difficult to decipher. This helped us forge closer links with the Arab countries, Chiang Kai-Shek's China and the Scandinavian peoples.

The communist world had not yet reached its present expanse. Today's satellites were, in 1947, occupied by Soviet troops. Many of those countries were unhappy and their diplomats, still loyal to their ideals, felt ill at ease in embassies in which some members were ready to betray them. They liked to see us and keep up a liaison that, as they well knew, was probably not going to last. Following a reception I occasionally found in my coat pocket a short message written in utter desperation. We could do nothing, and they knew it, but this opportunity to unburden themselves seemed to help them. In turn, we had to be careful not to fall into a trap or to compromise those who opened their hearts to us. I was always afraid of these messages and, whenever I found one, I excused myself to go to the washroom to read it and throw it away. Strangely enough, I was always able to detect the origin of the message. The content was sometimes very useful in allowing me to foresee certain events.

The Chinese ambassador, Mr. Fu, and his embassy counsellor, became very good friends of mine. I was often invited to their embassy. One day, he told me that everything was over for them because Mao Tse-tung's troops were going to come to power with the help of the Soviet Army. He could not predict what his future might be. Mr. Fu was a good man who could feel things coming with that serenity often exhibited by Orientals. I saw him for the last time when we left the Moscow railway station. He gave me at that time a miniature jade vessel as a good luck charm. I was deeply touched. I can still visualize him as he saw me off. Many others left me with the same impression. The faces of these people loyal to their fate and country were revealing. I still remember that picture of despair that nobody could explain but I understood only too well.

Aware that international relations were becoming increasingly difficult between East and West, Ottawa began to be concerned. In 1947, things had taken a turn for the worse. Verbal attacks against the West were vitriolic (and all-encompassing: the Pope, Canada, the U.S., all were targets). In that atmosphere, "spy mania" reigned. Moreover, there was a great deal of tension in Germany where, at any time, one of the many incidents occurring daily could have ignited the powder keg. As a result, our embassy tightened its security. The ambassador was not replaced and General Charles Foulkes, then Chief of the General Staff, decided to recall me. He did not want to leave me in the USSR with my family in the eye of the potential storm. He sent me a message on December 27, 1947, asking me when I could leave Moscow. I was prepared to return, but in view of the temperature and of the difficulty of travelling with children, I would have preferred to leave in early spring. At that point, I could not see myself travelling throughout Europe, a good portion of which was occupied by the Soviets, or returning through Finland and the Scandinavian countries. However, I had a very good friend in General Smith, the U.S. ambassador, who offered me his plane in mid-February to go from Berlin to Paris. We therefore would only have to take the Moscow-Berlin train, which is what we decided to do as soon as possible. In early January, I was able to confirm that February 1 would be the date of our departure . . . provided the Soviets co-operated.

The month of January 1948 went by quickly, one farewell reception on the heels of the other. Our exit visas arrived on January 15. On the evening of the 27th, in the presence of fifty or so friends who had come to the railway station to bid us farewell, we embarked on the train to Berlin. It was to be a long trip for our young children. What could one do with them inside a compartment for over three days? In addition, we had to switch trains in Brest-Litovsk, as the Russian rail gauge was wider than the European one. Everything went well. My wife took care of the baby while I entertained the other two children, reading them stories and drawing little Walt Disney characters.

Outside, it was cold and one could hardly go out at stopovers. Near Warsaw, the train suddenly started going very slowly. I then noticed men climbing onto our railway car while others handed them boxes that seemed to contain dynamite. I told my wife and children to lie down under the seats and I went out in the corridor to see what was going on. You could hear people running on the roof. Fortunately, nothing else happened. When a Soviet general went by me, I asked him whether this was "a demonstration of friendship." He did not seem to appreciate my remark. We finally arrived in Warsaw—emotions and all. An hour later, we were on our way to Berlin, where we landed next day and were welcomed by General Pope and his lovely wife. Twenty-four hours later, on February 2, General Smith's plane took us to Paris. Colonel Dollard Ménard, our military attaché in France, welcomed us and took us to the Hôtel Napoléon, on Friedland Street. Simone was seeing Paris for the first time. We all had a good day's rest before starting our visits. After one week, the family embarked for London. Upon our arrival at the Dorchester Hotel, Simone sighed: "My God, it's good to be home." We were still thousands of miles from Canada when I heard that cry from the heart, and I knew exactly what she meant.

The impact of the Moscow stay on my career was quite significant. It made me much more confident in my capabilities, and it also made me understand that Russia, with all its many facets that I was able to perceive, had not strayed much from the mainstream of its history; the communist philosophy had merely accentuated certain characteristics that were already there. The Tsars and their courtiers had not really disappeared. The Russians had gone from a despot with a moth-eaten Orthodox philosophy to an atheist philosophy, which, like its predecessor, had no notion of fundamental freedoms. As the Marquis de Custine put it in his letters from Russia, "The Russian only sees two things, the cradle and the grave . . . he is laughing and crying at the same time." And, further on, "If your son is unhappy in France, send him to Russia and you will make a good Frenchman out of him."

Control of the people through spying completely terrorized them. They were told they were free, but they could only improve their standard of living by jumping into bed with the Communist Party. The people had also a difficult time improving their living conditions, because it was virtually impossible for them to buy (non-existent) consumer goods and because prices, controlled by the state, made such goods as there were inaccessible. The privileged of the system at the time of the Tsars were the descendants of the great families raised to respect orthodoxy. Now, their counterparts came from the privileged classes via the Komsomol (Young Communist League). The peasants were as poor (if not more so) than before 1917. The main building of a 1947 kolkhoz was no better than would have been the case in the 19th century. Women had retained their privileges, which included, among others, the right to load hay with pitchforks and to do back-breaking physical work. The Russians had lost their churches and priests, which were replaced by propaganda centres (Agitpunkt) where agitators sermoned them unceasingly. The greatest differences in comparison to the pre-1919 era were the philosophical justification of violence and the internationalization of the Soviet doctrine (which no longer had much in common with either Marxism or Communism).

The Soviet Union has invented nothing that would indicate the emergence of a "new man." Athletes are the government's favourite sons. Aside from being very few, artists who perform internationally are a distorting mirror of the people themselves. The workers and the masses are only slaves serving a privileged class. The Soviets have added nothing to the Russians' patriotism, for the people have always loved their country. Whether against Napoleon in 1812 or Hitler in 1942, they have shown the same courage and received the same reward: "the cradle and the grave."

Even the simplest peasant is a charming, remarkable person. He is both high in spirits and fatalistic. He submits because he cannot do anything about it. The Party man is a liar and a scoundrel. The privileges accrue to him because he is loyal to the dogma. He is cruel because Lenin told him that the end justified the means. Workers of the world, unite! Yes indeed, to give the privileged the right of life or death over those around them.

During my stay in the USSR, I often recalled a thought I had sometimes in

1944, in Italy, while we were crawling up the peninsula so slowly and painfully that it seemed the war would never end. I knew, though, that the Soviets were making increasingly astonishing advances towards the heart of Europe. Being already strongly opposed to Marxist philosophy, I thought that we should have stabilized the Italian front and invaded the Balkans, with Turkey's favourable complicity, in order to reach Central Europe via Vienna, thus participating in the liberation of large areas that Yalta was subsequently going to abandon to the USSR. Events turned out differently, at a time when the whole world was prey to confusion. The misfortunes of Eastern Europe therefore continued in spite of the German defeat.

I left the USSR happy to be finally able to breathe the freedom of our own political-economic systems, no matter how imperfect they may be. I was also happy to have remained loyal to my Christian faith, even if those who claim to have it are sometimes far from perfect. Having been received among those people, I came back. To adopt Custine's saying I was a better Canadian than ever, swearing to fight, without weapons (as much as possible) or hatred, this philosophy, under whatever guise it might present itself to me.

7

Quebec, London, Ottawa, 1948-1953

After a few days in London the family returned to Canada by ship. From Halifax we went to Montreal where Simone's parents were awaiting us. After a good celebration, we had to start thinking of our trip to Quebec City, where I was to succeed Paul Bernatchez as commander of Eastern Quebec area. The Canadian Army, headquartered in Ottawa, was divided into five regional commands, the two largest of which—Quebec and Ontario (called Central)—were subdivided into areas.

Upon our arrival in Quebec City, we lived temporarily at the Château Frontenac before moving in early March 1948 to the commander's residence at 59 Saint-Louis Street. This move turned out to be more complicated than expected. Our furnishings had been quite sufficient for the small, six-room dwelling we had had in Moscow. Our new residence, however, resembled the old private mansions, where one could house a dozen staff on the top floor. In the end, we only used two of the three floors available. The ceilings were thirteen feet high. Each room measured, on average, 450 square feet, while the second-floor hallway had another 500 feet. We quickly found that our entire furniture could fit into just one of these huge rooms. Moreover, the windows were ten feet high by four feet wide. Nothing we possessed matched this new setup. We therefore had to buy furniture, drapes, curtains. We were quite happy with the rugs the Army agreed to lend us in order to round out our meagre possessions in this area.

When we went to Paquet's store, we found that the total of our potential purchases would vastly exceed my bank account. An old friend of mine from Trois-Rivières was the manager of the local Bank of Commerce. With nothing but my word as collateral he lent me the funds required, equivalent to six months' wages. I was not overly concerned because I was to receive shortly an allowance for my wartime service, which would enable me to reduce that debt by half. Everything was finally ready and we had a house-warming with approximately forty guests. This marked the beginning of a happy and fruitful stay in a city which, after Moscow, seemed like paradise to us. In the meantime, our two school-age children had started attending Miss Aubry's lycée.

I still had no car beside the one provided by the government, which could not be used for other than official functions. Fortunately, my salary was over $20 a day. After paying off the bank loan during the first year, I bought a small English car, a Morris Minor, which cost about $2,000, and with this acquisition our comfort was complete.

My superiors wanted the successor of Bernatchez (who had been posted to Ottawa) to establish, like him, good relations with the local population. In addition to being born in Quebec City, Simone had a distant cousin from Trois-Rivières who had left his mark: Prime Minister Maurice Duplessis. Paul Sauvé, a provincial minister, was a wartime comrade of mine. We therefore quickly became a part of the social life of Quebec City.

I barely knew Duplessis since I had not followed the beginnings of his political career. I knew, though, that he was a sports fan, although to my knowledge he practised no sport. We knew in Trois-Rivières that when he could help the young practise a sport, he did not hesitate to devote his time and money to that cause. In my mind he had remained that generous man who had many times helped the youth in his area.

It was thus in 1948 that I started forging real links with Duplessis. In my position, I had to deal a lot with his government. I had to provide some military pomp and circumstance for the opening of the legislative sessions as well as assistance for the civilian authorities—which would have to be provided on some occasions during my stint.

Duplessis knew me before my arrival in Quebec City through the newspapers and conversations he had often had with his Trois-Rivières constituents. At our very first meeting he said he was proud to be dealing with a fellow "Trifluvian." His secretary, Miss Cloutier, was an old acquaintance of mine. Indeed, her brother owned a restaurant near the cathedral in Trois-Rivières. It was a popular meeting place for the local youth in the 1930s, and Maurice Duplessis' future secretary had often served us there. Thanks to her but also to the goodwill of her boss, it was easy for me to meet with the Premier when necessary. Two or three times I entered his office ahead of one or more waiting Union Nationale ministers, which flattered me somewhat.

Duplessis was a nice man, and I greatly enjoyed being in his company. He loved baseball. One day, he invited me to a game when his beloved Yankees were playing. Another time, we made a bet with each other on a Yankee-Dodgers game. The Dodgers won. Sometime later, Simone (whom he used to call "my cousin") received a huge fruit basket in the centre of which was the amount he had lost. For all these reasons, I went to his funeral in Trois-Rivières in 1959. It was a suffocatingly hot day and in full dress uniform, I stood up to the incredible heat and shared the mourning of the people of Trois-Rivières.

To conclude this aside, I shall add that I always admired Maurice Duplessis. However, we had absolutely no political links. I now find that some people often level vicious accusations against him or his government, when he is no longer around to defend himself. The period during which he governed Quebec was not one of darkness, as some glibly state. A product of the seminary of Trois-Rivières, influenced by Bishop Laflèche, Duplessis was a man with deep roots who understood the people of Quebec in his own way. He governed according to the circumstances of the moment, without great designs for the future. This seems to be what Quebeckers wanted at the time because they kept re-electing him.

I would certainly not want to leave the impression that my time in Quebec was spent in the offices of the provincial government. My functions at that level were only an infinitesimal part of my activities. What a change with respect to the rather boring (and tense) life I had led in Moscow! My new tasks were focused strictly on administration and organization. My efforts were devoted primarily to two goals: setting up the R22^{e}R comfortably on a peacetime footing in the Quebec Citadel and reorganizing the militia in my area, ensuring its training at Valcartier.

My office, located in the Post Office building on Buade Street, was spacious and well organized. I was always there and always busy. To mention a major concern first: the Citadel was decrepit and virtually in ruins, its maintenance having been badly neglected since 1914, owing to lack of funds. Fortunately, Paul Bernatchez had obtained $150,000 to restore the men's barracks. This was clearly insufficient, but that was all he had received.

At that time, the unemployment rate in Quebec City was high, although still below today's levels. There were already some subsidies that attempted to correct the situation. The member of Parliament for Quebec East was none other than the Honourable Louis St. Laurent. I quickly learned to benefit from the situation. I took advantage of an opportunity to tell him, in highly unorthodox fashion, that I had work to be done that could keep many workers busy. I obtained another $150,000. With $300,000, I could prepare an overall plan. My engineer, Coulombe, was put in charge of the project and he and the draftsman, Plamondon, started to sharpen their pencils. I had decided that we would use no architects or contractors to manage the worksite. We were going to be project managers, no matter how hard we had to work. In spite of my many other tasks, I would personally visit the site, on average twice a week.

Coulombe was competent, imaginative and hard-working. His draftsman was an artist who knew how to put our concepts on paper. When allowed to run with the ball, he came up with solutions that exceeded by far what I thought was possible and always within a reasonable budget. The best example was the restoration of the Jebb redoubt housing the NCO's mess, with its unique staircase. Taking advantage of other grants under the same federal programme, I later undertook the restoration of the Connaught Barracks and of the historical residence I was occupying, which was just about falling apart. I was very proud of the results achieved because all the buildings involved were part of a heritage that no one had yet started to protect in an organized fashion.

At the R22^{e}R, there was a visitors' fund that had been set up by Georges Vanier when he was lieutenant-colonel. It contained $1,500 administered by a committee chaired by the area commander and comprising four other members, including the commanding officer of the regiment, Lieutenant-Colonel Guy Roberge. One day, he came to my office to ask me to call a meeting of the committee. I was not even aware that the fund existed. I thus found out that Major Georges Guimont, a veteran of World War I, was its secretary. I summoned him so that he could give me some explanations about the fund. A very meticulous man, Guimont brought me his minute book as well as the statutes that specified what the money could be used for. I then recalled Roberge, who wanted to use a good portion of the $1,500 to repair the Vimy Cross, which was rotting away. It was suggested that we take advantage of the opportunity to place the cross on a granite base with a suitable inscription. The cost estimate was $1,400. At that point, I asked how the money had been collected. I was told that tourists were charged 25 cents for a guided tour of the Citadel, the guides being members of the regular forces. I then called together the committee, which approved the necessary amount.

An examination of the statutes, however, led us to conclude that using members of the regular forces as guides should, henceforth be forbidden since that was certainly not their function. How could we then replenish the visitors' fund? After a little discussion, I suggested to the members of the committee that we should organize things on another basis, namely, as a non-profit organization that would hire veterans as guides. Since I was the commander, they all agreed. But, deep down, nobody really believed in the feasibility of such a project. In the meantime, Roberge retired and Gilles Turcot took over. I told him about the matter. At that time, the men's mess, which needed expansion, moved to the casemates, which freed up the old gunpowder store. I asked Turcot about the suitability of turning that building, which had been constructed under the French regime by Chaussegros de Léry, into a museum. Gilles received the idea enthusiastically and began estimating the costs. Lieutenant-Colonel R. Vennes, a friend of the regiment and commandant of the local Officer School but also an architect, offered his services and those of his firm free of charge. The project was launched and Gilles gathered some veterans.

Informed of the project, Mayor Lucien Borne encouraged us to pursue it to help boost tourism in Quebec City, but he could not assist us financially, and we knew that. Vennes brought us his plans and estimates. Gilles submitted them to one of his friends, contractor J. Rourke, who agreed to do the work at cost. We nevertheless had to find about $10,000 to cover the cost of restoration and furnishing. My bank manager, once again, had faith in me.

There was still a big problem: what should be placed in the museum? While Gilles supervised the restoration, I once again appealed to Major Georges Guimont to collect exhibition items. He could not believe his ears, and it was without much optimism that he undertook to recover old items of some value. His appeal to the generosity of the people of Quebec, however, was well received. Still, what he was able to find for us was not enough. Through my good friend, Brigadier Jack Price, who had himself contributed to our effort, I contacted the curator of the McCord Museum of McGill University in Montreal, who agreed to lend me a collection pertaining to the military history of Quebec City. We had won. We then decided to raise the admission fee to 50 cents. Based on a conservative estimate of the number of visitors, the financing of our project seemed assured. In fact, the museum admitted during its very first season twice as many people as we had estimated. We were thus able to finance everything: the restoration, the overhead, the wages of the guides under Georges Guimont, whom I had the committee hire on a full time basis. When the committee was later assembled in a plenary meeting, all it had to do was review the decisions made and read a balance sheet showing a surplus of over $10,000.

Like myself, Lieutenant-Colonel Gilles Turcot took the restoration of the Citadel to heart. With an ally of this calibre, we quickly transformed the Citadel into a barracks envied by all. The basic architecture of Colonel Dunsford, of the British Army, was protected by men like Coulombe, Plamondon and Turcot who managed to retain, in spite of the modernization, the old, historical appearance of that magnificent monument.

The last restoration I undertook was that of the Champ de Mars. At its centre, prior to our intervention, was a brick stable. One evening, Gilles and I led a tactical exercise with militia officers in the Trois-Pistoles area. Gilles' wife Helen reached him by telephone to tell him that the stable, used as a garage for the Governor General's car, was in flames. She added that the fire trucks were unable to pass through the gate into the interior of the Citadel. She assured me that no one was in danger. Once she told me that, I said: "Let it burn!" Upon our return, I found that the walls were liable to collapse, and I therefore had the garage demolished. The car of the Governor General, who had a residence inside the Citadel, would henceforth be parked in a sector of the casemates. I then asked Plamondon to prepare for me the drawings of a ceremonial staircase to be installed at the entrance to the Champ de Mars. All that was left to do was to obtain the money required for its construction and for the levelling and paving of the parade ground that had now been cleared.

A few days prior to the fire, I had received from Prime Minister King's office a message asking me to suggest a place where two historical plaques could be placed in order to mark the spot where a conference between major allied political and military leaders had been held during the war. Since these were President Roosevelt, Prime Minister Winston Churchill and Mackenzie King himself, I said to myself that here was perhaps a chance to slip through my staircase project. Before replying, I decided nevertheless to consult the Governor General, Field Marshal Alexander. He accepted my proposal immediately, with a knowing smile. As a good soldier, he knew full well why I went to him. Indeed, following his recommendation, I received permission to proceed a few days later.

During the restoration of the Connaught Barracks we discovered the bones of American General Montgomery's soldiers killed on December 31, 1775. The U.S. consul was informed, and at my suggestion, the remains were buried along the road leading to the Citadel. The consul, Mr. Carols, placed a plaque on a stone detached from the cliff where these unfortunate men had been killed. In order to mark the event properly, he proposed that the inscription should be unveiled by the Chairman of the Honorable Artillery Company of Massachussetts, which was in fact a circle of retired officers who were financially very well-off. They came to visit us at their own expense, held a parade and offered a buffet at Château Frontenac. One of them gave a Parker pen to any passerby who smiled at him in the street. Altogether, a nice (not overly serious) ceremony and an opportunity to honour our American friends.

Upon my arrival, in 1948, Major-General R. O. Morton, G.O.C. Quebec Command, entrusted me with responsibility for the entire Command regarding the summer training camps at Valcartier. I knew Morton well and liked him. We had other opportunities to work together. He was bilingual, but his French was still somewhat limited, and he was thus happy that a French Canadian would be able to continue, after Bernatchez, to take care of his reserve troops, which consisted mostly of francophones. I would like to add, for the record, that his nephew Desmond would later be one of the first graduates of the *Collège militaire royal de Saint-Jean* and, subsequently, an excellent military historian. To return to our story, the job with the militia was not going to be an easy one. It had been foreseen that Valcartier was going to receive the Quebec units for two weeks. Moreover, the qualification courses for young militia officers and NCOs would be offered there; the R22^{e}R was to provide instruction to the members of the C.O.T.C.

All of this would take a great deal of my time. I therefore decided to move the bulk of my headquarters over there. It was no secret that the camp barracks were in very poor condition. We had high hopes, though, of preparing the necessary space for all our activities by spending some money and doing a lot of work. For some reason, the Valcartier camp had been declared "surplus asset," and was well in the process of being demolished. The kitchen facilities (refrigerators, doors, and so forth) had already been removed and the hospital was being demolished, when, quite angry, I stopped all that. Fortunately, the infrastructure had not been touched, and the stores and shops were in operational condition.

For our summer programme to be successful, we needed everything that was there and then some. The restoration to operating condition of the Valcartier facilities turned out to be very useful when we mobilized for the Korean War two years later. For the time being, the funds provided in the budget were insufficient. In order to stay within our allowance, I therefore used the R22^{e}R's pioneer platoon, the part-time and full-time civilian employees of the Department and materials salvaged from the demolition. This did not prevent a few skirmishes with the Treasury Board, which nevertheless quickly buried the hatchet, undoubtedly because of the good overall relations it had with our Department. Thus, in the midst of all these difficulties and in spite of the short time available, we were able to fulfil our mandate for 1948, although not in the best possible manner.

One should recall here that after the war of 1939-45 the government had reduced the strength of the Army from nearly half a million men to fewer than 25,000. Matériel and armament had been disposed of high-handedly. Once again, this indicated an unforgivable lack of perspective on the part of the government. The world situation was far from sufficiently improved to justify such a gesture. The Gouzenko affair should have given our parliamentarians some food for thought. Returning from the Soviet Union, I had a less optimistic view than our political leaders about the general context in which we were living. Our army had in effect been returned to its pre-war role of providing a professional training framework for the militia and, in times of crisis, for those who would be mobilized.

Since the war, the R22^{e}R had done no serious training, limiting itself to ceremonial duties. The arrival of Gilles Turcot at the head of the regiment brought it back to reality. Between early summer 1948 and mid-September it became vigorous again. Apparently soft and gentle, Turcot had the strong hand of a good commander and under his rule many things changed. Around a better-led regiment, the 1949 camp looked more promising than the previous one.

In addition, I spent a lot of time with the militia. I began by inspecting the units of Quebec City. They had an advantage over the others in my area, namely excellent barracks in the two permanent arsenals and the temporary buildings left by the war. The officer and NCO corps were made up of experienced veterans, and the recruits benefited from that experience.

During the winter, after meetings with Major-General Morton, who maintained his summer training policy, two of his staff officers were placed at my disposal: Lieutenant-Colonel Paul Garneau and Captain Duncan MacAlpine, who had to prepare the 1949 summer programme, which was going to be more realistic and coherent than that of the previous year.

This assistance freed my hands somewhat, and I was able to devote my attention to the units outside Quebec City. Major "Tony" Poulin, who was accompanying me, organized three long inspection tours. Tony, who knew me well, did some invaluable preparation work. We first went to the Lac Saint-Jean region, then to the Eastern Townships, then to the Chaudière, Lower Saint-Lawrence and the Gaspé.

I learned a great deal on this tour, and I was able to correct some problems immediately, while others were settled through budgetary action. One of the issues I was confronted with was surprising. It arose shortly after my return to Quebec City. One morning, I received a letter from a Gaspé militiaman asking me why he could not withdraw his pay directly. I did not immediately understand what he meant. Nevertheless, I had the military police investigate. The report I was given was highly revealing. The commander of the local militia was the owner of a general store. He received the pay of all his men and deposited it on their accounts with his store. I immediately relieved him of his command and ordered him to hand the money over to his men. I quickly put a stop to this disgusting practice which, as I learned a little later, was common in Gaspé. Attempts were made to make me change my mind, particularly by Lieutenant-Colonel J. D. Boswell of Quebec City and my quartermaster T. R. Burnside. Discreetly but firmly, I let them know who was in charge.

Towards the end of 1949 and early in 1950, things were moving along fast. In spite of a certain routine, the pace remained frantic. The restoration of the Citadel continued, the support to the militia units was improved and their numbers, although still limited, nevertheless made substantial progress.

The regular Army had just been given the task of defending the Canadian North and the order to train its men as paratroopers. At the same time, I lost

Lieutenant-Colonel Turcot, who was posted to London. I had a hard time choosing his replacement, and in the end, I settled on Major Louis-Frémont Trudeau, who had served with me in Italy. His task would be a difficult one. In order to help him, I decided to follow the regiment to Rivers, Manitoba, where the R22^{e}R was to receive parachute training. To me, it was a revelation. After five years of social and administrative life, my physical condition was not as good as at the end of the war. When I saw the men of the R22^{e}R emerge without any sign of fatigue after strenuous physical exercise, I felt rusty. But I was not going to give up at the age of 35. My sense of duty forced me to make rapid progress. The young corporals had fun watching their area commander sweat. I got my own back when the time came to jump from a plane. I was always the first of the stick, and before jumping, since I could not appear to be afraid, I stared into the eyes of the others in deadly silence. After the fifth jump we received our wings. The return to Quebec by train was a three-day party.

Having to take in hand the militia and to pass the parachute course brought me back to the grassroots, so to speak, in very close contact with the officers and men who were about to take over from us. In Quebec City, daily routine took over, although new projects were launched. Since we lacked housing for our families, I began by restoring historical houses owned by the Department of National Defence in Quebec City. This included mine, at 55 Saint-Louis street, in which we were able to create three dwellings. (We moved to number 4 Côte de la Citadelle, which had just been restored and was a convenient and comfortable residence.) But these three new dwellings were far from sufficient. Following a discussion with Prime Minister St. Laurent, some land was purchased at Ste-Foy in order to build approximately one hundred more. This did not meet our most urgent needs, though, and we had to find something in the meantime. I considered Valcartier where several old buildings could be restructured. The minister authorized us to go ahead on the condition that the future occupant would do the renovation himself. Rent was set at $16 per month. Many considered this a bargain. Under the supervision of our engineers the work began, and about sixty families soon moved in.

At that point new problems arose. First of all, there was no school closer than ten miles and no grocery store. In addition, there were few recreational opportunities. Something had to be done. In order to solve the school problems, I asked Bishop Roy whether he knew some nuns who would be prepared to run a primary school. He told me that the sisters of Notre-Dame-du-Bon-Conseil would perhaps be willing to do so. I contacted them and they agreed to come provided they were given appropriate housing and a decent school. These requirements being truly minimal, the work was undertaken without delay. Without a budget it was the children's fathers, under the supervision of the engineers, who altered the buildings for their future role. We also opened a mess that provided basic material comfort.

Another problem was somewhat more difficult to solve. It was virtually impossible to find day care for the children, particularly the babies. After a great deal of hesitation, I decided to open a daycare centre. This was a major undertaking. I quickly realized that the Department was absolutely not ready to accept the responsibilities this implied. For a while, I was not quite sure what to do. Then, tacitly, I left it up to the parents, who understood that I would look the other way, provided they organized things among themselves. With the assistance of a registered nurse, they used one of the now-vacant temporary residences and turned it into a daycare centre, which made everyone happy. The situation was saved, although Ottawa read the riot act to me when they got wind of the facts. Nobody, however, dared close down the centre.

During the second half of May 1950, two great fires enabled our soldiers to reveal their many talents. Returning from a brief stay in Chicoutimi while travelling with Simone by car through Laurentides Park, I heard on the radio that a serious fire was raging in Rimouski. As soon as I arrived in Quebec City, I tried to contact the provincial authorities to find out whether our soldiers could be of any assistance. It was Sunday and the ministers were unavailable. Moreover, I was aware that Quebec was known for its reluctance to appeal to the military authorities.

But the situation was serious. Rimouski asked me for assistance. Unfortunately, I could do nothing officially without the permission of the provincial Attorney-General, whose business it was to contact me directly for aid to the civil authorities (different from aid to the civil power, which was used in October 1970, for example). However, I could get things underway, even though I might have to cancel everything if our intervention were deemed unnecessary. I therefore made an appeal through the local radio station in order to recall to Valcartier our men who were on weekend leave. Thus alerted, they began to gather all the equipment we had that could be used either to fight the fire or to relieve the problems of the victims. All the material (a fire-fighting water pump, pickaxes, shovels, field stoves, tents) was loaded onto trucks and the convoy got underway early Monday morning.

I arrived in Rimouski on Sunday by plane. Flying over the area, I saw the extent of the damage. The west of the city was in flames,and a strong wind was pushing the fire eastward. Next day, the Mayor of the City, Doctor Victor Lepage, and his council agreed to sign a form authorizing me to have my men serve under the control of the local authorities. This provided cover while I awaited the official request that Antoine Rivard was to send me later. In any case, through prudence and out of respect for the formalities involved, we waited until I received it before we went into action.

Our soldiers responded well. They mounted the field kitchens in the local arena where both firefighters and the displaced population could have meals. Using their vehicles they also participated in the evacuation of the sick from the hospital to the agricultural school. In order to prevent the fire from jumping over to the roof of the cathedral, they blew up the neighbouring orphanage, which was already burning at the top. The effect of this was to stop the fire in that area. They controlled the flames that had begun to eat away at the technical school.

There were several incidents worth mentioning. The hoses we had brought with us were not compatible with the city's equipment. We were only able to use our fire-fighting pump in the immediate vicinity of the river, because it could at least use that source of water. The local prison was emptied of its least-dangerous inmates and those approaching the end of their sentence, so they could join the firefighters.

Some parts of the city were evacuated, as was the liquor store. In the burnt areas there was the occasional safe that had withstood the fire and protected its contents. It was decided that the military would guard these various points against potential looters. During the night, a Toronto journalist attempted to cross a guard post and our men, armed but without ammunition, prevented him from doing so. Next day, there was a headline in the *Globe and Mail* saying that the town was under martial law. Some people in Canada wondered whether or not we may have "overreacted" to the situation. These concerns quickly disappeared.

Food trucks soon began arriving from the United States, particularly from Maine. Money was also sent to help the local victims. In the name of the King, Governor General Alexander sent to the local workers, who had lost everything, tool boxes that enabled them to return to work quickly. He also came to inspect the place, but no local official was there to receive him. Even the local bishop had something else to do.

The fire was more or less under control when we found out that Cabano was also burning. Canon Cyr, the priest in Cabano asked us to come. By telephone, Rivard agreed. The experience we had just been through came in handy. Thus, I had roadblocks set up on all roads leaving Cabano. Vehicles carrying household goods or objects that could be stolen, were stopped. If proof of ownership could not be established the goods were sent to a field where the owners could later recover them. It takes strange people to try and take advantage of someone else's misfortune. We helped restore some order in the city before leaving it—it was almost completely ravaged. We lent a great deal of equipment to the Red Cross which, long after our return to Valcartier, was still able to use it in the two stricken areas. On May 25 and 26, I accompanied Mr. St. Laurent on visits to Rimouski and Cabano, to express his sympathies to the local people.

These were not the only occasions on which we assisted the authorities. Earlier, we had fought a forest fire near Saint-Antoine-sur-le-Richelieu, and we had brought under control the sector near Issoudun where an aircraft had crashed, killing all its many passengers. Each time, in spite of my good relationship with the Quebec government, people created difficulties or hesitated to call upon our services. In Valcartier and Quebec City, our military men, good French Canadians, natives of the stricken areas or having relatives there, had trouble understanding such an attitude.

The summer of 1950 arrived without any major events. Some 150 men of the R22^{e}R acted as extras in an American movie recounting the highly romanticized events of 1837. The militia summer camps started, and then, suddenly, on June 25, Communist North Korea crossed the 38th parallel. On June 28, while the North Korean army was consolidating its positions around Seoul, the United Nations asked its member countries, including Canada, to participate in the effort it was preparing to undertake in order to stop the North Korean aggression. If I remember correctly, I received the order to prepare the mobilization of a battalion well before the Prime Minister announced publicly, on August 7, that the army would add its presence to the naval and air elements Canada was already providing in Korea. The Canadian Army's contribution was going to be about equivalent to one infantry brigade, and this a mere five years following the brutal demobilization I mentioned earlier. Obviously, sending 7,000 men to Korea while the army had a total of only approximately 16,000 would further seriously deplete the home front, which was not particularly well covered in any case.

In my sector, the R22^{e}R, although quite ready, was reserved for the defence of the Canadian North. I therefore had to start from scratch and set up a new unit, which was to become the second battalion of the R22^{e}R. Luckily, since I had sufficiently restored Valcartier over the two previous years, the second battalion could be lodged there. For our purposes, the most logical plan would have been to mingle newcomers with members of the first battalion of the regular army. What complicated matters was that Defence Minister Brooke Claxton announced that the majority, at all levels, would come from the militia. Who, among the militia, was going to leave his job to go fight another war after having been demobilized only five years earlier? Among NCOs and men some were no doubt going to come along. Among officers, I was afraid that we were going to receive primarily those who had not been able to adjust to civilian life or who were unemployed. That was just about what happened. We then had to upgrade the discipline quickly and retrain them professionally. It was not an easy task. I was relieved to be told that we could put in some regular army officers. The commander, however, had to come from the militia. Whom should I take, who would be of a sufficiently high calibre to assume command without retraining? I knew only one, a man who had served under my command in the 6th Brigade during World War II and of whom I had since lost sight: Lieutenant-Colonel Jacques Dextraze. He had been working since his demobilization, as I learned later, on forest operations for the Singer Company. I proposed his name to Major-General Morton, who forwarded it to Ottawa. After a preliminary examination of his file, General Foulkes contacted me to ensure that the choice of Dextraze still suited me. I approved without reservation and Ottawa contacted him. Dextraze accepted and set out to join his new battalion at Valcartier. He arrived there in early October and officially took command on October 10, following a large parade on Charest Boulevard, attended by Louis St. Laurent, accompanied by General Thomas Tremblay (the spiritual father of the regiment) and myself. The second battalion then embarked for Fort Lewis (Washington State, U.S.A.) to complete its training before leaving for Korea. Thanks to an excellent staff and to the dedication of Louis-Frémont Trudeau, his officers and NCOs, another mission had been successfully accomplished.

But I was not going to see the battalion's departure towards the western United States. On the previous day, November 21, 1950, I embarked on the S.S. *Franconia* at Quebec City, sailing for London. Let us go back a little. One morning in August, feeling ill, I had gone to the military hospital. An hour later, Doctor Amyot Jolicoeur gave me a general anesthetic and removed my appendix. The same evening I was up and about, and five days later I returned home. During my convalescence, which took another ten days, the Chief of the General Staff, Lieutenant-General Foulkes, sent me the message that I had been chosen to spend a sabbatical year at the Imperial Defence College in London and asked me whether I had any major objection to that. I replied that I was very satisfied with the decision . . . and in good shape (I had already resumed my activities at Valcartier). Two weeks later, the news was announced officially, and Colonel Maurice DeRome arrived in Quebec City to replace me on a temporary basis. I was the first French-Canadian officer to be admitted to that college.

My niece, Irène Rousseau, crossed the Atlantic and stayed with us in England. In London, we were pleased to see again Gilles Turcot, a member of the Canadian military delegation in Great Britain, with his family. We settled in at 13 Chapel Street, in the immediate vicinity of fashionable Belgrave Square. From our residence, I could reach the College as well as Buckingham Palace in five minutes. Our three children were admitted to the French Lycée in London. While awaiting the beginning of the course (January 1951) but also during the free moments during the course (weekends, leaves) we had an opportunity to travel through England. There was London with all its beauty and possibilities. The Opera, the St. James Theatre, the famous cinemas in Leicester Square, the Folies Bergères (where we discovered a compatriot who was going to become a friend; Jacques Labrecque). We went to superb concerts at Albert Hall and Town Hall. We saw exhibitions of all sorts, art galleries, Kew Gardens, and historical sites such as the Tower of London. When friends from Quebec stopped by, the family was happy to have them discover Eton, Oxford, Windsor Castle, Hampton Court, ending the tour at the Talbot Inn, at Ripley (where Lady Hamilton used to meet her lover, Admiral Lord Nelson). We also visited other places. To the north of London, we went to Saint Albans, built on the ruins of a Roman city. There, we visited the cathedral where Edward the Confessor had been dean. In Kent, we passed by Dickens's house, magnificently preserved, where one could see his collected works. There were also little statues representing the characters he had created. I had liked Dickens since the time I had gone to college in Kitchener. It was by reading his works that I had learned a good portion of my literary English. Furthermore, I was attracted by his heroes because, being young, I often identified with them.

I was not in England, however, only to play tourist. The Imperial College was an institution established after the First World War. Candidates came there from the entire British Commonwealth in order to study subjects such as public administration, strategy and international politics. This enabled each of them to familiarize himself with British civil institutions and also to become acquainted with civil and military colleagues (from the three arms) with whom, some day, he might well be called upon to serve or fight.

During the course, we welcomed great leaders of every nationality. Churchill, Attlee, Noel Baker, Eisenhower and the ambassadors of the countries represented in London came to meet us and to speak to us on specific topics. Moreover, we were divided into teams of eight members each which had to find solutions to political, economic and military problems of the kind usually analyzed by the top of the political pyramid of our democratic countries. I remember one question our group (number 6) had to study: the lessons of the past. In our report, we reviewed the constants of British foreign policy and its military strategy over the last two centuries, before dealing with the specific lessons the last war had taught us, including psychological warfare and the support to groups which, from within, had resisted the enemy we were fighting. Our conclusion agreed with that of Lord Tedder in "Air Power in War." A country had to understand that modern war was more than just a series of battles. It was a test of the will and strength of an entire nation. In order to be well-prepared for that test, the nation and its armies had to be aware of the latest technological innovations and their possibilities. Their grasp of the situation, at any time, had to be based on a correct assessment of the real nature and scope of wars as well as on the potential of the nation and on the lessons learned between 1939 and 1945.

Like all the others, this group exercise was highly instructive, and some of the conclusions we reached after some discussion were to stay with me for ever. In addition to mandatory subjects, we were free to study a particular subject in greater detail. I decided to study the problems caused by borders because, according to a theory I held, 90 per cent of serious world problems were the result, directly or indirectly, of needless friction between peoples divided by borders.

The summer of 1951 was therefore largely devoted to verifying the correctness of my theory during a long and fruitful trip that took our entire group of students to the Mediterranean and just about everywhere in Africa, where there were already many territorial conflicts which have continued to this day. In particular, as I write this, such conflicts are going on in Lebanon, Chad, at the Iran-Iraq border and in southern Africa.

This extraordinary journey took us to Egypt, Iraq, Iran, Saudi Arabia, ex-Italian Somalia, Ethiopia, Kenya. In this last country, I had the opportunity to study an interesting situation. The Masai lived in south-western Kenya at that time of the year. The people of that tribe are in general very tall, intelligent and sensitive, and they speak a dialect different from that of the other Kenyans. We spent two marvellous days with them, including a night at Kenya's game park where I was able to see some lions chasing gazelles. For many centuries, the Masai have taken their cattle grazing on a plateau that lies in both Kenya and Tanzania. To them, there is nothing illegal in going from one country to the other. In fact, they do not even have a sense of country as we know it in the West. Furthermore, they have no acceptable alternative. It is impossible to climb higher in the mountains, for pastures are rare, while descending into the plains meant to be subjected to all kinds of diseases but particularly to the terrifying tse-tse fly. For the time being, the two countries turned a blind eye to these annual border violations. But who knows what lies in the future?

From Kenya, we went to Rhodesia before returning via Uganda, then up the Nile to sail from Khartoum to Egypt. I had known Egypt since the war. In 1951, a revolution was underway and instability was in the air; the country was divided. Three years later, Nasser succeeded in bringing about a lasting consensus. From Egypt, we crossed to Cyprus, which was at the time an earthly paradise. Then on to Greece where there were border conflicts, particularly with Yugoslavia and Turkey. We finally returned to London.

As a result of my collection of data, I could write my final report. Throughout these travels, I often wondered to what extremes human stupidity could go, and I never found a sure-fire, definitive answer. In fact, I wonder whether there is one.

My stay was near its end. Prior to my departure for London, I had been given to understand that I would return as Chief of Staff at the Western Command Headquarters. Around November 1951, I was told that these plans had changed. The minister had been approached to approve my appointment as Vice-Quartermaster-General, at Army HQ at Ottawa. This fitted quite well into my career plan because I had never yet served in Ottawa. At the very centre of our system, having been a area commander, I would be in a better position to know the magnitude of the issues the Quartermaster-General faces as the operational army constantly seeks to obtain various services from him. According to the Chief of the General Staff, Guy Simonds, one advantage of my appointment would be that this would bring another high-ranking francophone officer to Ottawa, where they were few in number.

On December 10, the minister approved my appointment. Twelve days later, I arrived in New York by ship.* Between then and the time when I assumed my new position, that is, January 4, 1952, Simone and I had no time to linger. The year-end holidays, the new home to be found and its setting up made real recreation opportunities rare.

In order to explain the nature of my new job a little, I must dwell briefly on the three major branches at Army headquarters, which extended to all the lower levels of the hierarchy. The first branch is the general staff and covers the major area such as operations, intelligence, training. The second is that of the Adjutant-General, who deals with personnel matters (selection, recruiting, etc.) and with personnel services such as pay, dental and medical care and the messes. Finally, the Quartermaster-General is responsible for housing, transportation, provisioning, clothing, ammunition, engineering services, and so forth. The Vice-Quartermaster-General, a brigadier acting as the deputy of the Major-General, is deeply involved in these matters of supply at all echelons.

My attention over the next twenty months was devoted primarily to two major subjects. I will mention first the one that took the lesser part of my time but was dear to my heart, the one that was going to have a massive medium-term (and, I hope, long-term) impact, and to which I was going to return at the very end of my career. This was the place francophones must occupy within the Army and, particularly at that time, the training of French-speaking officers.

However, before coming to that point, let us go back a little. The experience of the two wars had shown, among other things, that we had

* Simone and the children had returned to Canada before the beginning of the 1951 school year.

been ill-prepared to receive francophones in our Army. But for the existence of the R22^{e}R between the two great wars of the century, one would be justified in suspecting that, in 1939, Canada would have had to face the same general problem as in 1914. At least, in the later war, we had been able to count on the solid presence of francophone infantry battalions throughout the war. Through thick and thin, some artillery units had existed, as well as medical units. In the air, one squadron had had a majority of francophones among its flight crews, but they had all worked almost exclusively in English. In the thick of combat, the francophone senior officers had been unable to do much to improve the representation of our people in branches other than the infantry. Among ourselves, we nevertheless often discussed alternative solutions for the postwar period.

My absence from the country between 1945 and 1948 had not allowed me to act. Bernatchez, though, had taken the matter well in hand during a stint in Ottawa prior to taking command of Eastern Quebec area. He had attempted to persuade the authorities that the Army had to be opened up to francophones by creating opportunities for them in various units. Among other things, he had requested that a school be set up in Quebec where francophones could receive their basic training in their own language. Moreover, he had suggested that a francophone armoured squadron and artillery battery be created in the standing army. The Chief of the General Staff had been made aware of these recommendations but very little had been done. Certainly the massive demobilization mentioned earlier did not favour the establishment of new units. Nevertheless an all-arms training school was finally established at Saint-Jean in 1949—a first success. (Up to then, and this was to continue until 1950, the R22^{e}R had a detachment there to train its recruits. This "privilege" was therefore being extended to the other army recruits who would then go to the artillery, the tanks or elsewhere, obviously after they had been taught English.)

Then came the Korean affair. Since the effort initially agreed to by Canada was not enormous, there was no difficulty in filling the ranks of the R22^{e}R for Korea, except in one area: the officers. Indeed, approximately ten bilingual anglophones were included in the battalion, through sheer necessity. But one had to look beyond. Who was to say that, as in the two previous conflicts, Canada was not going to choose to increase its effort? How long was this war going to last?

Canada resumed mobilizing troops by tens of thousands. For the first time—if we exclude the Boer War—during a conflict our Prime Minister was a French Canadian. Furthermore, the Minister of Defence, Brooke Claxton, represented a county in the Montreal region. His parliamentary assistant in 1950 was Hugues Lapointe, the son of Ernest Lapointe and an ex-officer of the *Régiment de la Chaudière*. He was later replaced by another francophone. Claxton's Assistant Deputy Minister Paul Mathieu was, like Lapointe, a francophone ex-officer who had distinguished himself during the war by commanding the same regiment.

I don't know whether this string of coincidences played a role, but the fact is that Bernatchez, who was in Ottawa in 1950 as Assistant Adjutant-General, was appointed chairman of a committee to study "bilingual problems"—an euphemism that really meant the situation of francophones and the use of their language in the Army. In November 1950, that is, immediately prior to my leaving for London, Paul, who was doing his investigation, suggested to me that I might discuss unofficially with Monsignor Parent of Laval University the translation of the Army's manuals, with the direct or indirect involvement of the University. I contacted him, but the idea was not pursued any further.

The report of Bernatchez's task force was submitted in February 1951. I am not going to discuss it here since the Department of National Defence is about to write a major study on the history of francophones and their language in the Canadian Forces after 1946.* The historians assigned to this project will have had access to many documents and to correspondence that I have never seen. A small comment of appreciation, though: aside from the establishment of an anti-aircraft artillery unit at Picton in 1955 and from the fact that the 3 R22^{e}R was formed in 1951 as part of the Canadian military effort within NATO, one might say that the Bernatchez Report had no tangible impact, but it deserves praise for calling a spade a spade, explaining at length why French Canadians did not enlist. Moreover, our superiors promised— although, admittedly, they are always ready to make promises in this context but little inclined to action—that this report suggesting the establishment of French-language units outside the infantry would be acted upon during the next reorganization. (Every two or three years, the Army is reorganized, always for good reasons: post-war demobilization, commitments in Korea and to NATO. Still to come: preparation for nuclear war, integration and unification).

In 1951, an important debate began in the House of Commons. Young Léon Balcer, a Conservative Member of Parliament from the Trois-Rivières area, who had served in the Navy during the war, seized the numerous opportunities available to speak on National Defence in order to propose, in the spring of 1951, that French-language units be created outside the infantry within the Army, and in the Air Force and the Navy as well. He also

---

* This study, undertaken by Drs. Jean Pariseau and Serge Bernier, has now been published under the title *Les Canadiens français et le bilinguisme dans les Forces armées canadiennes,* Tome I, *1763-1969: Le Spectre d'une armée bicéphale* (1987), and is being translated into English.

proposed, regarding the shortage of francophone officers, that a third military college be established in Quebec, reserved for francophones who would be able to study there in French. Once again, I will not deal with all the details, since Jean-Yves Gravel has done it very well in *Le Québec et la guerre* (1974).

I nevertheless had to act on this matter in two ways. First of all, when I was in London, I met Ernest Côté, who was a neighbour, so to speak. Côté, an Alberta francophone and R22^{e}R field officer, had conducted himself brilliantly during World War II. His role in the preparation of the landing plans of the 3rd Division in Normandy had earned him a promotion and had brought him to Ottawa Headquarters, where he had been one of the rare French Canadians, as Deputy Vice-Adjutant-General. After the war, he had returned to civilian life, taking a position in the federal civil service, where he was to reach the highest levels. But in 1951 he was in London as First Secretary to our High Commissioner. In London, we saw each other almost every day on a friendly basis and, over drinks, we discussed this and that.

One of the topics that kept recurring was the representation of francophones in the Forces. I had thus expressed to him, as well as to others, my admiration for the student-officers graduated by the Royal Military College (for example, Generals Tremblay, Bernatchez, Gagnon, Richard and Harry Pope, whom I have already mentioned, all of them first-class soldiers), but also my own regret that I had not studied there. Another important detail, in view of what was to follow, was the fact that I had been a member for two years of the student-officer selection committee, where I had noted that French-Canadian candidates, often graduates of our classical high schools, in many cases had insufficient English, no scientific background and no preparation for military life. Indeed, we had in Quebec nothing comparable to the private anglophone colleges such as Ashbury or Upper Canada. Ernest agreed with me. In my opinion, in order to achieve something we had to seize every opportunity that the current situation provided. Balcer's initiative and the ensuing debate in Canada both in the papers and in Parliament paved the way. I therefore prepared a memo for the Chief of the General Staff, Guy Simonds. I must say that he had no great sympathy for the francophone cause, mainly—as he said—for reasons of efficiency. I must add that we were in perfect agreement on virtually all other points. And in order to dispel any doubts on this matter, let me say that he was a great soldier whom I admired and respected.

My memorandum was written with the assistance, and using the legal style, of my friend Côté. The concept I developed in it was that of a military academy. I opposed—wrongly, I now admit—the idea of a French-language military college because I believed at the time that French Canadians had to be able to measure themselves against the other officer-cadets, that is, those graduating from the RMC. We did not have enough of a military tradition, our schools were not oriented towards a potential military career, and our high school graduates often had only limited English. My military academy concept corrected these three problems by requiring admission to the academy after the ninth grade. For four years, study would be in French at the same time as special emphasis was placed on English. The courses would have to be designed so they would lead to acceptance at RMC, and our people would be surrounded by a semi-military atmosphere (uniforms, inspections, parades). The proposal did not provide details (for example, where the academy might be located), but it attempted to explain why the Canadian Officer Training Corps, open to francophone university students, had failed. Basically, it was because that programme kept its participants outside the military environment. Many had used it simply to get their studies free.

The memo, dated November 5, 1951, was sent to Simonds. In turn, Côté sent a copy on a highly confidential basis to Jean Lesage, then Parliamentary Secretary for External Affairs. Lesage was the only one who replied, by November 20. He objected to my proposal on three grounds. First, the fact that boys would be enrolled in the programme so young meant that the overwhelming majority would not be ready to make a final, lifetime career decision. Secondly, there would be an immediate outcry in Quebec against the fact that young French Canadians would be anglicized. Lastly, I had claimed in my memo that it was imperative for all Canadian officers to be from the same mould, that is, that of RMC. Yet, according to Lesage, this argument was invalid because there were already two moulds, the RMC in Kingston and Royal Roads in Victoria. This led me to conclude that the government's mind was already more or less made up. The tone of the last part of Lesage's letter led me to believe that if there was to be any movement, at the Canadian government's level, towards an opening for French Canadians, it might take the shape of a third military college aimed primarily at admitting francophones and training them in their own language.

On December 10, 1951, knowing that I was preoccupied by my inpending return to Canada, Côté replied to Lesage without consulting me. But he sent me a copy of Lesage's letter and of his own reply (which I approved). In general outline, Côté was saying that the military academy would be comparable to the commercial academies that were flourishing in Quebec, that the political problem of being accused of anglicizing French Canadians would indeed be there, but that in fact it would have no substance because the institution would have its own curriculum (French, religion, etc.) while emphasizing English and the sciences and mathematics, so that the graduates would be culturally francophone but also bilingual and oriented towards a military career. Finally, he noted that Royal Roads was merely a branch of the RMC. Indeed, the Royal Roads officer-cadets all had to spend their last two years at RMC before being commissioned. Still, according to Côté—and I supported him—we had to avoid splitting our armed forces along linguistic lines; francophones had to find their place within a unified force in war as in peace.

All of this had given me some new insights. Lesage's arguments were worth considering. Côté's were well known to me. I began questioning some parts of my original idea.

In January 1952, during my first meeting with Simonds following my return from London, it turned out that he had not received my letter. He asked me for a copy, which I gave him next month. In the meantime, fearing that the whole thing would die down, I approached an excellent friend of mine, Ted Bullock—I will write in greater detail about him later, and of his role in the advancement of francophones within the Department—who knew Pierre Asselin, St. Laurent's principal secretary, well. Through them, I made my ideas reach the top—and there they stayed. Although my proposal had not been accepted, I had become involved in the issue of the shortage of francophones without publicly attacking (which I could not and did not want to do) Balcer's designs, which I found too daring. The winner was going to be him, or politics. Indeed, it was only on June 12, 1952, four days before two by-elections in Quebec (Brome-Missisquoi and Roberval) that Claxton announced in the House the creation of a bilingual military college at Saint-Jean.

Through my work as Vice-Quartermaster-General, I was already involved in the issue. A few weeks earlier, Pierre Asselin had telephoned me to say that we would have that college, that it would be bilingual and that it would admit candidates from the three branches. I immediately started thinking about where it could be located. The idea of an academy had been in my mind for a long time. At first when I thought about a location in the Eastern Quebec area, I could see it housed in the renovated Citadel because the R22^{e}R would have gone to Valcartier. But in 1952 I thought that another solution might be preferable. I was familiar with St. Jean, where I had served in the 1930s. With the opening of the Korean front, I had had to increase the capacity of the Canadian Army Training School (CATS) which was located there and which taught basic training to the army's francophone recruits. At the time we are speaking of, a small detachment of the R22^{e}R had been withdrawn from there. A quick study proved to me that the CATS could very well move to Valcartier: this would vacate the place for the future college. I was ready when, a little later, the Adjutant-General, Major-General Slim Macklin, called me to ask whether there might be a place in Quebec where we could open a military college.

As soon as the official announcement was made, I received the personal authorization of the minister, who had summoned me to spend whatever was required to implement the project. Things had dragged out for months and even years, and then suddenly, smack in the middle of the summer of 1952, we had to establish a college that would start its academic activity by next fall. Things nevertheless went well. My decisions or requests went via the Quebec command, then under Paul Bernatchez, which simplified matters. I was able to retrieve the invaluable Coulombe, who quickly managed, with the assistance of a francophone RMC professor, to determine the main requirements of the college.

The first classrooms and sleeping quarters were prepared. A chapel was set up on the top floor of the administration building. I was not involved directly in the rest of it. Nevertheless, that college was going to be "profitable" for me right away. The Deputy Chief of the General Staff, Sparky Sparling, had told me that recruiting would not bring us more than ten francophone applicants. I had made a bet with him, saying that there would be at least fifty. After those fifty, Sparling would have to give me $1 per additional applicant. Fifteen hundred young men presented themselves at the initial selection. Sparling never paid up.

I was involved in this area as well, being chairman of the selection committee of the first CMR officer cadets. The total enrolment had to comprise 60 per cent francophones and 40 per cent anglophones. The decision had been made by others that all applicants having grade 12 education or its equivalent were eligible. CMR would train them for three years, and the last two years would be spent at RMC. Finally, bilingualism would be mandatory not at admission but gradually, and for both anglophones and francophones.

I had been told that I should be the first commandant of the college. I agreed with that, of course, but I would have preferred someone who was a little more "academic" than myself. The problem resolved itself: RMC was headed by a brigadier and it was the senior college. CMR—much like Royal Roads—would therefore have a colonel at its head. A friend of mine, Marcellin Lahaie, was brought back from Germany and promoted to that position. He had all the qualities required, including the education and organizational skills.

The college was ready on time. I had contributed to it and I was happy with the result, for an important step had been made with respect to francophones. It would be up to me, later, to go further.

Occasionally, Ottawa colleagues consulted me on other aspects of francophone affairs because I was, at the time, the senior francophone in the capital. In May 1952, it was recommended to the General Staff that a school be established in which English would be taught to all the Army's francophone recruits who did not already know the language. The

Vice-Chief of that branch asked me what I thought. My reply, dated May 30, opposed that concept for several reasons. For instance, in certain infantry units, a unilingual francophone does not have to know the other language before reaching the rank of corporal. English would be necessary for those who intended to become signalmen, but not for all. I recommended that we select a number to be taught English rather than submit all francophone personnel to anglicization. I took the liberty of going further and suggesting the beginnings of an overall framework within which my compatriots would function, predicated upon the premise that the Army's francophones should be kept in Quebec, as far as possible, by creating—among other things—French-language units outside the infantry. We would thus be preparing for the future, in order to avoid the problems that had emerged during the 1914 and 1939 mobilizations, for these units could then provide the necessary leadership, in the various specialties, to the newly mobilized. I added that "with such a policy, clearly presented and widely publicized, French Canada would quickly seize the opportunity it is given."

The table included with my brief shows the percentage of French-language officers and men we had in Korea, in Germany (with NATO) and in the army in general. The striking fact is that 22 per cent of the men were francophones as opposed to only 11 per cent of officers. I stated that this situation would not be changed by teaching English to all francophones, but only through "the renewed interest created by a new policy concerning them." Should we fail to achieve the expected results, we could always look for another way of getting francophones to join the army.

Some will probably find this digression lengthy, particularly since it had no immediate concrete results, except for the fact that the "anglicization" school did not gain a foothold in the army. The direction of my ideas is by now, no doubt, clear to the reader. Nor should the reader think that I was the only one in 1952 to think this way. There were many other francophones— including Bernatchez—and some anglophones, including Ted Bullock.

In the meantime, my job as Vice-Quartermaster-General included other activities, which were much more important in the very short term. Because of the requirements of the Korean War, Simonds had wanted an infantryman rather than a specialist in that position. At that point, we had about 8,000 men in Korea. We had to see to their administration, to ensure that they had appropriate weapons and ammunition, rations, means of transportation, and ongoing provisioning in goods and equipment. For winter clothing, for example, we at Headquarters had to take steps at least three months ahead—that being the minimum lead time required to order winter uniforms, ship them to the Far East and ensure their timely issue to the men.

I quickly learned to know the cogs of the machine of which I was a part. I soon knew all the agencies that existed between our decision-making office and the front. This allowed me to establish our basic supply policy for Korea, which was to be maintained roughly intact up to the end of our presence there. My experience in that position was perfect as far as learning all the complexities of large central offices was concerned.

Strange situations arose that had to be solved rapidly. It will be recalled that the first contingent for Korea had been recruited largely outside the regular forces. On the other hand, the second contingent was made up primarily of regulars. Because of the different recruiting standards for height—the regular forces recruited from 5'8" and up, until 1950, whereas the 1950 contingent included many soldiers 5'6" tall—there were occasional shortages of winter uniforms for the second contingent, which included too many "tall ones." The situation was quickly corrected.

This stint in Ottawa acquainted me fairly closely, for the first time, with a Minister of Defence. However, with Claxton, I had mainly social contact. I accompanied him on some of his trips. The minister favoured a certain unification of the three branches. He created the position of chairman of the committee of the three Chiefs of Staff, and he set up many inter-service committees. I was a member, as the Quartermaster-General's deputy, of the Logistics Committee. Although I became excellent friends with the representatives of the Navy, Air Force and the Research Council, and although I did believe in the feasibility of improved co-ordination among the three General Headquarters, I thought that these committees were a waste of time. I did not hide this view from Claxton, who always found good reasons to keep them going. He also ensured that the two military colleges (the Army's RMC and the Navy's Royal Roads) were unified, that each received officer-cadets from the three branches. Finally, as a footnote, it should be mentioned that in 1952 Claxton had received very coolly the proposal to open a military college for francophones. In my opinion, he even attempted to get around the proposal by discussing with Cardinal Roy and Father Garneau the feasibility of opening a faculty of military science at Laval University. Made aware of this manoeuvre, I informed my friend Bullock about my fears that such a "civilian" alternative might be approved. He immediately informed Pierre Asselin and Jean Lesage. Claxton's project did not get very far.

After I had spent more than a year and a half as Vice-Quartermaster-General, Simonds summoned me to his office and offered me the command of the 25th Brigade, which was fighting in Korea. Simone and I found this offer impossible to refuse. During my absence, she and the children were to stay in our new home in Ottawa.

8

Korea, 1953-1954

The news of my appointment was made public in January 1953 and I left my post in Ottawa on February 12. From then until the day I took over command of the 25th Brigade, I made time to study the files concerning our presence in Korea. In March, I did the rounds of several Quebec Chambers of Commerce with a lecture entitled "Communist Strategy in the Far East." I thus had the opportunity of getting an intellectual grasp on the question, which was a very useful exercise. Moreover, I was able to assure my listeners that our fighting men were performing well and had good equipment.

On March 21, the Amicale du R22ᵉR organized a dance in Quebec City in honour of Simone and myself. In April, I left Ottawa for Tokyo, via Vancouver. In the Japanese capital, I visited the Headquarters of the U.N. forces, commanded by an old acquaintance, General Mark Clark, of the U.S.A. I then called on the Canadian ambassador and met the Japanese official responsible for his country's external affairs. At that moment, it will be remembered, Japan had not yet signed a peace treaty so that the country was still officially under occupation. The government was only provisional, and its "ministers" were really more like members of a management committee. As it happens, I was one of the very few foreigners to have made such a courtesy visit. I was received in a very affable, even friendly, manner and was invited to take part in the beautiful tea ceremony.

Above all, I felt that my interlocutor was pleased with my gesture, which I had made quite spontaneously, with no ulterior motive. However, this courtesy on my part would prove useful to us.

The peace treaty was finally signed in February 1954. The Japanese then regained full sovereignty over their territory and, at the same time, full control over the enforcement of local laws. From that time on we were obviously under Japanese jurisdiction with respect to infringements of the local criminal code. However, my visit had apparently made such a good impression that the authorities did not try to pick on our men without good cause. Thus, we were duly notified of all their misdemeanours, and men who had been arrested were handed over to us. Our military code of discipline dealt with these cases in the most appropriate way.

After Tokyo, I went to Kure (near Hiroshima), the site of the Canadian base through which men and matériel passed before crossing over to Korea. It was customary to arrive there by ship before going on, very often by air. At Kure, the commander had a house, usually occupied by his adjutant since the brigadier preferred to be up at the front with his men. Here I was able to see one of the last links in the logistical chain of which I had been one of the first, at the other end, as Vice Quarter-Master. During my short stay in Kure, I had time to visit Hiroshima, which was in a state of total ruin. I then flew to Seoul where I introduced myself to the 8th Army Commander, General Maxwell Taylor. He had the Commonwealth Division under his command, including my brigade, which I immediately joined. During the last part of this journey—some sixty miles by road, I could see how widespread the devastation in South Korea was. The destruction was often total; even the forests, fields and marshes bore the scars of war. From the start, I found the people pleasant, an impression which was rapidly confirmed. But I already felt deeply grieved for them, crushed as they had been by the ruthless political decision that North Korea had taken in invading their lands.

My predecessor, the second to command the brigade, was Brigadier Bogert. He was an old friend who had prepared a fine reception programme for me, thanks to which I was able to meet the staff officers of the division, several of whom were Canadians. I then met the commanders of my units, whom I already knew. Then, after a private conversation, Bogert took me straight to our part of the front which we followed from left to right. We stopped at each platoon and observation post. We also visited the company and battalion command posts, as well as the artillery positions. Lastly, I made contact with my neighbours—the British on our left and the Australians on our right. This tour of our positions took six days. In front of and overlooking us were two Chinese divisions. But they were so far away that we could see the barrage coming and take appropriate action. The official hand-over took place on April 21. Only then did Bogert head for home.

Where were we in this war? Since the summer of 1951, armistice talks had been going on. The main topic was the location of the demarcation line, and it seemed obvious that the Chinese, here and there, were trying to increase their territorial advantage.

For our part, we faced some special difficulties. The first, and by far the most important, was the political situation: in other words, our orders were to wage a strictly defensive war. Thus, a brigade commander could not, on his own initiative, mount an offensive that would involve more than a platoon. To attack with a company, we had to obtain permission from the army corps commander—the divisional commander did not have that power of decision—and the corps commander had to have the blessing of the army commander to involve more than one company. One of the consequences of this during my term, was that I was unable to test either the defensive capability of my opponents or the offensive capability of my own troops. The other consequence was that if our enemy happened to dominate our positions, we had to let him snipe at us, with the ensuing loss of life which might have been avoided by capturing certain peaks from our adversary.

This first factor led to a second which I have already mentioned in passing and which I shall discuss again further on: ours was strictly "position" warfare. Thus, it taught us nothing about mobile warfare in general, nor about combined infantry-tank operations, in particular. The tanks, however, were useful: in the line, they discouraged the adversary from using his own (inferior) tanks; they served as fire support for the positions occupied by our infantry and could destroy from a distance the few bunkers that the enemy sometimes tried to put up in no man's land (I was able to put this specific advantage of the tanks to good use).

The next two factors were restrictive from the commander's point of view but not in terms of the overall situation. First, our air forces, in 1953, had total control of the air. That was discouraging as far as the experience that our troops might have been able to gain was concerned. Our men did not learn how to replenish their supplies against opposition from the enemy's air force; our camouflage was neglected; there was no need for anti-aircraft defence; our positions were not built to withstand aerial bombardment; lastly, since our reconnaissance planes could do what they wanted, our artillery had an unnatural domination over the enemy's guns. The enemy reacted by digging deep shelters in the hills and mounting night attacks. Since we did not have the initiative, we too had to fight at night.

Finally, the fact that we had no supply problems—everything arrived in great quantities and on time—meant that no one had the opportunity to plan his long-term needs and, above all, to exert strict control over what he received.

There were other negative points, though less important. For instance, our World War II veterans were not used to fighting one against thirty, as was the case here. Our tanks were almost useless in the Korean mountains, where there were no roads, while in the valleys the rice fields, bedded on clay soil, hampered their performance.

Moreover, units often changed position. The Commonwealth Division had occupied the place where we were for some time. Then, in December 1952, it had been replaced by the 2nd U.S. Division. On April 1st, 1953, the Commonwealth Division returned. However, the divisions of the different allies did not have the same complement of men or the same tactics. On reaching the line, we occupied our predecessors' trenches and shelters. Corrections then had to be made with respect to the arc that each ally's weapons had to cover, and that was quickly done. After that, we waited.

Our part of the front was considered the easiest within the Division because the enemy positions were about 900 yards from ours. However, we had a width of 4,800 yards to cover. The Division's front was 14,000 yards and the three brigades were in line. In my brigade, I worked with two battalions forward and one in reserve. But, on the whole, our line was thin, all the more so because my reserve was positioned just behind the right-hand battalion of the brigade to my left where there was an opening that had to be covered. To move this reserve might give the enemy an opening that he could easily exploit.

Given the circumstances (armistice talks; limited territorial ambition on the part of the Chinese, at this stage; good intelligence; superiority of fire), these remained minor points. However, two things greatly concerned me. First of all, at night, no man's land was under enemy control. Upon his arrival, Bogert had begun to challenge this predominance and I intended to pursue this tactic. Secondly, our defensive positions—especially our shelters—were not very solid. I also felt that the young officers were lacking in initiative: they arrived in their allotted positions and settled into them, usually making only minor adjustments. Then they waited. This was quite normal since the doctrine of the training these men had received was essentially based on offensive warfare; they had received little instruction in the art of entrenchment.

My left-hand unit, 3rd Battalion of the Royal Canadian Regiment (3 RCR) had just arrived at the front. Its commander, Lieutenant-Colonel K. L. Campbell, was busy familiarizing his men with the difficult terrain they would have to cope with (hills, ravines, streams) and also showing them how to patrol the sector against the Chinese and North Koreans.

The enemy was aware of our change of command and probably of the arrival of the young men of 3 RCR. The Chinese patrols increased in number towards the end of April, on the right extremity of the 3 RCR's position, which was an advanced ridge and a weak point in our line. By day, our positions were usually bombarded; however, the right of the 3 RCR got rather more than the others in the brigade. But it was hard to assess accurately whether the Chinese would try something. Was this merely harassment fire, or were they trying to pinpoint certain targets in preparation for an attack?

I had on my staff a British officer seconded to me by the Division's counter-battery artillery. His contact work with the rear was backed by great technical expertise. He would walk over the ground, picking up all the shell splinters he could find. From their identification, he drew certain conclusions, namely, that many of the shells fired against the right came from guns which could be used were this position to be attacked. My own conclusions were along the same lines.

In the midst of these analyses, General Taylor invited me to his HQ to meet his officers. For May 1 and 2, the programme included a dinner with the general and his staff, an overnight stay, and a familiarization tour the following morning. I agreed to go to Seoul. But I was so worried that I asked permission to leave again right after the meal, promising to complete my visit later. Taylor, who had seen many problem situations, pointed out that his units were constantly coming under fire that usually led to nothing more. I was not convinced and he readily let me do as I wanted.

As soon as the meal was over, I climbed back into my jeep which I had had specially equipped so that I could hear what information my HQ was receiving during the sixty-mile return journey. I thus realized that the Chinese fire against us had intensified quite suddenly. As I approached, this was confirmed; firing was apparently concentrated on C Company, 3 RCR, which was perched precisely on the advanced ridge mentioned earlier.

Back at my HQ, I immediately went to the officers' mess where there was a small party celebrating the departure of one of our officers for Canada. It was about 2300 hours when I closed the place and ordered everyone to take up their battle position. Then I began to revise our defence plans. My reserve consisted of the R22^{e}R, which had arrived from Canada three days earlier. But its commander, Tony Poulin, was an old comrade whom I trusted completely. I called him in, explained my fears and explained what I expected of him.

At 2345 hours, the barrage intensified against the RCR's C Company and, at midnight, the attack began. It was very predictable. Two strong patrols of the RCR (a dozen men in each) had already been engaged just opposite C Company's positions and had been wiped out by a superior enemy. Over the last few days, the latter had paid us frequent visits to gain an accurate picture of the target he wanted to destroy—for there was no question, for the Chinese, of taking over our lines. The barbed wire was now cut, and the Chinese plunged forward in successive waves against the 7th Platoon of the RCR. I told Campbell to take control of the brigade's artillery and sought the support of that of the army corps. At 0005 hours, our shells began to fall simultaneously far back on the Chinese rear and quite near on their assault troops. The American intelligence services tapping Chinese communications informed us that the Chinese HQs, two echelons above the units that were attacking us, were feeling the heat as our shells bracketed them.

In the meantime, our air force had arrived to light up the battle field so that soon after the start of the engagement, we could see as if it were daylight. About 0030 hours, the Chinese began to withdraw from C Company's position, which they had occupied. We did not counterattack, although Campbell had made all the necessary preparations to do so. I told myself that if the Chinese wanted to stay, we should arrange to make them pay heavily for it. Since we would obviously not allow supplies to reach the Chinese "occupation" troops, we could not expect our adversaries to make us the senseless gift of the lives of many of their men. Thus, in the early hours of the morning, after smoking out our positions, the last occupants left us. But they had demolished all our shelters and trenches in the sector of 7 Platoon, C Company.

Things could have been worse, however. On May 1, I had already signed a long memo revising all the arrangements which would have to be made concerning the companies in a defensive war. My predecessor had not had to undergo an attack but he had nonetheless made certain decisions along the same lines. From May 2 onwards, major changes took place, the most important of which was the setting up of a new patrol system.

Our positions were defended by minefields and barbed wire. Through these defences, paths were marked out for the use of our patrols. Moreover, our automatic weapons, mortars and barrage artillery had precise targets to strike in case of an alert. Since these objectives did not often change, the enemy had been able to approach our static defences, probe here and there, await our response and then mark on his maps the places that were well covered by our fire and those that were less so, or not at all. Because of the width of the front, it was impossible for us to give our line complete coverage. Thus, every night, as had been the case before the attack against the RCR, numerous enemy patrols along a particular sector of our front gave the Chinese a clear idea of our strong and weak points which they could subsequently avoid or use at the right moment.

All that had to be changed. First of all, the lines of fire of our defence would have to be changed frequently. In particular, our fighting patrols (ten men or more) that had gone out at night to occupy a few outposts would be disbanded and replaced by many more small groups of two men each . . . and a dog specially trained to signal unwarranted presences noiselessly; these dogs also gave confidence to these isolated, unprotected men. These small outposts would be dotted here and there in no man's land, out of reach of our defensive fire and off the beaten tracks, though staying close to them. Thus, equipped with a radio, the patrols could inform us of Chinese penetrations. It would then be up to our guns to fire at the right moment and at the right place, with the advantage of knowing fairly accurately where the enemy was. It should also be mentioned that, in case of battle, these men were supposed to stay where they were and supply us with all the information they could gather.

This tactic (combined with others that I shall briefly describe further on) produced excellent results for, very soon, the losses suffered by the Chinese patrols became too onerous for the results they obtained. We thus regained the initiative even though we did not mount an attack. Without going into greater detail, I may say that my battalion commanders had some very nasty surprises for the enemy advancing on the paths.

To achieve these results, I had to set up a patrol school under the masterly direction of Harry Pope. Other measures were also taken. Thus, I changed our defence system and added four tanks, which were placed below our positions, ready to give their support when needed. We hid them by day, and at night they patrolled the land near the former rice fields. I had frequent checks made of the positions of all our automatic weapons to make sure they were at maximum effectiveness. Moreover, I had our static positions redone, making sure that there was a good drainage system, reinforcing the roofs of our shelters, adding wire mesh lateral support to our trenches, digging nine-foot-deep communication trenches and covering them with barbed wire (a Chinese became stuck there, once, to his great discomfiture).

In the midst of these changes, the Chinese mounted a second attack, which failed, since they did not even reach our lines. A third, elsewhere on the Division's front, was no more successful. The 25th Brigade would subsequently be left in peace until the end of the fighting.

On our side, without mounting an attack, we organized an offensive type of strategy. Just behind us, there was a mountain that was slightly higher than those around us. Before my arrival, it had already been dug out from side to side to provide an observation post overlooking the Chinese lines. I had a very powerful telescope installed there. Our strategy was as follows: first, we photographed the enemy lines at a slant, from the air; second, we enlarged these photographs to a very large scale and subdivided them into squares; third, by day, our observers, all along our front, observed the Chinese with binoculars. If they thought they had found some target of interest (a bunker, for instance), they passed on the message to the observation post on the mountain together with the most accurate co-ordinates possible. Then, if the telescope confirmed the object, the precise location and nature of the discovery were marked on our maps.

Fourth and final stage: one misty morning, I had our sixteen tanks installed along the whole length of the front with three shells each, including one smoke shell. Each tank had its specific targets. I climbed up to my observation post to watch the show. I think I can say that the surprise was total. Direct hits were scored on the targets that had been detected. And our smoke shells indicated different ventilation outlets with which the Chinese tunnels were connected. An hour after the end of our "exercise," the Chinese replied by a very accurate bombardment—of our former positions. As a result we suffered no damage at all.

Unfortunately, at the beginning of July, because of the normal rotation of the brigades, we had to leave the centre of the division and move to the right. There too, everything needed rebuilding, but there was no time to do so. The rains came pouring down during the first half of the month and flooded everything. After especially heavy showers on July 14, I went to visit our former positions where our replacements were still quite dry—and thanked me for it.

We were now in direct contact with the 1st Korean Division. It had come under heavy attack for some days. General Clark asked me to help the Koreans, leaving me the initiative of how to do it. I therefore went to meet General Kim to discuss this subject and explain Clark's wishes to him. Kim was full of enthusiasm, but he lacked experience: two years earlier, he had been a teacher. He knew how to do two things, counterattack and use artillery, but without necessarily matching our own high standards. He then asked me what I could do. I was ready to lend him one of my regiments to replace the one he had just lost and to set up a small operational CP at his HQ, through which I could help him. He agreed, perhaps without understanding the full impact of his decision, and of the aggressive defence I espoused.

Clark had thought it wise to lighten the burden borne by the South Koreans by shortening their front. Thus, two of my reserve companies had already been installed on the right of the Princess Patricia's Canadian Light Infantry (PPCLI), enabling the Koreans to concentrate their men in a more limited area. Our help to this division was mainly channelled through our 81st Field Artillery Regiment. Lastly, since my small CP enabled me tactfully to assume real command of the Korean division, I made suggestions to which Kim immediately agreed. At that time, it was a question of recapturing about half a mile of ground lost to the enemy. To do so, I had the area that had been taken from us pounded by our artillery in a professional manner. Near our HQ, but further forward, I installed the last reserve company I had left. Since it was again the turn of the R22^{e}R to play this role, I had my friend Poulin at my side.

But the pounding of the South Koreans' former positions made the Chinese think. They soon found things uncomfortable and began to fall back. At this juncture, a new Korean regiment arrived. These fresh troops counterattacked with the help of our gunners, and the Chinese cleared out; the position was regained, and the R22^{e}R could return to its reserve status.

During this time, the Canadians all realized that our Korean allies were excellent, brave and fearless soldiers. Unfortunately, they had orders to use their artillery against the enemy at the very last minute, in other words, when he had reached their defensive positions. There was no question of trying to check their assailants' momentum or of trying to cut off their supplies by heavy shelling of their rear once they were far advanced. The result of such a practice was almost as disastrous for the attacked as for the attacker.

I subsequently suggested to Kim that we organize combined night patrols. He agreed but we scarcely had time to do so. In the midst of a period of relative tranquillity in our two divisions, we learned that the lengthy armistice talks had finally come to a head.

It was understood that as far as military matters were concerned, the commander of our division, a British officer, would make the decisions. We were merely expected to respond to his priorities. It was equally obvious, however, that from the administrative point of view the whole Canadian contingent (including the support sub-units, dispersed here and there) remained totally under my control. Moreover, all questions of a political nature could only be dealt with by Canadians. For this reason, the commander of our brigade was designated as the senior military officer in the Far East, answerable directly to Ottawa for political matters. I could also communicate directly with our Chief of the General Staff on any matter I wished. As an example, I might mention that an Australian proposal for harmonizing certain policies within the Commonwealth Division had been rejected by Ottawa because it risked making the troops too uniform, based on a common denominator that would have been British. At another time, it was suggested that our tank squadron be placed under British control. Under such an arrangement, the tank support for my infantry might have been provided by the Australians, whereas the Canadians might have supported the British. Here again, I gave an outright refusal. The signing of the armistice was also a political matter, hence my flat rejection of the suggestion made by my divisional commander that he sign it on behalf of all his troops. My refusal, which he immediately accepted, being fully aware of my rights, meant that all the participants of our division (other than the British) would sign the document putting an end to hostilities until the eventual conclusion of a peace treaty, which has not yet been achieved.

We had been ready to conclude this agreement officially for some time. But the Chinese wanted first of all to complete the building of the Peace Palace at Panmunjon. This would have the advantage for them of giving the impression that they alone would decide when the time for peace had come. They were certainly skilled at propaganda. But a far more serious disadvantage was that hundreds of people continued to be needlessly killed. Under these communist régimes, however, human life is cheap. It was a disastrously farcical situation.

On the appointed date we drove up in our jeep to the palace sector. Before being admitted we had to pass through barriers and complicated procedures that I would describe as "Red tape." Finally, shortly after 0900 hours on July 27, I entered this peace hall and took my place with my fellow commanders of the U.N. forces on the south side of the table on which the official signing would take place. We were a diverse group. Opposite us, the Chinese and North Korean generals sat straight and motionless, as if at grade school. Then Generals Harrison (U.N.) and Nam Il (Communist) entered this sacred place and swiftly concluded the ceremony.

I then went over to Munsan Ni where General Clark, by a stroke of his pen, confirmed the morning's settlement. At 1300 hours, it was all over, although hostilities would only end at midnight that same day. An interesting detail: from 2000 hours to midnight, the communists fired a record number (44,000) of shells at the 8th Army. All divisions, except that of the Commonwealth, were involved. For my part, after 1300 hours, I recorded an address in both English and French intended for Canadians and especially for the families of those whose bodies would remain forever in this other foreign field. Between April 21 and July 27, 1953, my brigade had had 49 men killed in action, due to wounds or presumed dead, 137 wounded in combat and 12 prisoners of war.

We had until 2200 hours, on July 30, to dismantle our positions, recovering as much wood and metal as possible. At dawn, on July 28, we set to work. For most of our men, it was their first chance to catch sight of the Chinese, the soldiers opposite them who were carrying out the same task.

With the role of our brigade changed, we remained ahead of the division, to the north of the Imjin, whereas our two sister brigades went to the south side and set about building their section of what was known as the "Kansas Line." My three battalions were fully occupied in filling the division's former front. By day, we observed the 4,000 yards separating us from the Chinese, and we installed observation posts, fences, and so forth. By night, we patrolled. Our aim was to prevent any possible surprise and, should there be an attack, to play a delaying role, thus enabling the rest of the division to prepare itself for battle.

We therefore had to adapt to this new life. We succeeded fairly well by conforming, in military matters, to the terms of the armistice. On three occasions, there were minor tensions: first, a patrol skirmish with the North Koreans who had come to sound out our positions, during which we took one prisoner. Secondly, one of our patrols strayed off course, fortunately with no ill effects, before the completion of the fence that was to serve as a frontier. Lastly, on January 20, 1954, the Indians—who were guarding all our prisoners of war—decided to open the gates of the camps where we were keeping them, a day before the fateful date on which an agreement was to be reached as to what would become of them. There was no chance of reaching such an agreement, for most of the prisoners taken by the U.N. troops did not wish to return home, whereas the Communists wanted all their prisoners back without giving them any choice in the matter. This infringement by the Indians of one of the clauses of the armistice was loudly exploited by the Chinese. Basically, however, they were quite pleased about it. About 325 of the 22,000 prisoners returned to the North. Most POWs had devised makeshift weapons (such as lances or wooden knives) for self-defence should anyone ever try to push them into the arms of the Communists. It must be said that our valiant friends from India, neutral though they might be, did not relish the hot potato . . . and decided to put an end to the situation.

In any case, fearing a reprisal of some sort, we remained on the alert for some days. But our conviction that this war was really over quickly returned. Indeed, since August 1953, our real enemy was boredom, which had already crept insidiously into our ranks before the hostilities had ended.

It was an enemy that was hard to conquer. My staff and I wracked our brains in an effort to deal with it. Little by little, we organized our peace mission. During the fighting, the sector had been completely depopulated. After July 1953, 800 people gradually returned to settle there. The fertile soil became productive again from June 1954 onwards; before my return to Canada, there was even the hope of soon having a surplus. However, before this could happen, everything had to be rebuilt since not one single building had been left standing. Our soldiers voluntarily organized a collection to pay for the building of a school and grain store. There was even enough money left over to buy material to clothe the children, who were in a state of utter destitution. Before returning to Canada I had the honour of turning the first spadeful of earth on the site of the future school. To make this a highly symbolic gesture, I made sure that men from all our provinces were present and had them trace the future contours of the building on the ground.

This function of "protector" was one that gave a certain meaning to our action. However, we had to improve life for our troops as well. The rest of my stay would be concerned primarily with that need, even though our actions would mainly benefit our comrades-in-arms who gradually took over from us. In order to house our troops better, the tents were winterized and often set on a wooden floor which helped to absorb the dampness of the ground. Large huts were built to house the kitchens, stores and most of the on-site work places. We also succeeded in hastening the delivery time of everything sent us by Royal Mail as well as increasing the number of postal arrivals per month.

We also introduced numerous leisure activities, including a cinema (showing six different films a week, using volunteer projectionists), a hobby shop, a library (I obtained French-language magazines and books through the French military attaché in Ottawa), a gymnasium, a post office, a souvenir shop, a mess, and a sports ground for several sports leagues. Seven women volunteers from the Canadian Red Cross took charge of the library and hobby shop.

During the Christmas festivities of 1953, we inaugurated a radio station which broadcast Canadian and American programmes between reveille and midnight (except during training hours). Our programming was very well received by unexpected listeners: Americans, Belgians, Turks and even Canadian sailors sailing off the Korean coast sent us their congratulations.

But that was not all. The units had to make sure that all the men spent at least ten days of their annual leave in Japan. The rest of these holidays were spent with the brigade. During their free time, our men built a recreation centre (Maple Leaf Park) which became a model that the Americans and British copied. Lastly, we made arrangements for an ecumenical church— used by both Catholics and Protestants—as well as a place for closed retreats available to the various religious groups who wished to organize such activities.

When this programme was completed, we realized that the number of our delinquents had dropped by 50 per cent. In any army, this is a sure sign of improved morale.

Apart from all this, we also had to carry out our principal tasks. One company of each battalion served in the forward area while the two others were kept busy in all sorts of ways including those just described. Before leaving Korea, I had time, for instance, to carry out a brigade exercise. But we also took part in several large divisional exercises. To keep the men in good shape, I organized competitions of forced route marches with full kit. My staff and I formed one of the teams. I must say that I had prepared myself fairly well for this before I left Canada by going for long walks in Ottawa. This had enabled me to lose forty pounds and to arrive in Korea in top physical condition.

At another level, officer training continued through lectures given by well-known visitors. And, above all, since we were now at an administrative phase of our presence in Korea, I made numerous inspections of units and subunits. I shall now allow myself to slip in one of the little anecdotes I promised you at the beginning. I had to inspect the brigade's support company commanded by Lucien Turcotte (who, since his retirement, has become the curator of the R22^{e}R museum). Lucien, I knew, always prepared his men so thoroughly that there was usually nothing for me to do except congratulate him on the fine appearance of his unit. However, just before

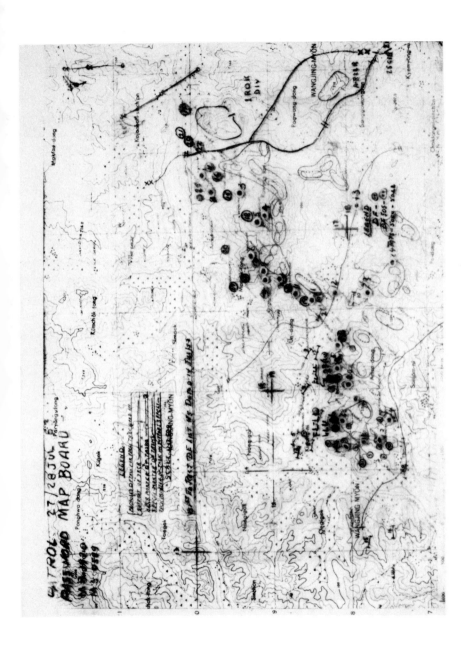

the inspection, I learned—I cannot remember quite how and why—that one of Turcotte's men had no socks. I therefore passed between the ranks as usual and, *by chance*, stopped before this chap and confirmed the fact that had been reported to me, to the officer's great discomfiture. At the time, I found it hard not to laugh.

My period of command in Korea was marked by many other tasks. I had to prepare suggestions with regard to Canada's military participation now that peace had returned. I also reorganized my subunits, trying to reduce the number of their members to a minimum. Meanwhile, a reorganization of the Canadian Army took place; its purpose was to deal with the situation caused by the great increase in the number of our soldiers since 1950. A division was formed, with its HQ at Petawawa. A Canadian Guards regiment was created including a bilingual 4th Battalion. A battalion of the PPCLI and another of the R22^{e}R became parachute units. The little effort made to satisfy the French-Canadian viewpoint in these changes was once more obvious.

These structural changes had little effect on the men's morale. It was other changes, which had an impact on their finances, that worried them a little. Under the pretext that they were no longer fighting—but with no regard for the special situation our troops faced in Korea (if only because of the numerous diseases they might contract there)—there was an attempt to abolish the privilege of supplementary rations, some allowances, and tax exemptions. Action on my part helped to correct this new situation partially: allowances and tax exemptions were maintained.

Towards the end of 1953, the Communists began to release the first U.N. prisoners of war. Only a few Canadians had been captured by the enemy during these three years of intermittent fighting. In spite of the brainwashing to which they had been subjected, they all gradually returned to us. In fact, only about 2 per cent of U.N. troops who had been taken prisoner chose to live in the communist world. I shall always remember the first Canadian who thus regained his freedom, Lance-Corporal Paul Dugal of Quebec City, with whom I spent several hours in Munsan Hospital.

Then, there were the numerous visits of dignitaries. General Simonds came very soon after my own arrival, from May 7 to 9, 1953. With him, I mainly discussed the type of relations we should maintain with the British within the Division. The following October, it was the turn of the Vice Adjutant-General, Brigadier A. E. B. Knight, to come and see us. He was mostly interested in taking note of our special needs. This list was long, but upon his return to Canada, he really did everything he could to satisfy us. From him, I learned that the tax exemptions would be maintained, that there would be an effort to offset—especially with more cigarettes (alas, yes! at that time, the more one smoked, the better one was)—the withdrawal of special rations, that a radio transmitter would soon be available, and that an adjustment in separation allowances should largely offset the loss of the combat allowance.

The other and undoubtedly most important visit was that of our Prime Minister, Louis St. Laurent, in March 1954. In October 1953 NDHQ had informed me of this possibility. When his visit was later confirmed, I was also told that I would be the principal organizer of his tour. Canada and South Korea had special ties during those years. Our country did not want to have a mission in Korea, but around August 1953, and without anyone knowing, a person was attached to our delegation in Japan to deal exclusively with Korean affairs. My role was to give him maximum support each time he came to Korea.

The South Koreans were extremely sensitive. The Geneva Conference, announced for 1954, was decided without them. President Rhee, whose country was to be one of the main subjects on the agenda, was not pleased: neither at the decision that the conference would be held far away from his country, nor that the USSR would take part in it as the host power. He launched into all kinds of actions, most frequently verbal, but nonetheless troublesome. One day, he talked about helping the French in Indochina. On another occasion, in 1953, he took the initiative of releasing all the North Korean prisoners his troops had taken, which made us worry about the consequences on the implementation by the Communists of certain terms of the armistice. The great majority of North Koreans were in no hurry to return home. So how, it was wondered, could the exchange be made? Finally, these fears turned out to be unfounded. Even so, Rhee's decision provoked some grumbling among my men, often quick to adopt certain British points of view. In this case, for instance, the British soldiers had little respect for Rhee and, generally speaking, for any South Koreans, whom they considered to be ungrateful. I had to remind our soldiers that it was nonetheless not our Korean allies who had begun this painful war.

My instructions concerning St. Laurent's visit were clear on one point: above all, he must devote his time to the Canadian Brigade. I therefore had to make sure that there were the least possible number of intermediaries between him and the Canadians. It was essential that St. Laurent and, through him, our country, should not look like a puppet of the Americans and British. In this affair, I had to parley directly with the Koreans or with Ottawa, when necessary, completely ignoring my usual hierarchical channel. Nonetheless courtesy demanded that I inform my superiors and colleagues, as well as our embassy in Japan, of what was about to happen. One of the political questions raised was the possibility that Rhee, at the official meeting which would take place, might ask St. Laurent's opinion concerning a threat he was brandishing, namely that South Korea would not go to Geneva. In this case, the Prime Minister was supposed to reply that the friends of South Korea would find it hard to understand such an abstention.

At any rate, St. Laurent arrived on March 7, 1953, in the early evening. He dined with the commander of the 8th Army, who also put him up for the night. The next morning, there was a short visit to Rhee and the laying of a wreath on the war memorial in Seoul. We then made a brief visit to the division before a light lunch in the brigade officer's mess, attended by 80 per cent of our officers.

After lunch there were various activities, including a tour of the Canadian units. St. Laurent officially opened our recreation centre where dozens of privates and corporals, representing all our units, were present and had the opportunity of seeing and talking with their Prime Minister. Before leaving us, St. Laurent recorded a statement, in both languages, concerning the state of our troops. It was to be broadcast over Canadian radio to the great pleasure of our men's families.

On March 9 I accompanied St. Laurent as far as Seoul. The next day, when he boarded the plane for Japan, a Korean army military band played "Vive la Canadienne" for him. The visit was a great success,and I congratulated everyone who had collaborated on it. A few weeks later, I sent a souvenir album to St. Laurent. I do not think he needed it to be reminded of the warmth with which he had been surrounded. About a year later, I had the confirmation that he had not forgotten any detail of our encounter.

One of the last memories I should like to recall concerning Korea was my relationship with the press and, in particular, with Bill Boss of the Canadian Press. Through an agreement made in 1951, Boss lived at Brigade HQ, unlike all the other press representatives attached to the Division. Upon my arrival, I therefore found that our journalist was the senior member of our officers' mess. He was also a friend and an excellent journalist. In 99 per cent of cases, his articles were flawless, and he did a good job of keeping the Canadian people informed. But his other writings could do a lot of harm. It was a fact, for example, that he sometimes used our warm (and open) hospitality to glean information to which he was not supposed to have access or else to seize upon a secondary opinion and improperly turn it into the central theme of one of his articles. Our relations became somewhat strained, since I did not intend to allow this little game to go on much longer.

A serious incident triggered the beginnings of a reaction. In Korea, in April and May 1953, we had tested the Patchett submachine gun, and our conclusions pointed to the acceptance of this weapon as a replacement for our Stens. However, the Patchett had many flaws that were listed in our report. As a result, it could obviously not become the new personal weapon our army needed to equip all our men. Nonetheless, on the Korean front, it was more satisfactory than the Sten. Without going into details, let us say that this had not been done under the cloak of secrecy, since the Patchett dated from the forties. The subject was therefore openly discussed in the mess. Suddenly, Boss sent his agency a very detailed article, which was published by various newspapers, on the result of our study. The annoying point was that our report had not yet reached Ottawa. Simonds was far from pleased and let me know it. However, he understood the situation since Boss had apparently acted in this way before. He asked me for a complete report and suggested that the time had come to take action in Boss's case.

The fact was that although the Patchett and the tests we had put it through were not secret, the report was. When I had learned the nature of Boss's article, I had intervened and spoken to him about it. But he had already sent it to Canada. This brings us to another aspect of the story. All correspondents' material was censored. However, the censoring was mainly done in Tokyo by the Americans, for whom certain subjects did not necessarily have the same importance as that accorded them by those principally concerned. Nonetheless, Tokyo had done its job by telephoning the Division, but had been told (without consultation with us) that apart from some details (range, degree of penetration), all the rest could be published.

Following this incident, I tried to take corrective steps, which had little effect for the moment. First, having asked the public relations office in Ottawa whether I could send Boss to the Division, I was told that such a move, after more than two years of his presence with the brigade, might be badly received and prove harmful for everyone. It was clearly pointed out to me, however, that Boss enjoyed a privilege, not a right. I was urged to act at my level to curb his potential access to aspects of our tasks which did not concern him. I therefore suggested to my officers that they should place a little less confidence in Boss. Nonetheless, the latter, by conscientious and tireless research, succeeded, in mid-June 1953, in piercing the mystery of the new patrol system that I mentioned earlier. He thought my ideas were brilliant and wanted to say so publicly. I tried to prevent him, but he sent his article off to the censor's office. As a precaution, I cabled Ottawa to say that if the text passed in Tokyo, it ought not to appear in the papers. I was finally able to block his article in Tokyo.

Almost at the same time, however, an article by Boss appeared in Canada in which he described the policy concerning the distribution of a special medal that the British wished to award, in limited numbers, to Canadians who had served in Korea. The subject, although confidential, had little strategic or tactical importance, but it showed me once more that our communication system was far from secure. The fact of being reminded of this by Ottawa (though politely) prompted me to act. In a memo dated June 26 I explained in a very positive way what our relations with the press should be and what they should not be. This last part seemed to offend Boss; at that stage, for various reasons known only to himself, he was on the point of leaving the brigade. Before his departure, he committed a further blunder by claiming to quote senior Canadian officers who had wondered within his earshot whether it was really worthwhile equipping ourselves with $3,500,000 of new tanks if the war was about to end? Naturally, Ottawa was again irritated, especially my successor in the post of Vice Quarter-Master General, whose department was responsible for such purchases. In this case, Boss was more or less acting in bad faith, for he knew quite well that this acquisition was not made in order to pursue the Korean war but rather to replace our 1940s vintage American tanks for which parts were hard to find. Moreover, we were all very pleased with the quality of our new British equipment, which was to be used outside Korea since the war was nearly over. I was unable to find out who had uttered the comment quoted by Boss or in what kind of tone. I was never able to clear up this question with him, and I did not see him again until November 1953.

Profiting from Boss's absence, I moved his replacement to Seoul. When the latter officially took over from the former, I brought him back to brigade while requesting my men to watch their tongues.

In September, accompanied by a delegation from the war correspondents' association, Boss visited Simonds office in Ottawa to discuss the Patchett affair and also the results of my memo of June 26, which, in his view, would prevent him from doing his job. The same day, September 18, 1953, Simonds cabled me to ask me to withdraw my memo. But from the tone of his exchanges with the correspondents, which he summed up for me, I felt that he was really on my side. He had clearly explained to them that classified matters—even though they did not concern operations—could not be dealt with by the press. His interlocutors had agreed, while giving him the impression that my memo had gone even further than that principle by almost setting up a second line of censorship in addition to the first, official one. Simonds gave in to this argument by exacting the promise that the correspondents would respect the limits stipulated.

With the signing of the armistice, all these questions became secondary. On September 22, I replied to Simonds that I had carried out his order but that, in my view, the Canadian people would have supported the steps I had taken. Let us imagine that, following such an article, the Chinese, now aware of our system, had also started using dogs to patrol near our sector. Such a countermeasure would have ruined our undertaking, in addition to causing, almost certainly, Canadian losses. Indeed, some of my officers had become so hostile to Boss by June 26 that my policy could not but help improve his relations with them. In any case, a lengthy conversation with Boss, on November 4 of that year, when he was on a short visit to us, cleared up many little misunderstandings that had crept between us since May.

Immediately after Boss's visit, in November, it would be the turn of a newcomer, Charles Lynch, to complain—wrongly—that the O.C. of our brigade public relations unit had not done his work properly. Lynch had not been informed of the release, by the Communists, of the Canadian prisoners. Thus, he had not been able to question them. He addressed his complaint directly to Ottawa and the Army's Director of Public Relations came down so heavily on my Chief of Public Relations, Major G. W. Pearce, that the latter threatened to resign. Pearce was an excellent public relations man and I had every reason to be satisfied with his performance. The conclusions of an inquiry concerning what had happened were forwarded to Ottawa where the tone suddenly changed. They had really gone off on the wrong track by only listening to a very partial version of the facts.

In spite of all this, I still repeat that the press has an essential and positive role to play as a link between a people and its fighting men, especially when the latter are far away. Our reporters, used to the freedom of expression in Western countries, must, in wartime, adjust to censorship, the necessity of which they understand, but sometimes they are not able to gauge its full scope. On the other hand, they might be working with military leaders who know little about journalism and who are unwilling to learn more about that trade and its potential. I do not believe that such was my case. However, it has been my experience that seeking improved mutual understanding between journalists and the military in peacetime could eliminate much needless friction under the tense circumstances of war.

The last incident I wish to recount is all to my credit, although it earned me a small reprimand. July 1, 1953, for Canadians in Korea, was Canada Day and not Dominion Day. I should remind readers that in 1946, 1950 and several times since then, there had been an attempt to turn the legal holiday of July 1 into Canada Day but with no success until 1983 when, at last, the amendment was made to our legislation.The term Canada Day was in current use by our troops; I had often heard it during the Second World War; the brigade in Germany had used it since 1951, and we in Korea had done so too. The overwhelming majority of our men were pleased to distinguish themselves in this way from the British under whom, at that point, they were still fighting and whose uniforms they wore.

The press article written in Korea concerning the preparations for our festivities laid particular stress on the title I wished to give them. There were two types of reactions to this. A young eighteen-year-old from Cape Breton wrote to congratulate me and even to propose a white, blue and red flag with a green leaf in the middle. He had apparently already submitted the idea to the Prime Minister, who had promised to reflect on the question. The young man asked me if I would not have such a flag made and use it in the brigade. This, of course, quite exceeded my authority, but I nonetheless sympathized with him. The "incident" I had created had a greater impact than I thought. The Vancouver *Province* approved my decision and also said that we ought to have a Canadian flag.

On the other hand, there was some outcry against my initiative. A disapproving letter sent to the *Ottawa Journal* prompted Simonds to write an unequivocal memo to his Director of Public Relations. In it, he stressed that the legal name of July 1 was "Dominion Day" and that this was the term that must be used. On July 14, Simonds' deputy, Major-General Sparling, sent me a copy of this memo. His letter, in the very friendly terms that Sparling used so effectively, suggested that it would be better for me not to provoke any further stories like this. But he only devoted the first part of his missive to this subject. He then dealt with other questions and did not refer again to his introductory paragraph. I was careful not to offend again for several years. Moreover, the Canadian population were gradually to fall into line with the nationalist sentiments of its soldiers.

All these somewhat trying events were almost forgotten when I boarded the plane to return to Canada in the early summer of 1954. On June 21, I was invited to stop off in Vancouver to address the local Canadian Club, and on June 23, I was in Ottawa. A new posting to the Quebec City area awaited me.

My successor in Korea was Brigadier Clift. I had known about this appointment since mid-December 1953. When Clift arrived, the new units were already all in place, our position was well defined and our role well established. Peace seemed assured. Our presence there was far less certain since, only a few months after his arrival, Clift was to supervise the repatriation of all our forces.

9

Once Again in Quebec,
1954-1958

On my return from Korea, I had two months' leave, which is not a luxury when one has been away from the family for more than a year. Since that free time was in July-August, midway through the school holidays, we decided to spend a few days at the ocean. Even though friends joined us, I remember mainly the good times we had by the sea, with Simone, my two teenagers and my little Andrée who had changed a great deal during my absence. She had become too big and too heavy for me to throw her up in the air as I used to do before going away. At first, Andrée seemed to have a little difficulty accepting her big girl status, then she got used to it.

Before the start of the school year, we moved again to Quebec City where I was to take command of the 3rd Brigade with its headquarters in Valcartier. The girls were at convents, Michèle at the Sisters of Saint-Joseph-de-Saint-Vallier and Andrée with the Ursulines. My son was going to the Quebec Academy.

My new command made me the head of all army units in Eastern Canada. My immediate task was to prepare them for NATO postings. Within the scope of that preparation was an important component, the possibility of nuclear war. A special committee had been set up in Ottawa to work on the subject. Simonds wanted me to think about the issue and to submit potential solutions directly to that task force. We had to adopt a new doctrine for the army which would be marked by mechanization and the arrival on the market of many new weapons during the next few years.

In many respects, I had the necessary war experience. Nevertheless, nuclear warfare was a fairly new field of thought. In Korea, the possibility of such a war had been slim. We talked about it sometimes among ourselves.

In fact, I have not known any responsible officer who would not have mentioned its possibility, one way or another in the mid-fifties.

So I tackled this task, which was both intellectual and practical. On the intellectual side, I read a great number of works on the subject, particularly those originating from the French Army. I discussed my ideas with my colleagues and tested them by means of exercises. The professionalism of the men and of the officers had to develop in parallel. For two years, we thus prepared to confront a nuclear attack or to take part in an offensive in which that terrible weapon would be used by our side. We gradually reached conclusions that were accepted by Ottawa because they were based on serious exercises. Nuclear warfare would be marked, for the Army, by rapid movement and wide dispersion. This may not seem like much, but to a military expert it implies a great deal. For example, the concept of dispersal means that the troops can be divided into very small units; hence arose the need to be able to trust the good leadership of our corporals and even our lance-corporals and soldiers. The training had to be adapted accordingly.

Everything considered, the work was an interesting, all-encompassing challenge. However, compared to Korea where I was active eighteen to twenty hours a day, seven days a week, it was equivalent to a rest period. Physical activity occurred mainly at the time of the annual concentrations at Gagetown, which were substantial. The exercise of the summer of 1957, for example, brought together more military men than any subsequent exercise up to the fall of 1982.

During my stint at the head of the brigade, I came to know certain subordinates, among whom was the very likeable Lieutenant-Colonel Armand Ross, who commanded 3 R22^{e}R. Ross was an educated, intelligent man who had come from the lower reaches of the St. Lawrence to fight during the Second World War in the *Régiment de la Chaudière* (he is the co-author of a history of that regiment, published in 1983). Like myself, he loved the operational side of our trade. We had many opportunities to exchange ideas regarding new tactics for nuclear warfare. We were not always in agreement, but there was mutual trust. I would even add, and I do not think that he would contradict me, that our relationship went beyond the usual exchanges between military colleagues of different ranks.

In March 1956, I went on a lecture tour in Quebec and the Maritimes at the invitation of the Canadian Institute for International Affairs. My speech dealt with the USSR and its expansionism. Before using the text, I sought Ross's opinion on it. He seemed to appreciate the whole thing. We lost sight of each other for some time since our postings took us to different places. We met again in the sixties to co-operate on a major task to which I have devoted all of chapter 14.

One episode of my long military life certainly deserves mention. It is my near-entry into federal politics in late 1955. As the reader already knows, I was not unacquainted with the Prime Minister at the time. In 1955, Alcide Côté, the Postmaster General, died. Apparently, the Liberal Cabinet had lost momentum since its last re-election. The members wanted to strengthen it by any means available and St. Laurent remembered me—mainly, I think, because of our meeting in Korea.

In July 1955, St. Laurent had someone contact me. He wanted me to meet him at Trois-Pistoles during his August vacation to discuss the details of my eventual entry into politics. The meeting did occur, not at Trois-Pistoles but at his summer cottage in St. Patrick, near Rivière-du-Loup, on August 17. One week earlier, at Camp Gagetown, the rumour began making the rounds that I had been sounded out by St. Laurent to become Minister of National Defence. It seems that that leak was owing to an indiscretion by the Prime Minister's son. The journalists who accompanied us in Gagetown picked up the rumour. At that point, I must say that nothing final had been decided, and that was the reply I gave to those who questioned me. But I added that if duty called me to enter politics, my answer would be yes.

By the summer of 1955, I had been a brigadier for more than ten years. Reaching that rank at the age of thirty-three was one thing; being still there eleven years later was another. Furthermore, I already had three years of commanding a brigade, two of them in combat. My military future seemed somewhat restricted. And basically, although I liked my profession very much, I was ready to enter politics if I had certain assurances.

I quickly realized that those around me and those who knew me well were split on the issue. Some told me that the mere fact of giving credence to my potential entry into politics was going to harm my military career, were that career to continue. Others thought otherwise and argued that I could certainly be a politician, but that the greatest need was for me to be in the Canadian Armed Forces. The francophones who made this last argument added that it was primarily as a French Canadian that my presence was required. In fact, the issue was blown out of all proportion. It was true that, given the situation, I would have found it difficult to say no to my Prime Minister. But plunging full-tilt into politics was, for me, out of the question.

Mr. St. Laurent explained to me, during our friendly conversation of August 17, which was held in secrecy—and I want to keep it largely confidential here—what he expected from me. Undoubtedly, I found the idea interesting. Some people quickly jumped to conclusions. Indeed, I received letters of congratulations addressed to the future Minister of National Defence (whereas St. Laurent was offering me the Post Office). The fall of 1955 was full of rumours regarding me anyway. There were many facts that ex-member of Parliament Lionel Bertrand has summarized quite well in his *Mémoires* (1972). St. Laurent was busily looking for a seat for me.

In Terrebonne as in Saint-Jean, the local associations opposed my being parachuted in. In the first case, Bertrand would have gone to the Senate—a position he apparently wanted. But his organizers were opposed to the arrival of a "stranger" at the time of the by-election. In Saint-Jean, the job was vacant—since Alcide Côté had died—but once again, they did not want any outside candidate. However, a well-orchestrated campaign to "draft" me was carried out under my name. On November 18, I received a telegram saying that a petition in my favour had been signed by hundreds of grass roots Liberals, by organizers and even by an ex-member of Parliament. But I had already decided to drop the whole thing and one day spent in Saint-Jean persuaded me that it was best to give up.

First of all, there was the split that my candidacy could have caused in the county. Then there was the opposition, even hostility, that emerged among some people around St. Laurent. Indeed, many ambitious MPs could see a ministerial position slip away from them to go to a newcomer. Thirdly, there was St. Laurent himself, increasingly rattled by the pack around him, which made any decision difficult for him. I believe that he had supported me without suspecting what reactions he was going to trigger.

For the record, I should say that among the Liberals in the county there were "collaborators" (with Duplessis) and "anticollaborators." Côté had sided with Duplessis and I think that I would have continued on that road. At any rate, my name was perceived as pro-Duplessis. The "collaborator" went on to win in Saint-Jean. A hard line Liberal who ran against him was beaten but resurfaced in 1960 on Lesage's provincial team.

After informing my fans that I was conceding, I met St. Laurent later, in November. His attitude was as nice and generous as usual. He assured me that we were to stay good friends in spite of the disappointment I had caused. He wished me a successful ongoing career.

The whole thing shook me a little. I came out of the process somewhat mauled. My opinion of politicians did not improve with my experience. Later, I was able to see better the web of complexities they must deal with on a daily basis. I resolved to follow the advice of my friend Bullock to continue doing my best with the brigade and to avoid making waves for some time. A great deal of ink had been spilled over this episode. I had been propelled centre-stage where some of my military colleagues did not appreciate seeing me, particularly when there were hints that I could sooner or later become their boss. I was prohibited from doing a recruiting tour that I had been supposed to do in the Eastern Sector, because too many people would think that my speeches were designed to earn votes. For several more months the newspapers wrote about the possibility that I might turn politician (they made me minister of Veterans' Affairs or Postmaster General) although I myself had completely given up the idea of leaving military life, particularly since Bullock, well-placed in Ottawa, told me that the old liberalism was dead. Furthermore, according to him, St. Laurent was no longer able to make decisions at any level. As soon as he decided anything, opponents within his own party gave him a hard time in order to reverse the decision.

In addition to all these reasons, there was a thought that had matured since late 1955. Could I have won a by-election? After all, A. G. L. McNaughton, appointed Minister of National Defence during the war, had never been able to get elected. Two years later, I could add two further questions: assuming a first victory (in any county), could I have held my ground at the general elections of 1957? Or during the collapse of 1958?

Besides, my career started moving again during the summer of 1956. I was contacted by Ottawa, and told that my promotion to major-general was assured. I was also asked, however, whether I was willing to let someone else have it before me, someone who, although older, had spent less time as a brigadier than I had. It was desired that he become a major-general before he retired. He was a good friend of mine who, starting as a cadet, had climbed through the ranks. I agreed but asked in return that I be allowed to go back to commanding the Eastern Quebec area. My goal was simple; I wanted to take a break and think about things. That job, which I had already worked at, would not be very difficult and I needed some time. My children were growing. Michèle was already 18, Jean-Ernest 16 and Andrée 13. It would be nice for my family to have the time to live well in Quebec City until my promotion and posting. Of course, this last-minute change disturbed some people. Dollard Ménard, who was to take over the area, had to accept—which he did gracefully—the task of replacing me at the head of the brigade. Some journalists still saw in my new appointment a springboard that would make me better known in Quebec and would soon allow me to enter the federal Cabinet.

My brief return to the Area HQ gave me an opportunity to tackle once again, this time more seriously, the issue of francophones in ourForces. When I commanded the brigade, I did my best to help "us." However, my priorities, as I had mentioned, were elsewhere. Basically, I did what I could when a problem arose. Thus, I had hardly returned from Korea when the commanding officer of the Guards, which had a battalion now designated bilingual, told me about some difficulties. An attempt had been made to bring together in that battalion bilingual francophones from outside Quebec and bilingual anglophones from Quebec. In reality, we were receiving increasing numbers of unilingual francophones and there was a shortage of higher ranks (corporals and above) able to understand them. Lieutenant-Colonel Sprung told me what the potential solutions were, though implementation depended on the personnel administration people in Ottawa. I forwarded those solutions to Bernatchez, G.O.C. Quebec command, who sent them higher still.

In the summer of 1955 came the problem of where to house the 3 R22^{e}R the next winter. Our higher authorities suggested the Citadel, while I wanted Valcartier. My reason was that this francophone battalion should not lose its operational effectiveness by being locked up in a place where it could hardly train properly in wintertime. Moreover, the maintenance of the place—snow removal, among other things—was much more costly, in terms of time, at the Citadel than at Valcartier. I was overruled.

In 1955-56, I tried to insist, once again unsuccessfully, to brigadier Fleury, my predecessor as Area Commander, that the streets of Valcartier be named after the most famous of our comrades of the French-Canadian infantry and artillery regiments who had been killed at the front and had not been decorated. I was merely recalling a policy I had drawn up in 1949 but had not been able to implement. On another front, I had launched the project of writing the history of our regiment during the Second World War (which was completed in the 60s).

Finally, I had noticed that many francophones learned the terms of the trade by rote. When one questioned them on some point, it became obvious that they did not understand the meaning of a certain words. This had become obvious to me during a winter exercise in Churchill, and I set up a committee to solve the problem. The conclusions were sent to Ottawa. As usual, I did not expect that anything concrete should come back from so far away. In the meantime, I did what I could.

In my area, I was once again able to participate to a greater extent in a concrete project that was unfortunately destined to fail in the short term. On October 26, 1956, Bernatchez asked me to study the feasibility of eventually receiving armour and artillery at Valcartier because, with the replacement of Simonds by Howard Graham as Chief of the General Staff in Ottawa, the overall outlook had changed. Graham was a friend of both Bernatchez and myself. He was open to the idea of changing the lot of francophones in the Forces. At the time when another reorganization appeared on the horizon, he no doubt remembered the commitments made in 1951 with respect to certain conclusions of Bernatchez's report on bilingualism in the Army. At any rate, Graham did not hesitate to take action.

The planned reorganization was to create new armoured units and release the artillery from its responsibility for anti-aircraft defence. It turned out, however, that Valcartier was not big enough to house an entire armoured regiment. As for the artillery, we had to settle for a medium battery. As a result, we were only given one squadron of the new 1/8th Hussars. As for Battery X, it would be part of the 3rd Royal Canadian Horse Artillery. The members of those two sub-units would often have to go outside Quebec to train and even to serve as higher-rank specialists in training schools that could not be located at Valcartier, once again owing to the lack of space. An armoured squadron would have to somehow manoeuvre in a sector that had just been redesigned for infantry use.

Bernatchez and I had many exchanges with respect to these modifications. We had to build more housing and schools at Valcartier to accommodate the hundreds of new soldiers and their dependents who were about to arrive. On the other hand, our young francophones would have to go on training courses and would occasionally even be posted to Gagetown. I told Bernatchez that the Department should publicly declare that there would be schools available there and that the personnel would be largely bilingual. This would facilitate our task by encouraging francophones to serve in that part of New Brunswick.

The money to improve the facilities at Valcartier was given to us for reasons other than those mentioned earlier. Ottawa was trying to reduce the rate at which members of the Forces were leaving and asked commanding officers for suggestions. I responded with a long memorandum recommending, among other things, that I be provided with the amounts necessary to build a community centre at Valcartier where families would be able to spend their leisure time together. Before the end of 1957, I was to see that new community centre as well as a curling ring built at Sainte-Foy and at Valcartier, respectively. As for a more complete welcome at Gagetown, Bernatchez received a formal promise that francophone elementary teachers would be hired as soon as the number of French-speaking children justified it.

My own specific actions in this matter were dictated by Ottawa. From Quebec, I had no input in the decision-making process that led to these thoroughly imperfect measures. My experience told me that one should not expect anything from the reform. Should we limit the military career of a francophone to an artillery battery or to an armoured squadron? What would happen to these sub-units during the unavoidable next reorganization? In short, all this generosity did not lead anywhere. As I had started explaining before I left for Korea, things would have to be handled differently by creating a framework ready to receive francophones, rather than first accepting them and later adapting the framework to their needs. The results of this latter system, with attempts being made to continue it under other forms in 1956-57, were not pretty to see. Young unilingual francophones, volunteers for the armoured unit, were sent to Gagetown. They landed in a completely alien environment and had to learn their trade in another language. Many became discouraged, discipline suffered and, too often, their bad conduct gave anglophones a distorted view of what francophones were all about. As to potential instructors, they went there knowing that some day, with luck, some essential services would be available. The same pattern was repeated with the artillery.

Finally, our two minor units got going. It is worth recounting two short anecdotes. Most of the gunners arriving at Valcartier came from Picton, where they had already served together in an anti-aircraft battery. The worst had already happened in some instances, that is, the parents, like the children, had started to assimilate. Except for some indispensable NCOs, however, all had voluntarily chosen to join the new unit at Valcartier. In fact, many francophones had been very disappointed with their reception in Picton. Some had even been refused housing because of their language and had lived many months, with their families, in military hangars. To us, all that had been revolting. And people occasionally still asked us why there were so few francophones serving outside the infantry!

The existence of the francophone 1/8th Hussars squadron led a French regiment, the *8ͤ régiment de Hussards*, to ask for affiliation with them. Since there was no precedent for linking French and Canadian units, any formal commitment was discouraged. It was suggested to Lieutenant-Colonel S. V. Radley-Walters, however, that he establish, if he wanted, the friendliest possible links with his French counterpart.

Thus the problem of the framework for welcoming francophones was far from settled. In 1957, one of the missing elements was still a genuine military base where francophone units could gather, train and mutually assist each other. The lesson of the shortage of space at Valcartier had not been lost on us. In March and April 1957, I wrote to my political connections in Ottawa to inform them of the situation and suggested a partial solution, namely, expanding Valcartier by expropriating thousands of acres. In the message I sent Hugues Lapointe and Jean Lesage, I pointed out that in 1949, as now, Bernatchez and I had made similar suggestions and that, in both instances, for apparently good reasons, our request had been refused, so that we doubted the sincerity of those blocking the project. I also emphasized the economic advantages linked to a greater number of army units at Valcartier, not to mention the advantages that the francophone soldiers in those units would derive from it.

My actions with the politicians were part of a pincer strategy. From within, we had sent our proposals upward. It was now up to the politicians to put the right questions to the minister for our arguments to be perceived in the right light. We were concerned with the future because, in the short term, all the decisions had been made favouring Gagetown in New Brunswick and Petawawa in Ontario, which had to be rebuilt in order to receive the Royal Canadian Dragoons. Lapointe nevertheless replied to me saying that things were well in hand.

Then the Conservatives came to power. As usual, there followed a period of indecision and the Valcartier expansion project was buried for lack of political support. This discouraged me, but I kept the idea in reserve for a better opportunity.

In December, I received confirmation that I would be promoted in 1958 to become, in April, the G.O.C. Western Command, headquartered in Edmonton. But Major-General Chris Vokes was approaching retirement and wanted to keep that command until then. I therefore learned through the newspapers, because Graham had not been able to reach me in time, that I would in fact become the first French Canadian to reach the important, strategic position of Vice-Chief of the General Staff.

Congratulations poured in from everywhere as soon as the news was made public around Christmas 1957. The French Canadians who wrote or spoke about any promotion were jubilant, sometimes ascribing to my new position more importance than it really had. My longtime English-Canadian friends, one of them reminding me that he was a Protestant and a freemason, did not lag behind and had even greater ambitions for me. As for St. Laurent, he let me know that it was one of the few Conservative decisions he approved of. My reply to the former Prime Minister, which I am rereading today, described fairly well what I had felt after the election of June 10, 1957. I had been briefly pessimistic, but later, noting that the new government was looking for francophone "big guns" in every area, my usual optimism had gained the upper hand. I added that I owed this promotion to a great extent to St. Laurent, who had often kept me in the foreground. I concluded that the Conservatives had been forced to draw a foregone conclusion.

When I wrote that reply on January 16, 1958, a great misfortune had begun to descend upon my family. Jean-Ernest was not long for this world. After our Moscow, Quebec and London stays where he had on each occasion shown great adaptability, he had entered Notre-Dame College on Côte-des-Neiges, in Montreal in September 1951. The next February, he was taken ill with rheumatic fever that kept him in bed for two months. He recovered fairly well, but his heart had been affected. He nevertheless remained a good athlete and was soon giving me badminton lessons; we sometimes also played squash or went swimming together. During my stay in Korea, he went to Saint-Alexandre College, near Hull, then he switched to the Quebec Academy, where his camaraderie earned him many friends. He was not the first in his class, but he managed quite well, with marks averaging between 75 and 85 per cent.

In Quebec City, he joined the cadet corps of the Academy in 1954. He became an instructor-corporal at Camp Farnham in the summer of 1955. The following fall, he was appointed commander of his cadet corps. It was with great pride that after inspecting it I had pinned on his chest the Strathcona medal awarded to the best cadet. In November 1957 he got two bits of good news, back-to-back: I would be promoted (the official confirmation came later) and he would be admitted to the Collège militaire royal provided his marks for the current year were good enough. Strangely, a premonition made him say that all of this seemed impossible to him. On November 20th, very early in the morning, he told me that he was not feeling very well. We took him to hospital where, after a few days of tests, leukemia was diagnosed. He was put on the "critical" list on November 25. This meant that we were allowed to visit him at any time. Over the following three months, Jean-Ernest had ups and downs, and his mother and I kept hoping for a miracle up to the end.

The inevitable, however, occurred on February 7, 1958. He left behind a family that loved him dearly. His fellow students inscribed a plaque recalling how much they had appreciated him. A multitude of people came to our home, where he lay in state, to pay their last respects. His cadet corps friends provided a guard twenty-four hours a day. Two striking images return to me. First of all, the picture of Jean-Ernest's shattered girlfriend who, for three days, stayed next to him almost continuously. Secondly, the visit of Louis St. Laurent, who came to see me in order to try to provide some consolation at this trying time. Finally, we took him with military honours to his last repose, beside his Grandfather Piché, at the Belmont Cemetery in Quebec City.

We had great difficulty, all four of us, in accepting the decision of the Lord. Many months were to elapse before we would recover.

10

Return to Ottawa and Command of a British Division, 1958-1963

I assumed my post in Ottawa on April 1, 1958, while the family remained in Quebec City in the Area commander's residence until June 30, when school ended. Our two daughters spent their following academic year in Quebec City, at the *Institut familial* and at the Ursulines, respectively, although Simone and I were in Ottawa. I remained Vice-Chief of the Defence Staff until September 10, 1961. The post was an important one because this was the Defence Staff branch in charge of operations. At the head of the 3rd Brigade, I had participated actively in developing the concepts regarding nuclear war, while from Ottawa I now had to implement certain things. Graham, who welcomed me with open arms, was only a few months from retirement. He wanted to initiate me in the higher-level functions and often asked me to replace him on the committee of the three Chiefs of Staff and the Defence Council.

In fact, I had undertaken my task as Vice-Chief many months before arriving in Ottawa. In mid-December 1957, I had gone on a cruise on the U.S. nuclear submarine U.S.S. *Sea Wolf*. I had concluded from that that the future of such submarines looked bright. Moreover, since the USSR had similar ones, it could—by removing a good portion of their gadgets—use them to land commando teams in isolated parts of our territory, such as Labrador or the mouth of the Mackenzie River.

In January 1958, I had participated in my first meeting of the Permanent Joint Board on Defence (PJBO). On that occasion, we had gone to the Cuban base at Guantanamo, where the U.S. Navy and the Marines had shown us their knowhow. This committee, to which I was going to devote a great deal of my time over the next few years, had been set up in 1940 by Canada and the United States to study the joint defence of the two countries. It was an advisory body that had no decision-making powers, only the power to recommend. A broad range of subjects was discussed. Each of the two sections representing the participating countries was chaired by a Foreign Affairs official. For Canada, the Vice-Chiefs of the three arms were members. With the Americans, the arrangement was quite similar.

Meetings were held every three months in a very informal atmosphere. The committee thus became an extremely flexible instrument for the exchange of views and information, as well as a forum for testing new ideas. Many defence-related matters were negotiated there, at a level very close to ministerial.

In 1958, the chairman of our section was Dana Wilgress, whom I had known very well in Moscow and whom I have already mentioned. Things went very well between us. His counterpart, John Hannah, became a friend of mine over the ensuing months. Our delegation also included Dr. L'Heureux, of the Defence Research Board.

The main topics we dealt with from 1958 to 1961 were the brand-new North American Air Defense (NORAD) agreement, the equipment and armament of the two countries, the nuclear armament policy and the Defence Production Sharing Agreement set up in 1959. Wilgress and I made great efforts to place this last activity on a solid foundation; the initiative had been agreed upon by the two governments, but the PJBD had to instill life into it. A lawyer from the Canadian Defence Production department, Bill Huck, worked closely with the two of us. He was a friend I had met thirty years earlier, in Kitchener. Our main achievement within the joint programme was to obtain the installation in Canada of a helicopter engine and parts plant. During the sixties, many U.S. helicopters in Vietnam flew with parts and engines that came from Canada.

With the Americans there were other kinds of issues to be settled as well. Thus, when they wanted to have two hundred additional people in Churchill in northern Manitoba in order to carry out certain military experiments in the Arctic, I had to write an explanatory memorandum, approved by the government (which was always—and rightly—sensitive to the quality and extent of the U.S. presence on our territory).

Another decision indirectly related to the United States was made in 1958, namely, to stop the project for the construction of the Arrow aircraft, which would have been the pride of our air force. Since a slight depression had undermined the Diefenbaker government's financial situation, the government singled out Defence and limited our budget to $1.5 billion per year. I must add that the government withdrew substantial amounts from the Army's pension fund. Approximately ten years later, we had to put back into the fund $300 million per year from our budget, for two years in a row, to plug the hole in the pension fund.

Finally, out of its own budget, our department was to be responsible in the future for the massive civil defence effort undertaken by the government during those crucial years of the cold war. Under those circumstances everything that used up a lot of money had to be reviewed, including the Arrow project. Within the tri-service committee where the issue was discussed, I was on record as being in favour of continuing the Arrow. Graham was against, but he was not the factor that decided the matter. It was Diefenbaker who finally abandoned this Canadian aircraft, thus agreeing on this point with the old Liberal government, which had reached the same conclusion in 1957, but had put off making it public, figuring it would make the announcement after the election that was going to return it to power. . . . The news became official on February 20, 1959. That potential masterpiece of aeronautics, the Arrow, disappeared,leaving in its wake a few thousand unemployed and creating a real tragedy for the Canadian aviation industry. The prototypes and drawings were destroyed, the skilled manpower left the country or the industry. It was after that decision that the Defence Production Sharing Agreement was born. Since then, we have been buying American military planes. Overall, however, our defence industry usually sells to the United States more than we buy from them.

As Vice-Chief, intelligence matters were within my field of responsibility. I organized a modest system to enable me to have fairly good knowledge of the atmosphere within which NATO General HQ operated at all times. It was always useful to know what the allied Chiefs thought. The other aspect of intelligence I was interested in most was electronic surveillance, which stretched all the way to Vietnam and allowed me to make fairly accurate forecasts regarding the likelihood of an upsurge in communist activity.

Between 1954, the end of the French presence in Indochina, and 1958, many things had happened. Tens of thousands of Catholics from North Vietnam had moved to the south. Léon Mayrand, a Canadian, had overseen the operation, which had gone fairly well. Those refugees had to be able to settle in, however. Our delegation had to be provided with the means to monitor that phase and its inevitable difficulties. Electronic listening posts had been set up in order to find out—and we did so quite effectively—what the North was preparing against the South, often in co-operation with communist sympathizers living in the South. Although listening did not change the facts, it allowed us to hope that we would always know enough to counter (how, exactly, remained to be determined) hostile initiatives from the North, designed to prevent the South from developing as we were entitled to believe it could do.

A commission to control the armistice between South and North Vietnam was also set up. Canada, India and Poland were members. There were Canadians in both Vietnams, in Laos and in Cambodia. By 1958, the reports we were receiving from there became increasingly worrisome. Hostilities grew between the two Vietnams. The South, as we all knew in the West, was not ready to withstand a major attack. We had to give it time to prepare.

On the ground, our men met with frustration after frustration. Each small control group included a member of each of the three nationalities present. Most of the time, this is how things went: a Canadian noted an incident that violated the armistice. In order for that act to be truly recorded, the Indian (India chaired the Commission) and the Pole had to approve it. The latter, however, never saw anything or was not available when the investigation required his immediate presence. The Indian, in order to avoid problems, agreed with the reasons given. When they went to the site of the event, twenty-four to forty-eight hours later—when the Pole was available—all traces had disappeared, and a Polish report blamed the Canadians for making trouble.

The Geneva Conference that had created this commission had ended without leaving a permanent secretariat. The Indochina Commission could accumulate as many facts as it wanted, but there was no one, at a level where decisions could have been made, to receive them and prepare a response. The North was violating the armistice left, right and centre, yet nothing was being recorded. One night, for example, all village heads of an area in the South were killed. This went unrecorded.

One of the results of this situation was the disenchantment of our men. It became extremely difficult to persuade those we sent there that they could play a positive role. Most of them, particularly the officers, had the impression that we wanted to get rid of them. Few believed that their career would be advanced by a stint in Indochina.

Fortunately, we were able, for some time, to improve our monitoring of events. George Ignatieff (who was of Ukrainian descent) was my External Affairs counterpart when the Vietnam question was on the table. Together, we attempted to see things more clearly. One of the decisions we took in 1960 was to withdraw our missions from Laos and Cambodia, two countries where nothing had happened for over one year. A few months later, however, war resumed in Laos. Loang-Prabang, the capital, as well as several outposts were attacked. The country seemed about to collapse when, in one of those surprises Khrushchev sometimes pulled on the West, the USSR agreed that the guarantors of the armistice should meet in Geneva. All communist activity suddenly ceased in Laos. Why? Because the conference was chaired jointly by Great Britain and the USSR. While the conference was meeting, the Control Commission would have been empowered to report any incidents to the Commission. The Soviets were not prepared to be put on the spot like that.

Ignatieff and I came up with something that nevertheless placed the USSR in a quandary. Our goal was to prolong the conference as much as possible, because we realized that this was the price to pay to keep peace in Indochina. I therefore sent to Geneva, with his whole family, one of the great experts of our electronic listening system, Brigadier Leech. Many people argued against that decision at the time in the belief that the meeting would be over within two weeks. By making demands unacceptable to the Soviets, we saw to it that the conference could not be adjourned quickly.

Our modus operandi was as follows. For a given area, I requested twenty-five listening posts instead of the three or four already in place. After lengthy talks, a reasonable compromise was reached. Then I had our people ask that each post have two helicopters. Discussions resumed. The meetings lasted for nearly a year. The British chuckled. They had a good idea what the reason was for our "extravagant" demands, although I had not told them about my strategy in order not to compromise them. Undoubtedly, the USSR suspected that someone behind the scenes had decided to play a little game. Perhaps it knew who the person was. At any rate, I used my knowledge of Soviet thinking to create a nice little farce using compromises (which we also made along the way) and the length of the talks.

Unfortunately, pressure on Canada to stop the whole thing was beginning to mount. The Diefenbaker government gave in, but not until I had left my post of Vice-Chief. A few short months after Leech's return, warfare resumed in Laos: the USSR was no longer in Geneva to receive the incident reports.

In the midst of these activities, there were others of varying importance. Thus, in April 1960, I had to produce a secret study of the impact of a reduction in Canadian civil and military personnel. The two options I was working on were of the order of 10 and 20 per cent, respectively. However, it was a later government that made the decision to proceed with the cuts. All this made great demands on my time, but in spite of a heavy schedule, I was able to get my pilot's wings for type L19 and L29 reconnaissance planes immediately prior to a posting that was to take me to Germany.

Before dealing with that, though, I would like to dwell on my relationship with an extraordinary man, Major-General George Pearkes, Minister of Defence during most of my stint as Vice-Chief. No newcomer to Canadian military affairs, Pearkes was a hero who had earned in World War I the highest and rarest decoration awarded by the British Empire, the Victoria Cross. Between the wars he had moved up the army ladder and, during the forties he was G.O.C. Western Command. He had later entered politics and became Minister of National Defence under Diefenbaker.

I have already stated that I was often asked to sit in on both the Chiefs of

Staff Committee and the Defence Council. That is where I first had direct contact with Pearkes. We soon became friends and our relationship kept getting better. There was something like a kinship of thought between us and the Minister had great trust in me. I often accompanied him on his trips. During one of them, to London, Ontario, Pearkes was asked as he disembarked from the plane whether he was happy with his appointment as Lieutenant-Governor of British Columbia. Surprised, Pearkes did not know what to say. I came to his assistance by pushing him in his car and telling journalists that we were running late. Pearkes then told me that he was not aware of such an appointment. I replied that there was no smoke without fire. With his usual smile, Pearkes nodded and said "I guess not." The news was true, and this was to be his last trip as Minister of National Defence.

Pearkes was extremely tired at that time. The people around him were quite difficult. His associate minister, Pierre Sévigny, more intent on socializing than on administration or policy development, did not help him. The aviation lobby had persuaded Pearkes to support the Arrow aircraft programme fully and this stand had isolated him within the Cabinet. The Navy and the Army also had programmes that Pearkes defended to the fullest. Within the fixed budget we had, however, it was impossible to carry them all out, and Pearkes had to bear the burden of the resulting conflicts. Moreover, his relations with Diefenbaker had become extremely tense following, among other things, the famous and highly-criticized NORAD agreement that Pearkes had, in my opinion, supported somewhat too quickly upon his joining the department. Big-hearted and loyal to the profession he had followed for over thirty years, the courageous, well-respected Minister was completely drained. He needed some rest, we well knew.

Pearkes had told me that on Labour Day in September 1960, he intended to go to Lake Simcoe. On the expected day of his departure from Ottawa, however, Diefenbaker had asked him to remain available. When I found out, I called Simone and we decided to invite the Pearkeses to our cottage on Lake Wakefield. Simone called Mrs. Pearkes who, concerned for her husband's health, accepted, admitting that it would be difficult to persuade George. I said I would take care of it. I communicated with my signals specialists, who assured me that excellent communications would exist at all times between the cottage and the government's operations centre in Ottawa. The Minister accepted the invitation on that condition. The two ladies left together in the early afternoon. Following a very difficult and hot work day, I brought the Minister to the cottage, where we arrived around 1700 hours. The weather was nice and cool at the lake and, after a drink, I announced that we would eat after 1900 hours. George said: "If you allow me, I'm going to rest a little." He was very surprised to wake up twenty hours later.

The lakeside atmosphere and his fatigue had won out. The balance of the weekend was spent sailing or around the bridge table. That brief stay was most pleasant. A few weeks later, when he left his post, Pearkes came to thank me for having given him a hand when he really needed it. He most generously returned the hospitality once he was settled in the Lieutenant-Governor's residence in British Columbia.

My relationship with the good General George Pearkes had been like that between father and son rather than between two generals of different generations. I have unforgettable memories of my contacts with him. With his successor, Douglas Harkness, I had fewer opportunities to fraternize. Anyway, in early 1961, I learned that I had been chosen for a posting that was going to take me to the Federal Republic of Germany for two years.

By 1961, Canada had been providing forces to NATO for ten years. In the northern part of West Germany, the Army had a permanent brigade within the British sector. At the time, the military strategy of the Allies was "gradual response," a doctrine with which I was well-acquainted.

I can only speculate on the reasons that made the British request, in late 1960, that a Canadian take command of their 4th Infantry Division, which was part of their Army of the Rhine, and with which our brigade often trained. What I do know is that Great Britain recognized that there were few Canadian officers left who had war experience. I suspected that this command offered to us was one of the means of pressure used by Great Britain to prevent Canada from changing the nature of its military participation in the Alliance. (I shall return to this question in chapter 15.)

As a result of the request, my name was proposed to the British, and they accepted it. With nearly four years behind me as Vice-Chief, I was available. Furthermore, I was still relatively young (47), I was energetic and my potential for promotion remained good. Finally, my immediate superiors had perhaps seized this perfect opportunity to send me away, for I must admit that many of the ideas I was advocating at the time were quite unacceptable to them.

This appointment, made public in March 1961 and effective in November, was a marvellous experience. It was the first time—and the only time to this day—that a Canadian had acceded to that position. Things augured well, since in 1961 Sir Richard Hull, one of my ex-instructors at the Imperial Defence College, was the Chief of the Defence Staff of the British Army, while Admiral Mountbatten, whom I knew and respected, was the Chairman of the Inter-service Committee.

Prior to our departure, all the administrative and financial arrangements regarding myself were made between our two armies. Michèle had just married a young R22^{e}R officer, whose future seemed promising. As for our younger daughter, she was already in Europe when we boarded the *Empress of Canada* on October 22, 1961. Andrée wanted to continue her studies in French. After a very careful survey, there remained three good schools on our list of possibilities, including the *Institut de la Légion d'honneur* in Paris. That was indeed her choice. The Institute had been founded by Napoléon the First in order to provide good instruction to the daughters of his new officers, who were themselves utterly uneducated. Obviously, this was yet another means to implant his new dynasty in the midst of the traditional, old European courts. The Institute was located at Saint-Denis-sur-Seine, to the northeast of Paris. In addition to providing excellent education, it was not too far from the place where I was to be posted from 1961 to 1963. It was through General Catroux, whom I had known in Moscow, where he was the French ambassador, that this opportunity arose. Since the children of holders of the *Légion d'honneur* were eligible for admission, and since I was a holder of that honour, Catroux had been able to have Andrée admitted even though she was not French. Upon her arrival in Paris, she stayed for a few days with Mr. and Mrs. Jules Léger, our ambassador there, who then took her to her school.

Simone and I therefore arrived in Great Britain by ourselves in late October. Even before having assumed my command—and this was to be confirmed subsequently—I felt that I was one of the most favoured Canadian officers in terms of career postings. In England, I made a formal visit to Buckingham Palace where I signed a special book: from that moment my appointment became official. During my brief stay at the War Office, I met many superior officers as well as colleagues I had met at the Imperial Defence College in 1950-51. I was told what was expected of me; among other things, reorganizing the division based on new principles laid down by the War Office and bringing to my unit some of the experience accumulated as commander of the 3rd Brigade, in which we had worked a great deal on a doctrine for the use of our forces in a nuclear war theatre. Furthermore, I was told that I had to participate in all the joint activities of the three British divisions in Germany.

I then crossed over to Germany to assume my command. On November 10, I was very warmly welcomed by the man I was to succeed, Sir James Cassell, whom I already knew well. I was given a service residence, a magnificent home approximately fifteen miles from my HQ. The War Office paid for three employees to maintain the commander's residence, the guest house and the garden, which was fenced in and well-guarded.

The HQ was in downtown Herford. My operational sector was to the south of the Cologne-Berlin highway, with a Belgian division on my right and a British division on my left. My units were basically British: three infantry brigades (including a Guards brigade) and an armoured brigade.

How were my young British soldiers going to react to this novelty—the first foreigner for many years to command, in peacetime, entirely British troops? Everything seemed to indicate that I would have no particular problems. First of all, the Canadian Army had patterned its organization on the British one. I was very well acquainted with the regimental spirit which was the basis of their (and our) successes. Also, I had been accepted at the higher levels, that is, they believed I would be able to do the job, something I did not doubt. During my visits in London, I was treated as one of them, and I did not feel at all like a foreigner. Once in place in Germany, I quickly received wonderful proof of their loyalty.

According to British tradition, which was what we practised, it was the NCOs who really led the troops. They were a very independent bunch. On December 1st, about two hundred of them serving in my division invited me to an official dinner in my honour. On that occasion, they did things perfectly. At one point, as was the custom, the senior NCO stood up to wish me welcome. On behalf of all of them, he said he was proud to be able to work with an officer who, until very recently, had only been known to him by his excellent reputation. His words and the hearty tone of his speech were, to me, a pledge of loyalty that I did not expect. Following the usual expressions of thanks, I talked with that NCO and asked him how it was possible for him to accept so readily a Canadian officer who, moreover, was French-speaking? His reply was typical of British NCOs: if the War Office has selected you, you must be the right man.

During my two years there I can say that my relationship with those men was perfect, as were their discipline and dedication. Among the Guards in particular these qualities were extraordinary (they still are, as witnessed in the Falklands). I could only be proud to have been a full member of that marvellous British Army.

Over those two years the work involved NATO troops with their particular problems. Since the soldiers were accompanied by their families, our battle plans had to take this factor into account. Throughout that period I had to adjust both to the top hierarchy and to my subordinates. My opinions were respected. I undertook to eliminate some outdated traditions. For example, the men who were part of the armoured corps that had taken the place of the cavalry of earlier centuries, were called "troopers." There was no harm in that. But to keep up the tradition the young soldiers had to get up at 0500 hours to go feed (check the radiators) all the mounts (tanks) of the units seemed somewhat quaint to me. To their great joy, I put an end to the practice. In general, aside from a few problems that were quickly settled with my first aide-de-camp and some little misunderstandings regarding the cost of lodgings, everything went smoothly.

I do not feel that it would be appropriate to discuss here the British strategy at the time, its positive or negative aspects. Suffice it to note that in that position, as well as in others I held before or after, I put in my best efforts, using my abilities and experience to the utmost.

One day, I went to Lunéville, in France, where there was a French brigade that was part of the same army group as my division. General Deysson greeted me in laboured English. The inspection was also done in that language although, when the opportunity arose, I addressed the men in French. At the meal, I told Deysson clearly that I was a francophone (I had already told him that once or twice before, but he was so engrossed in the details of our tour that he had not seemed to have heard me). After a few seconds, he burst out laughing. The conversation then turned to my nationality and how I had reached that post. A French Canadian at the head of a British division was quite mystifying to him. Nor was my name a clear indication, for if there was indeed, at the same time, a General Allard who was French, there was also another, British one, part of a long military lineage that went all the way back to the Normans.

In Germany we had many contacts with two German divisions. One of my tasks at the head of the 4th Division, Hull had told me, was to establish good relations between the British and the Germans. There was some stiffness between those two groups, a vestige, no doubt, of the last war. Since I was neither anglophone nor British, the hope was that I would be able to play, in the field, a role in the desired rapprochement. I therefore entertained many Germans (with whom I did not hesitate, when the opportunity arose, to talk about the years from 1933 to 1945). In my opinion, we had to stop playing the role of occupier—officially ended in 1955—and instead create links with the civilian population, to make it understand the solidarity aspect of our presence. Little by little, I became real friends with the mayor, the manager of the town of Herford and the director of the Westphalian Conservatory of Music. The Herford Symphony Orchestra was where the Berlin Orchestra placed its promising musicians. Records produced by the Conservatory were heard at my residence by guests with whom I had the friendliest of relations.

My stay in Germany was partly a cultural one. I helped with the Weser Music Festival that covered a whole season and was held in a dozen small castles along the Weser River. One day, when I was invited to City Hall for a visit by German industrialists, I recognized among the musicians who were playing the shepherd who, from time to time, brought his sheep to my park to "mow" the lawn. On those occasions, I had heard him play the flute, from my balcony. Seeing him in formal dress in the midst of the small orchestra reminded me of the extent to which I was immersed in music since my arrival in Herford. Obviously, this was not something I disliked.

During the summer of 1962, we organized a major European trip that included Andrée as well as Denise Auger, one of her Quebec City friends. We wanted mainly to go to Italy, which Simone had never seen. We had no money at all. I decided to buy a trailer that I hitched to our Peugeot. We entered Italy through the Swiss border and left it through the Austrian border. Between the two, we went to Como, Milan, Florence, Pisa, Sienna, Rome, Naples, Pompei, Ortona, Rimini, the Taranto Peninsula and Monte Cassino. I had planned this itinerary thoroughly in advance. In the mornings, I would ring a bell: forty-five minutes later, we had to be ready to leave. The trip was wonderful in spite of the strict schedule (which was followed throughout except on one occasion, in Rome).

We devoted one week to Rome. Colonel Tellier, our military attaché in Italy, was waiting for me. He left us his apartment and his driver, since he was himself going on leave in the north. In San Apollinare, somebody called me "signore colonello." It was the local beadle who had just recognized me. We visited Mrs. Berardi, whose house had cost us so many lives eighteen years before. We passed through San Fortunato and San Marino, that little republic which had not signed the peace with Germany after World War I and which had managed to avoid World War II.

We crossed into Austria at an altitude of 9,000 feet, through a high, snowy pass. After crossing part of that country, we returned to Germany and went to Bayreuth, where some friends had invited us to the Wagner Festival. We did not attend the entire festival, but during our four days' stopover, we heard, from a centre seat, two magnificent operas, *Tannhäuser* and *Lohengrin*. The same friends took us to a royal hunt in the Austrian Alps, in the course of which I shot a chamois. I have unforgettable memories of that episode and an excellent 8 mm film that I have viewed with pleasure many times. Back in Herford, I did my accounting: aside from what we had taken with us at the outset, the trip had cost us $500 (for four people and thirty days).

The time had come to send the girls to school and to resume the training of the division. It was around that time, if I remember correctly, that the journalist Hélène Pilote came to interview me in Herford for *Perspectives* magazine. The Canadians had therefore not forgotten me completely.

My posting was nearing its end when the Cuban crisis broke out. One of my roles, in case of problems, was to keep the access to Berlin open. The Cuban affair led the Soviets to close their roadblock at Harmsted. I had to negotiate to have it reopened and as a result, I had to spend a few days longer than expected at my post.

When we left the division, on October 14, 1963, we had a highly positive view of our experience. Simone had seen many new countries because, in my free moments, we had gone together to visit the castles of the Loire, Holland, Spain. Furthermore, she had contributed a great deal to the social work of the division. For example, she had often visited the Buchholz displaced persons camp, where she had spent some unforgettable moments.

As a result, she left behind a multitude of friends. Overall, both she and I could say that we had been spoiled, coddled even, by the British.

Germany, which we had visited thoroughly, marked us forever. As for the Germans, they filled me with admiration especially because of the culture that they had bequeathed to the world. I found them open and welcoming, even in Westphalia where we were posted and which was recognized as one of the regions where the people are the most reserved. Had my French-Canadian origin made them more open than usual? Or more curious?

When I left Herford, I took with me unforgettable memories while leaving behind many friends.

11

Unification: Prologue,
1963-1965

We left the 4th Division on October 15. Between that date and the 31st, we went for a farewell tour to London before embarking on the plane. We were happy to return home, in spite of some nostalgia, which we both felt, for Germany. Andrée had preceded us for the school year at the Sisters of the Holy Cross at Sainte-Rose de Laval. The following year, she started her studies at the University of Ottawa.

My job, starting on November 4, was to be the chief of Canada's entire civil defence system. I was also given another important responsibility, to study the potential reorganization of Army HQ.

The Conservative government had placed great emphasis on civil defence. Since our department had to co-ordinate this area, huge amounts had been devoted to it: training of the reserves (increasingly made up of civil defence specialists rather than soldiers), exercises, siren facilities (never used, not even for exercise purposes) everywhere in Canada, starting to build government nuclear shelters in the various Canadian urban centres and promoting individual or family shelters. These responsibilities had created some difficulties, however. What was the true role of the Army: military or civil defence? How should we use our budget? What amounts should be earmarked for our troops in Europe and how much should be set aside for civil defence?

When I took up my post, I was asked to study the issue of our participation in civil defence and to check where costs could be cut. This task alone kept me very busy. First of all, I had to establish a good contact with my Ottawa office (I was already acquainted with it, in general outline because of my old posting as Vice-Chief). Then I travelled from St. John's,

Newfoundland, to Toronto; I spent a few days in Ottawa, then I left again for British Columbia, returning to central Canada with stopovers at important spots.

What was the state of civil defence at the time? What there was, in 1963, was the result of lengthy studies done in the fifties, at the height of the cold war. Its development followed two levels, that of our department and that of the provinces, since the latter were to implement certain plans in case of nuclear attack. In my position, I had to provide liaison with the provincial governments and ensure that the regional HQs were fully staffed. The regional centres which—should a nuclear catastrophe occur—had to shelter the provincial governments were already in place, although at some of them the actual bunkers had not been dug. We verified the procedures the provinces would have had to follow. The entire system was based on the means of communication, which we had funded, and what there was was good. It must be pointed out that my predecessor, Major-General A. E. Wrinch was a signalman like Findley Clark, who had been my Chief of Staff from 1958 to 1961. In Ontario and Quebec, it was the provincial police—and elsewhere the Royal Canadian Mounted Police—who would control operations in case of need. In fact, these police forces covered all the regions and were connected to our communications centre in Ottawa, which was itself linked to that of NORAD at North Bay.

During my visit, I took note of these facts and of many others (supplies to be provided, role of the reservists who, after receiving warning of an impending nuclear attack, had to get together to prepare the re-entry, etc.). I now had to separate the wheat from the chaff. On the one hand, it was very expensive to maintain civil defence, which—we were all hoping—we would never have to use. On the other hand, this type of defence was part of the deterrent strategy because a hypothetical attacker ought to be discouraged by the fact that the target population is well-prepared to deal with a nuclear situation. Anyway, by various means, we managed to reduce our participation by a few million dollars without impairing the overall effectiveness. Many of our responsibilities were transferred to the provinces. Implemented in 1964, this system has since been reorganized to take into account new developments.

In Ottawa, we did many studies related to survival. One of them covered the path that nuclear fallout might follow from the United States, the assumption in this case being that the enemy would not attack Canada directly. It must be said that it is relatively easy to survive fallout if one is prepared. It is usually sufficient to be able to spend two weeks in a shelter well-prepared for the purpose, in order to allow specialized teams to decontaminate the worst hotspots and to let time do its work (the rate of radiation drops quickly, each day).

But what would happen if, after all, we were the target ourselves? We thought that cities such as Montreal, Toronto, Calgary, Vancouver and some others would be very likely strategic objectives. In that case, the problems would be immense. As an example, I recall that we looked at what would have to be done in Montreal in such a case. We concluded that in the event of an alert the city would have to be evacuated because the nuclear fallout shelters there were insufficient. How would that go, say, on New Year's Eve, when there would be office parties just about everywhere and when, at the time of the alert, tens of thousands of people would not be at home? It would be a mad scramble to reunite the families. Automobiles would break down and block traffic. The gas stations still open would be completely overwhelmed. In 1963-64, there were not enough bridges for the population to leave the island quickly. In any case, where would it go? Could the surrounding countryside house all these people? Which way and how far should they go to escape the potential fallout? Won't the attacker, undoubtedly aware of our plans, detonate his bomb at the very spot where he would be certain to kill a maximum of fleeing people? Faced with this problem and with our lack of means to solve it, we had to be realistic . . . and hope that the balance of terror would be maintained, thus preventing direct nuclear war and its effects, primarily fallout.

A trip to Sweden at that time impressed me very much. The Swedish measures in this field were far superior to ours: all public buildings and apartments had to have shelters; remote areas were also equipped with them; individual initiative was encouraged. With only a little warning, approximately 80 per cent of the population could at least be protected from fallout. Could we do as well? Yes, if we had the political will and were willing to pay the cost of such steps.

Today, when I think about the nuclear issue, I say to myself that small, irresponsible nations must be barred from having access to nuclear weapons. Indeed, I do not believe that the five powers that now have such weapons are prepared to start a conflict involving nuclear weapons. But the others . . .

My experience with civil defence, which covered only a few months, was very interesting. I understood what was involved in Canada and I contributed to rationalizing it. With the help of our specialized officers, an information campaign was prepared in English and in French. Through short films or recordings, I distributed information about what there was and why.

My other major task was to review the operations of our staff. Up to then, we had copied the British, as I have often pointed out. In 1963, they were themselves reorganizing. Lieutenant-General G. Walsh, who had become Chief of Staff of the Army in 1961, gave me the principles upon which my study had to be based: the reorganization was to reduce the number of committees at General Headquarters and increase the responsibility of the outside commands. I also had to find out how certain tools, such as computers and satellite communications, could help us. Finally, in what quick, rational way would the Army best be able to go to war?

My thoughts on the inter-service committee method, so well established since the tenure of Brooke Claxton, were well known. In order to make headway with my project, I therefore brought together a committee of communications specialists and National Research Council representatives, experienced, traditional staff officers as well as a few young ones who were prepared to sweep the slate clean. The discussion periods were very productive, particularly when the "young" and the "old" clashed.

When they got seriously down to work in Ottawa, I crossed over to Great Britain to see what was happening there. I had some knowledge of the British studies because I had been a "Britisher" only a few months earlier. But I had served at that time far from London HQ, and I now had to look at the matter in depth. My idea at that point was to apply in Canada (with the usual modifications) what was being done or contemplated in England.

After returning home, I examined with my committee the various theoretical concepts based on studies done since the early 60s on pay, personnel and training. Many of the recommendations made in those studies had begun to be implemented. We amalgamated these various data on the basis of the concept of what a staff should be.

My work, all of which was intended to provide advice, was not to serve any practical purpose. Indeed, we were now approaching the spring of 1964. My theoretical studies for a new army HQ were complete when, in March, Minister Paul Hellyer summoned his top officers of the three Ottawa HQs to inform them about certain decisions he had made and of which we had already been more or less aware for some time.

I will permit myself here a long, two-part parenthesis. The first one is made in order to stress that my interest in the francophones' place in the Forces had not flagged. During my stint with the British, I had nevertheless been able to note that, for operational reasons that were already predictable in 1957, the francophone battery and squadron of the 1/8th Hussars had been dismantled after being sent to Germany. In my role as British commander and even in the one I played since my return to Canada, all I could do was take note of these facts. It was very difficult for me to take initiatives. Anyway, in 1963, I managed to have Brigadier Dollard Ménard attached to my office. Ménard, whose health was quite precarious at the time, was surplus to strength. I had charged him with analyzing all the studies produced over the last few years on francophones in the Army. Based on that new report, I intended to undertake actions not yet quite defined. In the spring of 1964, Ménard was making very good headway, but once again new parameters had to be taken into account.

The second part of my parenthesis involves the studies that were being done on the armed forces since the 50s and which seemed to be designed to disgust any military man. The MacDonald Report, made public in the middle of the Korean War, was given more news coverage than our soldiers who were dying at the same time on foreign soil. Unfortunately, many events that hit the headlines at that time were ridiculing the administrative branch of the Army. Undoubtedly, there were reasons to laugh, but the MacDonald Commission had neglected the mitigating circumstances. The Army had barely been demobilized following the 1939-45 war when it had been asked to rebuild itself in order to take part in the Korean War and to participate in the North Atlantic Treaty Organization. These sudden, major fluctuations could not occur without a hitch, particularly since, by 1950, the 1939-45 army consisting of many high-quality militia officers (lawyers, accountants, engineers, etc.) no longer existed. These professionals had returned to their civilian functions once and for all. The members of the militia who responded to the call in 1950 were generally of lower quality. This sudden expansion had an unfortunate effect on the entire administrative system and on the professional quality of the new army's cadre of officers.

Could the Army overhaul its administrative system? The MacDonald Report had discovered shortcomings that we already knew. Some recommendations did not take into account the fact that the Army was still at war. Some others were simply ridiculous. For example, it was recommended that no project be undertaken without the Quartermaster General's prior review and approval. As soon as the system was implemented, requests for project approvals started coming in. Faced with that backlog, the Quartermaster delegated his approval authority to the Vice-Quartermaster General. As such, I had to approve them after having the Director of Engineers study them. These studies occupied many people and took approximately three hours of my time per day. This was very costly. Once, a request to put a lock on a door of a redoubt at Halifax fortress landed on my desk. The thing was to cost twelve dollars, six for materials and six for labour. I gave the go-ahead by phone, but tired of seeing the engineers' and my own time wasted like this, I had an analysis done on the cost of the entire approvals process. I found out that the approval of that particular project had cost more than $200. This was, of course, not the only instance where reality was stranger than fiction. What was one to do? That system operated for more than a year and was only corrected after I left. Thus, some of the subjects covered by the MacDonald Report had certainly not been studied sufficiently to justify some of its conclusions.

Once in power, the Diefenbaker government wanted to demonstrate, through a grand gesture, its intention to correct the administrative failings of its predecessors. It set up the Glassco Commission with powers of inquiry into all federal departments. The undertaking was praiseworthy, but when we were presented with the names of the military committee members, we found no one there capable of grasping the complexities of administering our peacetime forces. Following the cold war, the peace was entirely unlike the sad pre-1939 situation. I had been Vice-Quartermaster-General at the time of the MacDonald Report, and I was Vice-Chief of the General Staff at the time of the Glassco Commission. I therefore received the military committee of the Glassco Commission in my office, ready to discuss the various ways that the Army had of accounting for, controlling, using and replacing its equipment according to whether it was at war or at peace. These subjects, however, were not brought up.

In May 1964, when Hellyer summoned us, he wanted to talk about a reorganization resulting from the Glassco Report. My initial response was not favourable. In my opinion, the department was once again about to launch, without serious examination, something that could only harm rather than heal. Why did I think that? Perhaps because of a certain conversation I had had with our Minister, Hellyer, in 1963, when I commanded the 4th British Division. He had at that time communicated to me his ideas regarding the changes he wanted to make in the organization of his department and the armed forces in general. I had not been enthusiastic and the man himself had not impressed me at all during that first meeting. Since I was serving in the British Army, however, I had kept mum.

Hellyer had a few basic notions regarding the forces. He had had a stint in the Air Force during the war at a level at which he was probably unable to grasp the full scope of the operations of his branch. Then he had been Associate Minister of Defence for a few months during the last St. Laurent government. Once he became minister, his main advisers were ex-airmen who had fairly limited knowledge of the two other services. I will admit, though, that in the situation prevailing at the time, this lack of experience was not altogether a bad thing even if in limited, specific cases, it was a disadvantage.

After my return in November 1963, I had very little contact with the Minister—until the month of March 1964, to which we shall now return. At that stage, irrevocable decisions had been made without much prior consultation.

At the conference to which he had summoned us, Hellyer announced that there was going to be an integration of the three services (Navy, Army and Air Force), that this would reduce our personnel requirements and therefore the number of officers, and that there would henceforth be only one general headquarters, closely linked to the department. The general structure of the new forces would be based on functional commands, the composition of which would be announced gradually by the integrated General Headquarters. Officers forced to retire early would receive compensation that would allow them to have the same pension as they would have been entitled to normally. This was lucky for some, like Brigadier Dollard Ménard, who, after having been kept in his surplus position for more than a year, was finally able to retire with full pension four years before the expected date. He nevertheless had the time, in June, to give me in a few studies, the conclusions of which he had quickly modified in order to take into account the Air Force and the Navy.

In summary, I found in those documents the quantified confirmation of the problem that many of us already knew very well, namely, that the proportion of francophone officers diminished as one approached the top of the pyramid. In the infantry, they constituted 21 per cent of the cadres, whereas in the artillery the percentage fell to 5.5 per cent. It took no wizardry to conclude that, outside the R22^{e}R, a francophone infantry unit, there was no salvation for my compatriots. At the various staff schools, we were underrepresented. Among the other ranks (NCOs and men) we noted the same phenomenon. Altogether, the Army had 14.5 per cent francophone officers, owing to the major role played by infantry. With integration, however, according to Ménard's pessimistic conclusion, that ratio (of the total number of officers in the three branches) was going to drop to 7 per cent. Under the new system, francophones would only account for 9 per cent of the positions among the other ranks. (About two years later, I found out that although the situation was very unsatisfactory, it was somewhat less so than what that intuitive expectation had been.) Now that the three services were going to be united, those studies had to be repeated in greater detail although I was persuaded that the only thing this was going to prove was that the situation was worse in the Air Force and the Navy than in the Army. We shall dwell on this point later.

In the course of the decapitation announced by Hellyer, we lost Major-General Paul Bernatchez, who, having been seriously ill the previous year, had to retire one year before the mandatory age. This was a catastrophe, for I was now the only genuine French Canadian at my level. Some claimed that Majors-General Fleury and Moncel were francophones. Fleury spoke good French and had an attractive personality, but he was of Irish origin and education. Although we liked him, he could in no way claim to represent our aspirations. As for Moncel, whose ancestors were French, he was a Protestant and anglicized. There was no longer anything French-Canadian about him; he could not even speak the language.

Under the circumstances, I had to make a decision. On the one hand, there was a policy that had been clearly expressed by the Minister and his advisers. On the other hand, there were us, the old-timers: should we join the movement or leave? I quickly reached my conclusion: I would stay and support loyally, as one must, what was being prepared. One of the reasons for my choice was that I had to shoulder a major responsibility, that of the future of francophones. In the midst of all the rapid changes, my colleagues would indeed tend to forget their French-speaking compatriots. In my inner self, I was determined to carry alone the francophone torch that I had sometimes helped Bernatchez carry; not to abandon that cause unless my life were made impossible; and to turn it, if necessary, into a political matter. Having made that decision, all that was left for me to do was to continue doing the best job I could and to play the francophone card at the right moment.

Soon afterward, I left my post as chief of civil defence. In May, Hellyer informed me of my promotion to lieutenant-general. In June, I was told that within the new structure I would be Chief of Operational Readiness. The organization chart below shows that I was more or less third in line within the integrated HQ.

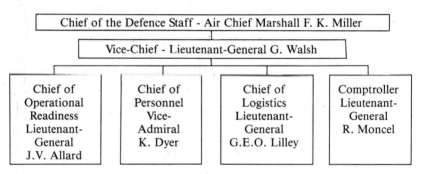

My position was to exist only during the reorganization stage, during which I had to ensure that our combined forces would be ready to respond in case of emergency. My staff was therefore an inter-service one and had to think primarily in operational terms. Since I had always liked the Navy and since I had also been a pilot since 1961, I found it easy to be interested in the specific requirements of each service.

One of the secondary roles connected to this position, as to that of any general staff officer, was that I was often asked to make speeches. On those occasions, I dealt with major current issues, the first one being the role reserved to our forces by the brand new White Paper on Defence. That document reiterated Canada's support to NATO as well as our continued participation in NORAD. Emphasis was also placed on participation in peacekeeping operations organized by the U.N., which placed added emphasis on mobility. Those three points were intimately linked to the overall strategy of our government, which was to help discourage the outbreak of wars. Finally, of course, we dealt with integration.

Regarding integration, which became effective on August 1, 1964, my numerous interventions throughout Canada and abroad (primarily in the United States) covered its major aspects. Henceforth, the organization of General Headquarters would be based on function rather than on the service, the goal being to reduce the excessive burden of administering the three services by eliminating duplication and integrating planning (most of us acknowledged the serious inadequacy of planning co-ordination between the three services). Thus, more men would be available to serve in operational units. We expected to reduce by 20 per cent our strength in HQs, in the various support units and in the training elements. Moreover, it was hoped to save one billion dollars over ten years, which could go to the procurement of new equipment. At that time, 14 per cent of the budget was devoted to acquisitions and it was predicted that that percentage would rise to 25 per cent by 1974.

My job as Chief of Operational Readiness was not the easiest one. The division of responsibility among the four branches was difficult to determine even though the old functions of the three major headquarters seemed to correspond to the new ones. In fact, the very nature of the tasks assigned to each branch prior to integration was very different, and this had a great impact when the time came to amalgamate them. Take training, for example.

In the Army, training was the responsibility of the general staff, that is, of Operations. The Army fought in regiments; the general staff, accountable for the competence of a given regiment in the field, wanted to have control over its training. In fact, each regiment trained its recruits according to standards set by the general staff. But those recruits were instilled with the very special atmosphere of each regiment and they became full members of their units.* On active duty, it could happen that a regiment would lose a substantial portion of its strength, while continuing to hold its position in combat. Later, it would be withdrawn from the front and reinforced to the desired level by being provided with new members who had received training according to the standards set by the general staff.

In my opinion, rightly or wrongly, the Navy and the Air Force operated quite differently. To them, war was above all a matter of machines. In both cases, the vehicle was available and one had to ensure that competent people were in charge. In those two services, thus, human competence was built up through training for which the personnel branch was responsible. When the men were deemed ready to carry out a specific task, they were transferred to

---

* A member of the Forces will say that he is a "Van Doo," an RCR, a Dragoon, etc., thus identifying with his unit and with its characteristic esprit de corps.

operations. A destroyed aircraft or ship generally meant the end of combat for the survivors until they were provided with a new vehicle.

There were two different ways, therefore, to perceive training. Faced with this discrepancy, the Minister decided in favour of the Navy-Air force system and against the Army system. The training of the three services would thus be the responsibility of the Personnel Branch. I was concerned for a while for our precious regimental spirit. In the event, it came through quite well. One of the results of that decision was to remove from my branch an element that I believed belonged to it automatically.

I was going to have enough things to do without this. My main problem was to ensure that our forces were ready to act quickly and independently of any mobilization. We therefore rejected the principle that had been the basis for our tiny pre-1914 and 1939 forces, namely, that they had to provide, in case of war, the officers necessary to the men who were mobilized. In order to reach the new objective, I thought of sub-dividing my branch into four: force development, operational requirements, operations and communications. My responsibilities were indeed many, ranging from the formulation of the logistic and operational concepts that our forces had to follow, to the control of the operations centre in Ottawa, and including the supervision of operational resources, naval hydrography, military cartography, meteorology, the communications system, and many other things.

During my stint in Operational Readiness, I set up an army tactics and organization council. Under the leadership of Major-General Roger Rowley that group had to produce a field duty manual that would cover all aspects of a doctrine common to the entire land army. The document had to establish the principles governing all army operations and training. It became a sort of Bible dealing with every kind of operation and each stage of warfare. In the United States there was a Combat Development Command that was dealing with future options; in 1965, that command was thinking about warfare in the 70s. Rowley, his co-workers and I had many contacts with these American experts during the various stages of producing our manual.

The first draft of that work was ready around February 1965. I sent it for translation immediately because I wanted the two versions, French and English, to be published simultaneously. After various peregrinations, Canadian Forces Publication 165 came out in March 1967. A major gap had thus been closed.

In the field of the reserves, always dear to my heart, I had the opportunity to act. A commission for the reorganization of the army reserves was set up. As mentioned, our reservists had been deeply involved in civil defence. Studies showed that they had therefore lost a good portion of their operational capability. The reserves had to be brought back to operational standards with emphasis on survival. Indeed, we believed that a good soldier could easily convert to civil defence. Although the reverse was always possible, it was more difficult. Our reservists took note of the new roles they were meant to play. There were four such roles: supporting the regular army, helping it meet Canadian commitments to NATO, assisting in the maintenance of public order, and supporting the regular forces in their civil defence responsibilities.

Prior to August 1, 1964, while the commission had dealt with the Army, two committees had studied the Navy and the Air Force. The government had ordered the total number of reservists to be brought up to 30,000, and the three reports had taken this into account. Those documents therefore quickly landed on my desk after August 1964 in order that co-ordination might proceed within the integrated system. I must admit, though, that the question of the future of our reserves had not been settled to my satisfaction by the time I left the Forces. We shall return to the subject later.

Another issue that required a great deal of my attention was equipment. It must be pointed out from the outset that in 1964-65 the Army was not acquiring matériel. What it would thereafter do would depend on the doctrine that was going to be adopted following our studies. In any case, as far as armour, artillery and the infantry were concerned, we had just gone through a major rearmament stage during which the Americans had helped us a great deal. We were soon going to look for new reconnaissance vehicles, and armoured troop carriers had already been ordered. Meanwhile, the artillery reviewed its organization on the basis of mobile, fluid battlefields. It was also understood that the sappers and signalmen were going to be modernized gradually; in the latter case, this was very important because we had troops in the Suez Canal, in Germany and everywhere in Canada with whom we had to stay in touch. Lastly, once the "Bible" was completed, we would no doubt have to acquire computers and helicopters (for troop transport, observation, medical evacuation, etc.).

The other two services were not in the same situation. The navy could not continue without new ships. Those ships had to be very sophisticated, including helicopter carriers that would be used for anti-submarine warfare. Vice-Admiral Welland took charge of the programme, which made very good headway and yielded the Tribal Class 280, four magnificent ships, each driven by two turbine engines. Two supply ships were also included, H.M.C.S. *Protecteur* and H.M.C.S. *Provider*. Construction started quickly and caused me no difficulty.

The Air Force did not advance so smoothly. The Minister asked me to chair a committee for the selection of a new aircraft. We received the proposals of the manufacturers who wanted to take part in the tender, then we studied the bids. The airmen wanted to have the Phantom F4, undoubtedly the best aircraft we had to study. But the politicians found that it cost too much for the tasks that it was to do. The new government policy was for Canada to have no atomic weapons. Why should one therefore acquire a means to carry such weapons? However, the other principles upon which the decision had to be based were ambiguous. There was no directive from Miller, who was an air force man. In the prevailing confusion, I decided to select an aircraft that was slower and less sophisticated than the F4 but capable of supporting the ground troops in a limited conflict. Although the airmen on the committee disagreed, the F5 was selected as the most cost-effective. The Minister approved our conclusion. Unfortunately, after 1970 the F5 was given no real aerial mission, one of the reasons being that the electronic sensors that we had planned on and which were to give it its effectiveness were never purchased. It therefore remained basically a ground support aircraft, in addition to complying with the government's nuclear veto.

In Germany, our Air Force was more or less integrated with that of the United States. The F5 did not fit in at all with our role in Germany. Either the F4, or an additional boost given to our CF104s, would have been a much more acceptable solution. The second one was chosen.

Did we really need the F5? Did we buy it to keep a portion of our aeronautics industry working? I must reiterate that our defence policy was full of ambiguities. Was the F5 the result of that? Quite likely that was the case, if one thinks about it! At any rate, the time has now come to regret the lack of courage of the Diefenbaker government, which had decided to abandon the Arrow five years earlier. George Stanley was correct in writing his "military history of an unmilitary people," as it is obvious that the Canadian government represents the great majority of Canadians, who, in peacetime, are utterly indifferent towards military affairs. We are a nation that will "participate," if necessary, without demanding adequate preparation from the government.

At the time, one essential part of my task was not going well, namely, the organization of my branch, which would remain virtually at a standstill during my tenure. Before diving head first into that job, I wanted to familiarize myself with the individuals around me within my integrated staff. I believed that the first step was for the people who were part of my organization to learn to know themselves, to learn to know each other and to discover the overall spirit that would enable each leader to co-operate with the other two branches and perhaps grasp the still-hazy concept of an integrated Forces.

During that initial contact phase, I often wondered whether the venture was worthwhile. I also noticed many things. I admired the loyalty Admiral Bob Welland, my deputy, showed towards the Navy; he shared my concerns even while keeping them to himself. The airmen were very different. Our Air Force was already "integrated" with that of the United States, whence it derived its strength and security. The senior officers of the Royal Canadian Air Force (RCAF) had nothing to fear from the ministerial project—indeed, they were all for it. They were calmly waiting to see the developments. For its part, the army, not yet affected by reorganization, was feeling unconcerned during those first months of integration although its system of command was going to disappear shortly. It seemed to have confidence in those leading it.

When I felt that the familiarization period had lasted long enough, I began structuring the organization of my branch. Obviously, operational responsibility was assumed on a day-by-day basis. Elsewhere, though, I ran into difficulties. There was no firm policy or well-defined intent from the Minister, and this had a negative impact. For instance, I believed in the need to proceed by stages: some decisions would be taken at my level, others would go to a council that would discuss the various options before finding a solution. The Comptroller, however, who had been given responsibility for organization and to whom I had to submit this type of proposal, did not perceive any need for stages. He had Miller's full confidence, so that the proposals Moncel rejected (including the one I have just mentioned) went no further.

One thing was successful, however: the operations centre, which had been proposed, designed and organized by three highly competent officers, one from each service. They had understood that it was of paramount importance that I have control over the events when necessary. The centre went into operation very quickly, in 1964. When I left, in 1969, it was still operating in the same format. This was a somewhat minor success in view of the general picture, although it was quite important in itself. My recommendations regarding communications were also well-received.

Overall, however, my work soon became frustrating. I therefore undertook an inspection of the troops. I began with a familiarization course for the CF104 aircraft at Cold Lake, Alberta. Once there, I did a full review of what a typical mission was on the European theatre, in addition to a training mission. Squadron leader Paisley, in charge of the course, was a superb instructor; it is certainly not easy, with a few lessons, to enable an L19 pilot to handle CF104s. The Air Force had thus done the right thing by putting me in the pilot's seat. Moreover, that experiment was one of the first tests of integration. Is it possible to make a land army officer (who is over 50) understand the technical, psychological and physical problems of the person who, with an ultra-sophisticated aircraft, must deliver a bomb on target behind the enemy lines? The answer seemed to be that a layman such as a land army officer could understand the elements upon which the airmen's professionalism was based, without however acquiring all the subtleties of their profession.

Following that stay, I visited our Air Division in Europe. When I arrived at Marville, France, I went to the Metz HQ and subsequently to Zweibrücken, Grostenquin, Baden-Soellingen. Finally, I went to our training base in Sardinia, Italy. That tour had two purposes: to make contact with the men and try to reassure them about their future; and to familiarize myself with the basic role played by our Air Forces in Europe.

Afterward, I went to see the land army in Westphalia. It was in the same condition I had seen it in two years earlier. Morale was excellent, and except for a few questions that I could readily answer, the situation was calm as people awaited developments. On another occasion, I went to Halifax where, with Admiral Landymore, the new commander of our naval forces, I visited the Naval Research Centre as well as his HQ.

In Ottawa, the proposed organization of logistics, personnel and comptroller branches had been approved, but there was still nothing regarding operations. During that long silence I was tortured by one question. Let me say first that I chose to listen and keep mum in the midst of the many rumours that made the rounds at the time. One of them became persistent, namely, that the three services would be unified and patterned on the U.S. Marines. In my opinion, that model was not suitable in view of the great Canadian diversity.

Before continuing, I would like to take a brief "political" step backward in time. Throughout my life, I have expressed my French-Canadian nationalism through the federal Liberal Party. But I have served well the Conservative Party when it was in power, although I did not like many of its characteristics. As a good soldier, I was perfectly straightforward and loyal, even though I knew, between 1957 and 1963, that no cultural reform would be effected by the "Westerner" ministers then in office. The first file that landed on my desk when I was Vice-Chief was a recommendation to eliminate the 3rd Battalion of the R22^{e}R; my refusal allowed the 3rd Battalion to continue to exist.

In 1964, however, in spite of the return to power of the Liberals, I was not at all reassured. The Minister's advisers were raising a lot of doubts. I worried about the francophones' future. The very existence of the only francophone unit, the R22^{e}R could be jeopardized if the "Marine" concept was adopted. The time had come, it seemed to me, in early 1965, to start a serious game of poker. Let me add first that I had made some verbal representations that yielded absolutely no results. On one occasion, when the top brass at Ottawa HQ were meeting to discuss the location, under integration, of the various military training schools, I had intervened in a way that had surprised many people. One fact seemed to be emerging at the time, namely, that there would be no such school in Quebec . . . as if by coincidence. My proposal, therefore was to reopen, on Mount St. Sylvestre, the radar station that had existed there during the war and to give there courses to all Forces radar specialists. I added that that training would be provided in French. Immediately, an anglophone pointed out that this was impossible because those who knew only English would automatically fail. Frankly, I had not thought that my trap would work so well. My reply could be summed up as follows: what would you do today with the unilingual francophones sent to take a technical course in English?

Things had not gone any further on that occasion, but I increasingly felt that the time was coming to assume my full responsibilities as the highest-ranking francophone in the Forces. On January 8, 1965, I prepared a long memorandum for Miller in which I mentioned the responsibility that I felt I had. I was very careful to link the idea I developed in it to the job I was doing at the time. I shall be very brief on the main points of my appeal because we will later return to the basic issues. I mentioned, of course, the example of the R22^{e}R that should be followed in other types of units. In order to avoid launching into such a project with our eyes closed, I asked permission to set up a commission of inquiry on the role and fate of francophones in our forces, a commission that would report directly to the Minister and some of the recommendations of which could be submitted to the Royal Commission of Inquiry on Bilingualism and Biculturalism, which had been at work for more than a year. I even specified to some extent the structure of that task force which would cover a whole range of subjects, including recruiting, selection, training, the availability of education for dependents. I added that, in my capacity as Chief of Operational Readiness, I had been studying for some time the problem of obtaining forces that would be truly national and effective. To achieve that goal we had to have the full support of Quebec and substantial participation by its population. My goal was therefore to enable my compatriots to see that the forces respected their rights and gave them a genuine opportunity to co-operate in the defence of their country.

The idea was to prevent the R22^{e}R from eventually being thrown into the melting pot that the U.S. Marine model would create. On the contrary, we had to study ways to expand francophone representation in branches other than the infantry in order to create truly Canadian armed forces.

Miller did not reply. After a reasonable waiting period, I repeated my initiative, asking whether he had received my previous letter, of which I attached a copy. His aide-de-camp informed me that Miller was leaving on holiday and would not be coming back for a month. After his vacation, I still received no answer. The time had come for me to do something dramatic. The decision was a difficult one, since the resignation I wanted to tender involved a considerable loss of pension. I wrote to my friend Jean Lesage, who had become Premier of Quebec. He assured me that if worse came to worse, he would have a position for me in the Quebec civil service, to which I would be able to transfer my pension fund. With that assurance, I sent my resignation to Air Marshal Miller. It had the effect of a bombshell and quickly landed on the Minister's desk. He summoned me immediately. I was given to understand that the question I had put to Miller regarding the unified future of our forces would force the Minister to reveal his policy prematurely, which he wanted to avoid. But he recognized the relevance of my questions regarding the future of francophones. After lengthy deliberation in the presence of a witness, he made the promise, in exchange for the withdrawal of my letter of resignation, to examine the issue and find a Canadian solution to the unification of the forces. As a result of this conciliatory attitude, I returned to my office and, before my co-workers Generals Henri Tellier and Marcel Richard, my secretary Paul Berniquez and many anglophones, I tore up my letter and threw it into the wastepaper basket. Today, I regret not having kept a copy of it. Anyway, that is what the situation was at the end of March 1965.

It was not at all clear what the government intended to do. Since the B & B Commission was under way and was studying Defence, I assumed that people wanted to await its conclusions before going any further. For the moment, I thought that Hellyer had salvaged the basics. (Would my departure have been acceptable to a government that tried to promote opportunities for French Canadians?)

During the interview, Hellyer and Miller had asked me to specify my views, without however committing themselves to launching my task force. Indeed, they did nothing of the sort. On two occasions, in April, I wrote memos to Miller regarding what the commission of inquiry I had suggested should be. It would be headed by a colonel who would have under him three lieutenant-colonels dealing with the historical, sociological and military aspects of the issue. There would be a secretariat and investigation teams to which experts would be attached. I proposed that a consultant be appointed for each branch, and even proposed three names, including my own for matters regarding the land army.

In the meantime, another one of my initiatives, closely linked to the francophones in the Army, namely, the expansion of Valcartier, was well under way. We have seen why that was necessary (chapter 9). Living in Ottawa, one gets to know valuable people. Thus, Jack Pickersgill and I had established a solid relationship. One day, I asked him whether he could get me an appointment with Prime Minister Pearson, whom I also knew well. The appointment was made and I arrived at the Prime Minister's office with a map of the Valcartier region. I explained to him for what reasons the base should be expanded and showed him, on the map, the exact sector that should be expropriated to meet potential needs, which were necessarily somewhat undefined at the time. Mr. Pearson responded very positively to my idea. In this case, I had decided not to debate that issue at HQ, as I felt once more that it could well end up in a dead end.

On April 26, 1965, Hellyer visited Valcartier and the surrounding grounds that could be used for an expansion of the training area. He took advantage of the opportunity to make a speech to the R22^{e}R declaring himself sympathetic to the francophone cause. He said that since he had started taking French lessons, he had become aware of the difficult situation in which French-speaking members of the forces had been involved with their families. He stated that he intended to gradually do things that would change our living conditions and ensure that more francophones would remain in the Forces. He had no specific steps in mind, but it would come. Certainly, francophones had to be allowed to improve their career possibilities.

To me, that visit and that statement proved that I had scored some points. For example, the Valcartier matter was finally about to be solved. But Louis-Frémont Trudeau, who commanded Valcartier and whom I had asked to keep me abreast of everything concerning the base, wrote to me on April 27 that he had found the speech too political as Hellyer had not committed himself to anything in particular and had not even mentioned the "fair share" francophones would be able to claim.

At that point, I could no longer direct studies or do anything else. A few days before this trip by Hellyer to Quebec City, I had to be admitted to the military hospital in Ottawa with severe back pain. I was to remain stretched out on a board for three months. I was almost fifty-two years old, and I was sure I had reached the summit of my military career. What I did not know was that this position—to which I was not going to return again—had prepared me to do much more.

For approximately one year, I had begun to see how three different staff systems could combine fairly harmoniously when the requirement arose. I had discovered a highly Americanized Air Force, a very British Navy and an Army that, particularly since the Korean War, stood between those two extremes and, therefore, in my opinion, was the most Canadian of our three arms. Fairly well aware of what was going on in the land army, I had busied myself primarily with the naval and air elements. As regards the naval side, a programme for the replacement of the units had been accepted. In the Air Force, a new aircraft was going to enter service within eighteen months. This long-term planning had been very demanding for those who had worked on it.

My position had been that of a Commander-in-Chief. I had had to examine all the issues (personnel, logistics, etc.) and stay constantly in touch with these various areas, as well as with the commands of the three arms which, in 1965, were in full transition. From the logistics viewpoint alone, I had had to deal with aspects that were completely new to me. For example, the Air Force inventory comprised approximately 600,000 parts that occupied hundreds of thousands of square feet of storage space, not to mention highly specialized sub-units responsible for an exacting level of maintenance.

Overall, I had had happy moments and others that had been much less so. The organization of the branch was still up in the air. On the other hand, army doctrine was well-advanced; we had developed excellent links with the Americans, thanks, among others, to Brigadier J. A. W. Bennett. He represented us well in the United States, and often came to consult with me in order to ensure that we were on the same wavelength before he presented some of our demands—particularly for equipment—to the Vice-Chief of the U.S. Army (whom he had cleverly managed to rope in). I had had a close-up view of the important role we could play in the standardization of weapons and communications. The United States, Great Britain, Australia and our own country had formed an organization that met every year, for this purpose, in one or another of these four countries. I also had the impression that the cause of francophones had made some progress in spite of the lack of obvious indications.

Lastly, other activities directly related to my regiment had been a source of great joy to me. One of the projects I had set up was completed on September 26, 1964. At the *Collège militaire royal de Saint-Jean*, the Governor General had unveiled a monument offered by the regiment, on which were inscribed all the major battles of the R22^{e}R. That monument was entirely of my design, including the concept, precise sketches and the co-ordination of the various stages of its construction (my friend Armand Ross, then commandant of the College had helped me with this last stage).

At the Citadel, on October 10, 1964, the memorial of the R22^{e}R, which I had fully supported for years and to which the French army had generously contributed two guns from the 1750s, rebuilt using the Europeans' ancient art, was inaugurated.

12

Commander of Mobile Command

During my lengthy stay in hospital, the Chief of the Defence Staff came to visit me; he was soon followed by the Minister, Paul Hellyer. The latter reminded me of certain aspects of our conversation which had led me, earlier in the year, to withdraw my letter of resignation. He then asked me if I would be willing to command a new organization to be known as Mobile Command. This command was to include the entire Army as well as certain sections of the Air Force which would support or transport these troops. The task seemed very burdensome to me, prostrate as I was on a wooden board with my back in such a sorry state. I asked for a week to think about it.

There seemed to be nothing spectacular in the Headquarters of the armed forces, apart from the disappearance of the Operational Readiness Branch which, I was told, would be decentralized at the command level (including Mobile Command). But, this suggestion of decentralization took my fancy. At the end of a week, I sent Hellyer an affirmative answer. A few days later—we were in mid-June, 1965—I was appointed General Officer commanding Mobile Command. Ten days later, I left the hospital and got down to work right away.

What we already knew of this new command and what we learned at various information meetings held at NDHQ in 1965 prompted me to say that Mobile Command would be the new HQ of the Army and would take in the current land units. But I was immediately confronted by several questions. What was meant by Mobile Command? A force to intervene in unknown theatres of operations? A force for internal stabilization? A force for the defence of the northern territories?

In Ottawa, a Central Integration Planning Group had been set up under the auspices of the Comptroller General. This group, which had been formed following the appointment of the commanders of the new commands, was intended to ensure that those commands would not implement structures incompatible with the reorganization at Headquarters in Ottawa. We therefore had ongoing consultations involving the commanders and this group, as well as the Chief of the Defence Staff. No one could or would answer my questions. The Chief of the Defence Staff merely suggested a meeting, outside Ottawa, where we should be far from the telephone, a kind of think-tank to discuss the problem. Obviously, this attitude left me somewhat sceptical. I found it strange that I should have been entrusted with such an important task without being informed of its basis or aims. However, I agreed to the suggestion and my office staff organized this "closed retreat." Major Fred Harris, my assistant, was the contact point. The chief organizer was none other than Major Ramsey Withers, a future Chief of the Defence Staff.

In 1965, I had already known Withers for eleven years. We had seen each other in Korea and later when he was with the Canadian Brigade in West Germany and I was commanding the British Division. In February 1964, he had brilliantly completed a course at the (British) Joint Services Staff College. In the summer of 1965, only just settled into a new posting in Ottawa, he learned that he had been transferred—officially, two or three days before me—to Mobile Command. Of course, he had absolutely no way of knowing what this force was which had just been brought into being on paper. I had complete confidence in Withers, and having a free hand, I had easily been able to "land" him. I would never regret it.

The think-tank, composed, among others, of Generals Anderson and Fleury, met near a lake not far from La Malbaie in the calm atmosphere of Quebec's great forest. Interesting discussions took place but without the emergence of any concrete solutions to my questions. The participants' good humour nonetheless showed that they had complete confidence in me as far as future events were concerned. Everyone went home satisfied in spite of the meagre result obtained.

Since no one was willing to tell me what road to follow, I concluded that it was up to me to make the decisions. I acted swiftly and energetically. I had long realized that it was not always necessary to await Headquarters' approval—nor, especially in this case, the Planning Group's approval—before taking action. On many occasions, I took initiatives that I considered necessary for the work and submitted their result for eventual approval. It was bulldozing, but the method worked.

I sketched a badge in September 1965 which would serve as a guide to my thoughts. The latter, touched up a little by the Chief of Personnel, Admiral

K. Dyer, is still in use and consists of a maple leaf, to represent the whole of Canada, and four arrows, indicating aircraft flying off in all directions. The background of this emblem is a white cross, clearly indicating the civilization to which Canada belongs. It was thus on these themes that Mobile Command was set up. Even though my basic philosophy was not always understood—or followed—I can say that the embryo I created subsequently grew to quite a size.

When Hellyer had visited me in the hospital, he had told me that the headquarters of the new command must be near an airport and, if possible, on land already belonging to the Defence Department. There were thus several options. However, since all the important Headquarters (which have a considerable economic impact on the area where they are set up) were, up to that time, outside Quebec, I decided to change this trend. We knew that Air Defence Headquarters, which was then at Saint-Hubert, would eventually be moved to North Bay. I could not settle in there right away, but the place had all the necessary facilities with its runway and fairly new buildings. My plan was willingly accepted: the few malcontents hardly got a hearing.

During the interim period, we moved to Longueuil where there was a personnel depot (which has since been demolished). We had all the space we needed there. In early July, the former occupants were transferred to St. Jean. The nucleus of my future headquarters replaced them. We were to work for many long hours at this place amidst the noise of the hammers and saws of the carpenters who were renovating our premises. But the Headquarters took shape quickly with a communications centre (its heart) which functioned very efficiently. On September 20, 1965 the installation of the command took place. At this stage, the organizational concept and needs of the command (among others, in temporary staff) was tackled by the Defence Council. Then, on October 19, the Headquarters was officially opened by Governor General Georges Vanier.

On a more personal level, on September 21, I succeeded in renting our home in Rockcliffe. It was not until October 4 that we moved into the residence that the commanders of the Quebec Command had occupied on Kitchener Street, in Westmount. Meanwhile, Simone, Andrée and I lived at the Windsor Hotel in Montreal.

The organization of the Headquarters obviously had to be related to the task it was called on to perform. But since this had not been clearly defined in high places, I had to invent one. I thus gave myself the responsibility of being able to deploy an element capable of commanding a division without the static Headquarters being paralyzed at all because of it. During the setting up of Mobile Command, the Headquarters of the First Canadian Division was absorbed; most of its positions were transferred to our main organization. Major-General Rowley, DSO, thus came to me from Petawawa. He was an excellent acquisition for, apart from being a former companion-in-arms and a true friend, Rowley brought with him an experienced team which, for over two years, had been studying the different kinds of warfare that Canada might have to wage (see the previous chapter). This group's contribution to the formulation of what our new forces were to be was incalculable and Rowley's experience enabled rapid progress to be made. The Major-General's contribution to the conception and organization of Mobile Command is not sufficiently known; I have no hesitation in saying that much of its success was due to him.

Before reaching a conclusion as to what Mobile Command should be, studies were carried out. Their objectives were to re-examine our wartime structures, bring them into line with the concept of a mobile force and the roles the latter might be called on to play, and to get our wartime strength approved, even though the forces had to be limited in peacetime (while taking into account the risks this limitation might involve). In the process, we had to consider what the government intended to do in concrete terms with its armed forces. Unfortunately, the various White Papers to which we referred had one thing in common: they were ambiguous where they should have been clear and clear where they should have been ambiguous.

Obtaining no satisfactory solution from either the government or NDHQ, I asked General Rowley and his staff to examine the potential troop needs of a division operating in central Europe, taking into consideration the weapons that were supposed to be in our possession in the 1970s and keeping in mind that Canada had rejected the military use of atomic power.

The evasiveness of the Liberal party in this matter must be mentioned here. During the 1963 election campaign, Pearson had said that Canada would respect its commitments of the time, unlike the Conservatives, who were then in power. And these commitments included nuclear weapons. However, Pearson added, a Liberal government would undertake an in-depth review of the country's defence. When Diefenbaker went down in defeat, Prime Minister Pearson and his minority government prepared a White Paper leading to the integration of the armed forces and announcing their unification. From the nuclear weapons standpoint, the agreements were initially observed, but the White Paper subsequently set out a new concept for the utilization of our forces, based on their mobility, so that they could serve with the U.N., with NATO, or within our own territory. A goal was nevertheless also sought: a non-nuclear role for our forces, both within Canada and within NATO.

This matter was of great concern to us, for the absence of nuclear weapons removed all semblance of reality from much of our studies. Would Canada agree to use these weapons at the last minute, or would it stick to its original decision if a conflict arose? If it did, Canadian troops would have to rely on the allies, for improvisation is impossible in this field. But a prior arrangement with the latter would be sheer hypocrisy in view of the Pearson Cabinet's decision. And without any agreement, the allies would probably have made no provision for our eventual needs. In wartime, should the political leaders persist in this course, the troops would have to refuse all outside assistance and very likely become the soft underbelly of allied defence. This situation would be totally unacceptable for a sector commander. This being so, what role would Canadian troops then play at the outset of a conflict that they would be waging alongside allies—which was a highly probable situation? How would our Air Force, without nuclear weapons, be able to play an effective role in Europe? Would our soldiers, without tactical nuclear weapons, become caretakers of munitions or stores, or the guards of airports or GHQs? This thought was enough to affect the morale of the high-calibre officers I had around me.

Our country's soldiers were loyal, silent, and realistic. They knew that it was useless to talk about armaments to a government whose intentions were basically pacifist and led by a Nobel peace prize winner. They made the best of this and chose the solution which would allow them, in case of war, to catch up as quickly as possible with the real situation. As in past wars, they would probably be forced to accept enormous sacrifices for a population that only takes an interest in its soldiers when obliged to do so by the enemy. Without realistic analyses of the situation, our servicemen would tend to follow decisions that others, such as the United States or Great Britain, would have made. On behalf of those who would have to go to the front, I rejected the obvious risk which the government sought to impose upon us, namely, at the time of a war in a European theatre, to have to add troops who would merely play the humiliating role of depot guards before being eventually wiped out in a battle for which they had not been prepared.

As usual, when it came to the defence of Canada, the government's policy of half-measures worried no one except the military personnel involved. In our view, it was not a question of rejecting Canadian policy or the government's intentions regarding the role that Canada should play within the Atlantic alliance. On the contrary, we believed that it was up to the population to judge the actions of its government and to place its trust in it or not. However, the Commander of Mobile Command, who had to accept the political situation, also had to act in accordance with his professional conscience.

I therefore gave firm orders about the roles that our Mobile Command HQ should have. It would have to be able, at all times, to provide staff officers for a division engaged in a nuclear war (even though this division did not have these weapons in its possession), those for an airborne unit able to intervene rapidly in limited conflicts, and those that might be needed to act in the northern sector under the responsibility of NATO. Moreover, provision must be made for administrative and logistics staff and a headquarters able to follow these various situations. Finally, we had to have an air group enabling us to adapt ourselves to these different circumstances.

The first of these roles was based on one observation (without nuclear weapons, the Canadian Brigade in Central Europe was a dragon without fire) and on two hopes: that the government would support it (although it did not do so officially, we were given free rein to plan realistically); and that in case of need, we would obtain the support of our allies, of which we were assured. Otherwise, it would be useless to leave Canadian troops with the British force in Europe, which was already weak.

To maintain itself in the state of readiness needed to carry out all the tasks in which its troops would participate, Mobile Command needed about 37,000 operational men, not counting the administrative staffs of the bases and regional headquarters. It had been (and still was) obvious that this level, under normal conditions, would not be easily attained. The budgetary constraints imposed on the Defence Department in conjunction with the large (and necessary) raises in pay which were expected in 1965 (although they would not be announced until October 1966) prevented us from transforming our dreams into reality. Moreover, the total strength authorized was inadequate. Finally, the armaments purchased were only sufficient for one overseas brigade and for the training of the troops stationed in Canada. The result? We had no reserves of matériel.

The Army, with almost no Canadian industries to back it, although the situation was then changing, was having difficulty asserting its interests. Indeed, in the sixties, this was one of our most serious problems. When it came to purchasing helicopters, only a joint production contract with Boeing, which agreed to obtain the dynamic system from York Gear of Toronto, and the hydraulic system from Jarry Hydraulique of Montreal, had tipped the scale in favour of the purchase of a very limited number of aircraft.

The Army was constantly faced with the problem of justifying its actions. Because of the lack of precision of our peacetime tasks, these were always hard to defend. For instance, the lowest civil servant might decide that the war in Europe could last no more than ten days. You were then asked: how many days would it take you to transport your guns, tanks and other vehicles to Europe? Ten days were obviously not enough. In this case, you then had to justify the operational use that would be made of these vehicles in Canada. The Army finally received the go-ahead for individual training, collective training being automatically sidelined. This attitude was all very well for the Navy and Air Force, but completely ridiculous when it came to the Army. The government was satisfied with the situation and its master, the public, was not the least bit worried about it.

It was therefore with all these handicaps that I had to reorganize my command, a task which I had accepted, first and foremost, to ensure that the Army would have a strong voice in the wake of integration. I think that this is what actually happened. What I had seen and experienced in Ottawa as Chief of Operational Readiness had convinced me that, in some way, I would have to impose an "Army" point of view during the integration process. The way this Army Headquarters was organized reflected my approach. I felt strong enough politically to get its basic plan and structures approved. Although my attitude was at times somewhat uncompromising, it would eventually render great service to the armed forces.

Without going into the details of my organization, I nonetheless wish to review briefly the form that the officering of the operational troops would take. At my request, Mobile Command would control the 4th Brigade in Germany. This formation, very well organized and effective for any conventional war that might take place in central Europe, might easily become useless in a nuclear context. Nonetheless, when the time came, it could be reinforced by drawing on the officers of regiments stationed in Canada. At Mobile Command HQ, we planned for the rotation of individuals, since the lack of modern equipment, even in Canada—as I mentioned above—militated against the rotation of entire units which, once in Europe, would need months to familiarize themselves with equipment which they had never had the opportunity of thoroughly mastering. This question could obviously be revised in the light of new government policies.

Mobile Command would also have an airborne regiment. We knew that the deployment of an infantry brigade overseas could take several weeks and even then only if it were already completely equipped and had received at least one month's thorough training. The light and rapid airborne regiment was meant to "fill the bill" between the time our government acceded to a request for intervention from outside and the arrival of the main body of troops.

There was never any question between 1965 and 1969 that this regiment could only go into action by being parachuted. The most likely situation would be an intervention in hostile territory where, if landing was impossible, the regiment could be parachuted in. The men would then make use of the shelter of mountains, reefs and lakes to obstruct the enemy while awaiting the arrival of the forces who would undertake the major tasks.

What we were seeking was maximum flexibility. One of the ways of obtaining it would be by the rotation of the members of this regiment. This was to take place over a maximum period of two years. All infantry officers and NCOs had to go through it before being eligible for promotion to the ranks of captain and sergeant. This regiment obviously did not follow the Victorian regimental system, since men had to be "fast in, fast out." In this era of the air force, I had to allow some compromise of the principle of the regimental spirit which, in any case, would be upheld in other regiments. There was thus absolutely no question of training professional paratroopers, except for the instructors who, of course, had to be very much at ease in this field.

This regiment was therefore designed to fill a gap in our strategy for modern warfare. In the minds of its planners, it was never intended to remain in the fighting line for more than a few weeks. After my departure from the forces, the regiment became a parachute unit that would be utilized alongside all the other units, but for special missions. In my view, those who took this course showed their complete ignorance of the need for the rapid reactions required by most present-day conflicts.

Mobile Command then had to give consideration to an essential need: the mobility of its administration. The Army and its air wing had to move hundreds of miles, swiftly and with minimum administrative backup. The Army's permanent bases on Canadian soil, such as Gagetown and Valcartier, were essential centres that had to continue to administer the Army, even after the departure of the units posted to a theatre of operations. It was at these bases that reinforcement units would be trained to support those on active service. For reasons of economy, administrative duties were assigned to the operational units. But it was essential to make sure that the administrative staff belonged to the static units so that the operational units might retain their mobility as their first priority.

In the original plan for Mobile Command, the utilization of the Reserve was included (while its training came under the specialized functional command). The idea I was trying to implement came from a lengthy study based on several inquiries carried out in the reserve units. In case of conflict, could they be mobilized in time to intervene? Faced with the new technical and administrative complexities, could the entire units still be mobilized, as was done in World War II? For the use that would be made of these units in peacetime, was it worth equipping them for an exhaustive training which would restrict them to merely supplying reinforcements, or was it better to aim at a new, complementary, regular/reserve role? In sum, was it possible, in the event rapid expansion were necessary, to guarantee the effectiveness of all the essential elements making up Mobile Command, short of having a reserve force whose training, in peacetime, would be aimed at carrying out certain tasks for which it would have to take full responsibility upon mobilization? My answer to this last question was affirmative.

Let us examine the situation in a little more detail. Let us leave aside the main centres, like Montreal, Toronto or Vancouver, where several categories of reserve army units could be stationed. But why, in 1965, as today, did we plan to station only specific units in small towns? For instance, Brockville had an infantry regiment, and Trois-Rivières a tank regiment. In the days when the army was almost mobilized from scratch, this made sense. But under the new conditions there was to be a professional army with a clearly determined wartime and peacetime policy, which was not only to provide officers for the new recruits but to respond from the very first days of a conflict with a combat brigade . Under these conditions, what grounds were there for deciding that Brockville should only produce infantrymen and Trois-Rivières only armoured personnel? In my view, this situation was quite ridiculous. Our reserve ought to have been able to use the professional talents of young engineers, lawyers, doctors, accountants, contractors and businessmen. With the minimum theoretical training and the normal training period undergone by all reserve personnel, it would have been relatively easy to make those men into staff officers to fill Mobile Command HQ requirements if it were suddenly called upon to deploy its strength.

The experience of the years 1939 to 1945 had shown how erroneous our method of mobilizing by regional units already was. At one point, there was a lack of technicians. The unit commanders knew that they had many specialists in their ranks, but it took a long time to convince the top brass to screen the men who had been waiting in England for two or three years for a battle that never came, before sounding the alarm in Canada. Indeed, many machine operators, electricians, welders and tradesmen of all kinds had enlisted as infantrymen, gunners, etc. instead of members of a technical wing because, in their immediate area, recruitment was carried out for one specific unit only.

When the occasion arose, I was to discuss this subject with the seniors of the Brockville Rifles, which were to be very receptive to my ideas. I then went into an experimental phase. As early as 1965, our command was able to send reserve reinforcements overseas to fill some of the gaps in the 4th Brigade in Germany. This proved a great success and seemed very promising. At that time, a lieutenant-colonel of the militia successfully replaced the commander of the PPCLI; young officers and NCOs did equally well. As for the troops, the situation was less encouraging. The regiments did not respect our requests to send trained men. Instead, raw recruits were sent out under the federal summer job creation programme. They certainly showed much good will but their inexperience completely spoiled our plan. I was stunned by the irresponsibility shown by the reserve commanders.

Nonetheless, between 1966 and 1969, I took certain measures to obtain the kind of Reserve I wanted. But instead of pursuing this path, of redefining the tasks of the Reserve and then reorganizing it so that it could take its place in the most recent context, there was a movement after my retirement to wipe out the little I had accomplished and to fall back to sleep by leaning on "the acquired knowledge" of the nineteenth century, which no longer has anything useful to offer in contemporary conflicts. This was doubtless one of the most bitter setbacks of my long career.

In spite of all this, I could claim, on May 30, 1966, that Mobile Command was well established. I therefore invited the Parliamentary Defence Committee and gave it a forty-five minute talk on the ideas set out above. This was followed by an hour-long question period which went off very well even though some Opposition members seemed to be trying to corner me.

At this stage, I had reason for pride. It was less than a year since Hellyer had approached me when I was in the physical condition that I have already described. Since that time, my officers and I had accomplished a gigantic task. Army headquarters and its five regional commands had been dismantled. Of the 2,650 servicemen of all ranks who had served in them, 570 were sufficient for Mobile Command Headquarters which replaced all these organizations. However, efficiency had suffered somewhat from the very considerable reduction in the number of officers. Even so, 2,100 positions had been retrieved by our units or freed for other tasks.

During our few months of work, we had planned to take over 433rd Squadron of Bagotville, when it received its new F5s. We had thus integrated—very partially, admittedly—Army and Air Force, the latter only in its role of ground support. Furthermore, I had succeeded in getting away to visit all our army units, in Canada as well as in Cyprus and Europe. I explained to them all what was about to happen, telling them that in future they would be responsible to a HQ at St. Hubert. This tour showed me that the Army was not worried about integration. I was popular and trusted, both for my way of commanding and for my traditionalism—which had its limits, however, as I have said. I wanted to maintain continuity in our units and this was well known. No, I would not be the grave-digger of their identity! That was a fact and had pleased people.

As to the command of Mobile Command, I must say that I had been surprised at the speed with which I had been able to take over in such a short time after the idea for the project had been presented to me. I had every reason to be pleased with the careful choice I had made of my senior and junior officers, as well as of my NCOs. The team had worked extremely hard and their thoroughness had impressed our units. Indeed, the latter had taken immediate steps to fall in with our new organizational and operational ideas.

In short, Canada, which was already the world leader in the concept of integrated armed forces, had seen the most important element of this concept, namely, a mobile command of an equally mobile, global force, capable of rapid deployment anywhere in the world to carry out peacekeeping or peace-restoring tasks or to wage a limited, conventional war. This command was the most important of all those that had just been created and the most impressive that our country had ever had in peacetime. About 25 per cent of Canada's total forces depended on it. The National Defence Headquarters (Ottawa) would assign to this Command its tasks, goals and the guidelines that were to be respected. On the basis of this general information, the commander would work out his plans and needs.

This force, which could face up to a variety of situations, also had to adapt itself to all sorts of climates and regions anywhere in the world. Hence training was required which, for some of its elements, would be carried out at various latitudes both in Canada and in friendly countries. Since part of the Air Force was to work alongside the Army, the geographical location of the support squadrons had to be chosen. Many air/land co-ordination exercises were to take place. Moreover, sound liaison had already been established with the naval element of the unified forces in case Mobile Command had need of it. Furthermore, it could count on the other functional commands. Should a problem arise that the commands were unable to solve among themselves, NDHQ would settle the question.

Our units were "housed" by bases instructed to supply them with all the administrative and logistic support they required, both when they were on the spot and when they were deployed on operations. It should be noted here that the commanders of these units were to have direct access to a specific sector of the St. Hubert Headquarters and that the base commanders were also to have their own links with us. Thus, they would not be subordinate to one another, while, at the local level, co-operation would be the rule. Our brigades were to become real combat arms, leaving the services to specialized battalions, detached from them but present near the front where necessary.

As to the formations that would eventually come into operation, these might be of various kinds: the Air Force alone, the Army alone, a signals unit or a combination of different units. If the latter—air-transportable at twenty-four hours' notice, which gave our forces a mobility they had never had before—happened to need a headquarters, it was up to St. Hubert to arrange to provide one. The HQ of this Mobile Command was divided along functional lines and was responsible for all the active operational units stationed in Canada. It had to see to their training, co-ordination, development and tactics, ensure the proper rotation of our men in Europe or under the command of the United Nations, answer the requests of Reserve units and civil defence organizations, develop and maintain the Canadian capacity to operate at the divisional level. Our command was not, in itself, an organization that could go overseas to operate. Why not? Simply because our country had agreed in advance that its forces would be part of larger international forces or operate under special commands. However, the administration and supervision of these troops would be our responsibility.

Sectors could be detached from time to time in order to assume specific tasks. Mobile Command was not responsible for the training of the Reserve and its planning for mobilization concerned only the units it already had.

The functions of the commander of this vast network are worth describing. We had decided that he should inspect and visit his units scattered all over the world—from the Northwest Territories to the Gaza Strip. Over the period of a year, 134 working days, according to our calculations, would be used for this function alone. He would also have to prepare and supervise the execution of the major exercises that might eventually involve all his men. Furthermore, he was to organize an important annual conference at which operational problems would be studied. Every two years, he was to see that operational command post exercises were held. And, of course, he must at all times supervise the work of his HQ staff.

It was immediately obvious that the "boss" would need the help of senior and experienced assistants (in addition to his personal staff). Indeed, operations would be in the hands of a major-general as well as the operational support branch. Lastly, the Comptroller would be an experienced colonel.

In concluding this part, I must add that, in spite of this enormous organizational task, which took up most of our time between July 1965 and May 1966, we managed to carry out several exercises and produce lengthy reports dealing, for instance, with the morale of our troops.

During my time with Mobile Command, the lot of francophones was not forgotten. I had been given clearly to understand, at my interview following my abortive resignation, that it would be far better do to things to improve the lot of my fellow countrymen than to produce studies: in that task, it was added, I would readily be given support. In 1965-66, I had installed the HQ of the largest of our commands in Quebec: this should serve as a centre of attraction. Obviously, it was not sufficient. In my little speech at the official opening, in October 1965, I had added that I saw a more important role for Valcartier and that I would make special efforts to get more francophones to join our ranks.

In regard to Valcartier, the game was well and truly won. On September 23, the decision was made, in Ottawa, to enlarge this base by about 40,000 acres. There were many excellent reasons for this. The base was well situated and its enlargement would give it the necessary flexibility for the combined exercises we wanted to hold. The new weapons we were to receive and the principle of mobility required a vast amount of space. Naturally, some of the people whose lands were expropriated—though few in number—protested. But in the House of Commons, on February 22, 1966, except for a few difficult moments for Hellyer and Cadieux (the latter had become the

Top) Visiting a South Korean orphange.

(Left) A group participating in the demanding marching exercise.

(Right) Centre front, the Canadian military cemetery in South Korea.

(Top) Assuming command of
Eastern Quebec area. At right,
His Honour the Mayor of
Quebec, Mr. Wilfrid Hamel.

(Left) With Jean-Ernest at
the cadet camp in Valcartier,
summer 1957.

(Right) Dr. John A. Hannah
(centre) and the Honourable
L. Dana Wilgress (right),
respective chairmen of the
U.S. and Canadian sections o
the Permanent Joint Board
on Defence, look on as an
Elgin Air Force Base officer
describes parts of the compl
missile facilities. Air Provin
Ground Center, Elgin AFB,
Florida, January 1960.

(Top) Jaguar and driver (Cpl Smith). The British Army knows how to do things in style!

(Left) Staff-Sergeant Paul Berniquez served with me in the 4th Division. I had had this faithful secretary with me from the time I was in Korea until I became CDS. Paul ended his career in the 1970s, as a captain, with only one regret: he had never been able to make me into a good golf player.

(Right) A good-bye from some British friends, October 1963. From left to right, Generals Darling, Butler, Pearson, Allard and Wheeler.

(Top) Monument given to the CMR by the R22ᵉR, Fall 1964.

(Left) My eldest daughter, Michèle, about the time she got married.

(Right) My daughter Andrée after receiving her officer's commission in the Canadian Navy.

(Top) This is where integration took me, in the first phase.

(Left) New naval flag being dedicated. I'm not happy, as my face and clenched fists demonstrate.

(Right) Paul Hellyer addresses guests at the farewell before my departure from Ottawa to go to Longueil, August 1963.

(Above) With Frank Miller, July 15, 1966.

(Below) The members present at the first Armed Forces Council. Seated, from left to right: Vice-Admiral Ralph L. Hennessy (Comptroller General); Lieutenant-General William A.B. Anderson (Mobile Command); General J.V. Allard (CDS); Rear-Admiral J.C. O'Brien (Maritime Command); Air Marshal Fred Sharp (Vice-Chief). Standing: Air Commodore G.G. Diamond (Air Transport Command); Air Marshal E.M. Reyno (Personnel Chief); Major-General M.R. Dare (Deputy Chief Reserves); Air Vice-Marshal R.C. Stovel (Training Command); Major-General R.P. Rothschild (Matériel Command); Rear-Admiral H.B. Burchell (Technological Services); Air Vice-Marshal M.E. Pollard (Air Defence Command).

(Above) Visit to Halifax, August 1966.

(Below) With Archbishop Makarios, 1967.

(Above) Companion of the
Order of Canada, November
12, 1968, presented by
Governor General Roland
Michener.

(Below) With Dr. Fazil
Kuchuck, 1969. The situatio
in Cyprus had hardly
changed since 1967, but our
uniforms had been modified

Minister's associate after Cardin had been appointed Minister of Justice), everything went off quite well.

Subjected to the ground support flights of F5s or helicopters and the noise of simulated combat, the close neighbours of the base could scarcely have been happy. Once Valcartier was enlarged to the size I had suggested to Ottawa, there would be no more obstacles in the way, for instance, of accommodating entire artillery and tank units there. It was then up to me to sell the idea that these units should be francophone.

We have now come to more long-term projects over which I had little influence from my base at Longueuil. Nonetheless, I did what I could, as Hellyer and Miller had suggested I should, a year previously. Major R. Monette of the artillery wrote me a letter—at my request—on October 18, 1965, in which he described the problems encountered by X Battery: not enough francophone or bilingual officers in the artillery; several men unable to speak French, which meant that this supposedly bilingual battery had to work in English. On the other hand, some francophones had difficulty understanding English and found it hard to adjust; there were family problems caused by men being uprooted, for it was impossible to pursue a career as a gunner and always stay with X Battery. In spite of everything, Monette still believed in the idea of a French-speaking regiment. My reply of November 5 reflected this view when I wrote that I hoped to increase opportunities for francophones in the Forces.

At the end of October, I organized an important ceremony at Valcartier to mark the official incorporation of this base within Mobile Command. The guest, Jean Lesage, gave an inspiring speech in which he declared that co-operation between his government and the Defence Department must be better. Among the spheres of cooperation he mentioned were roads, education, hospital care and training. Unfortunately, I arrived after Lesage's departure. Nonetheless, having learned of this quite new approach—after years of Duplessism—I returned to my office to draft a series of letters and memos. I thanked Lesage in one of these; addressed myself to the provincial deputy minister (Claude Morin) in another to say that I personally welcomed this opening. Then, I turned to Ottawa to which I addressed four memos, each devoted to one of the themes in Lesage's speech. In them, I suggested concrete ways of establishing this co-operation. For instance, the basic training of certain naval technicians might be given in French, in Quebec, to francophones who had opted for these special trades. The same thing would be available for motor mechanics. I knew that Ottawa was having my suggestions studied. But by May 1966, nothing had come of them. Lastly, to close this question for the moment, let us say that on April 22, 1966, I had the opportunity of explaining to the Royal Commission on Bilingualism and Biculturalism, during its visit to Longueuil, my ideas concerning the place that francophones and their language should have in our Forces. My readers already know the themes on which I based my arguments.

These ten, very intense months spent in setting up the Command were interrupted by a holiday and business trip to Sainte Lucie, in February 1966. The Queen paid a visit to the island during our stay which brought us an invitation to a fine reception we shall not easily forget.

13

At the Summit, with Unification

Several weeks before my presentation on Mobile Command to members of
the Canadian Parliament (May 30, 1966), the Chief of the Defence Staff,
Frank Miller, informed me that the minister wished to see me in Ottawa.
Upon my arrival at Miller's quarters, I was asked to go to Hellyer's office,
alone.

The latter gave me a very warm reception. And he asked me the following
question: would I be ready to serve under Robert Moncel, if he were to
replace Miller who should be leaving his post the following July. Moncel was
my junior. But an analysis of my position told me this: I was nearly 53 years
old, and normal retirement age was 55; I had had serious health problems in
1965; I was "in exile" outside Ottawa, and therefore far from general
decisions affecting the Forces, with a consequent loss of influence. All these
factors, which I had considered months before, had already led me to the
conclusion that my career would end at my present rank. In fact, I expected
nothing more from the Army. The little guy from Sainte-Monique de Nicolet
had already received from it far more than he had ever dreamed of. Was I
not the first French-Canadian to have reached the rank of lieutenant-general
in our Army? It was therefore easy for me to assure the Minister of my
complete co-operation should the situation which he had just presented to
me become a reality. I told him plainly that, at my age, I no longer expected
promotion. Lastly, I added that, in my view, Moncel was an excellent choice.
In all, our conversation was quite short. Returning to Longueuil, I said to
myself that the Minister had been very kind in consulting me on such a
decision, which he was in no way obliged to do.

But rumours of a different sort were soon making the rounds. In mid-May

1966, I accompanied Miller to Paris for a conference on the potential impact on NATO of the French initiatives announced the previous March. I was greatly interested in attending a meeting of this top-level committee and to see how this system, in which several nations could intervene, actually worked. Whenever I participated, at my level, in the progress of the alliance, I was always struck with amazement at how well the diversity of interests of these countries could be overcome.

In the plane on the way back, Admiral Landymore, during a private conversation with me, maintained that I was the most likely candidate to succeed Miller. In reply, I told him what I knew about Moncel. But Landymore replied that this choice had been rejected after due reflection. To change the subject, which I found somewhat embarrassing, I reminded Landymore that we were to meet soon at Longueuil to tackle several subjects of common interest, including that of collaboration between our two commands. Landymore did not seem to be too anxious to get off the subject of rumours.

A few days later, as planned, Landymore stopped at Longueuil. He had come from Ottawa and immediately told me of the persistent rumours circulating about me in the dark corridors of Headquarters. I said I believed none of them and we got down to work. That was how things were at the end of May 1966 when the Minister summoned me once again. This time, his office had contacted mine directly. Later, Miller confirmed that the meeting was to take place at 2 p.m. the next day. The Minister's welcome was just as pleasant. In the presence of his associate, Léo Cadieux, he began by explaining that he had had me followed for some time by various journalists and had thus come to realize the great popularity I enjoyed with the troops. He then went on to say that he had chosen me to succeed Miller and that Pearson backed this choice.

Let us go no further for the moment. Let us say, first of all, that the surprise I should have felt was somewhat muted by the rumours that had come my way since my last visit to Hellyer's office. Secondly, let us add for the record that the *Quebec Chronicle* of June 1964, reporting my appointment as Head of Operational Readiness, had speculated on the fact that I had a good chance of becoming Chief of the Defence Staff (CDS) in 1966 and that I would thus become the first French-Canadian to attain the highest position in the Canadian Forces.

Many readers may now be asking themselves: why Allard? I might answer: Why not? But I shall try to go a little further than that. First, let us consider a long-term reason of considerable importance. I do not hesitate to say that a process of natural selection had played in my favour. Several soldiers with the greatest intellectual abilities were unable to remain in the reduced forces that Canada proposed to maintain after 1945: their talents would have been under-utilized. They had thus returned to private practice, to further studies or to other areas of government. The expansion of 1950 and subsequent years would not bring them back to us. Nevertheless, a good number of these excellent men with whom I was to be in competition stayed on. By learning on the job, I had been able to become their equal and to find myself in a position to reach the top.

Secondly, there were more immediate reasons that led our political leaders of the time to consider my name although, even now, I do not claim to know all of them. Strictly from the point of view of "military logic," I do not think it would be too pretentious to say that at this stage, this choice was obvious. I was the senior general in the Army. I had proved my worth in war and in peace. For this reason alone, which should have supplanted all the others, it was known that my appointment could not be objected to. It was quite certain that I would be able to carry out the task. There were several other considerations that probably entered into the picture either explicitly or implicitly. Was I not becoming a sort of symbol just when the celebrations for the Centenary of Confederation were being announced? Moreover, Hellyer may possibly have thought that he could thus win over many Quebec Liberals once the way was open for Pearson's succession, to which he aspired. And then, by acting in this way, the authorities were anticipating certain actions that would inevitably have to be taken once the conclusions of the Laurendeau-Dunton Commission were published. Lastly, there was the fact that the troops often saw me as a father figure. Surely this was a useful factor when progress would have to be made with unification, and quickly too, as the government wished.

Let us now return to Hellyers's office. I understood perfectly without anyone having to spell it out for me that the position of CDS was linked at that time to the thorny question of unification. From the top, I could influence many aspects of the latter, but I would certainly not get the government to change its mind on the actual principle. Moreover, there were the francophones and their future in our forces. In Longueuil, I had had to restrict myself to the land army. My return to Ottawa would give me an opportunity of influencing all three services, but only if I was allowed to have my way. The moment had once more come to lay all my cards on the table. My interlocutor was in for a big surprise.

Rather than accept the Minister's decision right away, I told him that I had certain conditions to make. The latter replied that such an appointment was usually accepted or refused without conditions. However, he was quite ready to listen to me. So I reminded him of the conversation we had had two years earlier concerning the future of francophones. Before accepting his offer, I wished to know what the Minister's opinion was on the subject and to obtain from him the guarantee that I would be able to set up, within as short a time as possible, the study group I had been dreaming of and which must have the means of examining the question in depth. I must also be assured that, before my retirement, I would be able to make concrete gestures, based on the results of the report, to ensure and guarantee equality of opportunity for the advancement of francophones at all levels, within the new structures that the armed forces were about to adopt.

Hellyer turned to Cadieux to see what he thought. The latter agreed with me. The Minister then asked me for an hour's reflection and consultation. Meanwhile, I went over to the Château Laurier for a drink. Upon my return, Hellyer told me that such a question, which committed the government to a specific policy, must be referred to the Prime Minister and probably to the Cabinet and to the Privy Council which had to confirm the appointment. But he and Cadieux assured me that they would present my point of view in a positive light to these two authorities. Satisfied, I repeated that I would accept the post if the response was favourable. We then shook hands and I received a password (which I have now forgotten) from Hellyer which he would send to let me know whether the government was in agreement.

Upon returning home, I described my trip to the ever discreet Simone. And I resumed my normal routine. Several days went by before the Minister communicated the password to me and indicated that the official announcement of my appointment would be made within about ten days. On June 23, a message to all units announced the news, saying that I would take up my duties on July 15, 1966. Assurances of support were soon coming from all sides. Some people recalled the predictions they had made to me years earlier concerning this happy outcome. Others kindly remembered my discouraged state in 1955 or the fact that I had suggested to them in recent months that my career was well and truly over. Above all, there was a great outpouring of pride on the part of many francophones.

At the same time that these messages began to come in, I had to make provisions for my successor at Mobile Command. I chose W. A. B. Anderson, who would consequently be promoted to the rank of lieutenant-general. We had been friends for many years, and I had absolute confidence in Bill whose reputation as a staff officer was unrivalled and who was fluently bilingual. Anderson hesitated a moment before accepting. But I needed him. In certain fields, we would have to present a combined front to the government. And this soldier's son understood where his duty lay. Because his mind was open on the question of new francophone units, I had obtained an inestimable ally for what was to follow. Before leaving him, I said: "Take care! The façade of the command looks fine, but the structure's shaky. I have built it up without solid foundations. But you're lucky because, at Headquarters in Ottawa, you'll at least have someone who'll listen to your requests."

On July 15, 1966, dressed as befitted my new rank of general, I took my seat in an Otter of the Air Reserve that I had been able to charter. Ottawa had replied to one of my messages that there was no other aircraft available to fly me to Uplands. At the airport of the Capital, there was no one to meet me so I took a taxi to downtown Ottawa. Upon my arrival at Miller's office, I found only himself,his wife, Colonel Raymont* (his executive assistant) and a photographer. Also present was my aide-de-camp who had accompanied me from Montreal. After the customary civilities, Miller asked the photographer to take pictures. Then he said to me: "Try my chair to see if it suits you." Taking him at his word, I went over and sat down, commenting: "It suits me very well but the back is a little soft." The conversation thus came to an end. Three and a half years of hard work had begun.

During these years, two major questions would monopolize my time: the first, which I shall deal with in this chapter, was unification. I shall explain this term very briefly by saying that it was a question of merging the three existing forces into a single force which would continue to assume the duties that the Navy, Army and Air Force had carried out up to that time. The second major problem, which I shall deal with in the next chapter, was that of the place of francophones in our armed forces.

So let us first consider unification. On July 16, 1966—the day after my arrival in Ottawa—Hellyer announced that Parliament would have to vote on a bill about unification. The Minister added that he would resign if he did not obtain the full support of the Cabinet on this question. I was strongly in favour of this law, for it would officially give to the Chief of the Defence Staff (CDS), the legal responsibility for all the country's military forces, united into a single service.

One of the causes, admittedly a minor one, of the storm brewing around unification was the loss of powers that each service believed it would suffer. When Bill C-90 was enacted, on August 1, 1964, the heads of the three armed services were eliminated. The CDS had taken over the collective authority held by them to control and administer the Canadian Forces, under the direction of the Minister of National Defence. However, the three services continued to exist legally and maintained certain differences among them that complicated the implementation of common standards and an effective system of personnel management. It was certain that, with the legislation on unification, this state of affairs would have to go; moreover,

---

* I was already acquainted with Bob Raymont, who stayed on after Miller's departure. Bob had been with Wilgress in London in 1945 when, over a period of two weeks, I was being prepared for Moscow. On a visit to the Raymont home I had, in the course of the conversation, expressed a personal view of Canadian military history and of the role played by the French Canadians. I later learned that Mrs. Raymont had been very taken by that presentation because she had until then known little about this country.

under the new law, the CDS would be responsible, depending on the nature of the affair, to the government, to the Prime Minister, or to his Minister (with respect to the organization and administration of his forces).

What disappointed me, over the following months, was the attitude of the official Opposition in Parliament, whose members behaved like school-children, basing their objections to unification essentially on questions of esprit de corps and traditions. These two elements were indeed valuable. I had certainly done all I could to protect them as far as the Army was concerned. But with me at the helm, there was no danger on that score. I had declared publicly, in English, in Kingston, on CBC television, that the R22^{e}R would never disappear. When I was with Mobile Command, I had also invited Admiral Landymore to back me up in this respect by protecting the Navy. Thus, instead of "politicking," Conservatives, New Democrats and Social Crediters would have done a greater service to the armed forces and to Canada by addressing the real questions. Narrowly defined esprit de corps and outmoded traditions, red uniforms and parades modelled on the British forces were no longer essential for Canada in view of the importance of the forthcoming law. Moreover, twenty years after the end of the Second World War, the new generation of servicemen might be expected to have a different attitude from ours.

Opponents of the law should have examined basic issues such as the transfer of officers between staff and combat positions. They might also have broadened the discussion and analyzed the usefulness and necessity of the Minister hiring civilians: to what degree and for what reasons should "civilianization" be extended? A more serious role that the Opposition might have played was to examine in depth the responsibilities of the Minister and those of the Prime Minister with regard to the security of the country as well as the role the armed forces should play. What was essential was the basic doctrine, the policy that dictated the quantity, form and size, of the country's armed forces. That was the nub of a discussion that never really took place.

Moreover, in my view, the opponents of the law would have found grounds for constructive debate if they had carefully read an article in *Canada Month*, November 1966, in which Hellyer tried to rationalize his proposals. In it, he explained that there was something basically inefficient in the tri-service system, each having a head who had access to the Minister and even, in certain cases, to the Prime Minister. He did not forget to mention, and rightly, the lack of adaptability in the committee system which, from the start, had been doomed to failure.

When the Minister, still in the same article, stated that "Airplane pilots will not be required to 'pilot' a ship; sailors will not have to repair airplanes," he was responding to the exaggerations of journalists and the ignorance of his political adversaries. He was absolutely right to denounce these persons. But when he added that "we are now becoming leaders in defence organization and thinking, not just followers," he made a serious error. I have already said that, militarily speaking, the Glassco Commission lacked depth and realism. No serious study, for instance, had been undertaken before the Defence Minister embarked on the policy we are discussing, which was different from that proposed by Glassco. The Minister counted on vague ideas of inaccessible advisors who, for their part, justified themselves by quoting—out of context—declarations made by Montgomery, Eisenhower or Mountbatten, who had said that unified armed forces would guarantee future successes. It would thus be hard to consider the Canadian Minister of National Defence as a serious forerunner as regards "the concept and organization of his forces."

There is no doubt in my mind that reform was necessary. But the Minister missed the boat, totally overlooking an opportunity to show up the inefficiency of the three services, which was the focus of his article, and to define the role of political power in this state of affairs.

Let's not kid ourselves: if successive governments had wanted to eliminate the three services at an earlier date, they could have done so. But not only had they let things slide, they had allowed a certain amount of inconsistency to develop to excess.

I shall explain this in greater detail. In 1949, this country had been officially accepted into the great western alliance, the North Atlantic Treaty Organization. For Canada, the commitment of participating in a common defence was new and presented numerous challenges. What could a country like ours offer to an alliance alongside three of the great powers (the United States, France and Great Britain)? Taking our demographic character and our national wealth into account, specific decisions had to be made. The heads of the three armed services suggested, in disorganized fashion, terms for participating in this alliance. Some were accepted by our legislators; others were not.

Thus, in 1966, although the Canadian Air Force was an active participant in NATO, it was not because of the presence of the Canadian brigade in the British Sector. The two were in no way related. Indeed, our First Air Division was integrated with the USAF, the latter having no direct connection with the British Army of the Rhine and its airborne counterpart, the Royal Air Force.

Let us now consider the Navy. This service also saw much of its role as dependent on NATO. Although backed by units of our Air Force, still stationed in Canada, it retained a fair amount of independence of action. But it had no solid link with the Army and no means for eventually helping the latter to reinforce its brigade in Europe.

In short, military experts acting in good faith and wanting to project a positive image of their country's participation to the allies advanced proposals that the government, also acting in good faith, accepted. And none of these officials had made the connection (or if they had made it, they had not had enough conviction) between the role of the Canadian Forces in the country's defence and their utilization within the alliance. Why should these three arms have to work in a disorganized fashion within the alliance and together in Canada?

I was not ignorant of the fact that the perfect model of a military alliance favoured the elimination of particular characteristics in favour of total conformity with shared objectives. We all knew, though, that reality was far removed from that ideal. The acceptance alone of the goals of an alliance was a major feat. Moreover, all countries insist on maintaining total control over the administration of their forces, and even over their use. Canada was no exception in this respect. With its airmen in the American sector and its army in the British sector, however, it was easy to see that in any major conflict we would have to grapple with even more problems than we had known during World War II as far as the administration and employment of our troops was concerned.

This situation had other implications as well. Our Air Force had gradually come under American influence. While this dependency was being created, a powerful American lobby was arising that gave the Air Force some clout with the Canadian government because, directly or indirectly, it was engaged in an aeronautics industry that far exceeded the requirements of the small Canadian Air Force and needed to export to the U.S. to survive. The airmen had grasped the strength of their position.

Because of the government's justified desire to keep our shipbuilding industry afloat, the Navy also had some clout with politicians, particularly, as is the case today, when the life-cycle of its armaments is nearing the end and its effectiveness is therefore greatly impaired. In the 60s, our Navy had an enviable reputation in its anti-submarine role, and the point was to avoid losing the technological lead we had in some areas related to that function.

The Army, for its part, had no lobby. Apart from its brigade in Europe, it was very poorly equipped. But it was the Army that had responded to all the government's appeals, which had led it to Kashmir, Korea, the Congo and Cyprus, and to many other missions around the world. But could it be present at the only encounter that really mattered, in other words, the defence of the civilized world in Europe, the reason why, in principle, it was maintained? We shall come back to this question.

For the moment, I shall simply summarize my reaction, upon taking up the post of CDS, to the concept of unification as presented by our Minister of National Defence. Unification from the administrative and personnel management standpoint was both justifiable and necessary. But, as it stood, it would not correspond to an operational need. Indeed, neither the Minister nor the officers responsible for carrying out his projects seemed to have correctly understood, either individually or collectively, the justification for and the consequences of the independence of the three elements of which our forces were composed. Those who had initiated the reform, about which they talked non-stop for two years, had not given sufficient consideration to its overall implications. There could not help but be some confusion under these conditions.

Nevertheless, the basis of the law was sound in relation to the goals it attempted to achieve. In the House of Commons, Hellyer got off fairly lightly. One after the other, he destroyed the false arguments of the opponents of unification who claimed that the esprit de corps would be destroyed or that the armed forces would become an international police force for the United Nations. The Opposition had decided to ignore most of the eventual terms for implementation of the future act. This indolence gave me a chance to present my own ideas to the Minister, who seemed fairly receptive to them. Thus, a few days after my arrival in Ottawa, he allowed me to state that none of our present military personnel would be forced to work in an environment other than the one in which he was then serving.

The first reading went off without too much difficulty, as is usual. The second, during which the bill was studied in committee, was stormier. On February 23 and 24, 1967, I attended Hellyer's testimony before the commission. Then, from February 28 to March 2, it was my turn. The Conservatives had decided to resist to the end, but I stood up to my "torturers," among whom were several courageous former brothers-in-arms. Some moments were actually quite hard. Thus, on February 28, I made my official presentation and then replied to questions. I believed I had mastered my subject. In any case, my Vice-Chief, Fred Sharp, assured me that I had.

On March 2, I had engagements everywhere so that in the evening, I ate a box lunch between Uplands and Parliament, where I was to appear for the last time. What a relief! The worst was over. Indeed, I had had constantly to think in terms of the law and not open new doors to the discussions by revealing what I wanted to do with this unification—especially with regard to the presence of francophones. The Opposition tried hard to make me swerve from my positions, but I avoided disaster. The parliamentary commission was soon to accept the law almost in its original terms.

As soon as this difficult moment was over, I took a few days' leave. This rest did me good. For since I had become CDS, many subjects, apart from this bill, had taken up my time. Let us go back a little!

Whether it was intentional or not, the coldness which, it seemed to me, had reigned during my arrival in Ottawa, played in my favour. I owed nothing to anyone. A second element of interest: several important positions had to be filled at the Ottawa HQ. The Vice-Chief, General Geoffrey Walsh, had reached the normal end of his career. However, Lieutenant-Generals Robert Moncel and Frank Fleury had preferred to take early retirement, as had Rear Admiral Kenneth Dyer. This was fortunate, in a way, since some of them had not intended to collaborate with much determination in unification. I was therefore short a Vice-Chief, a Chief of Personnel and a Comptroller. F. R. Sharp, E. M. Reyno and R. L. Hennessy (who skipped a rank, which scandalized many people) filled these positions. I believe I set a record in regard to the number of generals promoted in one day by a Canadian military leader. These new appointees were pleased with their promotions; they were highly competent and knew that they must follow me in order to pursue the program already under way.

These first vacancies had hardly been filled when another problem arose. Rear-Admiral William (Bill) Landymore made a public statement against the forthcoming reorganization of the Armed Forces. In acting in this way, Landymore came to the assistance of the Opposition. The latter were alleging that the introduction of unified forces would destroy the morale of the men who would thus no longer be able to serve their country within this new structure. This was, of course, a politician's exaggeration. I even doubted the sincerity of the senior officers who backed these senseless remarks.

Landymore had more or less sent me a signal. In a letter dated June 28, 1966, he congratulated me on becoming CDS, then added that I knew what he thought of the tremendous changes that were to be imposed on him. He ended by saying that, except on this matter, I would have his full support. Nonetheless, as a result of his outburst, he was rather hastily hailed in some quarters as the hero of the Navy. But whose hero, in the Navy, was he? That of the ordinary seamen? Of the Chiefs? Of the young officers? Or was he not rather the hero of the servants of the British Royal Navy and of the politicians who found it to their interest to see him thus speak out in public? The seamen, but above all the Chiefs, remembered an incipient mutiny which, in the late forties, had led to important reforms often oriented towards a "Canadianization" of our naval service. Had these changes settled everything? In my view, the important thing was the messages I was to receive (we shall see upon what occasion) from ordinary seamen and from a large number of petty officers, urging me to complete the job without taking the senior officers into account.

Under the circumstances, ought I to consider Landymore's gesture as insubordination? Even granting him the benefit of the doubt as to his sincerity at the time of his declarations, I had no other choice than to accept his resignation when he offered it to me. Although he was fairly young, Bill was entitled to his full pension. But I very much regretted this incident. I had a great liking for Landymore and was counting on him to give the Maritime Command (as I had done with the Mobile Command) the Canadian image which it should have and which I was championing. In short, his departure would serve no useful purpose whereas his presence might have accomplished so much.

A while later, Landymore stated to the press that before leaving his post he had carried out a survey of officers with the rank of lieutenant-commander and up, and that only three of the 367 respondents had supported unification. Moreover, he made the accusation that a text he was to present to a parliamentary committee had been "censored" by the Minister. I wrote to him on August 22 to ask for the names of the three "loyal" officers as well as for a copy of his original text. He responded, of course, in the negative to my first question but, in September, he sent me two texts: one original and the other "censored." And he was then forced to admit that Hellyer's revision had not changed the sense of his intervention. The Minister had, in fact, deleted comments which he rightly considered the responsibility of the HQ Chief of Personnel, who might himself be called before the committee.

Landymore's gesture obliged me to find a new chief of naval forces. I offered the post to J. C. (Scruffy) O'Brien, a Quebecker, but this valiant sailor was reluctant to accept. He was afraid his colleagues would turn their backs on him. I assured him of my complete support and of my presence, in the near future, in Halifax.

After Admiral O'Brien had accepted the post, the process of unification continued. I feel obliged to say, however, that the departure of several senior officers who, in 1966, opted for the same course as Landymore, was unfortunate and much regretted. The greatest harm was caused by the gesture in itself and not by the skill or experience we were losing, for the replacements were as well-qualified and as capable as those who, since 1964, had laid the foundations of the programme. The notable and positive difference resulting from these replacements was to be found in the far higher level of motivation apparent among the new group. To the present day, no one has explained the secret motivation of those who resigned after having agreed to implement integration which was inevitably to be followed by unification. What did they want? We do not know. Some say that they did not believe in the viability and effectiveness of unification. If so, they were wrong. Had they come to an agreement among themselves? For the moment there is no way of knowing.

These first obstacles that, as CDS, I very soon had to overcome were not the only ones. Against the background of what I have written in the two previous chapters concerning the years of integration (1964-1966), the reader can easily imagine the scope of the task that awaited me.

One of the things I had noticed, and which I had found painful, when I was Chief of Operational Readiness was the lack of communication between the senior officers of our forces. It must be understood that the latter had been trained throughout their career in very strictly compartmentalized structures and systems. Functions differed from one service to the other. Inter-service operational relations were limited. Finally, each man, in his own way, was proud of the role he had played during the war. I therefore decided to tackle this lack of uniformity and communication by setting up the Armed Forces Council.

This Council was merely an advisory body. However, by bringing together once a month in Ottawa the chiefs of the HQ branches and those of the main functional commands, which were often established away from Ottawa, an absolutely essential link was created. The new organization was to provide me with advice and recommendations with regard to all the military aspects of our Department, including integration, that had now been more or less completed, and unification, which was then well underway. Discussions on all kinds of subjects would keep participants well-informed of the tremendous changes that our forces were about to undergo. Today, I am entitled to ask myself the following question: if Landymore had been really well-informed about the developments that were actually taking place in the unification project, would he have made the statements that forced him to resign? He alone can give a satisfactory answer. Personally, I doubt whether this unfortunate situation would have arisen.

The Council was to be composed entirely of military personnel, but two civilians were imposed on it: the Deputy Minister could, in certain cases, advise us on what course to take and on the means available to the department; the Chief of the Defence Research and Development Council would serve as an adviser within his field of competence. Although I put up with this and with the reasons given to justify their presence, I was somewhat embarrassed by this gesture. I did not think the Minister had properly understood the need for dialogue between the military personnel. In my view, the senior officers greatly needed to be able to think and speak freely without the intervention of non-professionals. Their presence was an intrusion into the constructive dialogue I wished to organize and diminished the result for which I had hoped.

The deliberations of the Council were to serve as a guide; I alone would be responsible for the decisions I would take. But I obviously needed professional discussion, open to the three former services that I had gathered around the table. At this stage, we were dealing with the dismantling of a system that had existed since the creation of the office of the Chairman of the three Chiefs of Staff, a post without any authority. In place of these four persons, power was now concentrated in the hands of the CDS. On different occasions, the latter would have to deal with the Defence Committee and the Parliamentary Committee, apart from attending several special Cabinet meetings. People may find it odd that I described myself as a FINK (Flying Infanteer with Naval Knowledge). This said, I could not possibly know everything and needed the experience of my colleagues in the other services. The latter would be prepared to co-operate fully if they had complete confidence in me. That could only come about through numerous exchanges which would prepare me, when the occasion arose, to put forward their views adequately. The Council was to serve this objective, too.

Let us take stock of the situation when the Armed Forces Council was preparing to meet for the first time on August 10, 1966. That date saw the end of the integration process which had begun two years earlier, almost to the day. Now gathered in their single Headquarters, the staff of the three services were still trying to do the following: grasp the differences that had characterized them up to that point; give real consideration to their neighbours' points of view; and maintain a general view of the tasks that befell them.

Meanwhile, the Minister had tabled the proposal in Parliament. Despite the lack of a truly unifying objective for our forces, there was one advantage in that our entire system could react through a single person who could take full responsibility for decisions. And this person could only be the Chief of the Defence Staff, backed by his operational and functional Chiefs. But could the latter face up to their real responsibilities amid the forthcoming turmoil? On the operational side, the Air Force and the Navy, by their very nature, would probably be able to make the most of the situation. But the Army, in the state it was then in, apart from its 4th Brigade in Europe, would not be able to play a vital role in the eventuality of a European war before the day an allied counter-offensive took place if there was ever to be one. It was even possible that at the start of the war the Army would have to sacrifice its best elements, its European contingent. I should therefore have to recognize and accept this fact. This being noted, we knew very well in Ottawa that, in one way or another, the effectiveness of our forces, already far from their maximum potential because of the disparity of their tasks within NATO, would suffer somewhat during the period when unification was being gradually implemented.

Let us now consider some of the problems I encountered during unification. I am not sure that my appointment was very popular in certain military circles in Ottawa, simply because many people saw it as proof of my blind acceptance of government policies. I was certain of one thing: unification would certainly come about. Had not the government's firm policy on this point been announced in the message of April 2, 1964, which had been sent to all units to confirm officially the impending start of the first phase in the process, namely, integration? That did not mean that the past must be thrown out completely. Canadian servicemen love their past. The British influence was still there, even among the French Canadians of the only francophone regiment, the R22^{e}R, affiliated to the Royal Welsh Fusiliers. This British influence was deeply rooted in the Navy. Our airmen, however, seemed oriented more to the USAF than to the RAF. Nonetheless, the situation created by this traditionalism was thoroughly exploited by the Opposition and by the press. Unfortunately, to satisfy the need for sensationalism, these people had forgotten to read the speech of the Minister, Paul Hellyer, when, on December 7, 1966, he had proposed the second reading of Bill C-243. He had stated clearly—and this is reported on pages 44-45 of the Red Paper published on the occasion of this presentation—that the essentials of tradition would be maintained.

On this point, the Minister had scarcely helped his cause, at least for the time being. As I said earlier, some of the members of his entourage had studied the form that the "Royal Canadian Armed Forces (RCAF)" was to take and had concluded that they would resemble the U.S. Marines. The rumour spread. There had to be real ignorance of the Navy and the Army, as well as of their history and the justifiable pride of all those who had served Canada within them to believe that they would be satisfied with a copy of the U.S. Marines. Moreover, would this type of organization meet the needs of a country like Canada which was anxious to be respected and recognized as a medium-size international power? This proposal, if it had ever made any headway, would certainly have met with my complete disapproval. And if I had ever been forced to implement it, I would have given it a very different form from that predicted by these rumourmongers. I had presented my idea of what the Army should be to the members of Parliament who came to St. Hubert in May 1966. From the attitude I had taken there, the general staffs of the Navy and Air Force could easily imagine what their future would be. It would certainly not be the total elimination of the three services within an excessively centralized system, depriving each of its identity.

The real need for unification made itself felt with regard to the service and storage units as well as to the permanent and support bases. Having studied in depth the reorganization undergone by the Soviet armies, I had realized that this was a worthwhile model for us to adopt, as well as to adapt. This remained a gigantic task and the discussions at the Armed Forces Council were to become quite animated each time we tried to find a solution to a specific question. Should the Training Command run everything in its field or should it allow Mobile Command or Maritime Command or others to also give instruction? The opinion that finally emerged was to leave theoretical and basic training to the specialized command while the practical part might be assumed jointly by Training and the command involved.

The new structure of trades and classification for men and officers had been the subject of lengthy reports in 1965 and 1966. It was up to us to make the final decisions, to specify which posts might be filled by military non-specialists and which should be reserved for specialists. The final decisions on this subject would only be made in the summer of 1969. But in the meantime, what torment we went through! Take the case of storemen, for instance. Those in the Navy and the Air Force usually had no intention of running around in snow, rain, the burning desert sun or the jungle. If they had wanted to, they would have joined the Army in the first place. We had to establish, however, a single, unified trade of storemen which the older, pre-unification men would be entitled to join should they so wish. Those joining after 1968 no longer had this choice: they would serve in a unified system in which the basic training would be broad enough to initiate them to working in any of the three environments. Additional training would be given depending on postings.

The general logistics situation posed serious problems. The Navy and Air Force were established on permanent bases and, abroad, obtained their supplies from our allies. In normal times, the Army, like the others, lived on permanent bases. But as soon as it was sent off on an operation, the situation changed completely: it then depended on logistic units which followed it around. An extension of the permanent base system must therefore be provided through mobile bases. Would the logistics personnel, coming from the three different services to serve on our permanent bases, be able to adjust themselves to the needs of the Army? In my view, there was every indication of trouble here. Indeed, the "Army" concept had to be played down a little in order to achieve a better overall situation. Fortunately, Mobile Command was organized to live "on its own," or almost. Nonetheless, part of its efficiency would inevitably be lost. I hoped that, with practice, everything would fall into place to suit the obvious operational mobility required by the Army. And that is exactly what happened.

The question was to know how far the unified soldiers, having come from the three branches of our armed forces, would go when having to provide logistics for the Army in peacetime as in battle. But this question arose in another context as well. The pre-1968 "sedentaries"—mainly in the Air Force—did not want to go to a theatre of operations or on a ship. In a unified system, could the same men always be left on the firing line? Each time that a civilian or serviceman was placed in a "sedentary" posting, it perhaps created an injustice since the chances for the operational personnel to occupy such a position were thus accordingly reduced. If, at the same time, the number of sedentary posts was cut, the likelihood of the problem arising was considerably increased. Moreover, because of the complexity in numerous parts of the system, it might be better to keep certain people in a post either permanently or for long periods. But going too far in this direction was to be avoided so that, in case of mobilization, important decisions would not be made by civil servants who did not understand the full extent of the problems and perhaps even less the effects that certain deployments might have in special situations (Korea, for example).

The control of matériel was another major problem. The starting point, here again, was rather different. The Navy and the Air Force provided bases which, in turn, supported their operational elements. On the other hand, the Army supported men who were often living out in the wilds in extremely variable conditions or in the midst of often starving civilian populations which, to satisfy their most basic needs, were prone to steal from our primitive installations where security was almost impossible. Unlike the sailors and airmen who are housed and protected, the Army's property accounts suffered from such a situation: even computers sometimes seemed to lie. Faced with these problems (and many others), sailors, airmen, the civilians at National Defence, the Glassco Commission Report and the public service in general, all showed a great lack of understanding.

In the past, there had been too much emphasis on the administrative inefficiency of the Army: that had been easy and had given the public a false impression. It is nonetheless true to say that the Army had been slow to address the problems caused by its administration. Having assumed reponsibility for the reorganization, however, I wished to avoid the exaggerations that had followed the application of the recommendations of the MacDonald Report. The solution was to decentralize, while keeping a certain degree of control by means of clearly defined directives.

In spite of appearances, it was not easy to structure forces around existing units. Once more, the Army was in a different situation. The Army consisted of units or regiments representing cultural or geographical segments of the Canadian population. These units had considerable autonomy and were represented, understood and defended at HQ in Ottawa by their respective corps. This diversity was important: after all, there were as many differences between the Maritimes and the West as there were between Quebec and Ontario. Theoretically, savings might perhaps be made by using the American "melting pot" approach. But in the eyes of a man who generously offers his life to his country by joining a fighting unit, the system as it exists in the Army is very attractive, like it or not.

The Air Force and Navy did not observe these cultural or geographical barriers, but that did not mean that airmen and sailors were identical. Thus, the sailor encountered family problems that his colleague in the Air Force did not. His long periods of absence forced his wife to make full use of what I shall call the solidarity of the naval base to which her husband was attached. Moreover, all the sailors on a single ship, whether they be storemen or artillerymen, faced the same dangers; even the cook assumed a combat post when an emergency arose. This was less obvious in the Air Force where ground personnel were generally relatively safe as compared to those in the air.

From the many factors that I have just enumerated, it will be seen that there could be no immediate consensus about the kind of unification that was to be achieved, even among those who supported the principle. Personally, I was pursuing five objectives when the time came to define the role of the CDS of the unified forces: to obtain absolute control over the three services by dissolving the legal structure that each still retained; to build the new forces around their traditional structures, in other words, for the Army, around separate units, corps and groups; to fully recognize the traditional structures specific to the Navy and Air Force; to organize a fully integrated logistic system; to ensure Canadian control of the administration of all our troops.

In my view, once these objectives were attained, I should have all the flexibility I needed to support the still uncertain policy goals of the Canadian government. Moreover, this control would give me the means of setting up a truly Canadian structure reflecting Canada's ethnic situation by imposing linguistic and cultural equality between francophones and anglophones. There was no doubt that the forthcoming new structure would abolish a good portion of the British tradition upheld by the Air Force and Navy. Once again, my traditionalism had its limits.

I believed at the time that operational priorities must be as follows: the air defence of North America and anti-submarine surveillance. These two areas must remain effective in the midst of the changes. The task of preparing for a war in Europe could be postponed in favour of Canadianization which required the support of the whole Canadian population. I shall discuss this in the next chapter.

All these internal debates at the Armed Forces Council between senior military and civilian personnel at the Department of National Defence sought to define the tangible orientation that unification should take. These discussions took up much of my time. I shall return briefly to certain developments that were either initiated or completed between 1966 and 1969. What took an enormous part of my energies in the first months was to convince everyone of the value of the principle of unification while trying to get my listeners to understand that the details of its implementation were not as revolutionary as was believed in certain circles.

One of the demagogic attacks which Hellyer had to face may be briefly described as follows: the government was said to be pursuing a systematic policy of brow-beating in order to force the unification of its armed forces on a country and on military personnel who had been taken completely by surprise. Hellyer had the answer to this accusation, if only the public was willing to listen. Nothing was further from the truth, he replied, for, since integration (1964) all units had received a message explaining integration and announcing unification. This would not happen for several years, he had then announced. But in 1966, these "several years" seemed rather short to some people. The Minister's reaction was to say that even if the law respecting unification was passed in 1966—which seemed highly improbable —it could not be fully implemented before 1970. He was perfectly right. During the summer and especially the fall of 1966, he repeated this message on every possible occasion. His speech of October 3 to the Canadian Club in Toronto was typical in this respect. In it he mentioned the positive aspects obtained by integration, and while recognizing that some of the fears came from the ranks of the military with regard to their future, he did his best to reassure them. Pay had just been substantially increased, he said; sailors would remain sailors, and airmen would be kept in the air. Certain experts would be called on to serve in any one of the three branches, but those already in the forces could not be obliged to change their allegiance. Those who were willing to do so, however, would find in this move a way of broadening their horizons.

In his view, unification was essential to break certain useless inter-service rivalries—although these would inevitably continue, but to a lesser degree. Loyalty to one service would thus be replaced by loyalty to the Canadian Armed Forces. The latter would thus be better prepared to react to changes. Even though a common uniform was planned within a few years, identity as far as units were concerned would be maintained. In all, therefore, Canada would have *one* force which would be more efficient than the three combined, an improvement to which our country was entitled. He concluded by saying that the idea of unification was not new. What was new was that the politicians of the day had had the courage to put it into practice.

All this was true. During the inter-war period, integration had been tried out, but the Navy had not taken to the idea. Brooke Claxton, in his (rather ineffective) way, had taken the project a step further. Foulkes, the former chairman of the Chiefs of Staff Committee, had written an article in favour of unification in 1961. In 1966, we were in a period in which Canada was acquiring external and very visible elements of its personality. In the international role that our forces were already playing, surely they had need of a strong national identity? It should be said that it was usually the same people who had opposed the Canadian flag in 1965 who opposed the common uniform (Canadian and no longer British) in 1969.

Upon my arrival in Ottawa, certain signs seemed admittedly discouraging. Morale was low, hence the studies ordered—including the one I had carried out at Mobile Command. But there was more. Administrative costs were to be reduced because of integration. In July 1966—nearly four months after integration had been completed—this goal had still not been attained. The number of servicemen was supposed to be cut from 124,000 to 110,000, but there were no more than 107,000 of us. There were several reasons for this: the re-enlistment rate was low; more and more servicemen of the Second World War were retiring each year; it was a period of prosperity with a low unemployment rate. The substantial pay increase of October—one of the main recommendations of the studies on morale—would curb the drop in numbers and even bring about a slow increase until 1969. Unfortunately, in the process, some of the money that integration was supposed to release for the acquisition of new matériel disappeared; the rest was eaten up by inflation. So, in 1969, administration and personnel related costs would take up a larger proportion of the total budget they had prior to 1964. All the same, from the fall of 1966 onwards, the worst of the morale problem seemed to be over.

This was because I, like Hellyer, was moving around with my pilgrim's staff. My speeches and visits during the first months that I was CDS were all based on the idea of defending unification. I should add that, until the end of my career, I would first of all defend and then present our unification to Canadians in this country and abroad, as well as to foreigners visiting this country or in countries I visited. Generally speaking, I would emphasize the two principal results it produced: better utilization of personnel; forces with greater mobility and flexibility than previously attained.

But it was here in Canada that I had to win a real battle of Titans. I visited Halifax, on August 4 and 5, 1966, as I had promised O'Brien. When I had been Chief of Operational Readiness, I had learned quite a bit about the Navy. Now my task was to reassure my people. Everyone available was called out on the parade ground and I carried out a brief inspection. I then replied to questions that had been submitted, anonymously, on slips of paper. In all, there were 57 questions divided as follows: unification and organization, 7; morale, 6; careers, postings, promotions and conditions of service, 15; uniforms and dress, 15; pay and allowances, 7; pensions, 7. By the tone of some of these questions, I realized that its chiefs had turned the Navy against the programme. But the nature of the questions, above all, showed me that here as elsewhere there was a lack of information and that some people, having falsified things—purposefully or not—in their minds, had succeeded in passing on this distortion of the truth to all levels. I had learned to trust people's common sense, however. And the sailors quickly showed me that they were not lacking in it.

Nevertheless, I was not going to answer all their questions one after the other, so I collected my thoughts and told them that I would rather speak to them from the bottom of my heart. First of all, I told them they must not suspect that just because I was a soldier I "loved" them any less than I loved their land brothers. And on two points in particular, I was especially emphatic. The Navy, I said, was essential to the Canadian Armed Forces. Whether its command was here in Halifax, as at that time, or in Ottawa, as prior to 1964, would make no difference. The command would remain in Halifax and they would carry on with their most important traditions. As for uniforms, that would be a matter to be settled later.

For the moment, that was all. But back in Ottawa, I prepared a long letter for O'Brien in which I insisted on the fact that the senior officers of the Command had not played their part to date. They could have replied for months past to many of the questions I had been asked. Moreover, in some of my informal conversations with sailors of all ranks, I had noted that widespread and contradictory rumours were making the rounds concerning, among other things, uniforms. This must stop to make way for the other orders. Everything would happen in time but I could assure them that no one would be obliged to become a jack-of-all-trades, as far too many people thought. O'Brien was able to take his command swiftly in hand after my visit. Fears were dissipated—except those concerning the uniform. I was to obtain excellent collaboration from the Admiral until the end of my career and this included the arrival of a ship on which French was to be the working language.

A strange incident occurred after my meeting with the sailors. A press conference was planned. I was prepared for an attempt to corner me. This is essentially what happened, but I managed to extricate myself quite well. The Canadian Press representative, however, asked me three times and in different ways if I was in Halifax to prepare the way for an anxious Hellyer, who would then arrive to carry on the task of reassurance that I had just begun. Twice, I repeated that I had absolutely no idea whether the Minister intended to visit Halifax or not. The third time, I framed my reply in other terms: "My name is Jean Victor, not Jean-Baptiste. I am not announcing anyone's coming!" There was an outburst of laughter in the hall to the great embarrassment of my questioner.

Before returning to Ottawa, I also visited long range air patrol units which were to be merged with Maritime Command. There, as I had expected, I encountered no problem caused by unification. I took advantage of the occasion to visit a small unit at Shelburne where my daughter Andrée, who had become a lieutenant, was serving. I then returned to Ottawa, to the accompaniment of by newspaper articles which attracted attention mainly for their headlines which included the famous Jean-Baptiste remark. In actual fact, I never did discover whether Hellyer had followed me to Halifax.

Toward mid-September, I returned to Halifax. The tone had changed and I noted that there was no consensus concerning Landymore's gesture. I took advantage of the occasion to reassure all the officers who had asked me the question: Yes, the ranks of naval officers could be kept by those who chose to do so. On October 25, I was out on the West Coast to visit various messes for informal discussions. I wished to sound the situation out, to reassure and explain. The atmosphere, which was somewhat strained upon my arrival, soon warmed up. The next day, I visited the Comox air base where morale was high and optimistic, as I had found it at Greenwood and Summerside.

With regard to the Air Force, I thus found no major problem concerning unification. From the summer to the fall of 1966, I succeeded, with everyone's good will, in somewhat appeasing the Navy. Those who served with the Army in 1966 were a little anxious but trusted me completely. On the other hand, some "veterans" were often mercilessly against unification.

Guy Simonds, now retired, collaborated in a petition against unification: he feared that esprit de corps would disappear. A letter from me giving him details about what unification was and would be did not reassure him. On the contrary, his reply of September 11, 1966 showed that he had hardly retreated at all on any of his preconceived ideas. Some of the arguments he put forward, which were sound in another context, did not take account of the actual situation. On September 20, we met at the Reserve HQ of the Central Ontario Area on the occasion of a reunion of honorary colonels at which I was to speak. Simonds was in the chair.

I made what I thought was a good speech that was fairly well received, with the exception of Simonds, who, having the task of thanking me, seized the platform thus afforded him to refute my approach—sometimes quite viciously. Fortunately, after-dinner conversations showed me that I had received considerable support. Several of my interlocutors were unhappy about Simonds's attitude. The next day—and this was to continue for some days to come—many favourable endorsements were sent to me by those who had attended the dinner. My speech behind closed doors had effectively won a consensus, to my great satisfaction.

A month later, to the day, I stopped off in Vancouver to address the honorary colonels and lieutenant-colonels of the West Coast reserves. A representative of the Naval Officers Association was also present. The question period that followed was "tougher" than the one I had undergone in Ontario. We parted, however, with promises to co-operate as closely as possible.

I do not wish to imply here that everyone was against me, for that would be wrong. In November, a private discussion with Moncel and a speech to the Canadian Club of Montreal went off well. Major General Worthington, the father of the Canadian Armoured Corps, gave full support to my way of carrying out unification, which assured me of the support of this Corps after its members' reunion in Calgary, on September 28, 1966. In 1967, literally on his deathbed, Worthington renewed his profession of faith.* In fact, he asked my permission to be buried in the new green uniform which was then in the trial stage. This last wish was respected.

Other former officers such as Kenneth R. Patrick (Air Force), Foulkes, and Churchill Mann (Army), as well as R. W. Murdoch, went along with the movement and declared so publicly. An editorial in the *Globe and Mail*, on August 3, 1966, said that a visit to the different Armed Forces bases—which had been integrated, like the messes, on April 1, 1966—revealed that there was hardly any opposition to unification, not even from the Navy. The naval resistance came mainly from senior officers—about whom I wrote to O'Brien several days later.

The progress I was making was not without difficulty, however. I received a most vulgar anonymous letter, apparently written by a sailor, in September 1966. Since becoming head of the Forces, I was often obliged to defend myself against interpretations of my words or false quotations by the press in general.

On January 12 and 13, 1967, there was another important fight. The Defence Association Conference (DAC) was holding its annual meeting in Ottawa. I was present for Hellyer's opening speech and gave the closing address. On the morning of the 12th, we were confronted by a small anti-unification (and even anti-integration) majority. But the resolutions opposing the project were gradually defeated in committee. The change of attitude was obvious on the evening of the 13th when, after my address, Captain Owens of the Navy declared that it was now up to the DAC "to get on with the job." Nonetheless, I continued to "work" until 4:30 a.m. on the morning of the 14th, going from one small group to the other, softening up the strongest opponents and rounding off the corners. My efforts bore fruit even though some of the discussions were somewhat heated, although never impolite.

Finally, the law was passed despite the last stand of diehards. My role from then on would be one of information rather than of persuasion, and I would pursue it for years after the end of my military career. I must say that people still quite frequently attack "my" unification, whereas "my" French-language units seem be well accepted.

The law was to be proclaimed on February 1, 1968. On January 30, at 9 a.m., at the Armed Forces Council, I presented the message that I would be

* See his article, "Reorganization of Armed Forces Long Overdue. Annihilation could be result of keeping old Generals." *Ottawa Journal*, Tuesday, April 4, 1967, p. 7.

sending the forces on this subject. I remember saying to the members present that because the essentials had been preserved, the resignations of 1966 had been quite useless. At mid-day, I presented to the Commander-in-Chief, Governor General Roland Michener, the new emblem of the Canadian Armed Forces. I was very moved and had great difficulty in expressing myself. At 8:00 that evening, that is, just before the law was proclaimed, Michener was invited to dinner by the senior staff of the Defence Department. The following day, I took care to keep away from mess meetings specially held to say good-bye to the three former services.

A month and a half later, I paid a visit to "my" Navy, then on manoeuvres in the south seas. On March 12, I attended an exercise. On the 13th, on the aircraft carrier *Bonaventure*, I had to officially present the new naval flag to the Navy. The ceremony promised to be most impressive, on a calm sea and under a blue sky. But an unexpected event was to spoil my pleasure. This flag was supposed to be dark blue with a white anchor in the middle. When, on the ship's deck, I opened the box containing the flag, I found it—white with a blue anchor. The colours that had been chosen were supposed to preserve an old naval tradition. Who had decided on these changes? Paul Hellyer, without any consultation.

On the 14th, I left the *Bonaventure* where I had met with another little adventure. The members of the Chiefs' and Petty Officers' Mess had invited me to meet them alone, and discreetly. In the evening, after dinner with the officers, I retired to my cabin. An hour later, I went down to meet the petty officers. I did not know what they wanted of me, but I was ready to talk to them over a drink. They had a message for me which went something like this: we are with you and will follow you in the rest of the unification; do not let yourself be had by the admirals and other senior officers. Some, during the conversation, said they were ready to change uniforms, if merely to avoid squabbles abroad, where they were too often taken for the British. They recounted some of these incidents to me. Then they offered me a hat bearing the inscription "The Chief of Chiefs."

Upon leaving them, my faith in the ordinary seaman had been strengthened. Politicians and senior officers no longer had much of a mind for the battle. The heart of the Navy was beating in unison with the Canadian Armed Forces.

Apparently, and for certain good reasons, the senior officers hardly ever visited the messes below decks. I had even been warned about such a descent into hell. However, I renewed the experience on the West Coast the following June, this time taking a photographer along with me. I asked him to take a picture of my back—what I wanted was the faces of the men with whom I was speaking. If the photographs are looked at in order, the initial shyness gradually turns into broad smiles. In the meantime, I had told two or three funny stories, apart from treating them to a couple of rounds of drinks— In spite of the method used to obtain this transformation, I was convinced that two years earlier we had only noticed the surface waves which we had to face in the Navy, forgetting the powerful undercurrent which was running in the desired direction.

My last important encounter with the Navy was in June 1969 when, in Saint John, New Brunswick, Simone christened the H.M.C.S. *Protecteur*, a ship that had been designed when I was Chief of Operational Readiness, five years earlier.

I can say that when I left the Forces in 1969 the unification aspect of my mandate was completed. It had taken place in both the main spheres, as we have seen (among others, that of morale and the Navy) and in the smaller areas. For example, the Unification Act had to choose new terms. Several discussions were required to come up with the term Canadian Armed Forces. Similarly, the structure of the ranks, which I wanted to be applicable in both French and English, had to take our British tradition into account. That was why we had Brigadier-Generals* rather than Brigade Generals (Général de Brigade, in French).

As for the officers, I allowed the sailors the choice of keeping their former rank or taking the new ones. This gave satisfaction. Many of them, especially among the non-operational officers, elected to be up-to-date. If I had been in the Navy, I would personally have kept my title as Admiral. There was no such permission for the Air Force or the Army. In the second case, the change was not so radical. In the first, the tradition was not old. There were certainly two or three timid protests from senior Air Force officers. Then it was over. The Air Force had wanted integration, so it had to pay the price for it like all the others, however small that might be in its case.

At the same time, because of the rationalization of our services, some bases had to be closed. Right at the end of my career, it was decided to reduce the number of servicemen from 110,000 to 83,000. Which posts were to be kept? To what extent could the inevitable increase in the civilian part of the Department be accepted? They were all decisions requiring lengthy discussions, consuming much time and energy.

In one field, one of my hopes did not have the outcome—logical though my hope was—to which it was entitled: this was the grouping in Ottawa of all our command and staff colleges. I had a study carried out on this subject that was started by General Guimond and completed by Rowley. My idea was to group all these institutions at the Rockcliffe base in Ottawa. Our officers in training would thus have had access to two universities as well as

---

* Brigadier-Generals have more power than the old Brigadiers. They can thus order a court martial, whereas this type of decision could previously only be made by Major-Generals.

to all the vital centres of the federal administration. Senior civil servants, whether Canadian or foreign, would easily have been able to present their knowledge and experience in our schools. Other advantages: reduced administration and services, the possibility for the CDS and other senior officers visiting the classes to monitor the progress of the more promising officers (I had even thought of installing areas behind one-way mirrors where we could have discretely observed debates and eventually made a preliminary selection of promising personnel).

The study was nonetheless carried out. Unfortunately, Guimond chose to include the military colleges in his report, including the famous RMC at Kingston. There was an immediate outcry from the "Old Boys' Club" of this venerable and very traditionalist institution. I did not have time to undertake the necessary steps to steer the matter in the right direction and, after my departure, the project faded from Ottawa's political and military preoccupations.

Another failure: the cap badges of senior officers should, in my view, have consisted of laurel leaves surrounding the Canadian lion holding a maple leaf in one of his paws. The lion and the maple leaf had formed the emblem of Canada since George V, after the Battle of Vimy, had given it to us, saying that we had become a nation. Unfortunately, it was decided to change this badge several years after my departure. Elsewhere, there were belated and incomplete successes. In 1967, I had suggested to the government the creation of various military orders for merit, bravery, and so forth. I wanted each one to have a different chancellor who would have been an ex-serviceman. I wanted there to be a very special category of Grand Officers to group a very small number of special cases. I should add that I was always against the eventual honorary rank of Field-Marshal that had been proposed at the time of unification and which never materialized. Nonetheless, Pearson rejected my idea of a military order, for he had just created the Order of Canada. Later, this decision was reversed, which was a victory. The chancellor of the different military decorations is the Governor General, however, which, in my view, is hardly satisfactory. I still believe that ex-servicemen, appointed to head each of the military orders, would be in a position to determine who deserved the decorations. The Governor General would, of course, head these military chancellors.

I did have certain more conclusive and rapid successes, however. Chairs of Strategic Studies were opened in several Canadian universities; a system of unified stores was introduced (CANEX); I created a study group on officer development; and a new retirement policy was proposed. And, of course, I closely supervised the new uniform, of which I tried on a sample in January 1967. For the officers, should rank be indicated on the sleeves or shoulders? Solution: a clever combination of the two. Withers suggested that generals should have maple leaves instead of stars on the shoulder. To strengthen esprit de corps between senior officers—brigadier generals and upwards—I had a parchment designed which each received, from 1969 onwards, when he attained this top level at which specialization necessarily gave way to generalization. At the same time, I was pleased with the material improvements being introduced at the enlarged Valcartier base.

In short, in 1969, I could say that unification had in no way changed the essentials. Thus, airmen were still flying and were not asked to take over platoons of infantrymen. The major changes had taken place in the HQs, in the management of the three services at the administrative, logistic and budgetary levels. Much of that had occurred before my arrival. I had thus successfully completed a good part of what I had undertaken: continuity in change.

14

The Francophones

I shall now turn to a very important chapter in my life, without going into too much detail. First of all, my readers already know how my thoughts had evolved during my career with regard to francophones in the forces. Moreover, I have already mentioned the important historical study prepared by the Department of National Defence, the first book of which was published in July 1987.

Bernatchez and I had promised each other that, whenever we had the opportunity, we would try to redress the balance in the Army in favour of the francophones. I must say that after 1945, it was Bernatchez who was mainly able to take this course, except between 1957 and 1961, because of the position I held. When Paul left the Forces, in 1964, I carried on in the way I have already described.

Thus, for over twenty years, Bernatchez and I had done what we could. I cannot overlook the fact, however, that hundreds of our French-speaking compatriots, at all levels and in all situations, had also carried on the fight, each in his own way. Many had given up the struggle; others had chosen the path—in many respects dangerous, yet easier, especially in the Navy and Air Force—of anglicization. The great majority of francophones had come to do their bit only to discover that these Forces were not theirs.

Personally, I was one of those—not the only one, I wish to emphasize—who made sure that my children were educated in French, often at my own expense. This desire to preserve the essentials had been accompanied by a fierce determination to succeed in my work. In this, I had met with the success which had taken me to the top. Once there, I felt it my duty to pay back what I owed to all my French-speaking brothers who, alive or dead, had served me so well and enabled me to get where I was. I shall never be ashamed to say that it was the courageous men of the R22^{e}R in Italy who placed my foot in the stirrup; the rest followed.

I do not really know whether, before 1966, it would have been possible, however, to do what I was to undertake. Certainly, by that date, dozens of francophones had passed through CMR de Saint-Jean, and then through RMC, before joining us. This was in contrast to the three or four officers that the RMC had succeeded in turning out each year up to 1957. The number of French-speaking officers had thus increased considerably but, generally speaking, we were still underrepresented. Moreover, these new additions had naturally been divided up between the different services.

In my view, in 1966 there was no longer any question of the Department of National Defence continuing the inaction it had shown up to that time with regard to the place of francophones in the Canadian Forces. I was convinced that if they were treated fairly, French Canadians would take part in Canada's military ventures in the same way as other Canadians. Thus, what I wanted was to establish a situation that guaranteed justice. For this purpose, I had already obtained the Cabinet's permission, as we have seen, to set up a board of inquiry that I launched unofficially before I even reached Ottawa.

Indeed, as soon as I was sure of becoming CDS, I telephoned Colonel Armand Ross, who was then commanding CMR de Saint-Jean, and asked him to come and see me at Longueuil. During our meeting, in strict confidence, I told him what was going to happen to me. I then asked him if he would be interested in heading the board of inquiry that I had in mind. I still recall part of our conversation. I had suggested that a separate organization might even have to be set up in Ottawa to deal only with francophones. To this, Ross immediately replied in the words of the Bible: "No! If a house be divided against itself that house cannot stand!" In any case, that was not the immediate question. My friend Ross had been picked to serve on the armistice control commission in Pakistan. Everything was organized for his departure within the week. His reply to my question had thus been a sort of provisional "Yes." This was what I had expected, since I had already warned the Chief of Personnel in Ottawa to be prepared to change Ross' posting. I could thus tell him, as soon as he had given his affirmative reply, that he had no need to worry about the rest for I would take care of things. This was quickly done.

Another interesting element: Ross got on very well with Reyno, the Chief of Personnel. He therefore asked me to let him carry out his task under the Air Marshal's direction, to which I immediately agreed. First, I was thus spared this supervisory task. Secondly, I wanted it clearly understood that the inquiry I was soon officially to sponsor ought not to be considered as an instrument that would simply reflect my opinions. I had complete confidence in Ross. I was sure he would be able to get on well without me: if he ran into trouble, my door would always be open to him. Finally, a last important point: it was quite logical for the Chief of Personnel to supervise this study since it would be examining problems which, in any case, would be mainly his responsibility to solve. In addition, politically speaking, it was a good thing for an anglophone to be playing an important role in this study right from the beginning.

Ross was indeed equal to the situation. Reyno asked him first of all to draft his own terms of reference and specify his needs with regard to staff. In October 1966, I was able to present this job description, written by Ross and scarcely altered by Reyno, to the Defence Council for its approval. Ross then started work in earnest, assembling his study group which included anglophones and francophones from the three services.

He was expected to complete his task in less than a year. In actual fact, he submitted his report, in both English and French, in March 1967, scarcely six months after starting work on it. In the intervening period, he had been able to prepare a questionnaire to be administered to all francophones in the Forces, receive their replies and analyze them. Moreover, he had sent investigators to the commands, bases and units to interview anglophones and (especially) francophones concerning the situation experienced by the latter. Lastly, he had paid personal visits to certain foreign armies where different linguistic groups existed side by side, as well as to the G.O.C.'s of commands to whom I had written to enlist their full support for Ross and his men.

While this essential work was going on, I helped the cause in my own way whenever the opportunity arose. On a visit to Valcartier, in August 1966, I told the troops, in front of the press, that we had decided, at NDHQ, to create a favourable climate for the professional and cultural advancement of French-speaking servicemen. It was neither the first nor the last time that I made such a statement in public. As soon as the journalists reached me, in June 1966, after learning of my appointment, I had emphasized this particular point of my speech, along with that of unification. And I often had the occasion, both verbally and in writing, to inform questioners who, more curious than others, wished to know my opinion on the matter. I remember that in August 1966, I partially anticipated the Department's programme by writing to someone in Montreal that the Forces would be divided into units with official names in either French or English.

I must say that I had strong moral support. The openly expressed intention of the Liberal government, since 1963, to put a little more French into its civil and military administration was one example. Hellyer and Cadieux certainly did not put any obstacles in my path. Other support was less obvious but just as useful. Our HighCommissioner in Australia, Arthur Menzies, wrote me on June 30, 1966, to say that my task to enhance the bilingualism and biculturalism in our Forces would be enormous but that he was 100 per cent behind me. And he mentioned specific areas where action might be taken.

But the person I wish to mention here in particular is Ted Bullock. Since the last time I mentioned him (Chapter 9), he had come quite a long way. For a few years, he had been living for long periods in London, where his wife was pursuing an international career as a musician. He himself was doing research for his book on the Canadian Pacific. When I visited the British capital, I usually called at Ted's house, a place where there was always plenty of activity. We would talk of this and that, but often of the results obtained by the CMR de Saint-Jean. Bullock had served in the Defence Department for a long time (not to mention the various positions he had held on the Minister's personal staff), either as a full-time soldier or on temporary active service. In 1949, he had been re-engaged in the latter capacity and, in that post, had tried to analyze the relational problems between French Canada and the three armed services of Canada. He wanted to find solutions to these problems and help in implementing the recommendations he would eventually make. Unfortunately, he left in the summer of 1951, quite discouraged and far from having carried out the last part of this task. He had succeeded, however, in sensitizing many people to the problem. In July 1951, he exchanged letters with Claxton, which I considered important and ahead of their time on several counts. He later entrusted me with copies of these documents which I have assembled in Appendix B.

Bullock, as well as many active servicemen—francophones, for the most part—became people on whom I tried out my ideas. From the reactions of these specially chosen interlocutors, I obtained what I was looking for. Moreover, thanks to them, I could be sure of not finding myself all alone should this battle not turn out as I wished—admittedly, a highly improbable situation.

Between October 1966 and March 1967, strong in my convictions and in the support I received from above (Hellyer and Cadieux) and from my staff, I took preliminary steps to prepare for the implementation of the recommendations of the Ross inquiry. Two lengthy reports dealing respectively with the unified structure of the trades for the men, and classifications for the officers, had been prepared prior to my arrival. Each contained a short chapter on bilingualism and biculturalism (B&B) in our forces, one of which favored the status quo (we had enough French-language units—FLUs), while the other was very open. I was asked to comment on these reports, on which the important decisions would have to be based. My comments on the chapters dealing with B&B generally emphasized that further studies should be carried out in some specific field or other before our plans were finalized. My HQ colleagues also wrote their comments on these two reports but had nothing to say on B&B. I believe they had already realized that it was the Ross Report that would have the final say on this issue.

At this point, the question of B&B was thus temporarily shelved by tacit consent, although things were to work out rather differently at other times. In November 1966, the Laurendeau-Dunton Commission expressed the wish to meet us to discuss the conclusions it intended to submit to our government concerning the armed forces (these conclusions appear on pages 346 to 356 of volume 3 of the Commission's Report, published in 1969), and we personally agreed to this proposal. In preparation for the meeting, which was to take place in January, I decided that we would present a common front. For this purpose, the senior HQ officials would receive a copy of the draft of the commission's recommendations for discussion. Comments would be collected and we would work out our conclusions, to which everyone had to rally during a meeting which was to be held a few days before the discussion with the Royal Commissioners.

Many of the notes written by my anglophone colleagues were fairly negative. Several arguments were made against the extension of French as a working language and the increase in the number of French-speaking units: esprit de corps would be affected; our forces would be divided along linguistic lines; the careers of francophones would be affected if their service was limited to French-speaking units. Ross confessed his disappointment to me shortly before the co-ordination meeting which he had attended for his own information. I told him not to worry, that I would be at the "rehearsal." Indeed, I felt I had to be there, and forcefully so. After the meeting, Ross came to see me to say that he had been a little startled when, at a particular moment, I had banged my fist on the table. It was true that, at that moment, I had heard just about enough. Having taken the floor, I briefly summed up the situation of the francophones in our forces. I do not remember my exact words, nor even whether everything I am now going to mention was said at that time. But, in any case, the lot of francophones in the forces I had known can never be described too often. They had to speak English if they wanted to serve anywhere else than in the infantry, and even as infantrymen, if they hoped for promotion, they could not avoid speaking English. Pursuing a career in one or the other of the three services meant being posted anywhere in Canada, often to a place where education and services in French were non-existent. To enlist at the age of 18 in the Navy or Air Force was almost equivalent to abandoning one's culture and language for good. For, in these two services, training was given outside Quebec, often in far-away places from which the servicemen, because of the poor pay, could not easily get away. In the circumstances, some obvious and very natural consequences, moreover, were that these young Quebeckers married anglophones and brought up their children in English, the latter often being unable to converse with their paternal grandparents. I did not attempt to trace how this state of affairs had come about over the years, nor did I try to distinguish between measures that were intentionally assimilatory and those that had come about because of inescapable circumstances, although they had the assimilation of francophones into the English culture as one of their consequences. Quite simply, it was essential that the necessary steps be taken to change this situation.

All the same, after my intervention, I steered the discussion on that January day in 1967 back to the subject we were supposed to be dealing with, namely, was it possible or not for each of the recommendations that we had before us to be implemented as formulated or with variations? We did not accept them all, but I may say that our response to the Commission was very positive indeed. In fact, we would be anticipating some of these proposals and acting in such a way as to respect not only the government's main objectives but also the operational principles of our forces—the latter aspect perhaps not having received all the attention it should have from the Commission's experts.

Still anticipating the future, I asked my old friend Colonel Marcel Richard, who commanded Camp Valcartier in 1966-67, to prepare a study for me on the future needs of the base, in terms of men, buildings and matériel, should it receive new artillery and tank units that would also be French-speaking. Always faithful and efficient, Richard had already sent me two short but well-documented reports by the end of January 1967, and, at my request, he advised me of his ideas for a school where the technical trades could be taught in French.

In March 1967, Ross completed his report. The document was a summary of the condition of francophones and the status of the French language in the Canadian Forces. Ross avoided (cleverly, in my opinion) mentioning the (often flagrant) injustices that existed, which had been reported to him and with which we were very familiar. Rather, he presented the situation in a way that was both general and precise, in addition to suggesting ways of improving it. His 131-page account, divided into 19 chapters, covered subjects as varied as the Quebec educational system, recruiting figures from 1961 to 1966, the training methods and career organization of francophone personnel, their social life in the Forces, and the potential resources in French-speaking manpower for the Armed Forces. In all, he succeeded in giving an accurate picture of the subject. The report ended with 39 recommendations.

To carry out its task, the committee based its study on the preliminary report of the B&B Commission, published in 1965, which contained certain charges against the unilingualism of the Forces (especially as far as the Navy and Air Force were concerned). The authors had had certain problems with their data gathering. There were no accurate figures in 1966-67, from which the exact percentage of francophones in the Forces could be determined. The report recommended that records should be organized according to mother tongue in order to correct this omission. Similarly, there must be consensus on the levels of bilingualism of servicemen, which would be helpful for administrative purposes.

The Ross Report on its part suggested that CMR de Saint-Jean should award diplomas and that training should be given to francophones in French. It called for a new "integrated" glossary to replace the old English-French military dictionary published by Col. Chaballe during the Second World War. There was mention of creating mainly French-speaking units and bases, thus giving francophones an opportunity to work in French, in the same way as anglophones had up to then been able to work in their language. It said that to require francophones, upon joining up, to learn English, went far beyond the government's policy on bilingualism and maintained that the policy concerning educational facilities offered to the children of francophone servicemen, where an appropriate school was not available, should be revised. The point was also raised that the very great majority of francophones who had attained the rank of general had come from the R22^{e}R. It was easy for the infantrymen to say, jokingly, that this situation was normal, since they were "smarter than the rest," but this theory was hard to accept for francophone airmen and sailors. I should add that the R22^{e}R has in fact supplied more generals than any other Canadian regiment. The recommendations thus touched all fields of activity from the recruiting and selection of francophones to their social life in the Forces, including the various stages of their training, their postings, and so forth.

There was no question of the report being put on the shelf. To prevent this I had to have an action group which would have complete responsibility for all the tasks related to B&B. In practice, its primary function would be to follow up the Ross Report. Colonel J. O. A. Letellier, Director of Organization at NDHQ, was chosen to direct this group. I had known him for a long time. He was born in Ottawa, while his wife was from Trois-Rivières. After serving on the Minister's personal staff during and after the war, Armand Letellier had commanded 3 R22^{e}R from 1957 to 1960 and had then gone on to become deputy head of the Staff College in Kingston. Sound of judgment, solid in discussions and on paper, very knowledgeable concerning the functioning of the NDHQ, he was the man I needed for this task. He quickly set to work. In May 1967, he had already started work on certain letters concerning his future Secretariat, but he would not be transferred to my staff officially until several weeks later. In January 1969, that is to say, a few months after Letellier's retirement, this Secretariat which, in my view, clearly demonstrated the Defence Department's wish to implement government policies with regard to B&B and to solve the numerous problems affecting the representation of francophones in the Forces, was transferred to the Chief of Personnel. It would subsequently be known by various other names—today, it is the Director General of Official Languages.*

Through the roles assigned to it, the Secretariat thus began to co-ordinate all the bilingual activities of our Department as well as to act as an advisory body with regard to the problems encountered by francophones in the Forces. I wanted to get out of the rut of "language teaching" and "translation" to which bilingualism had always been confined in our Department.

Thanks to the diligence of Letellier and his staff, I was able to appear before the Defence Council in November 1967 to propose three major changes, based on Ross's recommendations: the reorganization and relocation of mainly French-language units and bases; the creation of a French-language training centre; and the provision of educational facilities for the dependent children of francophone servicemen.

Before going any further, I should like to say a word about one aspect of this part of my activities: secrecy. While the Defence Council had agreed, in October 1966 to the setting up of the Ross enquiry, it had also refused the publication of a press release that was ready and waiting—announcing the study that we were about to undertake. I can no longer exactly recall all the arguments invoked, but one of them, probably referring to my speech at Valcartier, held that the whole business had already received enough publicity. In any case, having already obtained the essentials, I did not think it worth fighting over details.

Later, the Minister's personal staff ordered the printing of only one hundred copies of the Ross Report. Its distribution, controlled by my office to start with and then by the Bilingualism Secretariat, was done parsimoniously and copies were marked "Confidential," which prevented recipients from discussing the contents. The Laurendeau-Dunton Commission received its copy only in December 1967. These efforts to keep the report under wraps caused some uneasiness in Ottawa itself—not to mention in the units scattered across Canada. I heard rumours about this. Indeed, everyone knew that something was in the wind, but few knew exactly what it was. All kinds of things were justifiably imagined and rumours were rampant. Some

---

* Letellier's ten-year experience has been recounted in *DND Language Reform: Staffing the Bilingualism Programs, 1967-77* (1987).

people asked me outright why I did not trust them. Others concluded that the Chief had decided to take decisions over their heads to avoid discussion. This situation would gradually be defused, but in spite of this, I never really knew why there had been such an emphasis on silence. Perhaps there had been a wish not to confront the public with a study which largely paralleled that of Laurendeau-Dunton. Perhaps Hellyer, who was having enough trouble with the Opposition over unification, had decided to avoid further criticism. However, he did not want to bury the programme, for which I had his full support throughout his term of office—that is, until October 1967, when Cadieux took over from him.

But let us now return to the main question, proceeding by stages. I shall first of all mention a failure, perhaps only a partial one. Only the future will tell, for the reader will see, in the final chapter, that I continued to work until 1983—quite successfully in my view—on the case that I am about to reveal to you. At only one point, in Ross's Report, had I intervened "a little too much": namely, where he talked about improving the conditions of education in French for the children of francophone servicemen. I had long entertained the notion that the solution to this question might be a boarding school, located in Quebec, near Valcartier. Servicemen transferred outside Quebec need have no qualms in allowing their children to follow a programme of studies there which would be approved by Quebec. Following Lesage's visit to Valcartier in February 1966 (see Chapter 11), one of my memos to Ottawa had put forward the idea in a very concrete fashion. I spoke of this possibility to Daniel Johnson in May 1967. At my request, Ross had included this suggestion in his report. Letellier, charged with preparing the documentation for the Defence Council, had also had to include it in accordance with my instructions, but, I believe, without much conviction. The Defence Council asked to reflect on the matter. Finally, the whole project was shelved, to be replaced by a first element of solution that was more generally applicable and more flexible. Indeed, from April 1, 1968, anglophone or francophone servicemen who were unable, at their place of posting, to obtain for their children the education that they needed or desired (for instance, if there was no school in the children's language or no facilities for handicapped children) would be eligible for a grant of up to $1,300 per child—a sum that would be increased over the years. The second part of the solution was more important. With the agreement of the English-speaking provinces, a vigorous plan was launched to set up French-language schools on almost all the main Canadian bases; the results of this approach would mainly be felt after my departure.

The French-language units and training centre came off somewhat better. In October 1967, the Council asked us to reformulate and define our proposals with regard to these, and things progressed fairly fast since our report reached Cabinet level by about mid-January 1968. Approved in March, it was announced to the press on April 2, 1968. By creating French-language units (FLUs) and organizing a minimum of training in French, we hoped to extend, as far as possible, the use of French in the military units stationed in Quebec as well as the range of military trades practised in that province. A certain number of anglophones would belong to these FLUs; they would have the opportunity of improving their French (the reverse was also planned although it had in fact existed on a very wide scale for over two centuries in Canada). The francophone training centre would be located in Quebec.

It was hoped that many benefits would be reaped from these measures. The careers of francophone servicemen would be more solidly established. By eliminating the initial handicap that English had constituted up to then, the new measure would very likely extend the length of their careers for francophones. According to Ross, as recruits francophones represented about 27 per cent of the Forces—in other words, a percentage very close to their proportion in the Canadian population—but they left the Force so rapidly after that period that they barely constituted 16 per cent of the total strength in 1967 (a little more than Ménard had calculated in 1964—see Chapter 10). The precise goal sought here was to increase the percentage of francophones from 16 per cent to 28 per cent. Concerning this last point, it should be noted that this proportional increase was not explicitly recommended in Ross' Report. The study group, however, had been set up to examine the participation of francophones—implicitly, in proportion to their numbers in Canada. At the Defence Council on December 18, I clearly stated that the goal of the desired modifications was to raise the presence of francophones in the Forces to 28 per cent and to solve the educational problem of their dependents. I reiterated this on many occasions, either verbally or in complementary orders to the programme. The Minister repeated the figure of 28 per cent in his press conference on April 2. This objective would be retained in all subsequent expansion plans and included in the 1971 *White Paper on Defence* (p. 50).

The declaration of April 1968 brought other advantages for francophones. Those who, for family or educational reasons, could not serve outside Quebec, were to see their career opportunities increased. Those who were stationed outside Quebec would enjoy a more generally congenial climate, for cultural affinities would exist within homogeneous groups such as, for example, the crew of a ship or a commando battalion; opportunities for education in French also became available in these centres. With these first projects, francophones began to find solutions to the problems facing them when they joined the Canadian Forces.

All this had been fairly easy compared with the distressing obstacles that had been raised in my path each step of the way to unification. Moreover, I had taken care to relate the two subjects. According to its proponents, unification was to be the factor that would permit the constitution of genuinely Canadian forces. My own point of view was similar to this general presentation.

I clearly recalled the firing of McNaughton, brought about by the British because our general quite rightly did not wish Canadians to be separated from each other in battle. What I also remembered was the almost unanimous front that the British and English Canadians had managed to form during the war to oppose (unsuccessfully) the creation of the Alouette Squadron. In any case, from 1968 onwards, my conception of a Canadian force would make Canadians autonomous. Differences concerning the kind of participation of French-Canadians, for instance, would in future be fought out amongst ourselves. Whether this force served with the British or not, there would be no further foreign interference with regard to our "ethnic way" of participating.

But to reserve 28 per cent of the posts for francophones, whereas in 1967 they did not even hold 16 per cent, and to create new FLUs were two factors which meant that the number of anglophones as well as that of their units would obviously have to be reduced. This would mean a relative loss of power for anglophones. How would this be accepted? I can reply as follows: fairly well to start with but after a few explanations much better. To add to the problem, the government announced almost at the same moment a cutback in the number of servicemen. This decision alone meant that the Canadian infantry, not counting the FLUs, would have to be reduced from six regiments to three. The same thing was true also for the other services.

Here are a few examples of how the "selling" of my pro-francophone policy proceeded. At the end of May 1967, when I already had a good idea of what was to happen, I visited Belleville, Ontario, to attend the regimental dinner of the Hastings and Prince Edward Militia Regiment. Howard Graham, who had been my superior when I was Vice-Chief, was present: I knew he supported me and would be able to calm his men down, if necessary. I stated my views quite clearly. At the end, some of my listeners assured me that they themselves, as well as others, had been very anti-French-Canadian (not surprising in this traditionally Orange area). But, they added, my speech had convinced them and they assured me of their support.

On December 21 of the same year, I met the honorary colonels of two active infantry regiments, the Canadian Guards and the Queen's Own Rifles, which were to be put on the reserve list. They were obviously trying to maintain the status quo but finally rallied to my arguments, later, in 1968.

A few words concerning the Queen's Own Rifles and the Black Watch.

The name of the former played a certain (but not major) role in its disappearance. In 1956, when the time came to choose the Canadian units which, under the aegis of the United Nations, were to keep the Israelis and Egyptians apart, the latter had refused our suggestion of sending the Queen's Own. It will be recalled that the French and British had imposed their military mediation in a way that seemed more like an act of destabilization of the Nasser regime. The name and our uniforms of the time were far too similar to the reviled British for the Egyptians not to take offence. In 1967, faced with the task of having to reduce the number of infantry regiments and of seeing that our Army was Canadian in every detail (whenever possible), the names of infantry units to be eliminated that immediately sprang to mind were the Queen's Own Rifles and the Canadian Guards, the latter endeavoring to be an exact replica of the British Guards that I had known well between 1961 and 1963.

The decision to eliminate the Black Watch from the regular force came about in a painful way. This regiment was excellent in every way. It had been under my command in Korea and, later, when I commanded the 3rd Brigade in Valcartier. Despite its Scottish traditions, the Black Watch had many French-Canadian members. I wanted to keep it and was even prepared to eliminate one of the R22^{e}R battalions to do so. By maintaining the Black Watch, however, I would have gone against our principle of keeping the three active regiments that the Army had maintained between the two World Wars: the Royal Canadian Regiment, the Princess Patricia's Canadian Light Infantry and the R22^{e}R. The decision therefore was not a straightforward matter, and not everyone on my staff saw the situation in the same light as I did.

That was how things stood when I left for Europe to attend a NATO meeting. Upon my return I found that my interim replacement, Fred Sharp, had signed the document striking the Black Watch from our permanent force. That hurt, and I said so discreetly. But the decision had been made, and it had been approved by the Minister, so I had no choice but to support it.

To the R22^{e}R, which would remain an active unit, I made quite a different speech from that presented to the anglophone units required to disappear from the permanent force. In October 1967, I told the members of this regiment that the new FLUs would have the same problems that the glorious R22^{e}R had experienced in its infancy. But I wanted to be able to count on the men of the R22^{e}R to help these units succeed: we should need every effort on the hard road ahead of us, but I assured them that all the obstacles would be overcome.

Elsewhere, my admonitions took another turn. The chiefs of the commands proved very co-operative, especially the chief of Air Defence, who, on January 24, 1968, sent me a very important study concerning his francophone personnel and the bases and units that could become FLUs. I was so pleased with this document that I had it circulated among his colleagues who set to work in their turn. But I gradually got the impression that they in fact saw these FLUs as bilingual units. Several days before April 2, I drafted a very clear letter to correct this trend. The Chief of Air Defence balked a little when well-founded rumours reached him in February 1968 to the effect that the French-speaking air unit would be a squadron composed of the quite new CF-5s. Since the role of these aircraft was mainly that of ground support, this squadron could be easily integrated with the combat group whose creation we were shortly to announce at Valcartier. Tactically and strategically, that made sense. But . . . over a third of a new CF-5s in action would be at Bagotville, in an FLU. That was a little hard to take for the old English-speaking Royal Canadian Air Force. They got over it quite quickly, however.

It was once again in the Navy that things did not go so well. There, many francophones, often very anglicized, were against the plan of an FLU. The main reason given—a ship cannot function in French—was totally without foundation. O'Brien was obliged to throw his prestige behind the project so that Pierre Simard could carry out the study that I had asked him to undertake, in a normal way. The latter, a competent sailor, a member of my staff whom I now assigned to command this naval unit, thought that his unit would be bilingual rather than an FLU. He would maintain this mistaken attitude until after my departure. Every inch a sailor, he had a hard time accepting the needling of some of his brother officers. Then, certain retired naval personnel denounced my whole policy as quite mad, and Simard felt personally targeted. But progress never stops, as they say, and the nostalgic had to rally round over the next few years.

I consider it important to stress certain points which marked the path that brought us to April 2, 1968. On March 21, Pearson wrote to our Minister to specify certain conditions which must be respected in implementing this programme. I did not agree with all of them and wished to tell the Prime Minister so in a letter, but in the hierarchical scheme of things, Cadieux stopped its dispatch. He was able to convince me that we had gained the essential and that should certain details ever be raised, there would be time enough to react. In any case, in his letter Pearson had accepted the goals we were trying to achieve and thrown an important new element into the fray: this programme had been accepted by him and only another Canadian Prime Minister could change the guidelines he had just laid down. In my view, that meant that the FLUs, whose creation we were shortly to announce, had received an unconditional guarantee for the future. It would now be impossible for just anyone, at any time, in order to satisfy short-term objectives, to destroy what had taken us so many years and so much suffering to obtain. I must confess that that had been my greatest fear up to then. The small tank and artillery FLUs that we had set up in the late 1950s had disappeared five years later. Such occurrences must never be allowed to happen again. When I wrote a farewell letter to Pearson, who left political life in April 1968, I thanked him and sincerely congratulated him on what he had done for French Canadians in the Forces.*

We had prepared the forces to receive the public announcement of April 2. Indeed, the day before, a long message in both languages explained my views, asked for everyone's co-operation and gave the exact wording of the following day's press release (see Appendix C). The period of secrecy was well and truly over. On April 2, I had occasion to receive several encouraging telephone calls. Positive letters arrived over the next few days, as well as the inevitable—and necessary—interviews.

After that date, we more or less settled into a routine. On April 11, a letter reorganizing Mobile Command because of the new policies, including the FLUs, was sent to the chief of this Command. The new units, about which the press release of April 2 had remained somewhat vague, were named one after another (see the list in Appendix D).

The following is an example of how the naming process worked. It will be recalled that I had absolutely insisted on the official name of the FLUs being French—and not bilingual. It will be remembered that I had begun my career in the *Régiment de Trois-Rivières* (RTR), which had become, during the war, the 12th Armoured Regiment (Three Rivers). In 1946, the 12th disappeared and the RTR reappeared as a reserve unit. My aim in 1968 was to create a francophone tank unit, the *12e Régiment blindé du Canada (12e RBC)* to which the battle honours of the RTR would go. Along the same lines, I wanted the RTR (Reserve) to become the *12e RBC (Réserve)*, abolishing its regional relationship to Trois-Rivières in name but not in fact. Lieutenant-Colonel Duquette, who commanded the RTR, gladly accepted my proposals. Thus, the new FLU would already have had a war record and would be supported by a reserve unit solidly implanted at Trois-Rivières. I acted in more or less the same way with the *5e Régiment d'artillerie légère du Canada*, as well as with other FLUs, whenever possible.

The concept of FLUs led to interesting situations. The Commander-in-Chief of the French Air Force, General P. H. Maurin, after paying us a visit in June 1969, suggested twinning the *433e Escadron* at Bagotville with a French unit. There was no question of my rejecting this request as my

---

* I had asked that a photograph of Mr. Pearson be hung in the Citadel Officers' Mess in Quebec City with, on the back, a copy of the letter I just mentioned. The picture disappeared a few months later and all our efforts to find it were in vain.

predecessors had done in the 1950s with regard to the 1/8th Hussars. But the project, in fact, went no further because of the policy followed by France for some years with regard to NATO and our own country. All the same, very close ties were established between French units and our FLUs.

On July 13, 1969, two months before my retirement, I managed to bring together most of the francophone troops at Anse-au-Foulon, in a great and highly symbolic demonstration. The Governor General and our Minister were present. It was the *Ottawa* which conveyed me to the Anse where it moored during the parade of the *5ᵉ Groupement de combat*. On this occasion, Michener presented its colours to the *12ᵉ Régiment blindé du Canada*. I must say that at that moment the events of 1943 when the armored corps had dropped me, swiftly passed through my mind. In 1969, there was a place (and always would be) for francophones in this combat group. After the presentation of the colours, a formation of CF-101s from Bagotville—the CF-5s were not yet operational—symbolically flew over our heads.

The day finally ended with the official opening of what we called the Francotrain—in other words, the Training Division for francophones— which was to be located in Quebec City, detached from its Winnipeg command. In spite of grave shortcomings with regard to bilingual instructors, we had succeeded, in April 1969, in opening an *Ecole Technique des Forces canadiennes (ETFC)* in Saint-Jean, Quebec. This would put an end—and for the best—to another idea that I had entertained for a certain time: that of training our francophone technicians in Quebec's specialized schools (trials had been carried out, moreover, including the training of ten francophone soldiers, in 1965, at the *Ecole de l'automobile de Québec)*. My goal was to bring the ETFC, the recruits and the language schools (in which English and French would both be taught) to Valcartier. Plans had been made along these lines until my departure from the forces. In the end, however, it would be Saint-Jean, where these schools had been temporarily established, that finally housed them all. Major plans were, however, already on the drawing boards to modernize Valcartier. This base, where the *5ᵉ Groupement de combat* settled in, would be completely altered after my retirement, but in accordance with the initiatives I had taken when I was serving. Today, Valcartier is among the best equipped and most efficient military bases in the world. What a change in comparison with the dilapidated state in which I had found it in 1948!

Another project on which I worked until September 1969 was that of obtaining permission for the CMR de Saint-Jean to award diplomas. In May 1968, the academic Director of the College, Dr. Benoit, met with me to talk about this project. By August 1969, most of the problems were settled. Indeed, a year later, the CMR, through a federal-provincial agreement, was authorized to award diplomas in certain subjects on behalf of the University of Sherbrooke. Whereas all officer-cadets had previously had to pass through Kingston, today cadets from RMC or Royal Roads come to Saint-Jean to complete their studies. There again, what a change compared to 1950-51 when the battle over the opening of the CMR had begun!

What I have described above is based on the programme launched in April 1968. In the fall of 1967, it had been understood that we should rapidly take a first step to follow up the most important recommendations of the Ross Report. Once this first step had been taken, the next ones would take place gradually in order not to compromise the efficiency of the forces or the career plans of the military personnel then serving. Little by little, we were to submit other projects to the Cabinet based on the Ross Report and Laurendeau-Dunton Commission's findings. A few days after the press release of April 2, Cadieux sent me general directives on this subject. I explained these in some detail to my subordinates who had the task of building this great program.

In June 1969, a tentative plan was ready for discussion at the Council. But by then, a new element had come on the scene, the Official Languages Act (Bill C-120), although assent had not yet been given. We were psychologically prepared for it whereas, until the mid-sixties, anything to do with bilingualism literally sent the machine into a panic.

Thus, as elsewhere in the federal agencies, sixty days after royal assent, the Department of National Defence had to present a bilingual image to the public in the Ottawa area (posters, announcements, services to the public). Elsewhere in Canada, a process had to be started to apply Sections 3 to 6 of the Act, which required bilingualism in statutes, laws, orders, regulations and judgments. Legal proceedings, including trials, had to be made possible in both official languages. The Department had to project a bilingual image outside Canada as well. On August 29, the Chief of Personnel was able to send to the headquarters and bases a long message prepared in English and French which summarized Bill C-120 and how it would affect us.

On the following September 9, at my last appearance at the Defence Council as CDS, I presented for approval a directive entitled "Long-term bilingualism program in the Canadian Armed Forces." In it, I summed up what the Forces had already accomplished, especially since 1968, and stressed the fact that section 36(3) of Bill C-120 stated that the CF were subject to that Act. Steps must therefore be taken to implement on a long-term basis every part of the Act, with intermediate stages.

The basic principles of the plan were as follows: no injustice should be caused to servicemen then in the Forces; the latter should include, at all ranks and in all classifications and trades, a percentage of francophones proportional to their demographic weight in Canada.

So that all servicemen in the eighties might compete for the highest civil or military positions, which, it was rightly supposed, would be bilingual, it was important to ensure that anglophones might take French courses and that they might also have the opportunity of working in that language. Indeed, by 1980, all officers and senior NCOs had to be "functionally" bilingual. The plan was therefore to last for a ten-year period and included intermediate stages to which certain objectives were related. It was hoped that this time lapse would prevent injustices.

Another aspect of the proposed directive is worthy of mention. Bill C-120, by the requirements it laid down, increased the number of positions in which bilingualism was necessary, on both a short- and medium-term basis. Until bilingualism had been extended to a good number of anglophones, it was wise to keep in service the essential machinery, the FLUs. For, by attempting to comply with Bill C-120 too soon, we might run the risk of francophones monopolizing all sorts of bilingual positions, which would have undermined the implementation of the Ross recommendations, the FLUs and, perhaps as well, the goal of raising the number of francophones to 28 per cent at all ranks and in all trades and classifications. I had foreseen this situation by issuing a directive, on the previous January 13, in which I stated the priorities for francophone postings. Briefly, these priorities were as follows: FLUs; French-language trade training centres; training centres for pilots and other air or naval specialties; various staff colleges and schools; NDHQ, especially in the personnel branch; Training Command; Mobile Command; Maritime Command. On the other hand, low priority was given to the posting of francophones to the often sought-after posts of military attachés or personnel detached to other allied forces. The directive stressed that it could not be used in any way potentially detrimental to the careers of francophones, whose advancement it was expressly designed to improve. Thus, in my programme I mentioned this directive and the fact that it must be maintained.

Appendix A of the draft of my directive specified the "Stages in the implementation of the long-term bilingualism program in the Canadian Armed Forces." It spelled out the goals it hoped to attain: in 1970, anglophones posted to FLUs should previously have taken French courses; in 1971, the CMR would have to conform to Quebec standards with regard to conditions of acceptance; in 1974, new FLUs should be created at Bagotville; in 1975, graduates of all colleges directed by the Forces should be functionally bilingual; in 1978, candidates selected for the staff colleges should have this same qualification; in 1980, that is, at the end of the plan, functional bilingualism would be required of all officers and senior NCOs:

administrative and military procedures, including procedures in all services provided to our servicemen's dependents, would be available in both languages.

This summary is, of course, incomplete. It gives an idea of the spirit that was then animating me and the goals I hoped to attain, taking into account Bill C-120 on the one hand and, on the other, the possibilities of the Forces as well as the directives which guided them.

The Minister approved the basic principles of the document (not to create injustice; 28 per cent of francophones everywhere). But he thought that the possibilities for implementation should be studied as well as the time lapse, especially with respect to the similar objectives then being developed by the Public Service. He therefore requested a plan in this regard which would be submitted to the Defence Council after the Forces had consulted the Minister's B&B advisory committee (a different body from my secretariat) and had communicated with the Government Secretariat on Bilingualism, attached to the Secretary of State. We therefore set to work again in this direction, but the final results of all this only became definitive in 1972, three years after my retirement.

On many occasions, I realized that people appreciated this effort to improve the lot of francophones. On August 27, 1968, the *Conseil de la vie française en Amérique*, at a meeting in Quebec City, congratulated me for what had been undertaken up to that time. In July 1969, the *Conseil international de la langue française* congratulated me for having requested the compilation of an English- French military dictionary which would not be contaminated by anglicisms or "franglais." In 1971, during the program "Cross Country Check-Up" on CBC Radio, thirty people questioned me on various subjects. "My" unification did not earn unanimous support; far from it. But only one listener attacked "my" FLUs. Since only three people expressed their opinions on this matter, including two who disagreed with this lady, I may conclude that, so far as anglophones were concerned, the whole affair had been well assimilated.

15

Top Gun

The period from 1966 to 1969 was intellectually the most intense that I have ever experienced. The demands of the work took up all my time. I have already talked about the two major projects to which I gave so much attention. Let us now take a look at some of the many other activities which made the days go by at a hectic pace.

When the question of analyzing the role that should be played by the CDS of the Canadian Armed Forces arose, I came up against two problems: the first we have already discussed, that of the three services, each with its respective role; the second, that of the exact place that the CDS—and, by extension, his HQ in Ottawa—should occupy in the nation's administrative structure. It should be said right away that, as of October 1, 1947, the Governor General is designated Commander-in-Chief of the forces and exercises his/her power through the Governor-in-Council. I tended to forget this in my early days as CDS, but quickly made amends. And, on January 30, 1968, I organized a little ceremony at which I presented Michener with the insignia of his office, which looked very much like a Marshal's baton. My short speech fully acknowledged the role of the Governor General in our system.

The Prime Minister is responsible for the country's security. In principle, the CDS can only have access to him by going through the Minister of National Defence; on occasion, the Prime Minister came directly to the CDS. Personally, I must say that I did initiate meetings with Messrs. Pearson and Trudeau without going through the Minister.

The CDS reports to the Minister of National Defence for the control and administration of the Forces. The Minister of Defence has jurisdiction over the Armed Forces; his department must administer the Forces, implement the country's defence policies and see that the general staffs respect these policies.

In these functions, the Deputy Minister has an important role to play. He takes a leading part, for example, in the implementation of programmes, in the allocation of budgetary resources and their control. After decisions have been made by the Cabinet concerning the tasks and organization of the Forces, however, the Deputy Minister has no say in how these orders are applied by the CDS, so he is not and must never be the CDS's superior. Thus, the Deputy Minister has nothing to do with operations, these being the responsibility of the Prime Minister, who lays down the general policy to be followed on behalf of the Cabinet and through the Minister of National Defence.

For missions conducted outside the country, the Governor-in-Council would likely appoint a commander-in-chief who would be directly answerable to it through the Minister of National Defence. The CDS would then have to support this military leader who would direct the fighting and be in complete charge of the theatre of operations. In a certain sense, I even had to conclude that the CDS might become less important than the chiefs of the functional commands, such as those of Mobile Command, Maritime Command or Air Command, who might well be inclined, for instance, to re-examine the question of unification. Thus, the relationship of the CDS with his commands, on the one hand, and with the government, on the other, might one day become quite delicate, or even difficult.

The events that I am now about to describe were shaped by the special link between the CDS and the Prime Minister. In March 1969, the British showed us the extent to which they took it for granted that Canada was still a colony. In order to go and fight against rebels in Antigua, British troops made a stopover at Gander without having previously asked our permission. Personally, I was not opposed to the idea of British troops travelling there via Canada. But Britain should have respected our territorial sovereignty.

Arrangements were made for me to see the Prime Minister to inform him of the incident, which he knew nothing about. Naturally, when confronted with the facts, our allies immediately apologized through their High Commissioner in Ottawa. They were good friends who had too easily taken for granted that the colonial situation of Newfoundland could be perpetuated indefinitely, even though it was twenty years since that territory had become a Canadian province.

A similar situation occurred when the Americans, without consulting us, decided to send a submarine through the Northwest Passage. We thought for a moment that our neighbours, following the application of a policy of successive encroachments, might lay claim to the Northwest Territories.

At the Department, we had made a fairly thorough study of this possibility and of the various ways of countering it. I personally explained to the Prime Minister that it was a question of very great importance and that we should make quite sure that the Americans did not start imagining that our North could be considered as unexplored territory and thus open to anyone. After receiving Trudeau's approval, we carried out an air exercise in the far North during which we distributed little Canadian flags to the native peoples of the islands. The gesture was limited, but it did have a certain impact.

This was a matter I had to discuss with the Prime Minister alone. Moreover, Trudeau was very receptive to my arguments. One of the consequences of the American gesture and of our reaction would be the establishment, after my retirement, of a Northwest Territories Headquarters in Yellowknife. This territorial command would lead us back a little to the former Army system: its first commander was Ramsay Withers. In spite of this, it would be fair to say that Canada-U.S. territorial disputes still exist concerning, among other maritime areas, the Beaufort Sea.

There are many indirect links between the country's Prime Minister and its Chief of Defence Staff. I will mention one example that particularly struck me. In May 1968, Trudeau, who had only recently assumed the office of Prime Minister and had not yet even called an election (which would eventually be held on June 25), announced that his government was about to overhaul the country's foreign policy completely. Now, in many respects, foreign policy and defence go hand in hand. We were thus called upon to study the military aspect of one of the alternatives, namely that Canada should become a neutral country. Our report was fairly negative because neutrality along the lines of Sweden or Switzerland had to be defendable, if necessary. But to fulfil this requirement adequately, the budget of our Department would have to be at least doubled: for instance, our air defence at that time was partly ensured by the United States.

I do not know whether the neutrality option had originally been proposed with the firm intention of getting it adopted. I personally believe that the Prime Minister was strongly in favour of it. Nonetheless, Canada remained within NATO and NORAD and abandoned, for the time being, the idea of becoming neutral, although our foreign policy certainly underwent a considerable change, which meant that a lower priority was accorded our military alliances.

This had an impact on Canada's place and role in NATO, matters on which the CDS had very little to say. It was his duty to see that the troops were ready to respond in accordance with the government's demands. But in 1969, there was much talk in Canada about reducing the numbers of our troops in Europe. On April 30, the Cabinet decided that its total forces in

Europe would be reduced from 10,100 to 3,500. The final decision would, in fact, settle on a number of approximately 4,000 men. Furthermore, should the Supreme Commander of the NATO troops decide that the remaining Canadians would have to play an offensive role in the overall strategy, Cabinet would have to give its consent before this decision could be executed. At HQ, these requirements set us to work on various recommendations. My own conclusion was that the time had probably come to unite our air and land armies in Europe. Indeed, France's decision to leave NATO had led us to transfer our air division to southern Germany, where we had taken over from the French. It only remained to place our soldiers in the same sector where the two services could work together. We would then appoint a commander-in-chief for all these troops. Now, in the plane bringing us back from Eisenhower's funeral in April 1969, Trudeau did me the honour of asking me what I thought Canada should do with its forces in Europe. I immediately expressed the opinion that our land forces should be withdrawn from northern Germany where they gave Great Britain the opportunity of sometimes speaking on our behalf. Whether Trudeau, at the time he spoke to me, had already made up his mind or not makes no difference to the fact that he chose the course I recommended. It was a question on which we readily agreed.

I consider it worthwhile to spend some time on this matter, during which I shall recall certain facts about the British style of our military life until the 1960s. In many ways, I feel obliged to point out that this situation had been salutary, our military men being second to none as regards their combat efficiency. But, as always, there was another side to the coin. Among other things, there had often been interference—direct or indirect—in the conduct of our affairs. As a young officer in England, I had not grasped the full significance of the firings of McNaughton, Worthington and others that the British, according to their evaluation criteria, had managed to obtain. The creation of the Alouette Squadron during the Second World War had earned us another unjustifiable intervention. In Korea, when I was commanding, an attempt had been made, as I have already described, to take greater control of our brigade. From all these lessons, the time had come to draw the final conclusion and relate them to the redeployment of our troops in Europe. Integration, unification, as well as Canada's whole foreign policy had already succeeded in largely putting a stop to the British influence which had sometimes stifled us.

I shall now describe one aspect of my method of operating as CDS. For, before explaining my point of view to Trudeau on how our troops in Europe might be united, I had consulted and received the support of a great friend, General Charles Foulkes, the former Army Chief of the General Staff and, later, Chairman of the Chiefs of Staff Committee during the 1950s. My consultation with him had been conducted through my special adviser, Colonel Raymont.

Raymont had served under Foulkes. Throughout my term as CDS, I had often, mainly through Raymont's good offices, consulted Foulkes on various changes that I wanted to make. Knowing that I had the support of this man who still had a great deal of influence both within the Forces and among the crowd of senior civil servants and politicians in Ottawa, I felt in a stronger position to face certain difficult situations, especially at the time of the great debates on unification.

As for the work of our troops with the U.N., I had no more—possibly less—room to manoeuvre than with regard to our soldiers serving with NATO. Even so, I had been able to involve myself completely in the withdrawal of our men serving in Egypt. The tension that existed between Egyptians and Israelis towards the end of the winter of 1967 was far from promising. The information that reached me from our military attaché in Israel was important and detailed. Among other things, it said that Nasser would very shortly request U.N. troops to leave his territory to allow the Egyptians to fight it out openly with Israel.

The moment approached and, after obtaining the approval of Hellyer and Pearson (who had won the Nobel Peace Prize for having been the prime mover, in 1956, in the constitution of this U.N. force), I took the necessary precautions. Ships, including the famous aircraft carrier *Bonaventure*, "secretly" sailed from Halifax for Gibraltar, officially for exercises but in fact to be able to evacuate our troops rapidly should the situation so require. At the same time, I sent our fleet of transport planes to various places in Europe and Cyprus from where they could fly to Egypt within a few hours. What I wanted to do was quite simple: namely, to have the maximum means of transport on hand so that forty-eight hours after Nasser had given us the warning, we could get all our men out, thus minimizing the risk that they might be trapped there.

Toward the end of May, the Canadian Ambassador in Egypt, who had just spoken to Nasser on the telephone, called me up. He informed me that the Egyptian President wanted our men to leave his country within forty-eight hours. I asked what Egyptian airport I might use for the evacuation. The reply was El Arish. It was thus at this place that our soldiers assembled and boarded two Hercules cargo planes that took them to Pisa, where they transferred to more comfortable aircraft that would fly them back to Trenton. Within thirty-six hours, we had withdrawn completely, and I am quite sure that the Egyptians did not expect such a well-orchestrated response. Our ships returned close behind, not having arrived in time to help in the evacuation.

There were several incidents connected with this operation. First of all, I wanted our ships to leave Halifax very discreetly. This was done. To my great dismay, however, I learned that through the special telephones installed on our ships, by means of which our men could communicate with their families, they were telling their wives about their mission. Obviously, it did not take long for the news to spread to the newspapers. So much for discretion. I expressed my disappointment to Hellyer. We should have to find a better way of monitoring what was said on these airwaves, otherwise the secrecy of any naval operation would be too easily compromised. We eventually succeeded in doing so, slowly but surely.

Three days later, I went to Calgary to give a speech to the Alberta United Services Institute, in which I dealt with the role of the Reserves. About fifteen times, during my talk, a man called out from the floor, "What about our troops in Egypt?" I did not know exactly what his question meant, but I thought it was in very bad taste that none of the organizers of this meeting tried to silence the intruder. On the way back to Ottawa, I stopped at Trenton, late in the evening, where the first of our repatriated troops had just arrived. Hellyer was also there. We spoke for a while with them, and found them very happy to have escaped from the hornet's nest that would become a death trap in the next few days for some of their colleagues, supplied to the U.N. by other countries, who had not been evacuated in time. Our fine reporters, at that time, frequently highlighted the fact that we had taken the time to retrieve our supplies of drink before leaving. The fact that the lives of their compatriots had been saved was overlooked.

While on the subject of the U.N., I now turn to the problems of Southeast Asia that I had so closely followed from 1957 to 1961 and, a second time, from 1964 onwards, as Chief of Operational Readiness and at the head of Mobile Command. In 1964-65, following a fresh outbreak of fighting in this part of the world, there was talk of reconvening the Geneva Conference. I was thus asked to prepare a document for our government in which I would examine this eventuality. I described what I considered acceptable: a permanent committee in Geneva which would publicize any incidents that occurred; a mission of five countries rather than three, although three representatives of different countries would be acceptable for investigations; and adequate means of transport. Finally, the government was to maintain its commitment to the pre-1960 conditions, but only for a limited period.

During my term as CDS, our mission to Vientiane, in Laos, would be disbanded since there was nothing more to do. But in Vietnam, things were getting bogged down. At this stage, it was already some time since the United States had come out in favour of the South, which was not prepared to assume its defence on its own. General Westmoreland, a good friend, would emerge from the ordeal in a sorry state; he was unhappy at having to waste excellent troops in a "war" in which political considerations constantly intervened. Thus, his men could not go into Cambodia, where the Viet Cong had support bases for their fighters going south. Perhaps this penetration might not have settled the problem entirely, but the American soldiers would at least have felt that they were able to take the initiative. In any case, from my position, I did what I could to help our neighbours. It would be very little. But the West was not ready to pay the price of freedom when the time came to do so; since 1973 we had seen the worst brutality take hold in this region of the world. One may well ask whether it was really worthwhile, in 1954, to have helped the tens of thousands of North Vietnamese to settle in the South. Less than twenty years later, they were abandoned.

In 1966, my main task was to keep up the morale of our men over there. They had the impression of being completely powerless as regards the ever-worsening situation. To a certain extent, they were right, for the Poles and Indians hardly seemed eager to do anything, and boredom lay just under the surface. The Canadian senior officers worked at administrative duties for about nine or ten hours a week while the observers were occupied for about five hours a week. Then there were the living conditions, either in isolated posts which were real dumps or in lodgings in the large cities, which were badly ventilated and run down. The work, as Brigadier-General A. G. Chubb wrote me in October 1966, was "soul-destroying." No promising young officer should be sent out there, he added. I immediately replied to Chubb that he should study what the implications were for Canada in (or after) a ceasefire. Moreover, I asked him to take an interest in the military situation, its tactical aspects, peace-making methods, and strategies used against the guerillas. Chubb's position could thus become very useful to us, as well as very interesting for him and his observers. In early 1967, I felt his letters had become more positive. He had his Canadian observers working along the lines described above and even carried his analyses of the situation quite far. Our training schools were thus able to discuss the anti-personnel weapons used by the North Vietnamese and give instructions as to what precautions should be used against them, based on the experience of the Americans. All this, of course, ran counter to what the missions should have accomplished. But it was this type of work or nothing at all.

As Chief, I had to keep abreast of the new technology. At the end of the twentieth century, technology is developing so fast that many things change within the space of three years. It was during my tenure that we were considering the feasibility of equipping our air transport with Boeing 707s to replace our Yukons, dating from the mid-fifties. Another issue was whether we should purchase Huey helicopters, whose engines were made in Montreal, while our French friends came to see us with their Mirage F1 fighters. Finally, we bought quite a different type of aircraft from them, the

Falcon, a version of a business jet manufactured by Dassaut for transporting small groups of VIPs. Just after my departure, we received the famous Voyageur helicopters, frequently used for search and rescue. In February 1968, the first CF-5s to roll off Canadair's assembly line were presented to us.

From 1967 to 1969, I was concerned with the thorny question of the Bras d'Or, a hydrofoil-equipped boat. O'Brien and I would support this case to the end. But in 1971 a political decision similar to the one that had condemned the Arrow twelve years earlier was made: the trials and production of this "flying" ship would be halted. We wanted to use the Bras d'Or for all kinds of tasks. Among other things, we believed that, well-equipped and well-armed against both submarine and air weapons, it would have been useful during the certain period when an attack had been launched but war had not yet been officially declared. For instance, a missile launched by a submarine towards our country would not necessarily mean that war was declared; it might be a mistake! What should be done? Our Bras d'Or, armed with small, fast antimissile missiles could have been part of an antimissile network which might perhaps have enabled us to destroy the enemy weapon without involving us in an act of war. To attack and destroy the submarine that had fired it, however, would be an act of war.

The protection of our territorial waters was important. In the sixties, our country was a pioneer as far as sonar was concerned. Some of the information at our disposal concerning the movements of Russian submarines was extraordinarily precise and useful. Innovations in this field were pursued and I even managed to make a suggestion which improved the quality of detection. Our Navy was also concerned with Soviet "fishing boats," which often resembled spy ships.

Related to this question was that of the control of our airspace. The USSR often set off our warning system to check the reactions of our air defence. These were excellent, although less spectacular than those of the Soviet fighter, which can very easily shoot down a civilian aircraft, as the world learned in 1983. Nonetheless, between 1966 and 1969, it was our CF-101s from Bagotville that were most frequently called on to respond to these challenges. To exercise their control in the far North—sometimes helping civilian planes that lost their way—our fighters had to be fitted with extra fuel tanks to give them sufficient range. Naturally, in addition to these emergency responses provided by our system for the protection of Canadian territorial sovereignty, there were added the routine air patrols that were carried out over both land and sea.

A less serious episode is also worth mentioning. On December 14, 1967, after long months of physical preparation for the pilot and technical preparation for the CF-104 that was used, Lieutenant-Colonel R. A. White established a new altitude record for a Canadian jet. He succeeded in reaching a height of 100,100 feet (over twenty miles). I had given my full backing to this other Centennial project which caused quite a stir. Unfortunately, we did not succeed in breaking the world record.

Things were forging ahead in other fields as well. Thus, in August 1967, I had our first Armed Forces track and field championship organized. The curious thing about it was the resistance shown to the idea. The whole thing was very hastily prepared, but the events went off well. I also arranged for handball to be played in the Forces, beginning with an experiment at RMC which added this sport to its sports programme. In May 1968, in Kingston, I attended an interesting match and hoped that handball would subsequently be extended to other units of our Forces (which is what actually happened).

The Centennial Year was, of course, full of activities. I was caught up in a round of official functions of all kinds which took up much of my time. For the Centennial, the Forces organized a tattoo that won universal admiration. Letters of appreciation came in from all over Canada and abroad. On March 21, Cadieux and I attended the dress rehearsal which certainly gave promise of the success that was to follow. Our forces thus showed another aspect of their numerous talents.

Other normal occupations of the CDS: being the active or honorary president of organizations of all sorts. Part of my time was devoted to that. Some of these presidencies were related to military matters and others to social life, the latter because of the fact that I was interested in certain subjects. I was asked, for instance, to be honorary president of the *Fondation Léo Roy* (the musician) in 1969 and to chair the finance committee of the *Théâtre lyrique de Québec* in 1968.

Another secondary preoccupation was my constant interest in the Citadel in Quebec City. I sometimes had meetings in Ottawa concerning the Citadel Museum or the memorial which, although almost completed, often needed improvements. In May 1967, one of the two chambers that the cenotaph contained was occupied by the body of Georges Vanier, who had died on March 5 of that year.

Public relations was another of my important activities and was conducted at different levels. First of all, there were the interviews for television, radio and the newspapers. Since these were quite frequent, it was normal that some "interpretations" should occur. This mainly happened to me in 1967. And each time, those at fault made the appropriate corrections or apologies. Secondly, there were the speeches to organizations related either directly or indirectly to military life, or merely interested in hearing the CDS. I remember the Richelieu Club in Chicoutimi where, on April 5, 1968, several separatists or sympathizers had questioned me somewhat negatively, but politely, about the place of francophones in the Forces.

Thirdly, there were our own magazines, such as *Sentinel* and the *Canadian Defence Quarterly*, which were the new bilingual organs of our integrated and unified forces. Last but not least, there were the trips abroad on business or as representative of the Canadian government. There were all kinds of reasons for these journeys. Some, to attend the funeral of well-known personalities and friends, were rather sad. Others were made in a more congenial atmosphere. It is about the latter that I shall now say a word or two.

In 1966, my first official trip abroad as Chief took me to France. Here again, I broke a tradition. Until then, the Chief had always made his inaugural visit to Great Britain. My French counterpart, Ailleret, whom I had met during my stay in Moscow, received us (Simone accompanied me) in princely fashion. Our stay was marked by courtesy and even happiness.

My visit to the monument to the Unknown Soldier was moving, for when I laid the ritual wreath, I thought of the depth of emotion that this monument represents, as well as of all the other "greats" of this world who had preceded me there. During this visit to France, I met the Minister of the Armies. I also visited several French military units at Brest (the Navy), at Metz (the Army) and the Dassaut aircraft works. An interesting stop was made at Saclay where I was able to note that this nuclear research centre had no cause to envy any of those I had seen in North America. I also held discussions with the three chiefs of staff. It must be said that the French, while debating a certain degree of integration for their own forces, were somewhat hostile to our experience. As if by chance, it was the French Navy that was the most reluctant. Other subjects discussed were the eventual exchange of military technicians and the transfer of some of our air units from Metz and Marville to Lahr in West Germany.

We stayed in France from December 4 to 6, during which time we had the opportunity to fly over Paris in an Alouette helicopter; dine, the day after our arrival, with France's leading military personalities; and go to the Palais Royal in the evening. During all this time, Madame Ailleret took charge of Simone, who just could not get over the welcome she was given. These very cordial relations we had with our hosts made the air crash that killed the whole Ailleret family in April 1968 even more sorrowful.

But meanwhile, relations between our two countries had become strained. In April 1967, on the occasion of festivities marking the 50th anniversary of the Canadian victory at Vimy, we went to France. The organization of the stay was rather poor. Relations between Canada and France were, admittedly, already difficult, the French wishing to play too great a role in Quebec. At Vimy, Cadieux had to wage a hard protocol struggle for Canada to be fully represented. Indeed, the British Ambassador in France had tried to make us play second fiddle, to which the French seemed ready to agree.

At Arras—the site of another Canadian victory in 1918—the mayor, Pierre Mendès-France, who was to receive us on April 9, was absent, having been called away on "urgent business."

These little troubles were nothing compared to the consequences of the visit that de Gaulle paid us in July 1967. As the first francophone in the position of CDS, I wanted to do things in a big way for this occasion. For his visit to Ottawa, we had planned a fine reception at the airport, followed by a motorcade into town, the laying of a wreath at the national memorial and a State dinner to be given by the Governor General. The first hitch: in the previous weeks, at the insistence of the French, it was decided that de Gaulle should set foot on Canadian soil in Quebec City. There was nothing inherently wrong with that, since his visit to Ottawa was kept on the programme. But let us see what happened next.

De Gaulle flew to Saint-Pierre and Miquelon where he boarded the *Colbert*. When he reached our territorial waters, a small flotilla, consisting of four destroyers and as many torpedo boats, came out to escort him. Our commodore in charge saluted the *Colbert*, according to naval tradition. No reply. Our man was furious, for such behaviour was just "not done." From Quebec City, I set off in a Cosmos, which I piloted for most of the trip, and flew to the vicinity of Anticosti Island, where I could speak directly to the commodore. I calmed him down and asked him to pursue his escort as if the "refusal" had never taken place.

The next day, July 23, de Gaulle landed at Anse-au-Foulon at 8:30 a.m. We were all there waiting for him—Governor General Michener, Minister Jean Marchand, and others when François Leduc, the French Ambassador, came up to me and said: "I hope they won't play the Marseillaise like a funeral march." Now, the "they" in question were the members of the very professional band of the R22^{e}R. They were joined by an honour guard every bit as expert and hand-picked by the R22^{e}R. Our bandsmen knew the Marseillaise well and played it marvellously. Was it very diplomatic to act as Leduc had just done? Was he trying to annoy me? In any case, these details, though insignificant when taken singly, began to add up. De Gaulle, for his part, had himself "received" in his own way. Indeed, an improvised band had been assembled on the *Colbert* to play his national anthem for him, his way. Then, he landed at Anse-au-Foulon where we received him royally with an artillery salute and the two national anthems—well executed. Since "O Canada" was not yet officially recognized, we were represented by "God Save the Queen," while our flag, still the Union Jack for the Forces, was run down as is customary on such occasions to touch the ground. As a result, several separatists from Montreal, headed by Michel Chartrand, let loose their vociferations and sarcastic remarks. The visit had got off to a fine start.

De Gaulle then climbed into his car. The RCMP, which was afraid the OAS* might attack de Gaulle while he was in Canada, asked me if I would overtake the General's car when we got to the Grande Allée, on our way to the Citadel. I agreed . . . all the eventual fun and games would have been reserved for Simone and me. At the Citadel, de Gaulle seemed to act like an automaton. It was in the coldest possible way that, about 10:10 a.m., he laid a wreath on the Memorial where Vanier is buried but which, in fact, represents all the men of the R22^{e}R killed in battle, mostly on French soil. I succeeded in putting protocol aside for a moment so that the son of General Vanier could be presented to de Gaulle.

De Gaulle re-entered his car and started on his way to Citadel Hill. At the corner occupied by the *Club de la Garnison*, he was taken in charge by the Quebec Government. For the time being, the Armed Forces had finished playing their role. On the Chemin Saint-Louis, the General was greeted by popular acclaim, but there was also an uneasy feeling in the air. For my part, I took a moment to evaluate the situation which scarcely reassured me about what was to come.

At 5 p.m., we were invited to the reception the French had organized on the *Colbert*. One of de Gaulle's aides asked us to come and meet the General. The procedure was as follows: a space was created around de Gaulle and only the person with whom he was to talk could enter this area. Simone was subjected to the same situation around Madame de Gaulle. De Gaulle usually spent very little time on these ''appearances.'' However, mine lasted over five minutes and many people thought we were having an important discussion. In fact, nothing dramatic happened. De Gaulle asked me if I encountered any special problems in my post. I replied in the negative for obvious reasons. Then we talked about the weather. There was nothing particularly pleasant about the conversation. Finally, the General let me go. A French journalist immediately intercepted me and asked me who I was to have kept the General talking so long. I sent the intruder away, telling him to consult the information services about me.

During this reception, Leduc came up to say he was very worried about the safety of his President and asked me if all the appropriate measures had been taken at the military airport in Ottawa, where he was to land. As I was not responsible for security, I asked him to go and see the RCMP. I communicated with the operational centre at NDHQ, however, where I was informed that everything would be well under control. As Leduc also feared that the French plane in which de Gaulle was to fly from St. Hubert to Ottawa might be sabotaged, I telephoned Mobile Command Headquarters

---

* The *Organisation de l'Armée Secrète* that was still making trouble in France over Algeria's recent independence.

where I was assured that the plane, once it had landed there, would be in complete safety. A while later, Leduc came to explain his anxiety: the French intelligence service had every reason to believe that certain OAS agents had crossed the Atlantic, eager for a revenge they had been nurturing for years.

At 7:30 p.m., we attended the dinner at the Château Frontenac given by the Quebec Government in de Gaulle's honour. I was seated next to the French military attaché, Colonel Laurent, whom I knew well. I took advantage of this to give him my first impressions concerning our guest, de Gaulle, namely that things were not going well but that I hoped the French President would soon realize that Canada existed.

The next event was interesting. De Gaulle's plane was at Ancienne-Lorette. The special fuel it used was not available and Laurent, who was to precede de Gaulle to Montreal in this plane, asked me if I could take him in mine. I willingly agreed. The hour we spent together made a deep impression on me. We naturally discussed the turn of events which I found far from satisfactory. Thus, I said, many eminent French-Canadians followed a different course from that of separatism. They made their mark at the federal level or elsewhere, thus advancing the cause for all. De Gaulle, by continuing to ignore these people in order, apparently, to encourage only the Quebec nationalists, might well undermine our work. In any case, for over two centuries we had got on quite well without France. Why, all of a sudden, did the latter find us so interesting? I ended with "prophetic" words, saying that I hoped someone, in a position to express himself publicly—Drapeau perhaps—would present this point of view to de Gaulle. In my position, I could not undertake this mission. But why had François Leduc not informed de Gaulle of these facts? It was his duty to do so.

Laurent more or less agreed with me. Together we boarded *Le Chevalier Paul*, moored at Montreal, where lunch awaited us. Monsieur Bourdasz, the French commissioner at the Expo Exhibition, seemed to have been informed of my ill humour. I must confess that, for all his kind attention, he did not succeed in softening my attitude. Laurent, for his part, telephoned Leduc to inform him of my apprehensions.

After this meal, I flew back to Ottawa. I immediately lay down to rest, while listening to de Gaulle's triumphal procession on the French network of the CBC. I saw the mass of humanity that welcomed him. I heard him cry, "Vive le Québec libre," immediately taken up by the crowd. The only problem was that this type of intervention was just "not done" on such visits.

The next day, I took part, with others, in a meeting of a special committee which had the task of advising Pearson as to what should be done about this speech. I myself was quite intransigent: de Gaulle must be told that we had had enough of his clowning. Back in my office, I asked about my engagements for the rest of the visit. I felt I had shown myself enough. Upon his arrival, I had wanted to impress upon de Gaulle the bicultural character of Canada and of its public servants. I had therefore taken charge of him, at Quebec City, as we have seen. But I could not accept what had happened. In Ottawa, I decided to cancel all the engagements that I had made. First of all, I made sure that the Canadian Guards—excellent on all scores—would replace the R22^{e}R at the War Memorial in Ottawa for the planned ceremony. I also refused to attend the state dinner which was to be held the following day. At the suggestion of my staff I phoned the Minister in Saint-Jérôme to obtain his approval for these two projects, and immediately received it. As to the personal invitation I had received to a reception at the French Embassy on July 27, I declined it without consultation. My aide-de-camp asked me what reason he should give the Embassy to justify my absence. "Tell them I have to repair the plumbing in my bathroom at home."

I then prepared to leave Ottawa for a two-day fishing trip to Goose Bay. I only left on July 28. Meanwhile, as everyone knows, on the 25th Drapeau had made the speech that I had hoped he would when I had had my discussion with Laurent. And de Gaulle had decided to end his visit in Montreal. The Ottawa stage augured ill for him.

Upon my return from Goose Bay, the Swiss ambassador, Mr. Gasser, invited me to dinner. Leduc was also invited and Gasser hoped to be able to reconcile us. It was all arranged for us to have a private conversation on the embassy terrace. I began the conversation by describing the visit as a disaster. We had so wanted to make a fine celebration of it. Then I ventured onto more delicate ground. I told Leduc that I had played my part. Had he himself presented the whole situation to his President? If he had informed him of the protocol that he was to observe and de Gaulle had refused to comply with it, then Leduc had no other course than to resign. But if he had not properly presented de Gaulle with the whole picture, Leduc should also resign. Why had this visit been such a lamentable failure? How could de Gaulle act in such a way in our Centennial Year? Was it done willingly or had he been put up to it by certain Quebec ministers? When I visit Brittany, I do not try to liberate that part of European territory from the French presence.

I think Leduc fully realized that I had not been exactly impressed by his performance nor by that of his master. Finally, he told me that from then on, our relations would be "more difficult." Leduc was soon recalled and appointed elsewhere. I certainly do not wish to suggest that my relations with the French Embassy had always been like this. We were, in fact, on excellent terms until this incident. Lacoste (Leduc's predecessor) and Laurent had been and still were very close friends. After Leduc's departure, things slowly resumed their former harmonious course.

One consequence of this episode. On July 27, Bernatchez, the honorary colonel of the R22^{e}R, wrote to Hellyer to ask that "O Canada" be played on occasions such as de Gaulle's arrival in Canada and that the Union Jack be quickly replaced. Lastly, he asked whether the dipping of the flag to the ground was a gesture that Canadians understood. In his view, they did not. In which case, should the tradition be perpetuated? On the first two points, he was soon to see his wishes realized. However, the ceremony with the flag was maintained.

In May 1968, I had occasion to spend a few days in France on an unofficial visit. We went to Beaulne, to the Vougeot vineyard where I dined with the *Confrérie des Tastes-vins*, which received me as a member. What particularly struck me was the kind of diplomacy being practised. The other guests of honour on that evening of May 11 were Willie Brandt (German), James Roosevelt (American) and Couve de Murville (French). During the speeches, there was no end to the praises that Brandt and de Murville mutually exchanged, but there was nothing similar between the Frenchman and the American. I found it strange that France's ally in hard times was thus left out in the cold.

It was during this stay in Europe that I met General Massu in West Germany on May 14. I let him know that, during some future visit to France, I should like to meet de Gaulle to discuss the whole matter of our departure from France and our installation in the French zone in Germany. In May 1968, it will be remembered, the French President had a difficult political situation to face. It was therefore not until the following July that Massu informed our commander at Lahr that de Gaulle would be ready to receive me when I came to Paris on official business. The next visit on the programme was to mark the jubilee of the 1918 Armistice. Colonel Laurent, back in France, wrote to me to say that he had been requested to accompany me. Everything sounded promising.

In August, Massu contacted me directly to ask if I still wished to see de Gaulle. At this point, I turned to our Under-Secretary for External Affairs, Marcel Cadieux, for advice. In September, I had his reply which mentioned the possibility of the "considerable political implications" of such an interview. Moreover, Canada was not yet quite sure in what capacity it would be present at the fiftieth anniversary of the Armistice or if it would be there at all. And what if de Gaulle received me without receiving our Minister—which was possible since de Gaulle had more or less ostracized us—reserving all his attentions for the Quebec government. Under these conditions, a friendly meeting between brothers-in-arms could be used for various ends.

Cadieux' advice was that I ought to delay my reply until the last minute. It would thus be too late to solicit an interview with de Gaulle. In short, this was the advice I had expected. Indeed, my letter to Cadieux had asked the question while proposing a somewhat negative response since the problems raised by the transfer of our troops had already been settled. To achieve this satisfactory outcome, French General Gauthier, who commanded at Lahr, had played a leading role, always proving most co-operative.

In the end, it finally proved impossible for me to be in France on November 11 since, on the following day, I was to receive the Order of Canada from the hands of the Governor General in Ottawa, and on November 13, I had to be in Brussels for a NATO Council meeting. To have added a special round trip to France on November 11 would not have been humanly possible.

My last official visit to France therefore took place from January 19 to 21, 1969. At that time, General Michel Fouquet was the Chief of the Defence Staff of the French armed forces. I particularly wished to visit the French military schools to study the teaching methods used over there. I did indeed visit their *Ecole d'application du matériel* in Bourges, their school for naval mechanics in Toulon, and the Air Force Technical School in Rochcfort. In Toulon, I realized that the Navy signallers received very advanced English courses, for it was the language of communication between ships of all nationalities as well as that of the operations that the NATO squadrons might one day have to carry out. Concerning my relations with the French armed forces, I have nothing more to say. But, once more, the political situation was to catch up with us.

De Gaulle proposed making me a Grand Officer of the Legion of Honour. I was unable to accept, however, for there is a rule for Canadian military personnel that all foreign decorations must be refused unless they are awarded in time of war.* This compulsory refusal set the tone of my visit since, in de Gaulle's eyes, decorations had a political character. Under the pretext that the Quebec Minister of Education (Guy Cardinal) was visiting France, the French Defence Minister persuaded journalists not to attend a press conference that I was to give. Several other previously planned events were also cancelled. I had already grasped, prior to this incident, that no one could say "no" to de Gaulle with impunity. Yet I had merely conformed to Canadian policy. My official relations with France came to an end on this note.

In April 1967, after the disappointment of the ceremonies at Vimy, which I mentioned earlier, we set out on a lengthy trip. We crossed over to Great Britain on April 10, where I visited Southern Command and RAF Transport Command. I noted that the British reorganization then taking place was

---

* For example, I was already *Chevalier de la Légion d'Honneur* for feats of arms carried out in Italy with French troops.

moving toward a "mobile base," very similar to our own Mobile Command. I was also shown new armoured vehicles that they would have liked to sell us. I personally thought they had too much hardware that would be difficult to maintain.

On April 12, Fred Sharp called me from Ottawa to tell me that I must return to the capital immediately to attend the swearing-in of the new Governor General. This was a major problem, but I was scheduled to be at Nicosia in Cyprus on that day. My aide-de-camp set to work right away. After numerous discussions between Ottawa, London and Nicosia, an agreement was reached at about 2:00 the next morning: I would remain in Great Britain where I would welcome Michener, who was to arrive in London in a few hours' time en route to Ottawa. At the time of our meeting, photographs were to be taken for publication in Canada. External Affairs fully understood that to postpone my visit to Cyprus would be just as serious as not being at the ceremony in Ottawa.

I was indeed at the airport to meet the plane flying Michener in from India. After the photo session, I flew to Lahr and arrived at 2 p.m., only an hour behind schedule. There, Air Vice-Marshal Lane took me on a tour of the installations that France had left us. They were not extraordinary, but the necessary alterations had been started. At Zweibrücken and Baden-Soellingen, which I also visited, the officers and men showed me that their morale was high. Finally, on April 16, I set out on my first visit to Cyprus as CDS. I had to travel in a Hercules, however, since the Yukon had been lent to the Governor General designate.

Upon my arrival, I was greeted by the Commander of the U.N. forces. I saw him again the next day, together with the Secretary-General's special representative. The latter, who claimed he had put an end to the troubles in the Congo, counted on achieving the same success here. In his view, it was a question of blaming whoever had to be blamed and of leaving no room for useless loopholes. I listened to him, but my own information gave me a less optimistic view of the situation.

I then met Lieutenant-Colonel Robinson, who was commanding our contingent over there. His men had only just arrived, but the corporals in charge of the observation posts were already fully informed about their duties. Their excellent performance was a pleasure to see.

The next day at 9 a.m., I was received by the President of the island, His Beatitude Archbishop Makarios. During my visit in the summer of 1951, after my stay at the Imperial Defence College, the British authorities in Cyprus had pointed Makarios out to me—he was then a political prisoner—in the courtyard of the prison where he was being held. On this day in 1967, it was thus the second time that I had "seen" this man. I was supposed to spend only ten minutes with him, but we talked until midday.

We were both born in 1913, about two months apart. Having made this discovery, we chatted about the special events that had marked our respective lives and noted several coincidences. But it was my interest in the island and my literary knowledge of it which intrigued him most. Since Makarios seemed little inclined to discuss other subjects, we started to talk about archaeological digs, their results and the impact they had on our knowledge of the island. I kept up very friendly relations with Makarios until his death.

Because our troops behaved in an absolutely impartial manner, I was able to have contact with both communities. In the afternoon, I therefore went over to visit the Turkish Vice-President, Dr. Kuchuk (Makarios and he spoke as little as possible). During our conversation, Kuchuk, surrounded by many mainland Turks, was ready to embark on banalities. He spoke enough French to do so and upon leaving him, I told myself that the problems were far from settled and that we had better prepare ourselves for a lengthy stay.

Since my Yukon had not yet returned, I had a day and a half at my disposal for sightseeing, often in spots where my presence seemed scarcely appreciated. For instance, I realized that they would rather not have seen me at the Abbey of Bellapais. The Turkish Cypriots were reluctant to show me the eagle's nest Castle of St. Hilarion. In Kyrenia, the same problem, but with the Greek Cypriots. In Salamis, the former capital of Cyprus, today half submerged, I was welcomed more warmly. The theater there and all the ruins were extraordinarily beautiful. Finally, I was able to visit Mount Olympus where a little 11th century church had been restored by the island's archaeologists. On May 21, I flew back to Canada. Two years later, with only a ten-day difference in dates, I made the Makarios-Kuchuk pilgrimage once more. Little had changed.

In September 1967, I made another long trip outside Canada. The purpose, among other things, was to participate in a tour designed to familiarize the various senior military authorities of the NATO countries with some of the territories covered by the alliance. This time, we went to Norway and Denmark. We were taken to the northernmost point of the Norwegian frontier where the Norwegians were living alongside the Russians. The latter, after the Second World War, had grabbed these lands, which had previously belonged to Finland. Referring to the studies I had made in 1951, I told myself that the USSR perhaps saw some advantages in having common borders with as many countries as possible. It could then create little incidents there, if only to test the other's reactions. In actual fact, Norway was nervous about the Russian bear. Denmark was less so, but knew very well that, should the worst happen, the country could well find itself on the front line.

We then went on to Germany where various military affairs occupied my time. It was there, on September 19, that I learned that Hellyer had been moved to Transport and replaced by Cadieux. After a three-day holiday in the French Alps, I arrived in Istanbul on September 23 for an official visit.

At the numerous meetings of the military partners in NATO, my Turkish counterpart General Tural and I had developed mutual friendship and respect. His welcome was extraordinary and consisted of two special events. The first took place on September 24 when he took me to Ankara to visit the Ataturk Mausoleum where I laid a wreath. The second was military in nature: I was taken to visit the headquarters of the Turkish forces as well as their operations centre, where the military installations on the various Turkish frontiers were explained to me. This was followed by a sightseeing tour: the presidential yacht took us through the Black Sea to the Bosphorus.

On September 27, I was involved in a diplomatic incident. I was visiting the town of Izmir to see Vice-Admiral Sarikey, who was commanding NATO's southern naval sector. At 4 p.m., I was to visit the Headquarters of the land forces of NATO's southeastern sector, commanded by American General Dick. But upon my arrival at the door of the latter, the Turkish interpreter who accompanied me and who had been assigned to me by Tural himself was refused entry. The American officer who had taken charge of me at the hotel managed, in less than five minutes, to show the full extent of his tactlessness. I immediately cancelled the whole thing. Dick called on me at the hotel to apologize and set another time. I refused any such arrangements.

The day had gone off well up to that point, however, with the military visit in the morning followed, in the early afternoon, by an excursion to Ephesus which I visited at some length and where I was shown where the Holy Virgin was supposed to have lived. An old monk told me the whole story, beginning with the discovery of the house. After 1945 German archaeologists had indicated their wish to excavate in this part of Ephesus. Since the Germans and Turks had been allies in 1914-18 and the Turks had remained neutral in 1939-45, the request caused no problems. The archaeologists dug and discovered the house in question, which was supposed to have been built by St. John. Now, St. John had in fact accompanied Mary and carried on his teaching in the Ephesus area in Anatolia. Naturally, this ruined house, within which a spring flowed, had had to be repaired and given a new roof.

All this had impressed me greatly. Back in Canada, at the first mass I attended, the priest asked me to read the epistle of St. Paul . . . to the Ephesians. In Anatolia, without realizing it, I had walked along the road which had eventually led to our Christian civilization. The remarkable thing was that it was at Ephesus, where Moslem Turks predominated, that not only was this house preserved, but also the Basilica of St. John, an historical monument containing the remains of the very first church erected on this site.

The next two days, September 28 and 29, were taken up by business meetings. On the 30th, the last day of my trip, part of the day was set aside for a tour of the old bazaar in Istanbul. Simone, who had joined me in Turkey, was able to take full advantage of the sightseeing part of my travels.

We then flew to England where I took part in meetings and made several speeches. On October 4, during the second session of the Atlantic Channel Symposium, I was informed that our government had requested the Department of National Defence to cut its budget by 15 per cent. I hastened my departure in order to be in Ottawa the next day. I found NDHQ in quite an upheaval. But, professionals that they were, my men had already started on the work. The problems are always the same in such cases. The planning and budgeting that had already been done had to be re-examined. Where should cuts be made? What would their consequences be? Until May 1968, we were to live in some uncertainty as to the future. It was only after attending a Cabinet priorities committee on May 2, 1968, that I was able to count on a stable—though reduced—budget that would enable us to plan several years in advance. I must stress that our financial participation in civil protection was greatly reduced (by 30 per cent) in 1968-69. This trend, which I had initiated in 1964-65, continued after my departure.

In late February 1968, I went to Puerto Rico. I visited various American bases and spoke with some Argus crews from our naval air force who were being trained there. I also met several local dignitaries. On February 26, I received a message from Ottawa announcing that I could extend my term of service for two years. This very good news would enable me to complete the task I had undertaken with regard to the French-language units and which augured well for the holidays I was to take in the Caribbean from February 28 to March 12.

The 1968 tour of the chiefs of the defence staff of the NATO countries focused on the southern flank of our defence zone. We made short visits to Rome, Greece and Turkey and returned to Italy. In Greece, I spent some delightful hours in the National Archaeological Museum in Athens (but it would take at least a month to see it properly). We were also taken to Mount Athos, a biblical site covered with almost inaccessible monasteries. The break with the rest of the world which the monks who live there have imposed on themselves is almost total. As a group, we also visited Greece's frontiers with Turkey, Albania, Yugoslavia and Bulgaria. The Greeks felt very much hemmed in and their policies, which often seemed to us to be very cautious, were quite understandable.

In Italy, I accepted a special invitation from my counterpart. I knew the country quite well. However, I began to sense Italy's problems that are so well known today. What had been rebuilt by de Gasperi was already ageing. My visits to the Italian armies allowed me to sound them out. They seemed to me to be regaining confidence in their ability. But the troops were marvellous for many other reasons. First of all, Italy provided me with an aide-de-camp in the person of the son of Madame Berardi. The latter accompanied me throughout a little nostalgic visit to our former battle sites, including the famous house where his mother still lived, near Ortona. In Ortona itself commemorative ceremonies were held for the 25th anniversary of the capture of the town by Canadian troops. During this stay, Simone and I were the guests of honour at a State dinner. We were also able to meet Pope Paul VI at Castel Gandolfo. Although he was not as impressive as Pius XII, I found him to be a saintly man whom the press violently, and quite unnecessarily, attacked.

On the North American continent, my three years as CDS enabled me to travel extensively, in all directions and for all sorts of reasons both in Canada and in the United States. I shall briefly recall three occasions—apart from those mentioned in the two previous chapters, closely related to unification or to the FLUs—which made a particular impression on me.

On April 22 and 23, 1967, I visited St. Catharines, Ontario,where, with local veterans, I was to commemorate the battle of St. Julian which had taken place in France fifty years earlier. Some of the local residents were French-speaking. They asked me whether I would come and take part in the official opening of the town's French-Canadian parish. I accepted enthusiastically even though I was unprepared for the occasion.

On the following June 1, on a visit to British Columbia, George Pearkes, who was then Lieutenant-Governor, and his wife, invited me to dinner. It was an opportunity to reminisce about the pleasant times we had spent together nine years earlier.

Another pleasant social occasion was the dinner we gave for Westmoreland on November 27, 1968. The American general was a man with little social life. As a rule, he refused almost all invitations. Our military attaché, who had sometimes invited him to dinner, had always been turned down. Very anxious to succeed where others had failed, he then suggested that I invite Westmoreland to our Embassy in Washington. If we chose a date during a lull in Westmoreland's timetable, he could hardly refuse. This was done and Westmoreland accepted. On the appointed day, the dinner took place under favourable conditions, even though Canada was then talking quite openly of considerably reducing its military participation in the Atlantic Alliance in West Germany. I do not know the precise value for us of having drawn Westmoreland from his lair. But I could say "mission accomplished."

There is a final subject that I wish to discuss in this chapter if only to round out my demonstration that the 24 hours in each of my days were well and truly filled. The affair in question began in late April 1965, when the Rector of the University of Ottawa, Father Roger Guindon, made an appointment to see me. Once in my office, he explained that his university was nearing bankruptcy since it could not receive provincial grants like other universities, because it was under the control of the Oblate Fathers and was thus considered part of a "religious denomination." However, approaches had been made to the provincial government and the reply obtained was that if the property and administration of the university were transferred to a Board of Governors with no religious affiliation, it could then request a charter as a government-subsidized university. It was to study this question that Father Guindon invited me, along with numerous other people, to sit on a committee to advise the Rector of the University. This committee was to become the Board of Governors if everything went off according to plan. But hardly had I been appointed than I fell ill. During my illness, the first provisions of the University of Ottawa Act (1965) were introduced. The Act, passed on its third reading on June 21, 1965, came into effect on July 1 of the same year. However, the agreement that had been made specified that the Oblates would receive reasonable compensation following discussions to be held once the Board of Governors was set up.

. The situation, in July 1965, was more or less as follows. The Oblates, who had founded the University of Ottawa in 1848, had accumulated a debt of $7 million in running it. In order that they might receive a decent compensation in return for what they were leaving to the governors, we had to present a clean sheet to the government of Ontario. I was very much involved in this operation.

Accordingly, we had an inventory of the assets made by independent agents prior to our appearance before the University Affairs Committee in Toronto. Our first three meetings with this committee were somewhat disappointing. Each time, some piece of information was missing or something prevented a decision from being made. But after the last of these appearances—we were then in 1966—the chairman of the committee, Leslie Frost, former Premier of Ontario and a veteran of the First World War, asked me if he and I could meet during the following week. One Tuesday, in the fall of 1966, I met him at the Royal York where he had invited me to lunch. We discussed this and that. Finally, I tackled the subject of the university. "Ah, yes," he said, "come and see me in John Robarts' office (the Premier) at 7:30 tomorrow morning."

Robarts immediately showed his readiness to find a solution. He saw no objection to the Oblates retaining control of a part of the existing faculties without receiving any provincial grants (this is known today as St. Paul University, and includes the faculties of theology and canon law). He was prepared to finance the new buildings that were absolutely essential for the development of the institution, but he felt that the province could not give our corporation the full amount estimated by the independent evaluation mentioned above. He asked me whether the Oblates would accept partial compensation for what would be transferred to the Board of Governors under a new charter. If so, what percentage would be acceptable to them? Obviously, I could not answer for the Oblates, but I suggested that I discuss this possibility with their Provincial, to whom I suggested compensation amounting to two-thirds of the debt.

A few days later, during a meeting with Rev. Father J.-C. Laframboise, the Provincial, we discussed this proposal at length, and finally agreed on this formula. I wired this approval to the Premier. The final transfer of properties took place in 1967.

On October 11, 1966, around the time this matter was being officially settled, the Rt. Hon. Gérald Fauteux, the chairman of our Board of Governors, resigned. My colleagues unanimously elected me to replace him. I accepted, even though I was already CDS and snowed under with work. The task was by no means easy, but I had extensive help. The Chancellor of the University was the excellent Madame Georges Vanier, whom I knew so well. And with my colleagues on the Board, we formed a good team. We had to prepare a comprehensive plan that would take into account the needs of each faculty, approve the plans submitted by the architects, and supervise the building, if only at a distance. I held this office for five years. When I left in 1971, we had about $100 million of buildings under construction (among them schools of physical education, sciences, law, a library). I am naturally very proud of this part of the work we accomplished, which is there for all to see. But we also set up a proper administrative organization for the university. The Ontario government, on its part, had agreed to pay us a 7 per cent premium on our grants to maintain the university's bilingual aspect, for it was acknowledged that it would cost more to provide teaching in two languages than in just one.

In January 1967 (I was still CDS), I told local journalists: "If I hear of any rumours of strikes among the students, I shall close down the faculty." Certain people were pleased with my firmness. Others, especially at the university—professors and students—did not find my intervention very amusing. It did not go any further.

At the time, the Minister of Education was Bill Davis. We had very good relations with him so that when he replaced Robarts as Premier, we had no difficulty in remaining on good terms with the Ontario Government. In this regard, I must say that my relations with that government have always been excellent. I am afraid I am obliged to make a less positive assessment with regard to my own province. We shall see why in the following pages. This being said, and to finish with the University of Ottawa, I may say that I am still a member of its Board of Governors.

16

Retirement and After

In February 1968, I had been allowed to continue for two years beyond my normal retirement date. I could therefore stretch out my career until June 12, 1970. Three major reasons caused me to cut that term short and ask Mr. Cadieux, on July 2, 1969, for permission to leave my post on September 15 (which was approved). The first reason had to do with intellectual fatigue. The second one,combined with the first, made me decide as I did. Since the beginning of 1969, job offers had been piling up on my desk. Lastly, I knew that what remained to be done, in the case of French-language units, was going to be done very well by my successor, Fred Sharp. Since I had devoted myself entirely to my work, the results in that area had been achieved rapidly so that by the spring of 1969 I had accomplished the bulk of my mission.

The reader might remember the kind of welcome I had received in Ottawa upon my arrival in 1966. I wanted to make sure that things would be done differently during the transfer of power to Fred Sharp, scheduled for September 12, 1969, at Uplands. For the occasion, 300 members of the three old services were gathered together in their common uniform. I made sure that francophones from the R22^{e}R were present. The entire guard was under the command of Lieutenant-Colonel Jean Riffou. Many guests from different areas of public life were in attendance, including Governor General Roland Michener and Defence Minister Léo Cadieux, as well as Cardinal Maurice Roy, Hugues Lapointe, Arthur Trudeau and Paul Hellyer. I was greatly touched by the ceremony. No one can leave a profession to which he has devoted all his energy for over thirty years without feeling some emotion. My feelings were clear to the participants. I also felt deeply the fact that General Charles Foulkes, who had been an excellent friend of mine and who should have been there, had died early on the 12th.

The review—in a jeep—and the customary speeches were held prior to our flying to our Sainte-Adèle residence in the Laurentians, where we celebrated my retirement in a more private fashion.

In what condition were the Forces I left behind? First of all, the francophone element had begun to find there a place that was going to expand in the years to come. In addition, the Forces were unified.

When Minister Cadieux, on July 31, 1969, sent me a letter accepting my request to retire, he added that my name would long be known as that of the man who had "made" unification. Paul Hellyer was another person who wrote to me on September 15. I had found out about his switch to the Department of Transport while I was in England. Upon my return, I had organized a farewell dinner at Rockcliffe in his honour. On the evening of October 24, 1967 (twelve days after that first event), I received him, again at Rockcliffe, at a more intimate soirée during which, as was often the custom in the Forces at the time, comic skits were performed. I wanted to ensure that Hellyer would be there when I was saying farewell to the Armed Forces. In my speech, I mentioned many names, including his, and thanked him sincerely for the leadership he had provided in the field of integration and unification. In his letter, Hellyer thanked me for that mention. He also noted that I had "Canadianized" the Armed Forces. And, in French, he wrote that "the guidelines established for greater use of the French language within the Armed Forces, designed and approved jointly, and which Léo Cadieux and yourself have systematically implemented, will make an enormous long-term contribution to the unity of our Canada." After mentioning Simone's highly effective background role in my life, he concluded by saying that, without me, he was not certain whether the Canadian Armed Forces could have been successfully unified.

If I mention Hellyer's letter at length, it is because, in spite of many differences of opinion between us, he had been on top of the situation. He had managed to persuade the Cabinet that his "integrationist" and "unifying" views were right. Once he had been given the mission to achieve results in those two fields, within a reasonable time frame, he had bravely confronted numerous reactions in that area. He had successfully completed his project, steering it carefully according to the situation and even altering major details of it (the arrival of the French-language units, for example) without losing sight of the ultimate goal. I am wholly persuaded, even today, that our forces could not have achieved their present efficiency if their three components had not been brought together the way they were in the 60s.

Unification was therefore accomplished; the French-language units and the B&B programme in the Forces were well underway. However, I was somewhat concerned about other areas. In 1969, NATO was a lesser priority for Canada than it had been before Mr. Trudeau came to power. The number of our soldiers was to be reduced to 83,000—it had already dropped, between 1963 and 1969, from 118,000 to 98,000. Our budgets were going to stay unchanged for three years. There was talk of completely abandoning the limited nuclear role that we still had.

During my last weeks as Chief, I insisted on two major points. The first one was that our Forces, although reduced, should be well-equipped and have "teeth." The second was that we had to reassure our allies, to whom we had announced a reduction in the number of our troops in Europe in addition to requiring that the Air Force and Army be brought together (a move I approved, as mentioned earlier) in the south of Germany, on the French border. All these changes were announced in the departmental statement of April 18, 1969, which resulted from Trudeau's May 1968 speech and anticipated the 1971 White Paper that the Minister was already working on. The public relations work I did following those announcements seemed successful, since the Supreme Commander of NATO forces in Europe wrote us, prior to my departure, that our military, after 1972 (when the concentration would be completed) would have an important role to play in the strategy, although that role would be smaller than at present.

I must add this, however. As I had publicly stated in August 1969 (this had earned me on August 22 a supportive editorial in the Montreal *Gazette*) abandoning our nuclear role was sheer hypocrisy. We refused to carry nuclear weapons on our aircraft, but we continued to participate militarily in NATO, which had a nuclear strategy. In case of necessity, we would leave the dirty job to the others, thus playing the role of Pontius Pilate. In addition, we had decided that our troops, to the rear of the potential front, would form a reserve. As such, they still had some importance, but we got the feeling from our allies that we were given that task in order to avoid having on the firing line, at the outbreak of hostilities, a Canadian contingent that would be unsure of the extent to which its chiefs would allow it to commit itself in a given situation.

I did not leave the Forces officially in September 1969. Indeed, since I was entitled to nine months' leave, my name was only due to be struck from the rolls on May 13, 1970. That date was finally postponed by four days because of minor surgery that had to be done on one of my hands. Even then, I did not abandon the Forces completely since I remained an Honorary colonel of the infantry corps until February 1, 1973, and of the 12th Armoured Regiment of Canada from December 1969 on. There was also the Board of the *Régie du R22eR* and all the honorary and protocol functions that often called for me to wear the uniform.

My working life was not over. As already mentioned, many opportunities arose. Mr. Cadieux spoke to me about a diplomatic posting that I could have taken up immediately upon my retirement. I was also offered various private sector opportunities. I chose to accept a proposal from the Government of Quebec.

During my last months of military service, senior Quebec officials approached me, in the name of their government, which was at that time led by Premier Bertrand. The position was to be Quebec's representative in New York. My goal was to continue working for Canada by participating in the development of the Province of Quebec. If that province were able to reduce its economic lag a little, it would once more begin to play the major role that it deserved in the affairs of the country. I was therefore ready to place my experience and—modesty apart, my prestige—at the service of that cause. A long article in *La Presse* of August 21, 1969, gave a very good indication of the state of mind I have just described.

Some of my advisers in Ottawa had strongly urged me to take a few weeks holidays when leaving the post of CDS. They believed that I had a great need for it. Undoubtedly too accustomed to action, I waved off this advice. On August 28, in Quebec City, I agreed with Bertrand on the date when I was to assume my posting. On September 3, 1969, a press release in Quebec City announced that I would assume my duties in New York by September 17. Obviously, I did not take much time to relax, and I regret it a little today.

In New York, my primary concern was to enable the province to attract investors while opening up American markets for all kinds of finished products made in Quebec. To that end, I began by contacting various U.S. organizations. I took many people out to lunch and was in turn invited to other luncheons. Within a short time, the editorial writers of the major dailies and the news makers at the New York Stock Exchange knew me well. I went to many places in New York and its environs to meet people who might be interested in our products. Among other things, I saw the various furniture wholesalers. We then decided to organize an exhibition to allow our people to display their products. At the same time, I helped anyone who came to see me at my office. All went fairly well, although I quickly realized that the Americans had required guaranteed delivery of the various goods they needed which many Quebec manufacturers had trouble meeting.

In other fields, I made suggestions, particularly concerning the type of publicity that Quebec was then using in the U.S. For instance, the province arranged a major public relations piece in *Business Week*, which was subsequently sent to the members of Congress. In my opinion, we should have proceeded differently by entrusting the publicity to a U.S. company which would know the market and by providing all our agents with brochures and audio-visuals on Quebec. On another front, I was able to have a lobbyist appointed—in the greatest confidence—in Washington for financial and industrial issues. He was an old friend, Arthur Trudeau, a retired U.S. Lieutenant-General, who, in spite of his Franco-American origin, spoke no French.

Finally, I took an interest in all kinds of secondary fields. At the request of Anaïs and Wilfrid Pelletier, I took care of the young Canadian students working at the various New York music schools. From time to time, I brought them together for a meal to which I invited a Canadian professional, such as Louis Quillico or Joseph Rouleau. The young people thus got to know each other while meeting some performers who had already made their mark in the world of music.

On October 28, 1969, I participated in Chicago in the opening of the new Quebec House. There was a problem: the person who was to be its head wanted total independence of the other legations. It would have been advisable, however, to co-ordinate our action, at least as far as the promotion of our tourism or the distribution of information was concerned. The Ministry seemed ready, though, to accept an arbitrary subdivision of our work areas in the United States, and even the fact that they would be completely isolated from each other.

I arrived, therefore, with a whole delegation led by Marcel Masse, Minister of Intergovernmental Affairs. Things went badly, for I realized that many of these people had trouble expressing themselves in English. When the time came for the press conference, there were only two of us Quebeckers left, although it had been agreed that all would be there. However, using the pretext that they did not speak sufficient English, the others failed to appear. I therefore became master of ceremonies as well as chairman of the press conference, an unfortunate situation since this "show" was of a rather political nature. The U.S. press was very favourable, whereas the *Toronto Star*'s reporter attacked me, accusing me of having almost betrayed the country by working for Quebec. I was furious that he could have conceived the notion that I had taken that posting in New York in order to foster separatism. I must admit, on the other hand, that in Chicago I occasionally did seem to be taking care of the intergovernmental affairs of a highly nationalistic Quebec government.

Another, more serious, event occurred shortly thereafter. A Canadian Broadcasting Corporation reporter, who was later president of the National Assembly, interviewed me for television. I realized that Mr. Guay was more interested in the separatist movement and those who planted bombs than in the economic development of his province. I simply told him to go back home, that I did not intend to continue the interview under those conditions.

A little later, Claude Morin met with me to talk about intergovernmental affairs. He asked me to establish closer links with the United Nations in order to create contacts with the francophone countries of Black Africa. I had not the slightest intention of pursuing the matter on my own. I called my old friend, Yvon Beaulne, who was then Canadian Ambassador to the United Nations. I spoke to him about the whole affair, and he told me that indeed I did not need to do much since Canada had excellent relations with francophone Black Africa. He added that he would take advantage of the earliest opportunity to invite me to his home when he was to have discussions with representatives from that part of the world.

Shortly after that visit by Morin, Jean-Jacques Bertrand asked a lawyer from Baie-Comeau, Gaétan Rouleau, to investigate this entire affair. I simply told Rouleau what I had heard, and I added that I was not prepared to play a diplomatic role but rather to promote Quebec industry. Rouleau then went to see Beaulne, who must have made his report. At any rate, I was fed up. I was very annoyed that the situation developed the way it did. I was unhappy that many perceived me to be one of those who were attempting, directly or indirectly, to separate the Province of Quebec from the rest of Canada. From that time on, I looked for a way of leaving the post that I had been so happy to accept a few months earlier.

Since I had only been in New York for a few months, I now had to find an excuse. I therefore sent Mr. Bertrand a letter telling him that I preferred to abandon the post because of a conflict of interest between my work and certain family affairs. This was obviously not the case, but it allowed everyone to save face. In the meantime, Bertrand decided to call a general election. Under the circumstances,he asked me to delay my resignation. Bertrand lost out and I had to deal with Robert Bourassa and other members of the new Cabinet in order for them to follow up on my decision, which was finally approved. I was almost happy to give up a salary of $25,000. Nevertheless, I found it difficult to leave New York, as I liked the city a great deal. I had just rented a beautiful apartment in a large building near Central Park.

I have since been accused sometimes of having spent a great deal of money to furnish the representative's apartment. I find it indecent that this point should be raised, particularly since I had nothing to do with it. I never asked the Quebec Minister of Public Works for anything; he hired a professional decorator, who submitted his plans directly to Quebec City. I only got involved in that matter when Mr. Beaulac consulted me, which he seldom did.

Some have attempted to make a great deal out of another event as well. I had taken steps to purchase a historic piano for Quebec, but I did not make that decision by myself. One day, Mr. Bouchard and Mrs. Morissette, two well-known pianists, visited me when they were on a mission for the Quebec government. I took advantage of the opportunity to ask them whether it was possible to buy a certain Steinway, which was interesting from a history-of-music viewpoint, for Quebec, since it had belonged to Helen Beillen, a great Canadian pianist and co-founder of McGill University's School of Music in Montreal; she had since died. Helen had been an extraordinary pianist whom I had known well, as well as her husband, Ted Bullock, whom I have already mentioned.* The people I spoke to took up my suggestion and the piano was sent to our apartment. Later, I was reproached for this as an undue expense.

When I left my New York job in June 1970, my problems with Quebec officials did not end altogether. In fact, my dealings with them were not completed until March 1, 1971, after I had been paid a certain amount of money that I was owed.

Back in Sainte-Adèle, in need of a job, I immediately contacted Ottawa. I quickly realized that my stay in New York had seriously undermined my credibility in Ottawa as well as in Quebec City. I therefore had to manage by myself.

For some time, though, I was subjected to some very special attention. The kidnappings of James Cross and Pierre Laporte had placed the authorities on alert. Apparently, I was one of the people the FLQ would have liked to kidnap. One thing was certain: at one point, two unknown characters watched my house for over 48 hours. I was also given a driver and a bodyguard for a few days. I had no fears for myself. I took steps to defend myself if need be, without firearms but with a chain that my commando courses had taught me to use effectively. In case of an attempt to kidnap me, my goal was to fight until I was killed on the spot rather than follow the FLQ people. At the time, Simone and I were primarily afraid for our two grandchildren, who lived with Michèle directly across from us. What could we do, for instance, if an attempt were made to attack them on the way to school? My fear for my grandchildren left me only when the crisis had ended.

After June 1970, I was mainly interested in the business side of my career. In business, I met with some successes and some failures, one of the latter being the result of some impetuous decisions made by the Quebec government elected in 1976.

In 1975, I decided to sell my property in Sainte-Adèle and return to the good old city of Trois-Rivières. Between 1970 and that time, some people had made further attempts to turn me into a politician. I must say that, being personally attracted to that, I kept up-to-date. I remember having received, as early as October 1968, highly specific reports from federal Liberal friends regarding the serious challenge posed by the new Parti

---

* Ted died suddenly at the Ritz Carlton in Montreal following my return to Quebec and a few hours after we had attended a football match at the *Collège Militaire royal de Saint Jean.*

Québécois. In fact, they even predicted the eventual electoral victory of that party. In 1969, after my retirement, an influential friend told me that he had suggested to Pearson in 1967 that I be made a minister. Pearson's written reply, which I have in my papers, says that he had already been thinking of that possibility for some time. In the fall of 1970, it was the turn of the routed Union Nationale to spread a rumour to the effect that I might become the "promised saviour." On November 10, 1970, I issued a public statement putting an end to all speculations. In 1973, specific proposals on this same topic were made to me. I gave no shred of hope to those who made it.

I stayed in close touch with military affairs. Years after my retirement, I was still granting interviews related to my years of military service. I also attended many protocol-related events to which I was invited in Canada and abroad. Primarily, though, I watched from afar the development of the French-language units. From March 1, 1969 until February 28, 1974, I was the honorary colonel of the *12ᵉ Régiment blindé du Canada*. In order to create that unit in 1968 I had had to remove the Fort Garry Horse from the active force, which, let it be said in passing, took the decision fairly well, as they understood the full scope of my project. Not surprisingly, I showed a very special interest in the 12ᵉ RBC during its first years of existence. I accepted the appointment as honorary colonel of the regiment precisely in order to ensure that the 12ᵉ would become a truly French-language unit. I did not want the English tradition to be perpetuated in that unit. I must say that I was going to be a little disappointed.

In April 1971, I found out that an anglophone was going to replace Savard, who was commanding officer at the time. I immediately objected in a letter to the Chief of Personnel. I had nothing against Campbell, who had served in the R22ᵉR and was an excellent, highly bilingual officer whom I had advised in 1958 to obtain a transfer to the Armoured Corps in order to assume command of the francophone squadron of the 1/8th Hussars. The problem was that by appointing him to lead the 12ᵉ RBC, the old way of doing things would be maintained, since Campbell's French, albeit very good, was far from excellent. My goal had been that the new French-language unit should quickly become a unit operating like the R22ᵉR as regards the working languages and the linguistic make-up. That was not going to be achieved by having anglophone unit leaders a mere three years after the creation of the unit. In July, the Chief of Personnel confirmed his decision to me and explained that he had no choice, since no francophone was ready to take over. He assured me, however, that it would be the last appointment of this kind in the 12ᵉ RBC. Although I was no longer in the system, I had enough information on the situation of the Armoured Corps to know that, with a little effort, an acceptable alternative could have been found.

Unhappy with this development, but unable to do much about it since I was no longer in the Department, I contacted Claude Ryan to advise him of my fears regarding the future of the French-language unit. In my opinion, the Quebec press could exert some pressure. A few days later, a reporter from *Le Devoir* came to see me. I did not hold back anything, and I repeated some of the points mentioned earlier, openly referring to the Campbell case and expressing astonishment at the fact that the French programme appeared to have been blocked since I had left. I noted that a monitoring committee outside the Department could be set up to watch how things were developing in this area. The article was published prominently on July 13, 1971.

Things stayed that way for a while until the Minister, Donald MacDonald, sent a copy of the White Paper to me on August 24 and asked for my comments. Six days later, I replied that I liked what I had read. First of all, this resembled fairly closely the presentation I had made to Trudeau in 1968. Regarding the role of the CF-5, I stressed that unless the country obtained certain electronic components that would enable the plane to provide surveillance over its own territory (in my opinion, the highest-priority use of that aircraft),we would be restricted to using them exclusively for ground support.

Most of my letter, however, was devoted to bilingualism and biculturalism in the Forces. I stated in various ways my fear that National Defence would soon return to the errors of the past. Some of my recent findings supported that. I mentioned again Campbell's appointment, which had brought us back to square one, precisely when a young francophone officer, Denis Turcotte, had just left the Forces and described, in a long letter to *Le Devoir*, the unfair situation francophones faced. To my mind, the French-language units had normal growth problems and the Department ought to have been ready, in these times, to accept for a while a somewhat lesser effectiveness of those units, if that was to lead to an improved situation in the long term. (I must admit that when I was in my post I said the opposite, namely, that the B&B programme must not render our Forces less effective. I had therefore left that well-worn path.) I stated that Ottawa had to have a branch devoted exclusively to the administration of the francophones, that the numerous postings of French-language unit com-manders should cease (three commanders of the 12^e RBC since 1967; at the 5^e RALC, a third commander was soon going to be appointed), that French-language units should not be used as language schools for anglophones (my visits to Valcartier had shown that the number of hardly-bilingual anglophones was enormous: twenty officers in the 12^e RBC in 1971), and, lastly, that technical training increasingly be provided in French because some of the young people I had met told me that they had chosen a non-technical trade since their English was insufficient. I concluded by thanking the Minister for his kindness in asking me for my comments on the White Paper.

For over two months nothing happened at the Department. Then, on November 12, I was informed of the case of a young Trois-Rivières militiaman who had been refused access to the Armoured Corps when he enrolled, under the pretext that there were no vacancies. On the 18th, I prepared a long letter to the Minister, starting with that event and going back to the past, touching upon the history of the old anglophone cavalry and mentioning again the Campbell case. I added that there should be an investigation of the accusations levelled by Turcotte against the 12^e RBC. In my opinion, they contained many half-truths but also some undeniable facts. If that situation was not changed, I was ready to resign as honorary colonel (that possibility had already been mentioned in the Le Devoir article of the previous July).

That letter was never sent because at the very instant when I was going to mail it, a long reply from MacDonald to my August message arrived. Obviously, experts had examined each of the points I had raised. They were able to reassure me, overall, regarding what was happening with B&B at National Defence. Above all, I found out that Armand Letellier had become, as a civilian, Director General of Bilingualism and Biculturalism. I even suspected that he had penned that very complete reply which satisfied many points . . . except as regards the 12^e RBC. The goals of a long-term programme that would take into account everything (recruiting of francophones by trade and classification, new French-language units, teaching of languages, including French to anglophones, and so on) were thoroughly explained. This calmed me temporarily, and I immediately thanked MacDonald for his goodwill, but I took up again the issue of the unjustifiable appointment of Campbell and I added the case of the rejection of our young Trois-Rivières citizen.

The latter issue was settled, although Campbell's case was handled less well since he remained in his posting until the end of his term. Since then, other anglophones have taken his place only too often, in spite of the promise made to me in 1971 by the Chief of Personnel.

Even after I left the honorary command of the 12^e RBC in 1974, I did not abandon all interest in B&B. At different times and places, I was able to note that the programme, as we had designed it in 1968 did not seem to operate as well as expected. In 1983, fifteen years after the creation of the units, I decided to do a little investigation on my own to find out the state of things. To my great disappointment, in spite of unquestionable improvement, I found that what I had set up was being frittered away and disappearing.

First of all, I noted during that investigation that a great number of officers (gunners, armoured personnel and others) at Valcartier were anglophones. We found them in an excessive number of important positions in those units, which were supposed to help develop the potential of francophones. In the Navy, almost nothing had been done to date to develop the cadres we were going to need at every level, not only to maintain the two French-language units that existed but also to increase the number of that type of naval unit. The Air Force was about halfway between the army and the navy.

Many of my hopes were therefore not yet realized in this field, *over fifteen years after the initial effort we had made*. Of course, and this was certainly praiseworthy, many anglophones had learned French. And it was also true that the great majority of those who claimed to speak our language did so fairly well. But it seemed to me that, in many cases, trained francophone cadres had been simply shunted aside in favor of anglophones who had just learned to speak French. This militated against the goals of 1968, which included the creation, with French-Canadians as essential factors, within those new French-speaking units, of the same spirit that was the foundation of the R22^{e}R which would give our people a chance to serve within a suitable environment, where their culture would be a living one, even while permitting, where required, learning English, which is essential for those who want to advance.

I spoke to many young people during my investigation. An NCO whom I considered to be a man of integrity told me, for instance, that he had been unable to pass a certain armoured corps course which was given in English at Petawawa because he did not speak the language sufficiently well. And the brave lad had not had the chance to learn English at the language school; he had applied without having the prerequisite linguistic skills. This was absolutely contrary to the principles we had established.

I knew well a young officer graduate of the CMR, who had prepared himself for the 12^e BC. On leaving St. Jean, he had gone to Gagetown to complete his practical courses. Like many others ready to serve in the armoured corps, he had failed because, in some people's opinion, he was not ready. It was upsetting to see that these young people who had been transferred elsewhere, where they had showed themselves competent, and yet—as if they had succeeded by a mere fluke—had not been allowed to serve where they wanted. The fact was that during the period when the officer involved went to Gagetown, the Commanding officer of the Armoured Officers School was a "frog baiter," who should never have been given that responsibility.

Moreover, I had been told a short while before of the possibility that the technical courses at St. Jean might be eliminated for reasons of economy. The way I saw it, there are no valid funds worth the savings when your duty is to create a country and train men and women to adequately defend it. I reminded the authorities of my proposal, made when I was CDS, that someday we should be able to provide all technical courses in French to francophones. We had to start at the basic level of training, which was very quickly provided in French. It would have been too costly in 1968-69 to advance this issue any quicker, and it was simply impossible because we lacked cadres. It had therefore been agreed that, even though the courses were to be given in English, we would set up modules within which unilingual francophones would receive assistance from bilingual persons. That measure, meant to be an interim one, was combined with another one, namely, providing a solid training in English to those who would *have to serve in that language*, in order for them to be properly equipped and to have full career chances.

Even now, in 1988, too many courses are still available only in English. An aggravating circumstance is that our young unilingual francophones must almost always take an English language course in their first months in the Forces, whether the requirement is immediate or not. What is particularly frustrating is that many of those recruits joined the Forces in order to "do something." To sit down in a classroom at sixteen or seventeen years of age to memorize basic English was a discouraging experience for many of them.

On the point of technical training in French, I have said that regardless of the costs involved, it was an investment in the future of the country. One only has to consider the number of technicians trained by our Forces who had later no difficulty finding jobs in civilian industry.

I am a good Canadian, one of those who feel at ease anywhere between the Pacific and the Atlantic. I have noticed, however, that—perhaps due to lack of knowledge—none of the ministers who succeeded Paul Hellyer and Léo Cadieux has stepped forward to handle these issues seriously. During the 1980 referendum, I stayed on the federalist side although, on some points, including that of the full recognition of our francophone existence, I was and I still am fairly close to the separatists. Unlike them, though, I believe that we must do what is required from within the present political system rather than from without. I hope that this book will enable Canadians to reconsider what they think the country must be, which is no longer the same as in the 50s, and to consider these issues even more seriously than they have up until now. If the present situation, both in the Forces and elsewhere, continues, I must say—to my infinite regret—that Quebec will probably have no choice but to follow its own path.

Concerning the armed forces, my hopes rest on the many francophone senior officers and NCOs who are today in command positions. They have all reached those positions through undeniable professionalism. In the course of their careers, however, which now often develop in an environment using French, thanks to the conditions we established in 1968, they have perhaps failed to perceive the full scope of the challenge that must still be met for present and future francophones. I want to reiterate to these French Canadians—and I know that many anglophones support me—that it is essential to create a strong francophone infra-structure in our Forces that will enable them to respond to any eventuality, and particularly to a general mobilization during which hundreds of thousands of francophones would be trained and led in their language in all branches of the Forces. Within the existing infra-structure, therefore, much remains to be done, particularly on the naval and air side as well as with respect to technical training in general. One must understand that, in Canada, francophones and their language are operational necessities. Today, so many of them have come to take the place of the handful of diehards that we once were, that it should not be difficult, if the will is there, to emphasize once again an issue that could play a crucial role in the survival of our country.

I will now deal with the education of our francophone servicemen's children. I will recall the proposal I made to my department on February 3, 1966 and which Ross took up in his report concerning the establishment of a boarding school at Valcartier. The matter had gone no further during my tenure. The problem was solved in two ways: through subsidies to parents posted outside Quebec and through French schools set up at some of our bases outside Quebec but run by our Department with the permission of the province involved.

In practice, those schools did not mean much, because there had to be a minimum number of students for each, and it rarely happened, except in Europe, that there were sufficient students for secondary classes to be organized. Even today, in Halifax, our courses in French to children stop before the secondary level.

What does the requirement of French schools mean? Here is an example. When we created the Airborne Regiment, it was agreed that it would be sub-divided into three units, called commandos. 1st Commando would be a French-language unit. However, the whole regiment had to be based in Edmonton. I refused for more than a year to send 1st Commando to Edmonton (it was at Valcartier then) because, in my opinion, adequate education in French was not available. There were indeed French schools in Alberta, but they followed the provincial curriculum, which could have caused problems when the students would eventually return to Quebec. Finally, I asked that the Chief of Mobile Command, Bill Anderson, go there himself, take the necessary steps and assure me that everything was settled in satisfactory manner before authorizing 1st Commando to join the two others. In my opinion, the availability of essential services in French throughout Canada was part of the price to pay in order to be a Canadian.

Subsequent to my leaving the Forces, when I noticed that the overall situation was far from settled, I attempted to add the right to subsidies to my concept of a boarding school. In 1978, I created a non-profit corporation that took over a school that the Brothers of the Christian Schools had to abandon at Mont Bénilde, near Trois-Rivières. Then we asked for a grant from the province in order to start up our project. The idea of a boarding school was maintained, but it would have been accessible to all those within the general population who wanted to send their children to a private school (not exclusively for the children of the military, as my original idea had been). In addition, I thought I would be able to reach an agreement with the Department of National Defence which would have enabled the children of the military, once or twice a year, to be taken from the school and sent to their parents (which was already being done for the subsidized employees of the federal Treasury Board).

Since the Quebec government was against the proliferation of private schools, however, we were refused subsidies. We took the matter to court and the case dragged on from 1978 to 1983. Finally, in the fall of 1983, we won our lawsuit and the government could no longer refuse to subsidize a new private school that had a serious concept to propose. In the meantime, I had resigned as chairman of the corporation, which had managed to stay afloat, with some difficulty, over the years. What will be done now? Only my successors will be able to say, but it seems to me that, in this area, for the first time, the future is promising not only for our own little group, but for other people as well.

I will now deal with the 1980 referendum, the last major event with which I conclude this chapter. I had absolutely no intention of getting involved in this serious political affair. I was not a politician and I did not want to become one, but there was an incident that changed my mind.

Of course, I had read the Parti Québécois manifesto so that I would know exactly what it wanted and what it promised us. I looked particularly at a section dealing with military affairs. I don't know who had prepared that part of the document, but one thing was obvious, as I could tell from my experience: it would be impossible, with the budget proposed for the defence of Quebec, to do what was suggested. Apparently a "liberated" Quebec would have stayed in NATO, as well as NORAD, in addition to ensuring the sovereignty of its territory and providing peacekeeping troops. I could not believe that this might seem plausible to the population. There had to be at least $1 billion per year in order to achieve the proposed undertaking, instead of the $165 million mentioned in the brochure.

I did nothing further about this finding, however. Then one day René

Lévesque spoke about the issue in Chicoutimi.* I could not imagine that a responsible politician would seriously attempt to sell the public on this defence programme. The last drop of my patience was exhausted when, in his speech, he called the Canadian military a farce. Immediately, I said to myself that I had to intervene. The least he had to be told was that he would have been better off following Canadian soldiers instead of the U.S. Army during the Second World War. He would then have noticed how well his compatriots, and particularly the French-speaking ones, had conducted themselves throughout the war.

Mr. Lévesque had no right to treat the Canadian military as he had just done, and much less the tens of thousands of them who had given their lives on alien soil during this century. Personally, I could not leave undefended all those men who had devoted themselves to our country, nor those who today are ready to make the supreme sacrifice, particularly since neither group can speak for itself in such instances.

At the first opportunity I had (having been invited to Louiseville by the member of Parliament for Maskinongé), I asserted that the Canadian troops were not a farce. I also stated, on radio and on television, that if Mr. Lévesque wanted to confront with me on television or the radio or before a public assembly, I was ready to debate his defence project properly. Moreover, I would demonstrate to him that the troops I had commanded, admired and loved had nothing in common with *opéra bouffe*. With a view to such a potential confrontation, I made a special trip to Ottawa to check some of my assumptions regarding the cost of the armed forces in Quebec. I was ready to enter the fray in order to seriously inform rather than to "politic," although my intervention, I suspected, would lead me to attack the myths that the PQ was trying to make us swallow in military affairs.

I continued to harass Mr. Lévesque in order to obtain that debate. But it was another man who offered to respond in his place, an old comrade-in-arms who had held the rank of brigadier. He came to Lévesque's assistance on the background question by saying that what the "yes" advocates were proposing for defence was easily achievable. He explained his viewpoint in April 1980 to a reporter from the *Gazette*, stating that an independent Quebec could form a defence force capable of implementing the "yes" military programme. That force would resemble Luxemburg's and would consist of militia. The air force would be equipped with helicopters that would intercept unidentified aircraft over Quebec for identification purposes.

---

* By the way, I have already mentioned that at the time when my job opportunity in New York arose, Lévesque had briefly drawn me in, in Chicoutimi in 1969, by implying in a speech that I was resigning in order to join the Québec forces because I was "fed up" with working for the federal government. This had earned him a public denial (see *Le Soleil* of June 17, 1969) to the effect that the rumour was ridiculous and that he had not spoken for me.

Following that article, I agreed to go to a press conference. For the occasion, I prepared a long text that was issued to the press. I followed that text closely during my presentation and I have attached it as Appendix E. But I could have added many other arguments and questions to that speech. I wonder how much it would cost today to have a small—"modest," in Lévesque's words—air defence for Québec? How much would the ships cost that would have to be there to defend our shores? And the various parts that the three services would require in order to maintain their weapons in operational condition? There is no point in talking of Luxemburg, a country smaller than the Island of Montreal and defended by a small infantry battalion. After all, we would be a country as large, say, as Norway or Sweden (countries that the PQ people loved to use for reference).

What would Quebec need in order to protect its sea approaches? Undoubtedly patrol boats, minelayers or minesweepers, and others. What aircraft would it use to guarantee its sovereignty? Whether they be F18s, which the Parti Québécois despised, or some other aircraft, they must be able to control the territory, including the Arctic. Many of them would therefore be required to ensure genuine surveillance of the territory. Even by taking the least expensive high-performance aircraft, the proposed budget would be exhausted on the very first day.

My last question to Lévesque and company: would the French-Canadian troops, which play an important role in the defence of Canada, remain with the province of Québec in a situation such as the one we were being led to in 1980? Would these servicemen not try instead to continue with Canada?

Another aspect had been mentioned in the *Gazette* article. The point was made for a defence partly provided by the Americans. I do not believe that we can honestly maintain our sovereignty by having our neighbours to the south defend us. Why would they do the job without requiring payment for it? Should one sincerely believe that the Americans would not exact some kind of toll? Quebeckers would undoubtedly find, as they already know, that the Americans are always ready to undertake tasks. But all the negotiations I have had with them, and they were many, have proven to me that, one way or another, one must pay for the services they render and that the final bill can be high.

In summary, in the military field (I will not speak about the other topics, where I feel less at ease), the "yes" people had tried to make us swallow a tall tale. They did not have the right to deal with that issue in that manner, given the general ignorance of the public in this matter. If that is the type of story they tried to peddle in every area, no wonder their call went unheeded.

Epilogue

As I finish this book, I remember the place where I started out: Sainte-Monique-de-Nicolet. I recall the difficulties of my childhood and my youth. I also recall the world outbreak of violence that physically or morally destroyed so many human beings. But it was also a turmoil which, on the other hand, enabled so many others to affirm themselves. Then, I see those tens of thousands of Canadians—men and women—with whom I served for over thirty years, in war as in peace, and all those loyal services that we rendered together.

My career owes its success to the continuing co-operation provided by those around me. Special mention must go to my family, who supported me so completely, particularly in the most difficult moments; to those of the R22eR, whom I had the honour to command for more than a year during the Italian campaign, those men who gave everything they had.

Nor can I forget those who served under my orders during the last months of the Second World War, when I was a brigadier: the Queen's Own Cameron Highlanders of Canada, *Les Fusiliers Mont-Royal* and the South Saskatchewan Regiment. Also, all those Canadians, anglophones and francophones, who demonstrated once again their great human and military qualities during the Korean War. All Canadian troops I have known in combat have shown a dedication, a bravery and a pride in being Canadian that were obvious wherever they went, to the greatest glory of our country. I also think fondly of the courage the British people demonstrated in the worst moments of their history, and of how happy I was to lead for two years the men of their 4th Division.

At the summit of my career, there were great challenges. It would have been simply impossible to meet them all, had I not been able to count on the understanding and active assistance of politicians such as Messrs Hellyer, Cadieux and Pearson. Thanks to them, our armed forces were able to shed the last remnants of a tradition that was out of date and acquire a thoroughly Canadian identity. In summary, I have great fondness for the people I have known during my life, both civilian and military, dedicated to their respective tasks, striving for a better future for all.

A look at my life shows that I was certainly not predestined for high functions by my birth, my childhood or my youth. And yet, I was "successful," as they say. I would be very happy if this book would help instill hope in a certain portion of our young people. Through persistence and conscientious work day after day in things both small and big, one can only advance, sometimes slowly, but always surely. It is my fondest hope that our young people in search of a future will find a less violent, less cruel outlet than war.

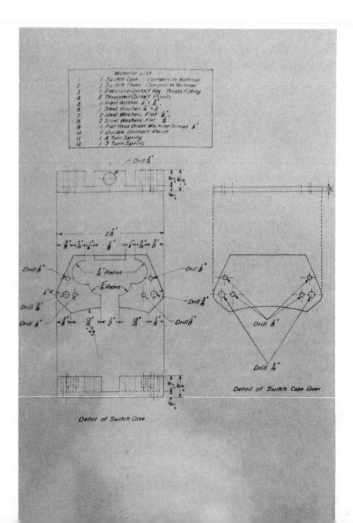

Detail of Switch Case Cover

Detail of Switch Case

Appendix A

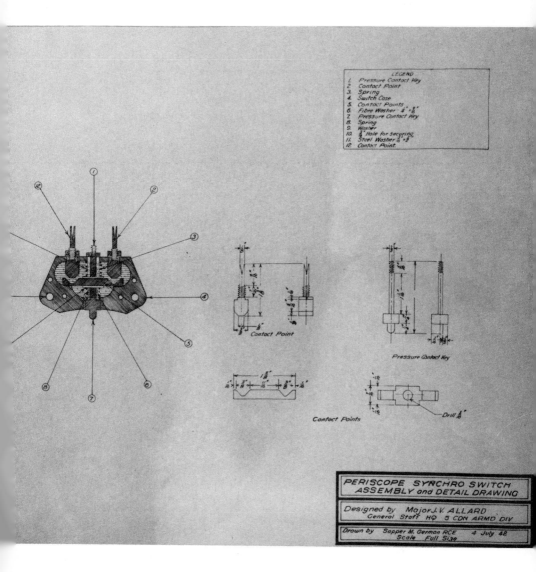

LEGEND
1. Pressure Contact Key
2. Contact Point
3. Spring
4. Switch Case
5. Contact Points
6. Fibre Washer
7. Pressure Contact Key
8. Spring
9. Washer
10. Hole for securing
11. Steel Washer
12. Contact Point.

Contact Point

Pressure Contact Key

Contact Points

Drill

PERISCOPE SYNCHRO SWITCH
ASSEMBLY and DETAIL DRAWING

Designed by   Major J.K. ALLARD
General Staff HQ 5 CDN ARMD DIV

Drawn by Sapper M. German RCE   4 July 42
Scale   Full Size

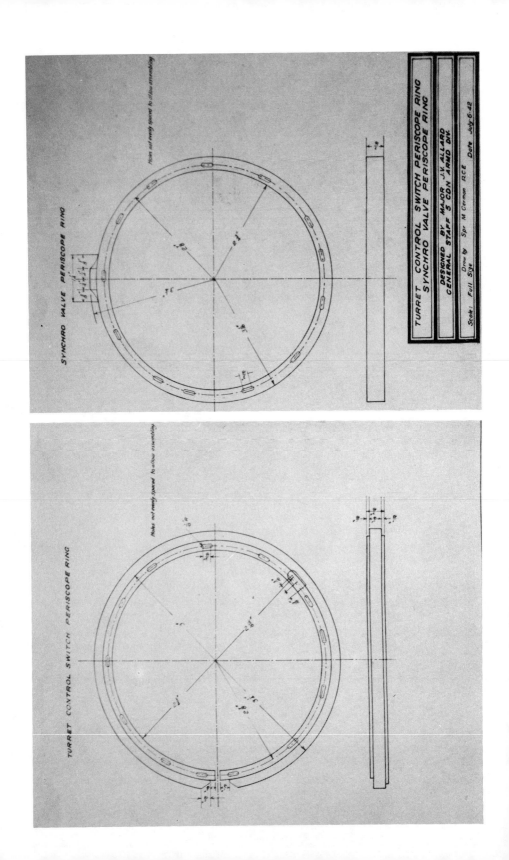

SYNCHRO VALVE PERISCOPE RING

TURRET CONTROL SWITCH PERISCOPE RING

TURRET CONTROL SWITCH PERISCOPE RING
SYNCHRO VALVE PERISCOPE RING

DESIGNED BY MAJOR J.V. ALLARD
GENERAL STAFF 5 CDN ARMD DIV.

Scale: Full Size   Drawn by Spr. M Carmon RCE   Date July 6·42

Appendix B

106 Cartier Street
Ottawa, Ontario
3 July 1951

The Honourable Brooke Claxton, K.C., D.C.M., M.P.,
Minister of National Defence,
Ottawa, Ontario.

Dear Mr. Claxton,

The enclosed letter, which I have taken the liberty of writing to you, will speak for itself.

It is perhaps necessary to inform you, however, that though I have worked very hard on the problem of relations between French Canadian and the Armed Forces during the 25 months that I have been on temporary active service in Eastern Quebec Area and Army Headquarters, I have at no time let that problem take my mind off the English-language side of recruiting advertising and publicity. While there was a tendency in the Department to consult me more freely about French-Canadian matters, I nevertheless carried all the weight I was allowed to lift on the other side as well.

English-speaking Reserve Force officers in Quebec City like Tim Atkinson, Gordon Ross and Brig. Archer will tell you that I did as much for them while I was there as for my own Regiment and for the Area as a whole.

Here at Army Headquarters, also, I initiated more than one practice which bore fruit. You are now receiving from Protestant clergymen across Canada, Col. Stone tells me, letters of commendation because the "Divine Service Book for the Armed Forces" was mailed to the pastor of every Protestant Church in Canada. This was an idea which I had great difficulty in getting adopted until I talked Bill Dumsday into asking you to direct that it be done. The Conference on recruiting publicity which was held late in May at AHQ between the advertising and public relations people was the result of long planning and very hard work on my part. There are various reports in files at HQ incorporating ideas and proposals which are the fruit of my 34 years of experience in newspaper, public relations, advertising, political, military and administrative service in all parts of Canada and overseas.

I was developing useful and cordial relations with Dr. Low and Ken MacGillivray, as I had done already with Bill Dumsday and Jack Mahony, when circumstances made it advisable for me to ask for my retirement.

I should like you to believe, Sir, that no officer in Canada would have been happier than I if it had been possible for me to continue in your service and to put at your disposal on a more suitable level and in a more effective manner the somewhat unusual resources which I have gathered in my lifetime for just such purposes as I think the Armed Forces have need of at this time.

I have the honour to be, Mr. Minister,

> Faithfully yours,
> T.L. Bullock
> Lieutenant-Colonel
> (Ex-R22^{e}R)

> 106 Cartier Street
> Ottawa, Ontario
> 3 July 1951

The Honourable Brooke Claxton, K.C., D.C.M., M.P.,
Minister of National Defence,
Ottawa, Ontario

Dear Mr. Claxton,

As I have now retired from temporary Active Service to the Supplementary Reserve, I feel free for the first time to communicate with you directly and in some detail on the subject which has long been uppermost in my mind.

My purpose in accepting a call-out in 1949 was to look into the difficulties in the relationships between French Canada and the Armed Services, to find out what could be done to get around those difficulties, and, if possible, to take a hand in the job.

I have been aware for thirty-five years of the political factors at play in this situation and it seemed wise to find out what military obstacles might lie in the way of a solution.

I read with admiration your statement in the House in May that French Canadians were to be given a more realistic status in the Armed Forces. I viewed with dismay certain things which were even then going on in the Services whose effect would be to discredit your statement in the eyes of French Canada.

Voluntary recruiting in French Canada has begun already to suffer again from the widely held and not wholly unjustified belief that French-Canadians cannot hope to hold key positions in the Armed Services even at Quebec Command Headquarters, let alone at National Defence Headquarters, and that the only Corps which is really open to them in practice is the Infantry. This impression has been allowed to spread and recruiting has fallen off sharply in recent weeks. The more this goes on, the more insistent will be the cry for compulsory service, and the sooner the Government will have to adopt it.

When that happens, whether we are at war or not, the three Services will quickly find themselves with about one-third of their personnel French-speaking, straight across the board on the lower levels, but without adequate representation in the higher ranks, and that is, in my opinion, the stage at which very real trouble is going to break out. This coming state of affairs has been pointed out at Headquarters and there are senior officers who have acknowledged in theory that it is a very real problem to be considered. But during the year in which I laboured in Ottawa on a very low level to do the little bit I could, I worked practically alone as far as definite measures were concerned and, though I communicated to Paul Paré at his request all that I was doing, the sloth of the organization as a whole in the face of what seems to me a vital principle was a fundamental factor in the growing sense of frustration and exhaustion which led finally to my withdrawal.

I am aware of communications which you have received from Quebec universities and other sources about this problem. We all know what can happen to such suggestions when they are referred for study to several echelons of a bureaucracy which has many ways of muffling the will of a responsible Minister. I could tell you instances of the thwarting of useful suggestions, even in Quebec Command, where the position is more critical than anywhere else. We must recognize that apathy and latent, almost unconscious hostility to French-Canadians are, in some quarters, dangerously effective brakes upon action.

Would it not be wise to have the whole problem up for thorough discussion now, while remedies can still be worked out, rather than wait for the inevitable explosion when the time comes to dump thousands of French-Canadians into a Navy, an Army and an Air Force not one of which is genuinely preparing to take them in on an equal footing?

That this matter requires urgent study is not an opinion which I have reached either recently or suddenly. As long ago as last year, I had private discussions of the problem with General Morton, Brigadier Allard, Colonel DeRome and others in Quebec and Montreal. General Morton, I have been informed, took it up directly with General Macklin; but the conclusion was, I believe, that committees already in existence could and would deal with it. At about the same time I had a long, private talk with Bill Dumsday on the same subject and suggested that, as it is as much a question of policy and public relations as of organization, he discuss it with you, possibly with a view to considering informal exploration of the situation on the Cabinet level. Bill told me some weeks ago that he had never done so, as he thought that General Macklin's committees would settle things all right.

There are, of course, two sides to the question: the problem of improving the position of French-Canadians in all branches and on all levels of the three services without seriously dislocating the general principles upon which military organization normally rests; and the equally grave political problem of creating a new relationship between the services and French Canada without arousing serious political tension in English-Canadian circles which traditionally consider that the Armed Forces belong particularly to them.

As whatever is done will have to be somewhat drastic in its effects, it is of the utmost political importance that it be presented to English Canada, and to the services themselves, as a measure of grave national equity and necessity, and in no sense "a plot to turn the Services over to the Vatican." At the same time, French-Canadians must be reassured that the plan is not a devious scheme to trick them into becoming English-Canadians.

There is no doubt in my mind that only a Liberal Government can tackle this problem realistically enough to solve it, and I should think that its solution would appeal very strongly to a party which draws so much of its strength from French Canada. There is no doubt, either, that the Minister who turns the trick, especially if he is a Quebec Minister, will ultimately find himself in a stronger position within the party than his colleagues. This, it seems to me, makes it doubly important to approach the question in a very broad spirit and to study carefully the political and public relations implications of each step before decisions are made and implemented. For one must have constantly in mind the political interests of Ministers who represent non-French-Canadian constituencies, and so the policy must be presented to the country as a whole as a belated and inevitable adjustment within a federal service in the truest and highest interests of Canadian racial unity and armed strength.

One must keep in mind, of course, Mr. Churchill's principle that "wars are not won by heroic militias," and I have tried in my thinking not to develop ideas which might impair the effectiveness of the Active Service. On the other hand, a close acquaintance with the military bureaucracy in peace time has pointed my attention forcibly to another statement of Mr. Churchill's in the same volume of his great work: "I have found it necessary to have direct access to and control of the Joint Planning Staffs because after a year of war I cannot recall a single plan initiated by the existing machinery."

Perhaps the time has come for Cabinet to set up a committee, directly responsible to you, as Mr. Churchill did under Professor Frederick Lindemann in scientific matters when "there was no time to proceed by ordinary channels," in order to settle some of the things which must be done if French Canadians are not to go on feeling that they are only hewers of wood and carriers of water in the Department of National Defence.

If the problem is still too involved for study by an official committee or commission, and since it is not deemed desirable to set up a Committee of the House of Commons on National Defence, might it mot be possible to organize quietly a qualified group within the Liberal party organization charged directly with the duty of studying and reporting party and public opinion for an effective solution?

French-speaking officers, among whom there is a very real fear of provoking retaliation if they speak their minds officially, might convey far more information to such a body than to an official committee; and English-speaking officers, also, might state their views more definitely to such a group than in the presence of official commissioners.

I have the honour to be, Sir,

> Faithfully yours,
> T.L. Bullock

C A N A D A

MINISTER OF NATIONAL DEFENCE   Ottawa, July 7, 1951

Lieutenant-Colonel T.L. Bullock,
106 Cartier Street,
Ottawa, Ontario.

Dear Colonel Bullock,

Thank you very much for your letter of July 3, 1951 on the question of service relations with French speaking personnel.

As you know, this has been a matter of personal concern to me ever since I have had this job and I have taken advantage of every opportunity to bring the importance of the problem and the necessity of finding satisfactory solutions home to all three services.

As you know, innumerable changes have been made along these lines. May I mention some of them.

(1) An order was passed requiring the recognition of O Canada.

(2) The Red Ensign was made alternative to the Union Jack.

(3) All three services were required to wear "Canada" on their shoulders.

(4) In the Navy steps were taken in advance of the Mainguy Report to provide for training of personnel in Canada rather than Britain, putting maple leaves on funnels, substituting for Rule Britannia and Song for Iolanthe in naval honours two French songs.

(5) Personal examination of every promotional list of the rank of Colonel or equivalent and above to insure that no qualified French-speaking officer has been passed over.

(6) Personal attendance at every possible service function in French-speaking parts of Canada.

(7) Insistence on letterheads, correspondence, door signs, orders, publications, reports, being in French as well as English.

(8) Personal investigation of every charge of discrimination.

(9) Personal exploration of every possible opportunity to secure the retention or return to the permanent force of French-speaking officers who had made good records for themselves.

(10) Enlistment of assistance of the Governor General, the Prime Minister and colleagues in the Cabinet at ceremonies and in speeches in drawing attention to features appealing to French-speaking people.

(11) Making every effort to feature French-speaking activities and successes in the armed forces, such as, for example, special references in speeches to the record of the 22nd and other French-speaking units, having the 22nd for the first time act as the guard of honour at the opening of Parliament, having French-speaking units furnish guards on the occasion of every important visit.

(12) Personal attention to all French advertisements.

(13) In the Canadian Services Colleges and the C.O.T.C. particular attention was paid to the possession of French.

(14) At the opening of R.M.C. and at the National Defence College and on numerous other occasions, as well as constantly with the Chiefs of Staff, I have emphasized that the possession of French is a definite military asset, which must be taken into consideration in making appointments and promotions.

I have enumerated these here so as to prepare a list which might be revised and added to in an effort to indicate that I personally am not responsible for the present position and that a great deal has been done.

The result is shown in the recruiting figures. For the first time in the history of canada French-speaking enlistments for the Special Force were in exact proportion to the population.

Lately we have been getting a very good number of French-speaking officers.

One can think of individual exceptions, but generally speaking the facts show that there is no discrimination.

I have had an examination made of the numbers of English- and French-speaking officers in the three services in the various ranks, as well as of their ages and years of service.

This shows that generally speaking French-speaking officers are younger and have less service than English-speaking officers of equivalent rank.

Also, the proportion of officers who are in the rank of Major and equivalent, or above, who are French-speaking, is very close to that of English-speaking officers, 24.3% of all French-speaking officers being in the rank of Major or above against 28.8% of English-speaking officers of the same category. The slight difference here is more than accounted for by the fact that there are in fact, relatively few French-speaking officers who have been in the armed forces prior to 1939, which is the case with the great majority of those who were in the rank of Major or above.

Here we come to the crux of the matter. The trouble is not due to discrimination in any sense whatever, but it is due to the relatively small number of French-speaking officers who joined the Active or Reserve forces prior to 1939. Since then, and particularly recently, the figures have been all right.

I know that there are other points, but what I am giving now are the facts.

I also recognize that it would be virtually impossible to persuade a good many French-speaking people that they are the facts. However, we must continue to try to bring out the facts.

We must also take other steps like those we now have for introducing French-speaking personnel to service life in a way which creates the best possible setting for their feeling at home.

The Army and the Air Force have courses for French-speaking recruits at St. Jean, Quebec. Some time ago I announced the intention of the Navy to have a similar course at H.M.C.S. *Montcalm* in Quebec.

We have been trying to work out some formula by which the same kind of thing can be done for candidates for commissions.

Three weeks ago I discussed this whole situation with His Excellency, Archbishop Roy, in Quebec. He was very sympathetic, thought we were tackling the job in the right way and said he would not hesitate to make any suggestions that occurred to him.

To create a third service college to deal with this would defeat the object of the service colleges and anyway, financially, would be quite out of the question. It is hard enough to justify having two as we have today.

Also, we are face to face with the fact that to a very large extent it is not possible to fight a bilingual war. This has been recognized in aviation, where English is the universal language of negotiation. It has been accepted as such for Air Force negotiations in all N.A.T.O. countries.

The same thing is true to a considerable degree of Navy and Army operations. You cannot conduct naval operations any more than you can fight a tank battle, in two languages.

Similarly, with regard to a good many trades, particularly related to the Navy and Air Force.

I appreciate your very helpful attitude and would be more than glad if you would let me have any comments on the foregoing or any suggestions as to what further steps should be taken.

Like you, I regard this as a matter of the greatest possible importance and appreciate your cooperation, as well as what you have done in this connection here.

I don't feel that at present a Cabinet Committee or any device of that kind would accomplish the purpose intended. What we want are ways of making it happier for French-speaking personnel in the armed forces, particularly the Navy and Air Force and convincing French-speaking people that everything possible is being done.

With all good wishes,

Yours sincerely,
BROOKE CLAXTON

106 Cartier Street
Ottawa, 4, Ontario
19 July 1951

The Honourable Brooke Claxton, K.C., D.C.M., M.P.,
Minister of National Defence,
Ottawa, Ontario.

Dear Mr. Claxton,

It seems to me that if the comments and suggestions which you invited me to offer are to be really useful to you in the light of the last paragraph of your careful and thought-provoking letter of 7 July, then perhaps it is well to start over again by referring you once more to the fifth paragraph of my letter dated 3 July:

> "Voluntary recruiting in French Canada has begun already to suffer again from the widely held and not wholly unjustified belief that French-Canadians cannot hope to hold key positions in the Armed Services even at Quebec Command Headquarters, let alone at National Defence Headquarters, and that the only

Corps which is really open to them in practice is the Infantry. This impression has been allowed to spread and recruiting has fallen off sharply in recent weeks. The more this goes on, the more insistent will be the cry for compulsory services, and the sooner the Government will have to adopt it."

The gist of my analysis of the situation lies in that paragraph, and all the arguments which are being massed in the French-language press and among French Canadians in general are based upon the assumptions which I report in it. If we are to "convince French-speaking people that everything possible is being done," then the Department's policy-makers and spokesmen should, if I may say so, (a) make themselves more familiar with what French Canadians are saying and thinking, and (b) show considerably more diligence, frankness and skill in explaining, to the French Canadians who direct opinion, how all that can be done is being done or is going to be, and why, in the case of impossible demands, those demands cannot be met.

I know that there are many Canadians who think that there is something mysterious and alien about the "French-Canadian mentality" and that there is not much purpose in trying to meet it, since it is a thing apart from ordinary Canadianism. This, of course, is not the case. Any officer of suitable prestige and rank who knows what he is doing will find French-Canadian publishers and editors more willing to meet his views than many English-Canadian publishers and editors you and I both know. In the twelve months which I spent in Quebec City I never experienced a bit of difficulty, not only in explaining our problems to the people of "L'Action Catholique," but in getting them to aid and abet the Army actively and constructively.

Where the Forces make their great tactical mistake in French Canada is in assuming that the people are automatically against us, and in neglecting to take the essential steps to bridge a gap which, in the first instance, was blasted into being by English Canadians for their own ends.

French-Canadian journalists are, in the main, rather better educated, better read and more flexibly-minded than their English-language colleagues, so that where the wave of a flag or the thump of a drum may move the Anglo Canadian emotionally to ones side of an argument, the cultivated and highly trained French Canadian editorial mind demands facts and pretty sound arguments.

Therefore, in their public relations particularly, the Forces should make it a point to see that there are always one or two men of outstanding calibre maintaining intimate relations with the French-Canadian press, radio and leaders of opinion. Since, in our native Province, prestige is a part of a man's presence, the practice of assigning junior officers to meet senior journalists defeats its own purpose from the very beginning. Frankly, Sir, the worst "store show window" in the entire Province of Quebec is the face that Quebec Command Headquarters presents to French Canada right now. There is not a government department, not a business, in the Province of Quebec which gives so strong an impression of having been deliberately organized to offend the people with whom it has to deal.

And how is the organization of Quebec Command Headquarters going to be made more suitable to the conditions under which it must operate, when those who select the officers to man it are themselves strangers to conditions in our Province, and have little if anything anywhere in their background to remind them, when they are making key personal selections, that they are dealing with a special situation?

May I come now to the text of your letter and, if you don't mind, try to answer it as if I were a well-informed French-Canadian editor to whom it had been addressed? For unless we may speak our minds freely to each other in discussion, surely there is not much point to this correspondence.

I do know that the subject we have written about has been a matter of personal concern to you, and that is why I wrote you in the first instance as soon as I could do it without violating Army channels too crassly. If I had not known that you are anxious to further the solution of the problem, I should not be wasting your time or mine. And I believe it is true that you have taken every opportunity which a Minister is given by his Department of bringing home the importance of this matter to your Forces. What I venture to question is whether you are kept fully informed of what is happening. But this it is not my business to determine.

Of the first three numbered sub-paragraphs at the bottom of the first page of your letter I should say that English- as well as French-Canadian opinion after the last war were, barring a noisy minority of super-patriots of the Kipling vintage, both equally anxious to see Canada's Armed Forces given distinctively Canadian characteristics. "O Canada" was, of course, officially recognized as a Canadian National Anthem at the unveiling of the Vimy Memorial in 1936 when His Majesty King Edward VIII saluted while it was being played. The Red Ensign was never hoisted in Valcartier Camp until long after the Union Jack had been hauled down in most other Army Camps in Canada. And surely it is not enough to stitch CANADA on the shoulders of Canadian officers who still wear pips of rank in the image of the insignia of the Order of the Bath when Maple Leaves would at least mean something to our people and would, it seems to many of us, fit more appropriately with the Crown of the King of Canada.

I think most Canadians were pleased when you made changes in the Navy set-up before the Mainguy Report was published. I knew nothing specific about the spirit in the Navy until I came to Ottawa some fourteen months ago, but I should say from my experience at Headquarters that there is a long way to go yet before that Service displays any noticeable seal to meet French Canada even part way—and I believe you are not unaware that right in the Naval Information set-up there is a decided resistance to our ideas. If officers charged with meeting public opinion are openly hostile to French Canadians, what must one think of others who are still more fully isolated from the facts of Canadian life?

Your paragraph 5 raises a sensitive point. It is true that there are quite a number of senior French-Canadian officers on the rolls of the Army. But if you will go over the list carefully you will see that a very high proportion of them have been carefully shipped out of the country, when they might be here helping to solve our problem, and posted to foreign lands where they are safely out of the way. At your Headquarters in Ottawa it is tragically easy to count the number of French Canadians in any Service who hold any position where they might exert influence or exercise practical authority.

A case in point is that of two capable French-Canadian officers, one a full Colonel and one a Lieutenant-Colonel, both with the DSO, who are rotting right now in Pakistan, replacing a call-out Major who was brought home to make an opening for their exile. I happen to know about this case since both those officers served in and wear the badges of my own Regiment.

We are all grateful to you, Sir, because of the time you spend with French Canadians every chance you get. Please believe that there is a very great affection for you personally in the French-Canadian units, and a great hope that some day you will find ways to help them more effectively.

Your paragraph 7 is, as I could recite in much detail and at considerable length, more honoured in the breach than in the observance, at Quebec Command Headquarters as well as elsewhere. The Army Translation Bureau is woefully inadequate to deal with even a fraction of the publications, reports and manuals which they should be getting out in French; a great many of the Army typewriters in the Province of Quebec have never had French accents on their keyboards, though RCEME could correct this easily at very little cost; and Part I Orders, even at the Recruiting Depot in Montreal, where young French Canadians come to enlist, are published in English only.

Cases of discrimination are very hard to prove. The French press is making quite an issue of one of them in the RCAF at the present time. If you spent a quiet evening in the R22^{e}R Mess in La Citadelle and listened to some of the tales that come out of Camp Borden you would realize that a lot that goes on in the Services never reaches the Minister's ears. Because, though I am an English Canadian and an Anglican I am also a true Vandoo, I could tell you stories, both of what went on during the War and of what has happened since, which you might find it almost impossible to believe. Most French Canadians know these things, and I think it does more harm than good to suggest that they exist no longer, when all the people most concerned, including the French-Canadian press, know that they do.

Your paragraphs 9 and 10 are, to my certain knowledge, happily correct. And fortunately French Canadians are responsive to courtesy and respect. But I question the usefulness of stressing secondary successes too strongly when basic ones are still to be achieved. I am a R22^{e}R officer myself, and we are all tickled pink when our Regiment is given precedence and honour. But we all know—and are all ready to make sacrifices to regimental pride in the broader interests of French Canada as a whole to that end—that, no matter how much praise is lavished upon the cream of 4,000,000 people who enlist in the R22^{e}R because there is nowhere else to enlist with self-respect, it would be far sounder if other Corps besides Infantry made room for our people on a basic of equal opportunity and equal recognition.

In the matter of advertisements, perhaps the issue is not as simple as it may seem. Except for yourself, Paul Paré, Armand Letellier and the Secretary of PMC, there is nobody in your Department now who is capable of directing and vetting a French-language recruiting campaign, and you all have other fish to fry. If Yves Bourassa's copy were in Chinese or Russian it could scarcely be more incomprehensible to the men responsible for "clearing it through" to your desk.

What the French-language press thinks of the "possession of French" at the Services Colleges is, of course, being published pretty forcefully these days and I have nothing to add to the very vigorous remarks which have already appeared in print.

I go along with you when you say that you are not responsible for the present position. We all know that it was deliberately created during World War I by Sam Hughes and his crowd, as the Shaughnessy correspondence I mailed you some months ago shows pretty clearly. Unfortunately, the Hughes heirs, a sort of Non-Conformist Apostolic Succession with a Tory tinge to it and a passionate seal for compulsory military service, have handed down their outlook and methods through tight, self-perpetuating channels squarely into our day and age. I expect a Grit Minister sometimes finds himself pretty helpless in their hands.

I am also ready to go along with you, Sir, in your statement that "a great deal has been done" with the qualification that a great deal more remains to be done, most of it more far-reaching than much of that which has been accomplished so far.

Your page three interests me very much indeed. I have studied it closely, and it would be a challenging exercise in technique and in understanding of the French-Canadian outlook to prepare these facts for presentation to the people of French Canada in a form which would convince them. There are tragically few men in the Services' recruiting and public relations organizations who understand the use of figures in telling a story that holds water. The Services' theory that any staff officer is competent to handle such highly specialized functions as advertising and public relations in a country like Canada seems to me about as sound as to put good Platoon or Company Commanders into the Medical or Dental Corps and expect them to run hospitals and clinics. Nor is the fact that a man has been a radio announcer or newspaper reporter necessarily any guarantee that he is properly equipped to deal with the intricate, delicate and very important task of interpreting the Services to Canadian opinion and Canadian opinion to the Services in a balanced and useful manner.

Your page four treats of the points which in my judgment are most in need of a fresh approach and an exhaustive re-examination, as it is in this area where there lies so much ground for misunderstanding and difference of opinion. If you will re-read the second paragraph of the third page of my 3 July letter, you will see that I am aware of the very grave difficulties involved in these aspects of the problem:

> "One must keep in mind, of course, Mr. Churchill's principle that 'wars are not won by heroic militias,' and I have tried in my thinking not to develop ideas which might impair the effectiveness of the Active Service. On the other hand, a close acquaintance with the military bureaucracy in peace time has pointed my attention forcibly to another statement of Mr. Churchill's in the same volume of his great work: 'I have found it necessary to have direct access to and control of the Joint Planning Staffs because after a year of war I cannot recall a single plan initiated by the existing machinery'."

You say, for instance, that it is impossible to fight a tank battle in two languages. I doubt very much if this assumption has ever been looked at closely. What is the difference between a battle and an infantry battle? I have debated this with George Bell more than once, and I am not sure that even George would not be willing now to try it out in practice before holding to the opinion he defended so categorically in the early days of our acquaintance. Nor am I convinced that, given bilingual signallers, a ship could not fight just as well with a French- as an English-speaking crew. I agree that there are certain levels of command in a battle, naval or ground, where you must have one language for the transmission of orders. But if your signals people are bilingual, surely the problem becomes a simple one on ship or regimental levels. I am afraid that in this case your Headquarters staffs have made up their minds to the verdict before looking at the evidence.

The problem of the admission of French-Canadian candidates to officer training courses in Corps other than Infantry is a complicated one from the very start by the position taken in the Services that Ontario standards of matriculation must be the norm for officer candidates from the entire country. As the Forces have been largely staffed in the past by Ontario men, or by men who contrived to meet Ontario standards, it is automatically assumed that the characteristics and skills which a man needs in order to qualify as "officer material" must fit the mould which has served so far. When Canada tried to take over control of the Canadian Forces from the Britishers who ran them in the first decades of Confederation, the controlling group resisted sturdily, claiming that if the Canadian Forces were officered by men who were not trained to English public or Canadian private school ideas and specifications, the Canadian Army would collapse in chaos. This same Family Compact spirit is now abroad in the current English-Canadian ruling group, who have made up their minds that any standards other than those by which they got in and maintain themselves would spell disaster to the Forces.

Well, I got to know a great many officers during the last War, both in Canada and overseas. And I respectfully submit, Sir, that I am far from satisfied that the rule-of-thumb specifications which the Canadian Forces require now from a candidate for commissioning represent a realistic gauge for ascertaining the value of a man as a leader of other men in the Services, either in peace or in war.

These are all intricate matters, and they are all interrelated. Canada, as any Minister of the Crown knows better than I do, is a complex nation, and is evolving in a different way from any other nation in the world. There are political, ethnic, social and economic facts in this country which set us very much apart. The easy way out of simulating evolution by taking old British ideas and diluting them with American ones, rather than taking the trouble to develop things of our own out of our own assets, represents in my mind a resort to stop-gaps rather than solutions. The Americans have gone a long way from the old European concepts of officer selection and training to which the British, the Germans, the French, the Italians and others have clung. So have the Russians. Perhaps the time has come for Canada, too, to do a little independent thinking about what kinds of leaders Canadians need in the Canadian Forces so that, preparing for emergencies, we can make the most effective and most economical use of our limited manpower and of all elements in the population with the least possible friction between groups.

Fundamentally, our problem is a problem of officers. And surely any system for selecting and training Canadian officers which can send only three French Canadians out of 83 Canadians to a Staff Course is, on the face of it, however stoutly its creators defend it, basically unsound and wasteful.

I can, of course, in a correspondence like ours, touch only upon the salients of the problem as I see it. I have never since the War sat on a level where I had access to information which would allow me to judge the reasoning which has entered into some of the decisions which have been made, so I can examine only the end results. I learned enough overseas and I have seen enough at Headquarters in Ottawa, however, to know that the scarcity of good officers in the Canadian Forces is not always compensated for by the wisest possible use of the abilities of those we do possess.

These are some of the fundamental problem which, I feel, will have to be overcome before the Department of National Defence has a really convincing story to tell in French Canada.

But, during the months it will take to settle these matters, even if they are tackled with the utmost diligence and vigour, the story which we do have to tell might, I submit, be managed much more skilfully.

For instance, I have to guess whether your clipping service is furnishing you full reports on the extremely well documented and sharply critical campaign running in French-language newspapers straight across Canada. I have often thought that it might be helpful to senior officers at Headquarters if the daily press summary, prepared and more or less adequately circulated by your public relations people, did not confine its extracts exclusively to the English-language press. This practice makes it all the easier for Headquarters personnel to forget the existence of such a group as French Canada which is so skimpily represented in the councils of the Department by living representatives. In all my associations with business people before the War and since, I have found that the men charged with administration are more anxious to know what is published in criticism of them than in praise, as it enables them to meet adverse opinion more effectively and to correct errors where they occur. The Armed Forces are the only organization I know whose public relations seem designed to hear from and to reach only the people who think as they do already. I understand that something is being done now to get French-Canadians into PR in the lower commissioned ranks in all three Services. But I am still of the opinion that it would be useful if some of the senior personnel in PR, the men who assign the duties and set the policies of their subordinates, were less obviously unqualified to direct usefully and wisely the relations of the Services with the press, radio and leaders of opinion of one-third of the people of Canada.

It occurs to me, as I know it has to you, that if a Cease Fire is arranged in Korea, the Armed Forces of Canada are going to need a pretty strong and sustained publicity campaign if they are to maintain enlistments in Canada over a long period at the levels you have specified. The main thing in telling a good story is to have a good story to tell, and the right people to tell it. That makes the planning of a good story doubly important now, if the deep-seated antagonism of French Canada to the Communists, which could be such an asset to the Services, is not to be neutralized by unfavourable reactions toward the Forces among people who would normally be on their side.

You may be surprised to learn that I am an uncompromising enemy of propaganda as it was developed and used by the governments of Nazi Germany and Communist Russia, and that during the months when I had a considerable voice in the reorganization of the press and radio of Italy I found nothing to admire in the methods which Mussolini had used throughout his public career. Freedom of public debate, based on free and copious information, are, I believe, the very life-blood of a free society. But I think one of the basic prerequisites of healthy democratic government is that the people should be fully aware of the policies and plans of their representatives.

I cannot subscribe, therefore, to the ruling school of thought in the Services which contends that press releases and photographs, set radio talks and paid advertising are the beginning and end of public relations.

The mechanics of publicity are fairly easy to master; what is less often grasped is that imagination, boundless energy and close, sustained relations on a dignified level with community leaders are fundamental for the dissemination of indirect publicity—the most effective of all forms of publicity and, given a realistic mind behind it, by far the cheapest in dollars and cents. The more varied the channels through which the facts reach the people, the more powerful will be the response of an informed and alert public opinion to the policies and needs of the nation.

Please forgive me, Sir, if I have repeated at such length and in different forms some of the thoughts which I submitted to you in my 3 July letter. I am now a bystander in these issues: but perhaps the view of a deeply interested outsider may have some value as a corrective to the routine policies of those who live and work in among the trees.

Once again, many thanks for your patience and courtesy in examining my views.

I have the honour to be, Mr. Minister,

> Faithfully yours,
> Ted Bullock

> 106 Cartier Street
> Ottawa, 4, Ontario
> 21 July 1951

The Honourable Brooke Claxton, K.C., D.C.M., M.P.,
Minister of National Defence,
Ottawa, Ontario.

Dear Mr. Claxton,

To illustrate the remarks in my last letter about bad Services public relations in French Canada I enclose an editorial which appeared in *Le Devoir* on 9 July 1951, and an editorial and an editorial page cartoon published in the same paper 12 July.

Le Devoir, as you know, enjoys a prestige among leaders of French-Canadian thought which is much greater than its circulation figures would suggest, and it is particularly influential among the clergy and the professional men, not only in Quebec Province but among the 1,000,000 French-Canadians who live in other parts of Canada.

As I am to be the featured speaker at the IVth Congress of l'Association Canadienne des éducateurs de Langue Française at Memramcook, New Brunswick,

5 August, and as my subject will be bilingualism in Canada, I wonder whether you consider it might be useful if I tried to neutralize some of these criticism for the benefit of the 500 leaders of French-Canadian education who will be my audience.

Another 1911 in the next Federal election in French Canada would be, in my belief, an unmitigated tragedy for Canada, and I cannot help remembering the rôle played by *Le Devoir* in that campaign on the Naval issue.

At that time, *Le Devoir* was alone. There are now numerous French-language papers in various parts of Canada who are echoing the current campaign for reforms in the Services.

Yours faithfully,
T.B.

Appendix C

FOR COMMANDERS FROM CDS

1. The minister has informed me that the Cabinet has now approved the plan for improving the retention of French-speaking Canadians in the Armed Forces and for fostering bilingualism. This item was discussed at Canadian Forces Council and a copy of the plan was sent to members 1 Feb.
2. The purpose of this message is to tell you what we are doing here to launch this new program and to suggest a line of action for your guidance. I am sure you realize that the success of the program depends on your leadership, and the LEADERSHIP OF YOUR COMMANDING OFFICERS.
3. First, I think it is important that you have my views. I have long been of the opinion that the Armed Forces have a deep responsibility and a unique opportunity when it comes to acting on matters of national unity. We have the advantage of being a well-structured and well-disciplined national entity dedicated by our very nature to service to country. I believe it is our duty to lead in such matters.
4. The implementation of the program will have its difficulties and will require your personal supervision as I realize that some members of the Forces have sincere misgivings about the program on three counts. First, they believe the manning of predominantly French-speaking units will present an insurmountable problem particularly with respect to senior tradesmen. Second, they believe that the program will tend to segregate French-speaking and English-speaking members of the Forces. Third, some French-speaking members of the Forces fear they will be restricted in their service to predominantly French-speaking units to the detriment of their careers, and may be located more or less permanently in one geographic area.
5. Undoubtedly, there will be difficulties related to the manning problem and it may take some considerable time before units are manned with the proposed ratio of French- or English-speaking personnel. Preliminary studies, however, indicate that the plan is feasible from a manning point of view. With respect to the objection that the plan will segregate English-speaking and French-speaking members of the Forces, I would draw to your attention that the program as a whole envisages a greater degree of bilingualism throughout the Forces by employing English-speaking and French-speaking members on a much wider basis than heretofore. Insofar as the fears expressed by some French-speaking members of the Forces are concerned with respect to career implications and restricted geographic location of service, I can assure you and you may in turn

assure your officers and men that the career progression of French-speaking members of the Forces will be fully safeguarded even if it results in a delay in reaching our long term objective for the plan.

6. We can expect considerable emotional reaction from both service and civilian sources and must be prepared for this. We must anticipate the problems and be prepared to solve them.

7. The following press release will be issued on Tuesday 2 April at 1330 Z. Text follows:

8. Quote "In accordance with the Government's policy on bilingualism in the public service, enunciated by the Prime Minister in the House of Commons on 6 April, 1966, and as a means of improving the retention rate of French speaking Canadians in the Armed Forces, the Department of National Defence will institute, beginning this summer, a long-term program leading to a substantial improvement in the bilingual character of the Forces," the Hon. Léo Cadieux, Minister of National Defence, announced today.

9. The program is based on the concept of two working languages; predominantly French-speaking bases and units to use french as a working language, and predominantly English-speaking bases and units to use English as a working language.

10. Mr. Cadieux said that the program provided for the establishment of French-language trades training, as well as the designation of a number of bases and units, covering a wide spectrum of military skills, in which the working language will be French.

11. To foster the use of a second language the ultimate aim is to have at least 20% of the strength of predominately French- and predominately English-speaking bases and units made up of members whose parent tongue is the other official language. This will not be possible in the initial stages, however.

12. He emphasized that the selection of units and bases for designation as French- or English-speaking in this program will not be restricted to any particular political or geographic division of the country. The object is to create a force in which both of the country's official language are in everyday use and not to divide the force on a unilingual or geographic basis.

13. Mr. Cadieux added: "This program will make the Armed Forces more attractive for Canadian youth whose parent language is French. They can expect to take a substantial part of their training in French and serve for a good portion of their careers in units where French is the working language. At the same time, this program will open the doors for both English and French speaking servicemen to learn a second language."

14. The minister continued: "The situation now is that while approximately 27% of the young Canadians who join the Armed Forces are from French-speaking homes, only about 15% of the total current strength of the Forces is made up of them. This is the result of a much higher release rate for French-speaking servicemen."

15. "This higher release rate among French-speaking servicemen is directly related to the difficulties they experience when they attempt advanced training in

English,'' Mr. Cadieux said. He said that another important factor was the lack of adequate French-language schooling for the children of servicemen serving outside of Quebec. This has resulted in some servicemen electing release when faced with a posting. Mr. Cadieux said that action has recently been taken to alleviate this latter problem by the provision of special dependents education allowances.

16. At present the only predominantly French-speaking units in the regular force are the three battalions of the Royal 22nd Regiment. Two are based in Valcartier, P.Q., and a third in Germany. However, bases and headquarters within the province of Quebec have some bilingual personnel on strength.

17. The new program has the immediate aim of increasing the number of units functioning on a predominantly French-speaking basis. However, English will continue to be the operational language of the forces above unit level and predominantly French-speaking air units will operate in the air in English, the air communication language throughout most of the world by international agreement.

18. One principal result of the new program will be that recruits whose parent language is French will be able to train and work in their own language particularly during their first critical years of service.

19. The initial steps in the program will be:

A destroyer, based at Halifax, will be designated as a predominately French-speaking unit this summer.

A CF 5 Squadron to be located at Bagotville, P.Q. will be classified as a predominantly French-speaking unit when it is formed early in 1969.

The new Airborne Regiment to be formed later this year and to be located outside of Quebec Province will be manned to approximately 30% of its strength with personnel whose parent language is French.

A French-language trades-training centre will be established at St. Jean, P.Q., in existing accommodation to provide basic trades training in certain selected Armed Forces trades.

20. Mr. Cadieux stressed that the program will be introduced gradually into the Forces and in such a way that military efficiency and career progression will not be prejudiced and with due regard for the rights and privileges of individuals. Unquote

21. I would like you to implement an information program of your own consistant with your individual situation. For example, you should brief key members of your staff and issue an appropriate message to your COS.

22. Generals Anderson, Stovel and Pollard and Admiral O'Brien, as the commanders most affected, may consider making themselves available to the news media for interviews in which they can expand on the implications of the program.

23. It is imperative that all commanders take a positive attitude in this matter. You should stress the desirability of the objectives and the part the Armed Forces can play in national unity.

24. You will note that the press release does not contain some information included in the plan. The location of the Airborne Regiment will be announced later. In the case of the Land Force units proposed for Valcartier I do not consider it

appropriate to release this information in advance of the release of information on the complete land-force redeployment.

25. I cannot overemphasize the importance of all of us getting behind this new program and making it work. I am confident you will do your part.

Appendix D

FRENCH-LANGUAGE UNITS SINCE 1968-1969

	Location
BFC Valcartier	CFB Valcartier
1er Commando aéroporté	CFB Petawawa
Le Skeena	CFB Halifax
Quartier général et escadron des transmissions, 5e Groupe-Brigade du Canada	CFB Valcartier
5e Régiment d'artillerie légère du Canada	CFB Valcartier
5e Régiment du génie du Canada	CFB Valcartier
433e Escadrille d'appui tactique	CFB Bagotville
1er Bataillon, R22^{e}R	CFB Lahr
2e Bataillon, R22^{e}R	La Citadelle, Québec
3e Bataillon, R22^{e}R	CFB Valcartier
La Musique du Royal 22e Régiment	La Citadelle, Québec
5e Ambulance de campagne	CFB Valcartier
5e Bataillon des services du Canada	CFB Valcartier
Détachement—Centre d'entraînement au combat	CFB Valcartier
430e Escadrille tactique d'hélicoptères	CFB Valcartier
Ecole Technique des Forces Canadiennes	CFB Saint-Jean

Appendix E

Gentlemen,

For obvious reasons, soldiers on active duty do not get involved in politics. But the soldiers are nevertheless citizens too and, as such, they are entitled to express their views, through the veterans, when the future of their country is at stake. Furthermore, thousands of Quebeckers now resting in foreign soil, primarily in France, have generously given their lives to ensure the freedoms that all Canadians enjoy today, and we believe that they deserve to be heard at this turning point in our history. This conference will not be a matter of erudite statistics and witch-hunts or aggressive attacks against those who do not share our views, but rather a forum that will enable us to state frankly our reasons for being in the NO camp. Initially, let us put in perspective the sacrifices made by a large number of Quebeckers during the two world conflicts; the members of the *Royal 22*^{e} *Régiment*, of the Chaudière, of the Fusiliers Mont-Royal, of the 4th Artillery Regiment, of the Maisonneuve Regiment, of the Trois-Rivières Regiment, of the Alouette Squadron and of many members of the Forces who served in the Royal Canadian Navy. To be persuaded of this, it is sufficient to visit the Canadian cemeteries in Europe. Those valiant defenders who fought alongside Canadians from the other provinces came from every corner of Quebec. Indeed, in the R22^{e}R, three Victoria Cross holders came from Rimouski. In the last few days, *The Gazette* has published an article that I must comment on. First of all, about fifteen days ago, at a meeting in Louiseville, I had attacked those who have written a defence policy in the White Book. Indeed, on pages 101 and 105 of the White Book, the Parti Québécois announced in its defence policy that this will hinge on three concerns; the first one would be internal security, the second one the security of the North American continent and of the West, and the third one its participation in UN peacekeeping and arbitration missions. The Parti Québécois policy proposal would maintain modest armed forces. For the last three weeks, I have tried to obtain an explanation of that policy. No member of the government has dared reply to me, but that reply was given to us via Brigadier Ménard, who told us that it would be easy to organize such a force. We shall reply, first, that Brigadier Ménard has only served at lower echelons and has no qualifications or experience to analyze the consequences of the stated policy and the goal of the press conference is to introduce to the public a group of veterans who have all served at all levels of Canada's military hierarchy, and to explain to the public the differences between the pious wishes of the policy announced and reality.

We will show you subsequently the progress made since 1914, following the organization of the first French Canadian regiment, the 22e, which, after having covered itself with glory during the war of 1914-1918, was maintained in the regular army in 1921. Although ministers Lévesque, Morin and Parizeau refused to elaborate on their promises, Ménard has nevertheless revealed their intentions. He told us that the Forces would resemble a militia similar to that of Luxemburg. This presupposes that the militia supported by an officer framework will constitute the cadre for a navy for the defence of the sea approaches and would be able to participate in the NATO forces within the Atlantic sector, equipped with the most sophisticated and modern ships. Please note that he was talking about part-time personnel. A land army, at least 1,500 men, is posted to Germany within the framework of the 1st Battalion of the *Royal 22e Régiment* and of the 12e RBC and the support artillery. An honourable participation with what he calls "helicopters." What a joke! What incompetence and what demagogy! To intercept, for identification purposes only, supersonic Mach II aircraft flying at an altitude of 30,000 feet and more, by means of an aircraft with a maximum speed of 150 miles per hour and a maximum altitude of 10,000 feet. Speaking of budgets, we have no recent figures, but in 1975 Parizeau had announced $164 millions for 1975-76. You know, this could not even provide a good scene with props for his comic opera. When last year, the Department of National Defence spent in Quebec, in Quebec alone, $564 million and for the current year, National Defence will spend approximately $756 million without counting purchases for the F-18 and Bombardier vehicle programs. But that is not all. Nothing is more expensive than a small army. First of all, to the figures mentioned must be added the cost of specialized schools, which, for climatic and topographical reasons, are scattered throughout Canada; they are very expensive and I do not even dare mention a figure. We must also add the logistics, which require considerable equipment and fixed asset investment. Nor must one forget the general headquarters to command those forces and a Department of Defence. Complexity and diversity require technical and other administrative skills, which a tactical general headquarters cannot meet and we can therefore say to Mr. Parizeau that his budget proposals are utterly unrealistic and that he can in no way repatriate the amounts required to duplicate the policy that his party will impose upon the people of Quebec, who have the right to know. We are often told that nothing is being done, that in Ottawa everything is motionless. I would like to speak to you for a few moments about what has happened since 1914. Many things have happened since 1914. First of all, I have spoken to you about the foundation of the *Royal 22e Régiment* and I have told you about many things that have helped French Canadians advance. I would like to tell you this morning that the *Royal 22e Régiment* alone has given the Canadian Armed Forces 23 general officers, a figure no other Canadian Regiment has equalled to date, including General Dextraze and myself. These being considerations that belong to the past, one should look at what is happening today and see how the French-speaking soldiers are doing in our armed forces. During subsequent years, we found that, although the number of francophones enrolled was in proportion to the French-Canadian population, the retention rate was lower than among anglophones. Instead of loudly clamouring that this was unjust, we decided to thoroughly examine the program in order to find out what the reasons were and to take corrective steps.

For nearly one year, a committee comprising approximately twenty almost exclusively francophone officers from the three services studied the situation, visiting the bases in Canada and in Europe where we had military personnel, including their dependents. The terms of reference of the task force were to study the situation and formulate recommendations for French-language personnel to have equal career opportunities to those provided to English-speaking members of the Forces. The program and recommendations of the committee were submitted to me at the end of 1967 and in early 1968. With Mr. Cadieux, we asked Mr. Pearson to authorize the establishment of new francophone units. Mr. Pearson gave us the go-ahead and told us in his letter to Mr. Cadieux that the policy he had just announced could only be changed by his prime ministerial successors. Mr. Pearson had thus raised the level of defence policy and reserved the right to say whether the units and his policy could be changed, such right being reserved to himself and to his successors. Following that approval, francophone units were created throughout the country. And I am going to name a few for you. First of all, in Halifax, the complete crew of a francophone ship was set up, but because we lacked officers, we had to delay somewhat the establishment of the others. Since then and under the leadership of General Dextraze, the program has continued and is now virtually complete. Throughout the Air Force structure of the province of Quebec, including radar stations and the Bagotville base, all cadres consist of francophone officers except, naturally, for some technicians who were simply not available. At CFB Valcartier, which has been increased by 55 thousand acres, we have formed, in addition to the *Royal 22e Régiment*, two battalions that now exist and that are there, we have formed the *5e Groupement de Combat*, which is a complete brigade group with its tanks, its artillery and its engineering units, its signals units, a helicopter squadron and finally the entire base, the entire supporting logistics organization. We have in place in Montreal the general headquarters of the land army, located at St. Hubert, which commands all the troops in Canada, and we have also set up, through all the schools I mentioned earlier, French modules so that the trainees who must go there in order to qualify may receive their training in French—and some speak of inactivity! I do not want to take too much of your time, but we believe that it is possible, in the light of our experience, to reach rational solutions to all the problems we have had. All of us and those who are here around me today, we have all been proud to serve our country and that is why I, with all my comrades, will say "No, thank you."

Index